The real Ireland

The evolution of Ireland in documentary film

Harvey O'Brien

Manchester University Press
Manchester and New York

distributed exclusively in the USA by Palgrave

Published by Manchester University Press
Oxford Road, Manchester M13 9NR, UK
and Room 400, 175 Fifth Avenue, New York, NY 10010, USA
www.manchesteruniversitypress.co.uk

Distributed exclusively in the USA by
Palgrave, 175 Fifth Avenue, New York,
NY 10010, USA

Distributed exclusively in Canada by
UBC Press, University of British Columbia, 2029 West Mall,
Vancouver, BC, Canada V6T 1Z2

British Library Cataloguing-in-Publication Data
A catalogue record for this book is available from the British Library

Library of Congress Cataloging-in-Publication Data applied for

ISBN   0 7190 6906 8   *hardback*
EAN   978 0 7190 6906 2
ISBN   0 7190 6907 6   *paperback*
EAN   978 0 7190 6907 9

First published 2004

13 12 11 10 09 08 07 06 05 04   10 9 8 7 6 5 4 3 2 1

Typeset in Simoncini Garamond
by Northern Phototypesetting Co. Ltd, Bolton
Printed in Great Britain
by Biddles Ltd, King's Lynn

This book is dedicated to Tom and Nora O'Brien, who picked me out of a crowd, who followed my every step, and who stood behind me all the way.

Contents

List of figures   *page* ix
Preface   x
Acknowledgements   xii

Introduction   1
The organisation of this book   1
State, society and nation   4
On documentary   9

1 **The lie of the land: primitives, poets and pilgrims**   16
Landscape, place and personality   17
Actualities and travelogues   21
Independence: the search for self and nation   30
Man of Aran   44
The country and the city   49

2 **Projecting the present: Irish society and social
   documentary**   56
Rhetorical form and national projection   58
Church and state and film   61
A Nation Once Again   63
Rhetoric, propaganda and *Our Country*   65
Docudramas and informational films   74
Tourism   84
Dublin   91
Parting ways: Northern Ireland, *Housing Discrimination* and
   documentary   95

3 **Projecting the past: history and ideology**   101
Historiography and ideology   101
The shape of history: Gael-Linn and Seán Lemass   103
An 'Irish' documentary?   107
Shaping history: *Mise Éire* and *Saoirse?*   110
The legacy of *Mise Éire*   117

Continuity and nostalgia   120
Revisionism and resurrection: historical documentary at the
    turn of the millennium   129

4 **The rocky road to change**   141
Old chestnuts, new growth   145
RTÉ and the winds of change   155
Radharc   158
Gael-Linn and Louis Marcus   161
Rocky Road to Dublin   170
The RTÉ rebellion and its consequences for the film industry   179
The quiet men   181
Unquiet times   187

5 **Uncertain spaces: postmodern, postcolonial,**
   postnationalist Ireland?   191
The fringes of Irishness: *Atlantean*   194
Mother Ireland   203
Inside and out: Alan Gilsenan and John T. Davis   208
The fall of the church   228

6 **Unto the breach: redefining the public sphere**   237
Taboos   241
Northern Ireland: the last taboo   245
Sport, music and the performance of culture   248
Dublin and the millennium   252
Docusoaps, *video vérités* and 'reality shows'   255

Filmography   263
Secondary filmography   334
Bibliography   337
Index   347

Figures

1 James and Joseph Horgan, circa 1915 (Jim Horgan/Irish Film Institute) *page* 26

2 *Eucharistic Congress 1932* (Fr Edward O'Donnell SJ) 34

3 Maggie Dirrane in *How the Myth Was Made* (George C. Stoney/ Irish Film Institute) 48

4 Liam O'Leary (Leslie Shepard/Irish Film Institute) 68

5 Seán MacBride in *Our Country* (Leslie Shepard) 74

6 Marie Kean and Joe Lynch in *Voyage to Recovery* (Dept. of Health/ Irish Film Institute) 83

7 The coffin of W. B. Yeats with honour guard in *W. B. Yeats – A Tribute* (Dept. of Foreign Affairs/Irish Film Institute) 87

8 Colm Ó Laoghaire and Vincent Corcoran making *Amharc Éireann* (Gael-Linn/Irish Film Institute) 105

9 *Saoirse?* (Gael-Linn/Irish Film Institute) 114

10 George Fleischmann during an early Irish television test (Irish Film Institute) 142

11 *The One-Nighters* (Michael Coppinger/Irish Film Institute) 154

12 Dolly MacMahon in *Fleá* (Louis Marcus/Irish Film Institute) 164

13 Peter Hunt, John Kavanagh and Louis Marcus making *Revival* (Louis Marcus/Irish Film Institute) 169

14 *Rocky Road to Dublin* poster (copyright © Peter Lennon) 177

15 Bob Quinn (Bob Quinn/Irish Film Institute) 202

16 John T. Davis and Beargrease making *Hobo* (John T. Davis/ Irish Film Institute) 217

Preface

You hold in your hand the first complete history of Irish documentary film. We could play games with that sentence, you know. We could contest every word, debating precisely what it means to be 'Irish', what is 'documentary', how 'history' is constituted and in exactly what sense 'first' is being used. The most interesting word of all, though, is 'complete'. History has taught us that nothing is ever complete, and let me be the first to point out that there are gaps in my research. In the course of the years during which I have been preparing this book I have viewed hundreds of films, and not all of them are included here. I have been treated with nothing but courtesy and friendship by the Irish Film Archive, in whose screening rooms I have been lurking almost since they opened. With the benefit of two years of funding from the Irish Research Council for Humanities and Social Sciences, I was even able to visit some of the more important archives in the United States, including the Library of Congress, the Smithsonian, the Museum of Radio and Television, and UCLA. Over time my research has also been serviced by the personal collections of friends and colleagues, and by endless hours of viewing from television.

In spite of all of this activity there is a large body of Irish documentary film out there which is essentially untouched. There are many films I have not yet seen, and many I probably never will. RTÉ's extensive archives are open only to researchers for whom commercial rates do not prompt a choice between viewing films and paying rent. A great many films even from as recently as the 1960s have been lost or destroyed, evidence of their existence now gleaned only from crumbling paper records. There is also the complex world of amateur film, which I have dealt with here and there in this book but which opens whole fields of debate best suited to another volume entirely. Finally there is the inevitable X factor which comes with being an explorer in a strange land. The terrain had been roughly mapped before I started, not least of all by Kevin Rockett in his contribution to the seminal book *Cinema and Ireland*, but that was only a sketch, and this book, though I believe it to be coherent and comprehensive, is but a series of brushstrokes in the landscape which is likely to be refined as time goes by.

It is for reasons like these that *The Real Ireland* is more than just a list of titles. It is an analysis of how documentary film developed in Ireland, and how the image of Ireland itself evolved alongside it. It is, as the subtitle suggests, as much about the evolution of Ireland in documentary film as it is about the details of who, what, when and where. *The Real Ireland* is not intended to close the subject of Irish documentary. The purpose of this book is to open debate on the role that non-fiction film has played in our understanding of Ireland, to provide a perspective from the wings of the 'discourses of sobriety', to borrow Bill Nichols's term, which define Irish society. As the study of non-fiction film has taught us, there is a more direct relationship between what is traditionally agreed to be negotiated reality and the type of film which claims to have a privileged relationship with its representation. The study of documentary film in Ireland is as much about Irish history, culture and politics as any book on these specific subjects. The fact that this book has an original angle from which to approach the issues, to my mind at least, only makes it more interesting.

Acknowledgements

There are too many people to thank for their support in the preparation of this book, but my most special thanks must be extended to the staff of the Irish Film Archive, especially curator Sunniva O'Flynn, who never once told me to go away and stop bothering her. My thanks also to Kevin Rockett, who oversaw my initial research. The Irish Research Council for Humanities and Social Sciences supported the preparation of this book as well as additional research, and the Centre for Film Studies at University College Dublin was my base of operations. Individuals whose names I would like to list in thanks include Susanne Bach, Ruth Barton, Margaret Brindley, Leon Conway, Eugene Finn, Tony Fitzmaurice, Peter Flynn, Rowena Kelly, Emma Keogh, Patrick Marsh, Antoinette Prout, Anne Sheridan, Mary Sherlock, Emer Williams and Liam Wylie, and there are many others who have played their part in one way or another who I hope will forgive my not naming them but accept my good wishes. I wish to acknowledge the love and support of all my extended family, my brother Barry and his fiancée Jackie, but most of all I must thank my wife Catherine, who makes everything seem possible.

Introduction

This book is concerned with how Ireland has been represented in documentary film. It is not just a history, though it is the first full study of non-fiction film in Ireland and it follows the evolution of the medium from the 'primitive' pre-documentary period to the present day. It is also about how ideas of Ireland have been communicated through documentaries, both on the level of content and in terms of the underlying structures of production and reception. It explores the relationship between concepts of history, politics, economics and culture, and notions of 'the real' which have affected the role and influence of non-fiction film. Following the model of documentary form proposed by Bill Nichols (1991), it charts the evolution of modes of representation in non-fiction film from an evidentiary or expositional model to the more reflexive types of films which question their own epistemological basis. Though, as shall be seen, Irish documentarists have yet to fully grasp the potential of this most recent variant, this can be related to notions of self and nation which have only begun to break down in the face of increasing multiculturalism and integration within the wider European community. This work follows recent writings in Irish Studies by Declan Kiberd (1995), Luke Gibbons (1996) and Richard Kearney (1997), in this regard. It shares with these authors the aim of deconstructing concepts of Ireland as represented through the products of cultural and political thought, in this case through documentary films.

The organisation of this book

In practice, *The Real Ireland* examines works of documentary not merely in terms of a discrete 'history' of the form, but in the context of the kinds of broader questions raised in this introduction. It is hoped that this will provide the reader with the means to contextualise the contribution of documentary to notions of Ireland and Irishness on the island throughout the history of documentary film, and to appreciate the complexity of the concepts of both 'reality' and 'documentary' involved. Each chapter contains a body of historical and textual analysis, usually supplemented by aspects of theoretical or critical enquiry which help to illustrate the issues involved. The book is organised primarily chronologically, though there will be references to films, movements and filmmakers from several eras in chapters where their contributions need to be noted.

Chapter 1 describes the initial stages of the development of non-fiction film in Ireland, beginning with the Lumière films of the late nineteenth century. It discusses the correlations between some of the earliest filmed images of Ireland and other forms of representation including painting, cartography and illustration. It explores ideas of 'place' and 'landscape' through the writings of Martin Heidegger (1971), E. Estyn Evans (1992), Bernard Nietschmann (1993), Tim Robinson (1993) and Brian Graham (1997) which suggest that interpretations of the 'natural' environment (both urban and rural) depend on cultural and political factors often embodied in representational forms. It points out how the documentary impulse need not necessarily find expression only in the more rigid formal conceits of the Griersonian model. Following the work of authors including Michael Renov (1993) and Sharon Sherman (1998), it argues that the separation of 'documentary' and 'poetry' into separate schools of self-inscription is culturally specific. As Renov and Sherman point out, sometimes films which seem 'innocent', 'primitive' or 'poetic' are as illustrative of social and political conditions as those which assume a more traditionally documentarian tone. The chapter examines several key films produced during the period prior to and immediately after political independence (achieved in 1921); a time at which, arguably, cultural and political concepts of Ireland were still being negotiated. It points out how film, as a new medium, offered a unique opportunity for filmmakers and audiences to investigate the emergent nation, but how, for the most part, it was often squandered or stifled by intellectual and economic prohibitions characteristic of that moment in Irish history.

Chapter 2 is concerned with what is termed 'projecting the present' after Sir Stephen Tallents's assertion that documentary film was 'the art of national projection' (Tallents, 1932: 41). It focuses on the spread of the Griersonian conception of rhetorical documentary in Ireland throughout the 1940s and 1950s and how this affected the understanding of the country. Employing the writings of J. H. Whyte (1980), Tom Inglis (1998) and Luke Gibbons, it describes how the ontologically determinate forces of church and state began to exert an influence over the production of Irish films and demonstrates how this contributed to the subject, style and type of argument put forward. It questions the democratic ideals proposed in some of the government-sponsored films of the day, and argues that, even in a film as nominally oppositional as *Our Country* (1948), the underlying structures of rhetorical form constrained the parameters of social discourse and ultimately contributed to the furtherance of orthodoxy. It also discusses how informational films of the era began to propose a vision of Ireland amenable to the need to promote the country as a tourist venue, and how this conception began to spread to non-tourist films.

Chapter 3 extends this critique to historical films. This chapter proposes that though debates were taking place within Ireland regarding its identity as a nation, films were produced within a rhetorical mode of representation which reinforced ideologically proscriptive notions of society, state, and nation. It demonstrates how historical documentaries such as *Mise Éire* (1959) framed their interpretations of Irish history within ideologically predetermined norms. It explores concepts of historiography, ideology and mythology as discussed by Robert A. Rosenstone (1996), Roland Barthes (1989) and Terry Eagleton (1991) and notes how these concepts both of history and of documentary's capacity to represent it in this way continued almost until the end of the century. The chapter concludes with a discussion of more contemporary historical films and illustrates that though some have been produced with a greater level of critical insight into the process by which history is a negotiated space, many still assume an unproblematic relationship between what is represented and what is real.

Chapter 4 deals with the gradual breakdown of the fixed ideas of Ireland and of documentary explored in the preceding chapters. It describes how the period prior to and following the establishment of a television service in 1961 saw the emergence of an oppositional sensibility. It discusses the output of a generation of filmmakers frustrated by convention, who sought new ways of looking at themselves and at Irish society. Though, as shall be seen, the emergence of such alternative voices offered Irish documentary an opportunity to embrace shifts in the conception of the form discussed by Nichols, the control of television itself became a political issue and ultimately limited the level to which new ideas could find public expression. This chapter uses Robert Savage's (1996) account of the development of Telefís Éireann (later Radio Telefís Éireann) to describe how the public service broadcasting model allegedly in use was, in reality, a site of friction between the state and those who presumed to represent the public. It shall be shown that the films of the period both made for television and for theatrical exhibition illustrated the division between those for whom documentary was a utility for distributing approved information and those for whom it represented an opportunity to expand the range of issues and ideas to which the public was exposed.

Chapter 5 examines developments in the final two decades of the twentieth century, raising issues arising out of postmodernism, postcolonialism and postnationalism illustrative of the challenges facing documentary filmmakers during these crucial years of change. It does not suggest that the issues raised can be accommodated by any one of these areas, but points out that the breakdown of social consensus was echoed by an increasing sense of the boundaries of the medium by a small handful of radical filmmakers such as Bob Quinn, Alan Gilesnan and John T. Davis. It delineates the schism between more formally and thematically radical works and those which, in spite of a century of evolution, continued to espouse conventional notions of the form and function of documentary film. The latter are the subject of the final chapter, which explores how ideas of Ireland began to shift to accommodate a greater range of debate in the public sphere.

Chapter 6 explores the range of issues discussed in the films of the millennial years in terms of what Habermas described as the public sphere, including those which confronted previously taboo subjects. It notes that many of these have only appeared with the decline in influence of the Catholic church, and discusses, with reference to Inglis, the consequences of increasing secularisation and the increasing dominance of the media. It also observes, however, that those few films which had the prescience and penetration to ask questions of the status quo before a consensus had been established and ratified by legislation or 'official' action were often subject to suppression, dismissed, or consigned to obscurity.

Clearly there are many questions to be asked about the evolution of Ireland in documentary film, and a great deal of ground to cover which has not been addressed directly before. That said it is worth pointing out that the work of writers including Kevin Rockett, Martin McLoone, John Hill, Lance Pettitt, Brian McIlroy and Luke Gibbons in the field of Irish film has been instrumental in establishing the groundwork and Ruth Barton has brought new perspective to debate with *Irish National Cinema* in 2004. At the time of writing, more work is under way. As I said in the preface, this book is not intended to close the subject of the role of documentary in understanding both Ireland and Ireland on film. It is intended to stimulate the desire for even greater levels of knowledge on the subject and to encourage reading, viewing and research into Irish documentary as the medium and the country continues to evolve throughout the twenty-first century.

State, society and nation

This book is centrally preoccupied with specific ideas of the relationship between representations of Ireland and the culture, institutions and social structures which actually exist there. It is worth clarifying, therefore, in what terms concepts such as 'state', 'society' and 'nation' may be understood in this context, and how the views of Kearney, Kiberd, Gibbons and others have influenced my position. Raymond Williams discusses the relationship between 'state' and 'society' in terms of the contestation between ideas of hierarchical structures and a general condition of belonging to a group of people who share a common system of life. He concludes that the term 'society' has meaning in both a general and an abstract sense. In the first instance, society is 'our most general term for the body of institutions and relationships within which a relatively large group of people live' (Williams, 1983: 291). Secondly, he notes, it is also 'the condition in which such institutions and relationships are formed' (291). This dual level of meaning allows us to speak of society not merely in terms of specific configurations of institutional power, but of a condition of existence and loose affiliation. As Williams also points out, the term is descended from its fourteenth-century usage as a synonym for 'companionship' or 'fellowship', which is distinct from his definition of 'state' as 'the apparatus of power', descended from its usage to describe the 'estates' of monarchy and nobility.

The Irish Constitution is quite specific in its definition of the state. Articles 4 to 7 of define Ireland as a 'sovereign, independent, democratic' (Article 5) state in which 'all powers of government, legislative, executive and judicial, derive, under God, from the people'(Article 6, section 1). Significantly, though power is hereby granted to the citizenry to designate its rulers and decide all questions of national policy, this power is expressly derived 'from God'. Article 6, section 1 also adds that it is only in 'final appeal' that the public has the right to determine national policy. Section 2 of the same article further qualifies the exercise of political power by the citizenry by stating that 'these powers of government are exercisable only by or on the authority of the organs of the State established by this Constitution'. Thus while supreme power derives from the citizenry, or, to use Williams's general definition, 'society', it is presumed that the organs of the state, using Christian principles as their guide, will administer the nation and protect the common good.

While on one hand this concept of democratic government is not uncommon, as shall be seen throughout this book, it is one which raises certain questions in relation to the definition of the nation, especially as it is represented in documentary films. Kearney observes that even the idea of popular sovereignty is itself problematic. With reference to Benedict Anderson's concept of 'imagined communities', according to which nation is never primordial but always the result of a fabricated concept of history and community, he asks 'who exactly are the people? Are they *a* people, *the* people, or peoples? Are "people" to be understood primarily as persons or nations? citizens or communities? regions or states?' (Kearney, 1997: 2). The nation, he observes, is often understood in several different contexts: as state, as territory, as ethnic group, as a migrant nationality transcending nation-state borders, and as a culture.

Gerry Smyth further notes that the nation emerged out of an intellectual and scholarly attempt to rationalise three key elements of human experience: social organisation, political order and a narrative of historical identity. This led to the rise of the nation-state, which was a particular response to the challenges presented in each of these areas that defined 'national' identity in terms of distinctive characteristics along the lines of those proposed by Kearney. Kearney notes that while not all of the contexts he lists apply equally to an understanding of Ireland as 'nation', they share a common goal of aspiring towards a sense of unity which provides a basis for solidarity. He explains that 'while nationalism, Irish or otherwise, displays a certain Protean, multiform and elusive character, it observes a common organizing principle – namely, the structural function of *unifying* a variety of elements (territory, language, statehood, tradition, history, race, religion, ideology) into a certain *identity*, thereby imparting to them a special function of inclusion and exclusion' (Kearney, 1997: 8–9). This notion of 'unity' is embodied in the tendency of nationalist conceptions to conceive of what Smyth terms 'the narrative of historical identity' in terms of grand narratives, or, as Kearney puts it, the 'Official Story of the Commisar' (Kearney, 1997: 63), to the point where it becomes increasingly difficult to acknowledge the metanarratives of disparate traditions or points of view within the mainstream. As shall be demonstrated throughout this book, this situation has resonances for the study of documentary, especially in terms of the conception of Irish history. It may also be applied in general terms to the manner in which the Griersonian documentary suggests a level of social cohesion and unanimity of perspective which has led some writers, such as Winston, to dispute its claims to referentiality.

Kearney applies elements of postmodern theory to his analysis of contemporary Ireland and proposes that the only model of nationality which can provide it with a future is a 'postnationalist' one. Postnationalism, he explains, does not abandon previously held concepts of self and nation, but embraces a multiplicity of perspectives and metanarratives. This includes those of groups within society which had previously been excluded, rather than a comprising a single, predominant interpretation of 'nationality' or national identity. He concludes by noting:

Citizens of these islands do best to think of themselves as 'mongrel-islanders' rather than as dwellers in two pure, god-given and rival nation-states. There is no such thing as primordial nationality. Every nation is a hybrid construct, an 'imagined' community which can be reimagined again in alternative versions. The ultimate challenge is to acknowledge this process of ongoing hybridization from which we derive and to which we are constantly subject. In the face of resurgent nationalisms fired by rhetorics of purity and purification, we must cling to the recognition that we are all happily mongrelized, independent, impure, mixed up. (Kearney, 1997: 188)

Though his argument has particular resonance given political develop-ments on the island of Ireland in the final years of the twentieth century, Kearney acknowledges that postnationalism is an aspiration rather than a certainty. This is the point at which Colin Graham interjects with the obser-vation that the flaw in the postnationalist concept is that 'firstly, its analysis and diagnosis are projected from a prearranged point in a teleology which has not yet quite played itself out' (Graham, 2001: 98). Secondly, he notes that postnationalism perhaps inadvertently reaffirms the centrality of the 'national'. Graham observes that 'its dependency on the maintenance of the conceptual value of the nation goes unrecognised. In this, post-nationalism philosophically dilutes postmodernism and uncomfortably straddles national and European polities' (98). Graham situates his own analysis of the particularities of Irish national identity within what he terms, (after Edward Said), 'liminal spaces' 'where the ultimate opposition of the coloniser and colonised breaks down through irony, imitation, and subver-sion' (86). This is a valuable precept, and we will return to it later as a gen-eral proposition for how a self-reflexive approach to documentary film might navigate such spaces.

Declan Kiberd and Luke Gibbons embark on projects similar to Kear-ney's in their analyses of literature and visual culture respectively. Kiberd's study of the relationship between ideas of Ireland expressed in poetry, liter-ature and the history of the state is centred on the premise that, as he puts it, works of art 'do not float free of their enabling conditions' (Kiberd, 1995: 4) and that there is an often all too direct link between representation and political reality. He notes that:

The imagination of these art-works has always been notable for its engagement with society and for its prophetic reading of the forces at work in their time. Less often remarked has been the extent to which political leaders from Pearse to Connolly, from de Valera to Collins, drew on the ideas of poets and playwrights. What makes the Irish Renaissance such a fascinating case is the knowledge that the cultural revival preceded and in many ways enabled the political revolution that followed. (Kiberd, 1995: 4)

Kiberd is indebted to writings on postcolonialism in this approach. He notes, for example, how Irish history follows the pattern described by Frantz Fanon (1963). In *The Wretched of the Earth*, Fanon described the postcolonial nation in terms of an attempt by an underdeveloped middle class and a col-onized intelligentsia to take over the running of the country from the colo-nial power only to find themselves, on one hand, following the template established by the colonial authority, and on the other attempting to rekin-dle 'national consciousness' by recourse to tribalism and myths of racial purity. Many writers on postcolonialism focus on the political discourse of the oppressed as expressed in literature through the inherited language and structures of the colonial power. Kiberd's book constantly returns to the manner in which Irish writers navigate the space between the English and Irish languages, between English and Irish culture, and even between different views of Ireland itself.

In his analysis of colonial legacies in Irish history and culture, Stephen Howe takes Kiberd's overall project to task, arguing that he has rather overstated the significance of colonialism and the applicability of Fanon and Said to the Irish condition. He notes, 'at the most rhetorically extreme, not only is colonialism presented as seeking to destroy Irish culture, but as making the place itself disappear' (Howe, 2000: 123). Colin Graham is likewise skeptical, noting that 'Kiberd's image of the "quilt of many colours, all beautiful, all distinct, yet all connected", wrapped around the shoulders of Cathleen ní Houlihan, is one striking example of how the hybrid can be reconfigured into old totalities' (Graham, 2001: 86). But even Gibbons suggests that postcolonial analyses of Irish history are sometimes problematic. This is not merely, as some writers he discusses have suggested, because, as a largely white and European culture, it is excluded from postcoloniality on racial grounds, but because the very suggestion of 'post' colonialism is false in the context of ongoing debates within Irish politics. Smyth addresses this by arguing that Ireland is still in a process of decolonisation, where, as he explains, both Northern Ireland and the Republic remain preoccupied with questions of political and cultural identity to the extent that a great deal of political will and public energy is absorbed by 'self-surveillance' (Smyth, 1997: 4).

Gibbons argues that studying transformation in Irish culture is not so much a revolutionary, postcolonial project of abandoning inherited ideas as a matter of re-envisioning them within a dynamic, contemporary framework. This approach echoes Kearney's formulation of postnationalism, and like Smyth, it suggests that assigning the condition of 'post' colonialism (or even 'post' modernism) to Ireland is premature. Gibbons argues 'the point here is that transformations induced by contact with the new may make active a transgressive potential already latent in the old, in the cast-offs and rejects of history' (Gibbons, 1996: 5). He elaborates upon this theme in his analysis of films, television, advertising, postcard art and some works of literature, and we will return to him throughout this book.

It remains to be seen how these ideas and the works of these writers may be applied to the study of Irish documentary. Indeed, though this concept of an unstable, shifting definition of 'Ireland' is central to the argument of this book, it is necessary to establish how 'stable' (largely nationalist and with quite fixed ideas of 'society', 'state' and 'nation') ideals were embodied in the non-fiction films made throughout the greater part of the twentieth century and the early twenty-first. The hitherto unobserved paradox is that the documentaries themselves were 'unstable' sites of meaning and inscription, and that the study of non-fiction film reveals the processes by which notions of 'the real Ireland' were conceived and debated throughout Irish history.

On documentary

Though, as John Corner notes, the word 'theory' should be applied with caution when approaching the study of non-fiction film, a few definitions are needed before we can usefully discuss 'documentary'. The itself term is a derivative of 'document', a word descended from the Latin *documentum*, meaning 'proof', and from *docere*, meaning 'to teach'. To term a piece of written material a 'document' is to maintain that it provides a record of events or circumstances which may be used as evidence that they transpired or exist. The process of creating 'documents' is a 'documentary' one, as is that of compiling them. Though legalistic in its roots, this current modern English language usage provides us with the first link between documentary film and what Bill Nichols terms the 'discourses of sobriety' (Nichols 1991: 3), by which he means systems of knowledge and social organisation including science, economics, politics, education and religion which 'have instrumental power' (3) in defining the nature of human social organisation.

Though Nichols notes that documentary is not equal in influence to these 'discourses of sobriety', he says it has 'a kinship' with them. Documentaries sometimes not only have bearing on general conceptions of the social and political world, but are capable of direct intervention in social process. Leni Riefenstahl's *Triumph of the Will* (1934) was considered so instrumental to the rise of Nazism that its maker faced prosecution for war crimes after the Second World War. Frederic Wiseman's *Titicut Follies* (1967) resulted in an official investigation of the psychiatric institute about which it was made and the film remains central to litigation on privacy because of the issues raised in making it. Errol Morris's *The Thin Blue Line* (1988) changed the course of a legal decision, freeing a man accused of the murder of a police officer over a decade before and forgotten until the film took up his case. These are not incidental connections, or fanciful academic apposition. There is a sense among writers about documentary that they are dealing with something politically challenging and socially relevant, much as there should be among those who make them.

The nature of the 'documents' which constitute a work of documentary film is also crucial. The raw material of the documentary film is not the illusory cinematic image, but the event it 'captures'. Documentaries are not presented as a constructed alternate reality, but as collected incidents of recorded actuality. Derived from the old French word *actualité* meaning 'entity', the word 'actuality' has a specific meaning. In common usage the term often refers to an item or section of documentary footage, usually a portion of a newsreel stored for archival purposes. Dziga Vertov refers to such items as 'film-facts', which may be used to build a work of documentary. He says that 'every instant of life shot unstaged, every individual frame shot *just as it is* in life with a hidden camera, "caught unawares," or by some other analogous technique – represents a fact recorded on film, a *film-fact* as we call it' (Vertov, cited in Michelson (ed.), 1984: 57). An actuality therefore is a perceptible moment, replete with multiple levels of action. When captured on film, this becomes a 'document' which proves on an evidentiary level (not taking into account potential manipulations of the profilmic or of the image for the time being) that something has transpired or exists. It may then be arranged by the filmmakers in accordance with their needs or desires.

The most famous use of the term is in John Grierson's all-encompassing, paradoxical definition of documentary as, 'the creative treatment of actuality.'[1] This pronouncement was the subject of a sustained critique by Brian Winston (1995). For Winston, the cultural and ideological factors which influence the filmmaker negate any possibility of the objectivity required to gain access to verifiable data and 'real' phenomena. Corner (1996) responds to this position by observing that Winston's assumption presumes that viewers of documentaries are unable to negotiate the space between documentary evidentiality and 'reality' itself. If we take 'actuality' not to mean the real, but instances of 'real' behaviour in specific circumstances, then we may begin to understand the inherent ambiguity of documentary film's 'documents'. It may be that the film camera's inability to give an unmediated reading is in fact the *reason* for its usefulness as a recorder of life.

Documentary cinema, by its very nature, represents an arrangement of data derived from 'reality' in the form of evidentiary exposition or interrogation. As Martin Moloney observes, documentary 'is supposed to dramatize life facts, to anatomize the problems of large masses of people, to comment on ideas' (cited in Bluem, 1965: 60). The key word here is 'anatomize'. Viewers are not expected to absorb the wholeness of human experience in a single document. 'Reality' must be broken down. Viewers must recognise in documentary a fragment of life, arranged in context, which draws on their current knowledge and contributes to their subsequent understanding of the 'real' world. Of course a person's conception of 'the real world' depends to a large degree on the ontological argument endorsed by the society in which they live. Ontology, briefly, is the branch of metaphysics concerned with primary conceptual matter – material objects, persons, numbers – facts which make up a theory of existence. An ontological argument may be related to a proposition (or an assertion) of the existence of a controlling force or system. Empiricism, for example, posits an external reality verifiable by scientific means which is known and knowable to the subject (person). Documentary is commonly perceived to operate within this tradition, offering as it does a methodology of observation which may be used to provide evidence of things as they are.

Yet because spectatorship operates on both sensory and cognitive levels, 'documentary' deals not so much with 'reality' or 'the real' as with a hermeneutic structure which negotiates epistemic space. We might usefully think of documentary as a set of organising principles and definitive practices which culminate in a conceptual framework wherein the viewer defines 'the real' through a continual process of negotiation between what is shown (sensory perception) and what is known (cognitive perception). Hence the nature of 'reality' is not so much a single, external, knowable state of being as defined by God or some other source of ultimate knowledge, but a realm of fluid interplay between observer, subject positions and ontology. In this light, documentary's claims to evidentiality are based upon the position it occupies in current definitions of social organisation, and very often it is the form, or mode of representation, which defines the film's relationship with the historical world. The difficulty is that very often viewers are not, or do not choose to be, aware of the formal strategies employed in representing reality.

Writing about documentary form is concerned with the structural characteristics of documentary films which affect their capacity to communicate information, present an argument and explore a subject area. Different writers emphasise different fundamentals: some focus on formal structures (Bordwell and Thompson, Michael Rabiger), some discuss variances on the level of subjectivity (Nichols, Corner), some deal in poetics (Michael Renov) and historicism (Richard Barsam, Erik Barnouw). Each provides inroads into what might be termed a theory of genre for documentary. The various tendencies, modes, impulses, categories and structures involved should not be viewed in isolation from one another. Form may be the result of interaction between all or any of them, and may also include a combination of historical and structural factors. Shifts in the nature of documentary itself, especially in terms of its social role, also affect the degree of 'creative treatment' which may be in ascendance at any given time, and this also impacts on the form used.

Nichols identifies four formal variances he terms 'voices'. He writes of these based 'not on a theoretical agenda but on the experiential effect that they have on a viewer' (Nichols (ed.), 1985: 258). He identifies four such 'voices': (1) the voice of God (also known as direct address), (2) *cinéma vérité*, (3) 'string of interviews' and (4) self-reflexive. In 1991, he refined these 'voices' into 'modes of representation', which he categorised as (1) expositional (2) observational (3) interactive and (4) reflexive. In 1999 he added 'poetic', 'participatory' and 'performative' modes. In all cases Nichols emphasises that these are not exclusive or necessarily confined to one historical period, though they arose in roughly chronological form.

To summarise Nichols's argument, a rough description of documentary history might describe the voice of God as a pragmatic, authoritarian type of film characterised by the work of John Grierson and the British documentary movement. These filmmakers, often operating with 'official' backing, produced films which concentrated on the solutions to social problems within a pedantic and sometimes romantic tradition (the 'poetic' mode). *Cinéma vérité* (or observational mode) might then be seen partly as a reaction to this type of film and partly as a response to technological changes which facilitated filmmakers such as Richard Leacock and Frederick Wiseman in their attempts to get closer to their subjects. The interactive (and participatory) mode then arose partly because the age of public television favoured the use of full-frame close ups of individuals speaking to the camera which allowed filmmakers such as Jean Rouch and Claude Lanzmann to construct their arguments more visibly through a combination of documents and opinions presented in a manner which allowed the viewer to participate in its construction. Finally, the self-reflexive (and performative) film might be seen as a conscious attempt not only to articulate the argument of the film maker, but to make explicit their presence as part of that argument in the postmodern age where all meaning is relative. Interestingly, the first instance of a film maker operating within this mode is Dziga Vertov, who predates all of the others.

In keeping with the structuralist dimensions of this model Nichols is careful to note that the chronology is not strictly linear, and that all forms of address continue to be used. He is also careful to point out that while realism and narrative might be considered to be formal systems which define documentary practice, that these are not modes or voices; rather, he argues, they are components of all four. These modes of representation are produced by differing degrees of emphasis (tempered by considerations of ideology) and by the decisions made by filmmakers. This brings up the inevitable question of subjectivity. If choices are involved, what lines are drawn between the personal whims of a decision maker and the 'objective' reality they are supposed to be documenting? Erik Barnouw gives probably the most succinct summary of the issues involved when he notes:

True documentarists have a passion for what they *find* in images and sounds – which always seem to them more meaningful than anything they can invent. They may serve as catalysts, not as inventors. Unlike the fiction artist, they are dedicated to not inventing. It is in selecting and arranging their findings that they express themselves; these choices are, in effect, their main comments. And whether they adopt the stance of observer, or chronicler, or painter, or whatever, they cannot escape their subjectivity. They present their version of the world. (Barnouw, 1993: 348) [original emphasis]

Documentary is a subjective medium because documentarists are human beings. An ethical and professional divide separates them from fiction artists, and an 'understanding' between all parties involved that a documentary *is* a documentary.

Anne Fischel further explains that 'often the determining factor is the quality of relations between filmmaker and subjects, the extent to which people can feel a common sense of purpose, and can trust that they will be heard and understood' (Fischel, 1989: 36). This idea of 'a common sense of purpose' links the documentary endeavour to an active formation of social reality (or perhaps, 'agreed reality') where the world of the film is taken to be a true representative of the world of everyday reality. There is a crucial distinction between the position occupied by the spectator in documentary and that of fiction. The world of documentary is the world of direct human experiences. It is not the constructed fantasy of a world which resembles our own and serves as an allegorical realm, but a place where the viewer is asked to occupy a position which actively engages them with a conception of 'real life'. This means that fundamentally, fiction manipulates and modifies reality from within its 'world' whereas non-fiction does so from without. Documentary film depends on the viewer's expectation that what is filmed in actual occurrence has not been entirely created by the film maker, however much they have 'shaped' it in accordance with their subjective point of view.

The emphasis in documentary is therefore upon an active spectator rather than a passive one. What Nichols terms 'procedures of rhetorical engagement' (Nichols, 1991: 26) are in effect. He notes, 'even if the images forfeit their claims to congruence, even if the documentary constructs what occurs in front of the camera as a representation of what occurs in the world, as do the films *Night Mail*, *Louisiana Story*, *Nanook of the North*, *Letter from Siberia*, and *The Thin Blue Line*, we still persist, as long as we assume it is a documentary that we are watching, in inferring an argument about the world' (25–6). There is, as Michael Rabiger says, a 'contract' with the audience (Rabiger, 1992: 9), or we could use the more euphemistic term 'understanding' whereby, as Fischel says, there is a common sense of purpose which allows 'documentary' to maintain a special status relative to agreed definitions of 'reality' and allows arguments to be drawn from the historical world. The question is not so much what the documentarist does as why. In using filmed actualities to construct a rhetorical argument about the historical world, is the documentarist serving the needs of narrative and false consciousness, as Winston would have it, or is this the ontology of documentary cinema and an essential condition of its existence?

There is more to be said, and I will refer throughout this book to the writings of Nichols, Bordwell and Thompson, Renov, Corner, Winston, and others. In general though, it is my contention that because it is definable not so much in its utterances (the films) as the processes which underlie it, the role and function of non-fiction film can only be understood through an examination of the society in which it operates. The evolution of Ireland in documentary is therefore as telling as the evolution of documentary in Ireland in terms of how we may understand the manner in which both are perceived. Though it is not my intention to argue that a single, definable identity can emerge from this discussion either for Ireland or for documentary, it is frequently necessary to argue that documentaries of specific periods reflect a dominant ideological (or philosophical, or ontological) conception of 'reality' itself which tells us something about the state of *things as they are* at that time. That we may, with the benefit of hindsight, apply models of interpretation which allow us to question the construction of these things is the great strength of documentary form. It is also for this reason that I have largely confined myself to films made in and about Ireland by Irish filmmakers. Without wanting to become too enwrapped in essentialism at this point, I think it is fair to say that the framework I have proposed necessitates the selective inclusion of films and television programmes originating outside of the country. *Man of Aran* (1934), *Ireland: A Television History* (1981) and other selected works have their place here, but in the main I have endeavoured to place these pieces relative to historical or critical arguments which require their presence. It is also with this overarching analytical framework in mind that I have excluded most of the films made by Irish filmmakers about other countries, including the multiple award-winning *Chavez: Inside the Coup* (2003). I should mention that such films (non-Irish films about Ireland and Irish films about other parts of the world) have been part of my ongoing research for some time, and there is much to be said about them. First things first, however.

Forearmed with the critical tools supplied by the study of documentary and with an awareness of the history of the form in other countries, it is my contention that we may assess Irish documentary in terms not only of the facts of the making of individual films, but of the evolving ideas of Ireland which they represent. Irish documentaries will not be examined under named categories or factors or modes or any other specific formulation. A discussion of documentary film should ideally incorporate elements of all of what has been discussed so far, but must also be cognisant of issues arising out of the specific historical and/or thematic questions under scrutiny. Thus while they will frequently draw upon the learning represented by theoretical and critical writings on documentary, this book will also incorporate a range of writers and theorists from disciplines outside documentary studies which are germane to the issues in question. Bear in mind all the while though that this book is not about documentary theory: it is about documentary in Ireland. It is not my intention that it should become bound up with ideas to the exclusion of textual analysis. Rather the analysis of non-fiction film which follows should present ideas within a framework which facilitates an understanding of the broader questions raised by the study of Irish documentary itself.

Notes

1 It is still uncertain as to when (or indeed if) he said this, though Winston notes that it was first attributed to him by Forsyth Hardy in 1946, then Paul Rotha in 1952. See Winston, 1999: 76.

The lie of the land: primitives, poets and pilgrims

Most of the earliest filmed images of Ireland were of its landscape. This is true of most places. The limited expressive capacities of cinema in the late nineteenth century resulted in a plethora of observational short subjects collectively termed 'actualities' or 'travelogues'. These urban or rural vignettes of people and places usually constituted the first non-fictional representation of countries visited by pioneer cineastes, and so it was in Ireland. Yet the use of the word 'landscape' in any discussion of Ireland raises many issues. For Luke Gibbons, the romantic evocation of Western Ireland in fiction films such as *The Quiet Man* (1952) and *Ryan's Daughter* (1970) represents a cultural and political distortion. He argues that the desocialisation and depoliticisation of the Irish landscape offers images of a pre-modern idyll in which the natural elements are contained by cinematic artifice. This provides the visual pleasures of both 'soft' and 'hard' primitivism, terms Gibbons derives from Erwin Panofsky.[1] It also creates a representational shorthand which can enable or disable understanding of the landscape in the context of a wider view of Irish culture. Moreover, as McLoone points out, these myths of the Irish landscape have been internalised and have been appropriated not only by filmmakers eager to contest their validity, but by nationalist ideologues who embrace them, proffering ideals of a proud people living in harmony and contest with a physical environment which endows them with a unique national identity (McLoone, 2000: 36–7).

While not wholly inappropriate in discussion of documentary, this basic approach to the meaning of landscape on film works from a supposition of conscious artifice consistent with procedures of fictive engagement. Even given the acknowledged interpretative subjectivity of documentary, the frames of reference for the analysis of non-fiction films are different. The status of documentary relative to the discourses of sobriety and the medium's role as an arbiter of social reality necessitate closer analysis of the raw materials employed in representing 'reality', namely, in this case, the landscape itself and the notion of 'place' which it suggests.

Landscape, place and personality

So what is landscape, and what do we mean when we employ the term in the study of Ireland in documentary? On one level 'landscape' is the profilmic environment. It is the physical subject of the camera's eye; that which is before the camera and is filmed. The location can be urban or rural, and subjects might include buildings, people, plants and animals. These features of an occupied living space become the basic pictorial elements of a cinematic image. It is frequently noted that such images are not neutral because the act of filmmaking constitutes a series of interpretational choices evincing and affecting a sense of perspective. Less often observed is that the landscape itself is also constructed, a signifier of habitation replete with meanings of its own.

The term 'place' also requires some elaboration. The combination of the physical topography of a location and the structures built upon it represents a conception of the relationship between an environment and its inhabitants. This relationship may be read as 'national' or 'cultural' given the weight of history brought to bear on the sense of being which comes with the act of dwelling. Patrick Sheeran notes that '"A sense of place", in one meaning of the phrase, is analogous to a sense of humour or a sixth sense, meaning a special faculty or mode of perception. Those who possess it delight in one another's company and spur one another on to even greater feats of finding connections' (Sheeran, 1988: 198). Though it is drawn from a landscape, the idea of place is a more specific formulation of the relationship between the land and its occupants. It is, as Sheeran notes, akin to a special mode of perception.

Some of the constituents of this mode of perception might be those discussed by Martin Heidegger. He writes of 'dwelling' and 'building' as conceptions of habitation which link what he terms 'the fourfold', namely earth, sky, divinities and mortals. His point is that in conceiving of any one of these four, the human mind inevitably locates it relative to the others; in other words our sense of place is relative to our philosophical conception of being. As such, Heidegger argues, 'We attain to dwelling, so it seems, only by means of building' (Heidegger, 1971: 145), by which he means that the condition of 'dwelling' in a place is more than simply building structures upon a landscape. It involves, he explains, conceiving of a state of being which connects us with the world around us on a metaphysical level. As such a sense of place is even more deeply intertwined with conceptual and contextual hermeneutics than literal depiction of the landscape can signify alone.

In his study of 'the personality of Ireland' (which is the title of his book), E. Estyn Evans attempts to integrate physical geography with cultural history. He emphasises the role of habitat in the formation of cultural identity, and details evolution of an identifiably 'Irish' Ireland from pre-Celtic times to the nineteenth century. His main contention is that the people who inhabit this island continually adapt to the terrain and the changeable climate, resulting in particular patterns of rural development and social organisation. His conclusion is not so much in the identification of a unique Gaelic type, but in contending that the land has played an important part in the formation of the cultural and political identity of those who have lived on it. He argues for an awareness of what he calls 'the visible heritage of cultural landscapes' (Evans, 1992: 82) which accommodates the shape, form and physical attributes of a geographical location into analysis of the nature of a place and the events which occur there; as he puts it himself, 'the land itself is something more than a picturesque stage for cultural achievement' (88). Cultural geographer Brian Graham takes this even further, arguing that the development of a consensus of identity on the island of Ireland will never occur until a common geographical framework has been established, 'defined by regional and cultural heterogeneity, notions of hybridity and the equality of rights of citizenship embodied in civic nationalism' (Graham (ed.), 1997: 210).

Tim Robinson points out that even the act of naming has implications for understanding both the inhabitants and those who map the spaces (physically or cognitively). He says that 'we, personally, cumulatively, communally, create and recreate landscapes – a landscape being not just the terrain but also the human perspectives on it, the land plus its overburden of meanings' (Robinson, 1993: 30). He argues that the act of putting words to a place is akin to a bolt of lightning which magnetises it, 'attracting observations and the accumulation of placelore' (31). He invents a new term to describe it: 'geophany', derived from the term 'theophany' meaning (according to the *Concise Oxford Dictionary*) a visible manifestation of God, a god, or man. The 'overburden of meanings' occurs as 'perspectives' accumulate. Bernard Nietschmann writes that 'the geographic montage of places that comprises a country probably maintains a people's collective identity as much as do language, religion, history or television' (Nietschmann, 1993: 6–7).

Nietschmann also observes that people are interested in 'places' because each is thought to have 'a special individual character that influences those who live there' (6) a character which inevitably features in their acts of self-representation. A process of negotiation and transformation occurs with any act of representation, evident even in some of the earliest visual depictions of the Irish landscape. Raymond Gillespie notes that the work of British cartographers and surveyors of the seventeenth century constitutes the first attempts to systematically record an impression of the Irish landscape intended for specific application. Cartography can been viewed in terms of colonialism, of course, as can the act of naming. This was explored in the play *Translations* (1980) by Brian Friel. John Breen notes that maps and texts produced in Ireland in accordance with the instruction and mandate of the British crown were intended to serve colonists and other imperial agents in their subjugation of the native population. These historical documents 'circumscribe the state of Ireland as the forces of colonialism and empiricism intersect' (Breen, 1994: 46).

I do not wish to dwell on the colonial/postcolonial debate at this point, but it suffices to note that mapmaking as a process is both politically determined and socially determinate to an extent which strongly influences subsequent thinking about the places 'mapped'. Drawings and watercolours by draughtsmen like Nicholas Pynnar, Thomas Phillips and Thomas Dineley, though they were primarily depictions of specific features of geography and topography, formed a collective representation, in Nietschmann's terms a geographical montage, of the country known as 'Ireland'. This work would have far-reaching effects in terms of the perception of the character of the landscape. Not only were they providing literal road maps for the forces of colonial occupation, they were ascribing qualities of habitability and hazard to a space hitherto viewed and occupied in terms now recorded only by what was being called 'folklore'.

A discernible documentary function beyond pragmatic inscription began with the engraver Francis Place. His attempts to record and integrate landmarks of particular political and historical significance into his sketches of Dublin served as important indicators of the social, religious and administrative life of the city. Like any documentarist, Place made choices and selections which, to him, provided important information about his subject. His choices of buildings, monuments and districts would later become the inspiration for postcard views, in terms of both the locations depicted and the perspectives from which they were seen. The work of nineteenth-century geological surveyor George Victor Du Noyer went even further. His drawings and watercolours were characterised by an exaggeration of scale and shape which lent a panoramic ruggedness to the landscape viewed. Du Noyer's work, still technically considered within the realm of scientific documentation, owed as much to the tradition of the picturesque as it did to empirical methodology.[2]

English artist William Gilpin wrote in 1792 that the aim of the picturesque genre was 'of not merely describing; but of adapting the description of natural scenery to the principles of artificial landscape; and of opening the sources of those pleasures, which are derived from the comparison' (cited in Kennedy, 1993: 165). As early as the 1790s, the representation of the landscape as an exaggerated idyll was commonplace, and not just in Ireland. Paintings in the 'picturesque' idiom evinced aesthetic and spiritual ideology. As Brian Kennedy puts it, 'a beautiful landscape evidenced the divine order underlying it; nature was superior to art, but, in the interests of the picturesque, the artist modified a landscape to improve its aesthetic aspect' (Kennedy, 1993: 166). Popular eighteenth- and nineteenth-century representations of Ireland were created in response to the demand for such sentimental, idealised and primarily rural scenes. As Gibbons observes, the popularity of this genre coincided with the desire of the urban middle classes and the aristocracy to escape the ravages of the Industrial Revolution. The problem was that the depictions became a self-fulfilling prophecy: as Gibbons notes, 'lacking the advanced social and political structures of the new economic order, it [Ireland] came to embody, along with other similar regions on the European periphery, all the attributes of a vanished preindustrial era – if not of a society entirely beyond the pale of civilisation' (Rockett et al., 1988: 203–4).

The advent of photography might have promised an emergence of the principles of documentary given the referential congruence between the photographed image and the landscape itself, but this was not so. Early photographs of Ireland were also postcard views which distorted the physical environment as much as paintings and drawings had. Carey Schofield (1994) notes that photographs of Irish peasants were often faked using friends of the photographer, usually in order to generate an expected image of the peasantry amenable to consumers. This is less surprising when it is remembered that photography was not employed in a documentary context generally until the 1850s, when Roger Fenton's photographs of the Crimean War and Matthew Brady's of the American Civil War assumed an emotional and psychological dimension beyond referential reportage. It was not until 1888, when Danish photographer Jacob Riis recorded images of poverty among emigrants in New York, that any semblance of issue-based social documentary emerged, and it would be forty years more before the same would occur in film.

The accumulation of perspective and placelore already evident from cartographical and illustrative representations makes evident the combination of elements and contexts contributing to perception of Ireland as a place. It is with film that Nietschmann's use of the term 'montage' begins to have particular meaning, even if in the years of early cinema it did not have the theoretical significance now ascribed to it. The earliest filmed images of Ireland share a lineage with these cartographical drawings and picturesque paintings. The films which will be examined in a moment form the basis of the cultural topography upon which we will begin to examine the formation of a documentary conception of Ireland on film. They are 'landscapes' in the purest sense of the word; referring not only to the depiction of the profilmic, but to the role it plays in the establishment of Evans's 'visible heritage of cultural landscapes' (Evans, 1992: 82). Considered as groups of images as well as single subjects in their own right, early films become 'geographic montages' (Nietschmann, 1993: 6) which give an indication of how Ireland was seen and known in the years around the turn of the nineteenth and early twentieth centuries. These films are also geophantic, to use Robinson's term, in that they represent the first identification of the place in the new medium and therefore inevitably influence subsequent recreations of the landscape on film. It is also arguable that these early films represent 'building' in a loose sense of the term as used by Heidegger insofar as they 'build' into a 'geographical montage' which illustrates the beginnings of the evolution of Ireland in documentary film and may help us to understand what it means to dwell there.

Actualities and travelogues

The films in the following section cover the years between 1896 and 1922. During this period non-fiction film in general was engaged in the literal depiction of events and scenes often termed 'views' or 'landscapes'. It was only with the making of *Nanook of the North* (1922) that the medium moved forward, coincidentally just as Ireland achieved political independence. It is an important phase in the evolution of Ireland in documentary film, encompassing the first films made and forming a bridge between what had gone before and what would follow.

Lumière in Ireland

The first cinematic images of Ireland were made by Lumière cineaste Alexandre Promio following the exhibition of the Cinématographe in Dublin, Cork and Belfast in 1896.[3] The Lumières' standard marketing strategy was to demonstrate the filming, developing and projecting capacities of their new machine by shooting scenes in the city in which they were exhibiting. The programme for subsequent public screenings would then include both the material they had just shot and subjects collected elsewhere. This policy gave many viewers their first impression of other countries as well as of themselves, and so it was that Ireland found its way to film for the first time in 1897.

There are some twenty-five films in the Lumière collection stored in the Irish Film Archive, which is not to say that others do not exist. While the films contain images of the countryside, the Ireland they represent is an urbanised, modern country with city streets, civic buildings, firemen, horse guards, and the ubiquitous train tracks which carried the camera from location to location. Filming primarily in Dublin and Belfast, with some phantom rides showing the outlying towns on the main train route between them, Promio did not attempt to examine the landscape he filmed in passing. Unlike those who would follow, he did not actively seek out a rural ethos. The result is that the first film images of Ireland portray a country in unison with the rest of Victorian Britain.

Ten of the scenes are taken on the train route from Belfast to Dublin. They mostly portray the train stations and the towns and lands immediately surrounding them within a radius of the customary fifty-three seconds of film. In most cases, the name of the station is not even visible. These particular films are of general interest for their use of depth of field to achieve a singular fade-out effect. As the train moves, the landscape furthest from the camera is in sharp focus and gives a clear portrait of whatever is in view: houses, cottages, public parks, etc. When a hedgerow or the wall of a station enters the frame, the image becomes, in effect, an abstraction. Nothing is clearly defined because of its proximity to the camera, and on several occasions the films end simply with ten to fifteen seconds of movement of this kind. Though the result of a simple physical fact (the hedges blocked the view) this may nonetheless be seen as a demonstration of the willingness to explore the limits of the stationary camera as a recorder of motion. In one case a rhythmic oscillation between scenes in and out of focus makes for a hypnotic portrait of this abstract landscape, and in another the rapid passage of rows of white picket fences surrounding the station seems more like a zoetrope animation than actual film.

Other films in the collection include the first use of what would become the signature image of Dublin city, namely O'Connell Street (then Sackville Street) taken from O'Connell Bridge (then Carlisle Bridge) with the statue of Daniel O'Connell, the General Post Office and the Nelson pillar in shot. The largest object in the street at 134 ft in height, the pillar was seen as a symbol of the colonial presence in popular views of the city sold in the nineteenth century. The pillar was a major landmark celebrating one of the heroes of the British navy. His position, standing tall above the principal street and looking down on Catholic patriot O'Connell at the end of it, made the monument an obvious target for satire (and, eventually, destruction by the IRA). It was also the site of a memorable scene in *Ulysses* (1922) as a vantage point from which old ladies spit upon pedestrians.

As a visitor to the city, Promio was quick to replicate the popular view of the street and the pillar. Though the latter was situated lower in the frame than the statue of O'Connell, it was in the all-important eyeline hot zone two thirds of the way up on the left-hand side. Framing, however, seems less significant given the added dimension of motion, which was what excited early film audiences in the first place. The image of the street features pedestrians, cyclists and horse-drawn vehicles moving within and in and out of the frame. This is doubly important because many nineteenth-century views of Sackville Street gave more prominence to buildings than to people. The depiction of the city as a landscape without living occupants had the effect of enhancing the grandeur of the colonial architecture. This also denoted the dominance of the elite over the general populace, which is especially significant given the decline of the city within the empire during the nineteenth century. It was considered 'second city of the empire' for part of the eighteenth century, but political unrest and the relative lack of industrial progress compared to Belfast in the nineteenth century saw a decline in its status. Such views, which were usually elegantly picturesque, omit the untidy details of actual occupancy in favour of edifices and monuments denoting colonial power. Their popularity was also indicative of the preference for fine art over popular forms of representation, including photography, in which realistic detail might spoil the view.

The cinema stood poised to overthrow the order of popular art, and in representing the people of Dublin as part of its landscape, the Lumière films reflected a change both in the representation of the city and in the prevailing conditions of reception. Though hardly advocating revolution or even intentionally intervening in the history of visual heritage, they signify the social and political development of urban culture between the early and late nineteenth centuries. While there is still no evidence of poverty or violence, which, as Kevin O'Neill observes, 'were clearly not in the artist's best commercial interests' (1993: 64), the Dublin pictured by Promio is of ordinary people, who were also the intended audience. The fact that over seven thousand people attended the first week of the second programme of Lumière shorts in October 1896 is testament to the mass nature of their reception.

The Lumière Irish collection also features firemen demonstrating their efficiency, a common theme in films during this period. In one example, firemen parade watched by a cheering crowd, many of whom seem as interested in the camera as the spectacle itself. In another, an action scene is staged on a corner of St Stephen's Green with a dramatic diagonal dividing the frame. The firemen race around the corner (again with cheering crowds) and past the camera. Afterwards, the audience themselves pile onto the street, several smiling at the camera. As with urban scenes in general, this demonstration of the efficiency of the fire services was an indication of the health and modernity of the city. This was also evident in films shot by Lumière cameramen throughout the world, including the seminal *Pompiers à Lyon* (1896). The genre would reach its apex with the more complex dramatic reconstructions of the first decade of the twentieth century, such as Edwin S. Porter's *The Life of an American Fireman* (1905).

The Dublin fireman films are also united by the presence of authentic Dubliners. These are not merely bystanders as in *Pompiers à Lyon*. Each of the four films features a group of cheering onlookers, who invariably run after the fire carriage when it moves out of shot. They are clearly entertained as much because the scene has been staged for the camera as they are by the event itself. Many of them are more concerned with the camera than the firemen. Again this demonstrates both the presence of ordinary people in nineteenth-century Dublin and the artifice of the 'actuality' (it has obviously been set up). Even more specifically contrived is the cavalry demonstration by the 13th Hussars. A total of seven films feature the neatly orchestrated manoeuvres of horsemen and steeds. As the fireman films demonstrate the efficiency of the emergency services, these films portray the unity and discipline of the British military. They also use striking composition, and even employ movement towards the camera. In one example they rush past, in a variant on *The Arrival of a Train* (1895), presumably intended to produce the reaction which famously greeted the earlier film.

Apart from the image of Sackville Street, the Ireland seen in these films is nonetheless an anonymous one. There is no particular 'uniqueness' or 'Irishness' which singles out the country from the rest of Britain. Other films in the collection feature boats in the harbour of Kingstown (now Dun Laoghaire) and barges filmed from a river bank which could essentially be from anywhere. Only one church is seen, and that is in the distance in an image of a bridge on which trams and carriages are the focus. In the same film, a man drawing coal rides past the camera then turns his head and stares with amusement, another fleeting glimpse of the attitudes of the natives to the presence of the camera. The continuity between Belfast and Dublin in the collection is further evidence that Promio did not have a preconceived notion of what Ireland should represent. The fact that Belfast was by now the more prosperous city is not clear. Given the lack of interest in industry, economy or politics in general in early films of this kind, it is not surprising that such distinctions were not made.

Even though these films would have been shown abroad, and would thus be for many people their first view of Ireland on film, they do not attempt to portray the country as a rural utopia (or dystopia), or construct any particular character or identity which might be termed 'Irish', even that familiar from paintings of the previous generation. Ireland is just another stop on the Lumière tour, an exhibition venue which differs little from others throughout Europe. Yet, in recording these scenes, Promio commits an act of geophany. With the hindsight of film history and an awareness of representational conventions, we can begin to piece together the significance of such seemingly 'random' scenes for later cinematic representation. The presence of the Dublin populace, the amused glances at camera, the political specifics of the monuments captured without inflection but with intrinsic added meaning, and the persistent (if momentary) presence of open countryside are signs of things to come.

Though several amateur and semi-professional filmmakers were active in Ireland during this period and that immediately following, the work of relatively few has survived. For a native equivalent to the Lumière films, albeit one which comes later in the chronology of cinema, it is necessary to turn to James and Thomas Horgan. In common with the Lumières, the Horgans were photographers by trade, though they were also trained as shoemakers (also the profession of Georges Méliès's family). They worked out of Youghal in County Cork, where they publicised their shoemaking and photography business with magic lantern slides and music. Realising that people enjoyed seeing pictures of themselves, they included their own photographs, taken locally, with more exotic views. This was a long-established tradition in the trade, as already seen in the Lumières' policy of film exhibition. It was often more important that the faces of potential patrons were included than that the details of the event itself were captured accurately: it improved the chance of a sale. This practice nonetheless had the effect of bringing about the first comprehensive acts of self-documentation by indigenous Irish filmmakers.

Following the arrival and subsequent success of the Cinématographe, the Horgans purchased a motion picture camera. They obtained a cinema licence in 1910 and opened the Horgan Picture Palace in Youghal, a six-hundred-seat purpose-built theatre. As with their photographic and lantern slide shows, they included films of local interest as part of the programme. They effectively ran a newsreel service through the 1910s and 1920s, albeit exclusively for patrons of their own cinema. The films are sometimes referred to collectively as *The Youghal Gazette*, a title which appears at the beginning of the material housed by the Irish Film Archive. It is not certain how much material was produced, but it is presumed that much of it is lost. The extant material has been loosely dated between 1910 and 1922 based on James Horgan's estimates and evidence from the films themselves.[4]

The Horgan material provides an interesting contrast with the Lumière films, not least because of its emphasis on aspects of Irish life not seen or sought by Promio. The films vary in style and quality, ranging in style from static views to edited sequences. All provide an early example of the recording of an image of Ireland by Irish eyes for Irish audiences from a period in which 'Irish' identity was itself in flux. The most fascinating film in the collection is an untitled shot of people descending the steps of a church. The building itself is unseen, but unmistakable long, grey stone steps are visible. The constant flow of human bodies from the top to the bottom of the frame is reminiscent of a key scene in Vsevelod Pudovkin's *End of St Petersburg* (1927) where the massed heads of Soviet citizens signify the anonymity of collective power. Obviously the Horgans did not have political ambitions on

1 James and Thomas Horgan were cineastes and shoemakers based in Co. Cork. They shot a series of short subjects in the 1910s and 1920s compiled into a newsreel shown at their cinema in Youghal. Pictured here are James and his son Joseph with some of their equipment, circa 1915

the scale of the Soviets, but the scene is an assertion of the same principle. It shows the large numbers of people attending religious services, and therefore their collectivity as members of both the communities of Youghal and the Catholic church.

Other films in the collection specifically emphasise religious rituals and events, such as the multiple-shot depiction of a Corpus Christi parade. One image features a procession of female communicants in white dresses framed in a fashion fairly typical of early films. The girls form a winding, snake-like pattern from top left to bottom right of the frame and are in continuous, dynamic motion like the crowds walking to the Odessa pier in *Battleship*

Potemkin (1925). Some scenes include decorated shrines, people praying, and the streets draped with bunting. Another film features the dedication of a local church, others feature worshippers at a local holy well. These films demonstrate the importance of religious events as community gatherings in turn-of-the-century Youghal, though they were not necessarily filmed for this purpose. They too have precedents in popular art from the previous century, including George Petrie's depictions of pilgrims in Clare and Offaly. From the Horgans' point of view, these were venues and events where their patrons were gathered in large numbers. They were also a form of spectacle ideally suited to the medium. Moving processions could be shot from several angles to provide visual interest.

In addition to shooting religious scenes, the Horgans were present at many secular events, including, in one case, a local flat-racing competition. The racing film, in the manner of Robert Paul's *At the Derby* (1896), features only a fragment of the actual race. It would have been of more interest to locals as a record of the atmosphere anyway, and gave the Horgans the opportunity to film groups of people. This was consistent with their marketing strategies, but it was also, like Promio's film of Sackville Street, making reference to themes in popular art. Depictions of crowds at sporting events were a favourite subject of Jack B. Yeats, who had been drawing and painting such scenes since the 1900s. Bringing images to life which were already familiar as paintings was also one of the Lumières' marketing ploys, seen in *Partie d'écarte* (1895), a variant on Cézanne's *The Card Players*. The Horgans' use of this gimmick was not so much a commentary or parody as the Lumière film was, but it does further indicate the general shift from still to moving images and the links between them.

A curious point arising from this and other films is that no scenes of Gaelic games such as hurling or Gaelic football appear either in the Horgan material or in other sources from this period. It is not known whether this indicates that racing was a more popular sport or if there was a reluctance to film Gaelic games due to the logistical and political complexity of doing so. The Gaelic Athletic Association (GAA) still had links with subversive organisations, and GAA events were a common meeting place for nationalists. Capturing the faces of wanted men on film would not have been in the best interests of either the subjects or the filmmakers.

In general, the Horgan collection documents a far more rural Ireland than the Lumières'. The cottages and donkeys which would later embody rurality are absent, but the films do emphasise the pictorial qualities of locations without structures. There are beach scenes shot from a hilltop which offer a panoramic view of the bay. Another film records the annual orphans' day out, at which several of the children appear to be swimming naked whilst well-to-do ladies stand nearby in full dress and with parasols. The countryside is often seen and in films such as those of the race meets, the rural character of the onlookers is evident from their clothing and features. The films are far from exclusively rural though, and do not attempt to omit or exclude aspects of modernity. The collection also features a scene of firemen in action observed by a crowd similar to those shot in Dublin, and there is a film of the arrival of a steam ship which disgorges its passengers, signifying as busy a port in Youghal as Promio had filmed in Dun Laoghaire.

The Horgan material is a fascinating combination of views of turn-of-the-century Ireland. While modern, the country they depict is more community based, more rural and more religious than the one recorded by the Lumières. This is not to imply that either view is more or less 'documentary' than the other. It is interesting to note though that the differences between them stem from perceptual positioning. In the case of Alexandre Promio, Dublin and Belfast were European cities which he visited and filmed for exhibition both *in situ* and abroad. For the Horgans, Youghal was their own locality recorded for exhibition to locals. The Horgan films are also arguably more 'exotic' than the Lumières' precisely because of their parochialism. The geographic montage of community and rurality brings us closer to the expected 'personality' of Ireland on film. Yet Youghal as filmed by the Horgans is also a place replete with inhabitants with a specific, visible relationship to the physical environment. Human and non-human subjects are integral to one another. There are no views of either land or municipal buildings which have extraneous meaning to be inferred from general foreknowledge. This is Ireland as lived in by the Irish on a local level. It is also Ireland as represented to and by the Irish.

Other early filmmakers

Throughout the first decades of the twentieth century, a number of prominent filmmakers based outside of the island made films in Ireland including British pioneers Robert Paul and Arthur Melbourne-Cooper. Paul made a number of films, including *A Cattle Drive in Galway* (1908) and *Whaling Ashore and Afloat* (1908). The latter is interesting because Paul not only captured the activities of the hunters, but represented the subjective experience of being on board their ship by mounting his camera on the deck. He was thus able to depict the labour of the whalers and give a sense of their point of view, the combination of which anticipates Grierson's *Drifters* (1929). The representation of manual labour in these terms is a significant shift from the idle (and idyllic) peasants of eighteenth- and nineteenth-century paintings, and again shows the progressive potential of the new medium. The film also features 'ashore' segments which show exactly the opposite. The land-based scenes depict a colourful working class not far from the stereotypes which subsequent producers would find or invent for fictional comedies. The whalers perform a number of dances and games for the camera, which while possibly part of their lives on special occasions or if suitably inebriated, were hardly essential for whaling, either ashore or afloat. The inclusion of these scenes is especially interesting given the debate which would rage much later when Robert Flaherty would be accused of altering the lives of the Aran islanders: at least he didn't make them dance.

Melbourne-Cooper's major claim to fame as far as Ireland is concerned is the direction of the travelogue *London to Killarney* (1907), which he shot while shooting the comedy *Irish Wives and English Husbands* (1907), the latter of which Rockett names as the first fiction film made in Ireland. The significance of the travelogue goes beyond mere historical footnoting. In August 1861 Queen Victoria had visited Killarney, an event which dramatically increased the region's tourist trade. The visit linked the Imperial centre with its rural periphery in terms of pleasure. As Donal Horgan observed, Killarney became 'the place where every self respecting Victorian visited' (Horgan, 1988: 64). Melbourne-Cooper's film demonstrated for the mass audience how, nearly fifty years later, it was possible for ordinary people to make the same journey as the late queen, using modern methods of transportation. The same factors may have motivated local filmmaker Louis de Clerq, whose *Life on the Great Southern and Western Railway* (1904) Rockett credits as the first indigenous documentary. This essentially amateur film documenting the now legendary rail route to that part of the country achieved national distribution.

Though the Horgan brothers were operating their 'newsreel' exclusively for a local audience, the first national newsreel service arrived in 1917, when the General Film Supply company began producing and distributing *Irish Events*. Rockett provides a detailed history of the relatively short life of this service (Rockett et al., 1988: 32–6). It operated out of offices in Dublin and was run by filmmaker Norman Whitten, who had trained in England under Cecil Hepworth. The country was already serviced nationally by Pathé and Gaumont, but *Irish Events* endeavoured to provide Irish news for an Irish audience. The footage shot by Whitten and his cameraman J. Gordon Lewis covered most of the important news and sports events of the period, the former of which would later provide raw material for the historical compilation film *Mise Éire* (1959), which will be discussed later.

Like many Irish-based filmmakers during this period, Whitten laboured under political conditions unfavourable to the development of a successful industry. Inevitably, the filming of news events during the time leading up to the outbreak of the war of independence brought him into conflict with the British authorities. It was the production of a documentary overview of the activities of Éamon deValera's nationalist party entitled *The Sinn Féin*

Review (1919) which finally prompted censorship by Dublin Castle, and by 1920 the company had ceased its newsreel operations altogether. Whitten returned to England after making a drama on the life of St Patrick in 1920, and remained working there until his death.

Independence: the search for self and nation

The years between 1916 and 1923 saw the struggle for political independence reach its climax, followed by a civil war which had lasting effects on the social and political landscape. Film production was a low political and economic priority during these years. Though the consequences of this policy for Irish film have been extensively documented in studies of fiction, none of them observe that the first major revolution in non-fiction was largely missed as a result. The pattern of actuality, travelogue and newsreel seen throughout the preceding decades in Ireland conforms to that worldwide. The combination of professional and amateur practitioners, both indigenous and foreign, was also common, and indeed necessary for the development of the form. But elsewhere in the world, a clear divide began to emerge between actualities and travelogues and more interpretative non-fiction films following *Nanook of the North*. Flaherty's use of actuality changed the way filmmakers conceived of the limits of the form, and by the time Grierson inadvertently christened the medium in 1927, significant progress had been made.

Soviet modernists had already begun to fragment and rearrange actuality to form montages not just of geography, but of time. Denis Kaufman's *Moscow* (1927), Dziga Vertov's *Man With a Movie Camera* (1929) and Esfir Shub's *Fall of the Romanov Dynasty* (1927) all demonstrated this. Brazilian Alberto Cavalcanti had used similar techniques to represent the modern metropolis in *Rien que les heures* (1926). Joris Ivens had studied a mechanical task as a rhythmic hymn to industrial labour in *The Bridge* (1928) and examined the patterns and effects of falling rain in Amsterdam in *Rain* (1929). Taking their cue from Flaherty, scientists and would-be scientists had begun making filmed ethnographic records of remote regions and peoples, and entertainers Merian C. Cooper and Ernest B. Schoedsack had made *Grass* (1925) and *Chang* (1927). Flaherty himself directed *Moana: A Romance of the South Seas* (1926). In a review of this latter film, John Grierson had labelled the new form 'documentary', and his own *Drifters* (1929) evinced a social democrat's concern with the plight of the working man which would inform the next step in the evolution of non-fiction film.

In Ireland, though the level of non-fiction production was higher than of fiction because of the demand for newsreel items and travelogues, the films remained arrested within a pre-*Nanook* phase of observing and recording without a real sense of context or consequence. The Irish Amateur Film society was formed in 1930, eager to make both fiction and non-fiction short subjects. Actor and fiction film director Richard Hayward tried his hand, as did amateur enthusiast and film critic Norris Davison, who would later assist Robert Flaherty on the preliminary research for *Man of Aran* (1934) as a trainee with the Empire Marketing Board. Amateur Desmond Egan also began making films in the 1930s, moving up to professional commercial projects after co-forming a production company in the 1940s. Jesuit priest Fr Frank Browne, who would later gain world renown as a photographer, directed several shorts and one documentary feature. The activities of individuals such as these are important although their work is not widely known. Though less technically and conceptually advanced than their international counterparts, entrepreneurial or merely enthusiastic non-professionals nonetheless produced work that embodies nascent steps in the conceptualisation of everyday life. It represents a search for self, insofar as the term may be applied in this context.

Sharon Sherman discusses this idea in terms of a folkloric tradition. She proposes that films and videos which capture ordinary activities can be used to understand societies. She argues that even material as innocuous as home videos reveals the need to define ourselves and our society by observing those around us. She writes, 'Folklore film confirms the experiences of people within their multiple subcultures, and viewers search within themselves for ways in which their behaviours are similar to or different from those of the persons depicted' (Sherman, 1998: 2). We will therefore take three particular examples of amateur/semi-professional films from the first third of the twentieth century which demonstrate the themes and tensions of the era: first, the work of renowned documentary photographer Fr Frank Browne, second, the British-produced *Aran of the Saints* (1932) and third, Desmond Egan's film *Harvest* (1934). Though these films do not constitute a definitive representation of cultural heritage or social identity, they demonstrate the processes by which these were negotiated during the period in question.

Triumph of the Catholic will: the films of Fr Browne

Fr Frank Browne was a Jesuit priest who supplemented his clerical duties throughout the first half of the twentieth century with a keen interest in amateur photography. His relationship with the medium began when his uncle, Bishop Robert Browne of Cloyne, inspired by Pope Leo XIII's encyclical *The Modern Art of Photography*, gave his nephew the first of a succession of cameras. Among his earlier efforts were a series of now famous images of the *Titanic* taken in 1912 on her maiden voyage between Southampton and Queenstown, where Browne disembarked. After the disaster, some of these were published and circulated worldwide. Despite this moment of fame, Browne remained concerned with clerical duties, including army chaplaincy during the First World War. He later documented the life of Ireland's major cities, and subjects such as the life of the Aran Islanders in the 1920s and the progress of rural electrification in the 1950s.

Browne's activities were initially supported by writing articles for Kodak's magazine of photography. At the behest of the then managing director of Kodak, George Davison, he was granted free Kodak film for life. With his uncle providing the equipment, he had little in the way of expenses to prevent him developing an experienced eye and compiling a massive collection of photographs. As his work became better known (though he was still strictly an amateur), he was commissioned by organisations including University College Dublin, the British Museum and the Church of England. Any profits he made from the assignments were funnelled into an especially created fund (nicknamed the 'Brownie Burses') which went towards the education of Jesuit scholastics in the art and craft of photography.

Fr Browne died in 1960 and his work was largely forgotten until 1987, when, following his discovery of boxes of carefully labelled photographs, fellow Jesuit Dr E. E. O'Donnell edited and published the first in the continuing series of books. Since then a new compilation of images has appeared roughly annually and more photographs and slides remain to be catalogued. His motion-picture work is still relatively unknown. Even given his growing popularity in recent years as a recorder of the changing hues of rural and urban Ireland, his films have not been widely circulated. Part of the difficulty is that it is still uncertain how many he made. Copies of four films are housed by the Irish Film Archive, but the existence of others is suggested by his correspondence and photographs.

Just as it had with photography, his involvement with film probably began with the help of his uncle. The Jesuit Order neither encouraged nor discouraged Browne's work, but it did not provide him with funding for equipment or training. Therefore, it is reasonable to assume that the bishop of Cloyne gave Browne his first 16 mm camera around 1931, when he made his first known film, *Castle Rising* (1931), a silent docudrama on an episode in the life of a historic building in East Anglia.[5] Though an amateur film, *Castle Rising* is interesting for its strong visual compositions and as an experiment for the photographer with a new form of expression. It follows a loose 'story' of two youngsters wandering around the ruins of a castle taking photographs until they 'witness' a scene from the past re-enacted in period costume. On one level it represents a classic docudramatist's attempt to bring fact to life by means of drama, but on another it is a cinematographic record of the historic site, which is photographed well with Browne's keen eye.

His most famous film, *Eucharistic Congress 1932* (1932), was a feature-length 16 mm record of the pivotal event in Irish Catholicism in the first half of the twentieth century, which it has been claimed 'witnessed a spontaneous popular enthusiasm for the Catholic Church in Ireland' (Lee and O'Tuathaigh, 1982: 192). Certainly the Eucharistic Congress was the biggest religious occasion yet seen in the newly founded state. How spontaneous the enthusiasm was is questionable. As was pointed out later in the documentary *The Best Catholics . . .* (2002), eager to prove its loyalty to Rome and utterly insensitive to the feelings of Protestants North or South, the government participated in a massive public demonstration of Catholic ascendancy throughout the country. It was as clear a statement as was needed of the religious ethos of the Irish Free State.

Fr Browne's film excels as a superficial recording of this event. Given the limited resources at his disposal, it does well to capture a sense of the moment. What the film lacks is a sense of the people. The feelings and reactions of the congregation to the congress are indicated only by superficial visual signifiers: faces of smiling children greet the arrival of religious dignitaries; the streets of Dublin are decked with bunting and shrines; the faithful wave papal flags. The film does not move beyond evidentiary exposition to provide either context or analysis of what we see. There are few close ups to disrupt the sense of distant, respectful observation. Dramatic images of huge crowds attending services provide basic information, but do not create a sense of how the people are reacting, or why. Browne is content to record parades and marches with his single camera and to edit them together in a roughly chronological sequence which extends to feature length. It is essentially an extended newsreel, and thereby assumes the character of an 'objective' and 'neutral' recording.

Paradoxically though, in assuming this very tone of objectivity, Browne's authoring presence becomes evident. This 'objectivity' is tainted at the source. *Eucharistic Congress 1932*, like the Horgans' footage of people exiting the church at Youghal, reinforces the notion of unity and community which underpins the Catholic church's sense of itself and its Irish congregation (which the congress itself was intended to promote and develop). The film presumes that those who view it share its director's faith, and indeed does not even entertain the possibility that they may not. Its nearest equivalent in world documentary of the time is Leni Riefenstahl's *Triumph of the Will* (1935), made only two years later at the Nazi party congress of 1934. The comparison is grossly unfair given the difference in resources and the relative influence of the church in Ireland compared to the Nazi party, yet what Riefenstahl achieved through coordination and orchestration was a greater sense of context which ultimately served the film's propagandistic aims. Its subtle embodiment of the dogma of the Nazi party in its visuals and structure was ultimately far more affecting than the mere recording of political speeches.[6]

2 Fr Frank Browne SJ's record of the Eucharistic Congress was a significant act of documentary at a time when resources for indigenous filmmakers were extremely limited. His sense of photographic composition is clearly demonstrated by this scene from the film *Eucharistic Congress 1932* (1932), depicting Taoiseach Éamon de Valera and the Papal Nuncio inspecting Irish Army troops

Eucharistic Congress 1932 offers an analogous demonstration of the presence and power of the church in Ireland, although it does this not so much by design as simply because of its director's point of view. The innocence of Riefenstahl's eye may be debatable, but Fr Browne's is less so. So thoroughly immersed in Catholicity is he that he is unable to even conceive of an alternative point of view. He sees no need to even attempt to propagandise the ideology of the church, nor indeed does he even see it as ideology at all. In filming these events, Fr Browne presumes that actuality speaks for itself. Though in doing so, he has selected and arranged profilmic reality to his own received, preconceived notions of what that reality is, it is clear that he intends only to film 'things as they are'. His mission was to document an event of immense importance to the Catholic population of Ireland, not to examine notions of Catholicism or of Ireland, and the film embodies rather than proposes ideas of Catholic supremacy.

This is best understood in the context of a folkloric documentary practice of the kind proposed by Sherman. The film is a tentative reaching for a sense of identity by virtue of observing people's behaviour at a major public event in which the viewer may recognise in the devotions of the faithful that which exists within himself. As Sherman notes, 'consumers and scholars discover that they are using folklore to document their own lives' (Sherman, 1998: 168). It is equally true in this case that this documentation of the supposedly external inevitably inscribes the personality of the documentarist. Given this, it is easy to understand why Browne is unable to step outside his own faith and education to critically examine the significance of the events for the ordinary people of Ireland or for the country as a whole.

The fragment of footage taken by Fr Browne for the Faculty of Agriculture of University College Dublin in 1933 is quite different. Evincing no religious context whatsoever, the film is, if anything, a hymn to man's relationship with nature. The film is untitled, but consists of three minutes of Irish forestry operations, including planting and felling. This film demonstrates a painterly sense of composition evident in Browne's still photographs, and is often reminiscent of the Soviet Naturalist tradition exemplified by the work of Alexander Dovzhenko, which we will discuss further in relation to *Harvest*. In Browne's film, images of workers ploughing and planting have an internal compositional rhythm which approaches poetry. The film was intended to supplement lectures, and details such as close ups of hands planting saplings were illustrations of technique rather than poetic symbols, yet they still retain a strong sense of the frame and have a documentary quality which goes beyond reportage.

The film represents a grasping for form; an impulse to organise the seemingly random profilmic environment into a system of images with which observers might understand the nature of their habitat and see the land more clearly than through eyes alone. It asserts the centrality of the land to a conception of Ireland, and not merely as a pictorial subject. Labourers tilling represent agricultural industry. The fact that they are planting and felling demonstrates a continuing interdependence between man and nature. This 'innocent' cinematic representation of an ordinary activity gives insight into behaviour of the indigenous inhabitants *and* speculates about its meaning, returning us to Evans's and Robinson's notions of national identity, and to Sherman's folkloric impulse.

Browne may have made other films throughout the 1930s, including the previously mentioned film of the Pilgrimage of Walsingham and a project commissioned for the Garda Siochána, the state police force, by General Eoin O'Duffy. O'Duffy, then Garda commissioner, knew Browne through the Irish International Salon of Photography (established in 1927) of which they were both members. O'Duffy was most famous for leading the ill-fated Blueshirt movement from 1933 to 1934 (after his dismissal from the Gardaí by then Taoiseach Éamon de Valera).[7] This important footnote in Irish history, a momentary glimpse of the links between Irish nationalism and European fascism, would have to wait sixty years for a documentary treatment, in the film *Patriots to a Man* (2000). Given his previous work, it is unlikely that

Browne would have been critical of O'Duffy (who had yet to take leadership of the Blueshirts at any rate), or of the organs of the state which the film, if it was made at all, was about. Browne may also have produced a film companion to his slides on the operations of a dairy cooperative in Cooraclare, County Clare, and possibly one on rural electrification. He travelled extensively and gave illustrated lectures on various subjects. He was also a close companion of a Mr. Byrne, a travelling cinema proprietor operating in the midlands, whose correspondence suggests he may have screened some of Fr Browne's films. The final film of which a copy exists is *The Waters of Providence* (1949), a considerably more professional documentary on the history of Providence Wollen Mills in Foxford, Co. Mayo, which is part of the tradition of social documentary and will be examined in the next chapter.

Ethnography with intent: Aran of the Saints

Though Fr Browne visited the Aran Islands in 1925 and 1938, and took a series of photographs collected as *Aran na Naomh/Aran of the Saints*, he is not believed to be the director of the film of the same name from 1932. Produced by the Catholic Film Society of London, the film was designed to emphasise the spartan lives and devout Catholicism of the Aran Islanders. The film was acquired by the Irish Film Archive from the Holy Ghost Fathers, indicating that its distribution was handled within the demesne of religious orders, presumably for screening to local congregations and to the religious communities themselves. Though it is not of Irish origin, the film is so defined by a Catholic point of view, like Browne's work, that it represents a reading of Irish culture worth exploring in some detail.

It is interesting that the Catholic Film Society of London should choose Ireland (and the Aran Islands in particular) to serve as an exemplar of Catholicity. It is also interesting that they should choose a rural community to embody these ideals given the extent of urban imagery in *Eucharistic Congress 1932*. Early on in the film, a title card informs the viewer that the islands are a place 'Where men preserve undefiled the faith brought to them 1400 years ago'. This sets the tone and context for what is primarily an ethnographic record of life on the islands. It records the behavioural patterns of the inhabitants and provides basic information on their lifestyles. In marked contrast to the roughly contemporaneous *Man of Aran*, it also shows evidence of the islands' links with the mainland and with the modern market economy, significant facts which will be discussed in more detail later.

The concept of ethnography requires further elaboration before the discussion may continue. Karl Heider provides a detailed introduction to ethnographic film, and is the primary source of reference for much of what follows. The premise of ethnography as a research method is that cultures are best understood through careful observation of everyday behaviour. It arose as a social sciences reaction to quantative and statistical methodologies and aspired to create a more responsive and reflexive means of conducting anthropological and sociological research. Apart from the complications which arise when adapting this methodology to film, Heider acknowledges that there are difficulties even with pure ethnography. Firstly, the ethnographer rarely if ever acknowledges their presence and the effect this may have on 'natural' behaviour. Simply by accommodating the researcher, the subjects inevitably make a mental adjustment which alters the rhythm of their lives. Hiesenberg's Uncertainty Principle is often invoked in this matter, which states in essence that an object under observation is altered by the act of observation. Thus, the premise of an ethnographic film is a false one to begin with.

This becomes especially relevant given the predisposition to grant the qualities of scientific inscription to documentary films discussed by Brian Winston (1993). Winston claims that the scientific methodology of observation has direct links with the capacity of the camera to film what it sees. He argues that documentary cinema has served science through sharing this common property, and traces the relationship between them to the arguments by French politician François Arago, who argued in 1839 that the French government should purchase the patents for Daguerre's photographic processes because they would benefit archeological research. The increasing need to acknowledge subjectivity from the 1960s on has, according to Winston, ultimately resulted in a postmodern morass where claims to scientific inscription are no longer worthwhile, though they are often assumed. In 1961 Jean Rouch and Edgar Morin claimed that their seminal *cinéma vérité* film *Chronicle of a Summer* (1961) was 'a study of the strange tribe that lives in Paris', though it was extremely self-reflexive and acknowledged its own subjectivity (as well as that of its participants).

A true ethnographic documentary is essentially a visual supplement to field notes and years of scientific research. Nonetheless beginning with footage of Aboriginal tribesmen, native Americans and other cultures, 'ethnographic films' began to find distribution both as commercial entertainments and as a source of scientific data in the early part of the twentieth century. They met with particular success following *Nanook of the North*, and producers were eager to find equivalent material in other places. The 'day in the life' structure and sketchpad characterisations of Flaherty's film established a formula quickly adopted by others including Merian C. Cooper and Ernest B. Schoedsack (*Grass*, *Chang*), Léon Poirier (*The Black Cruise* (1926), *The Yellow Cruise* (1929)), and Mr and Mrs Martin Johnson (*Congorilla* (1929)), to varying degrees of success and representational accuracy.[8]

Heider lists the important factors in determining how true to its subject and how ethnographic a film can be (Heider, 1976: 45–116). He emphasises that intentional and inadvertent distortion of behaviour should be minimal. An ideal ethnographic film should not intervene in the lives of the subjects either by accident or design. The filmmaker should merely observe from a vantage point which does not disrupt the natural rhythm of life. This seems straightforward and requires little further explication, but Heider draws attention to the fact that distortions to natural rhythms can occur both during shooting and after. Filmic distortions, which include not only the type of shot used (does the camera capture whole bodies and whole acts or only fragments?), but selection of data at the editing stage, are equally important. Filmmakers inevitably compress and compile months of raw footage. This compression alters both time and continuity. Events are rearranged to improve narrative flow. Scenes are constructed using footage shot at different times and even using different people or locations. All of this inherently alters life's natural rhythms without even taking into account how the pro-filmic itself has been affected by the presence of the crew.

Ethnographic film still endures because it attempts to deal directly with questions of habitat and habitation. With the increasing sophistication of fields such as anthropology, film has been a useful addition to research. It can also provide a sense of perspective which written data cannot. Robert Gardener (1996), himself an ethnographic documentarist, notes that it is in their capacity to document tensions between individual will and cultural constraint that ethnographic films retain links with observation. Like the paintings, drawings and photographs with which this chapter began, ethnographic portraiture such as *Aran of the Saints* and *Man of Aran* can still participate in the process of documentary even if they cannot and should not be accepted as texts in isolation. The essentialisms inherent in the form can prove reductive to the vision of society they aspire to create. As Brian Winston quips: 'If, as Jean Rouch put it, "anthropology was the eldest daughter of colonialism," then the ethnographic documentary, irrespective of its style, was revealed as a bastard grandchild' (Winston, 1999: 83).

Aran of the Saints is concerned with an ostensibly isolated community. Paradoxically, the point of the film is to indicate its integration within the Catholic church. Though the film demonstrates a degree of composition comparable with the work of Fr Browne, it has a much stronger sense of cinematic organisation. Its general aims are almost identical to *Eucharistic Congress 1932* but its form is quite different. It is mostly concerned with observing 'natural' behaviour and picturing the landscape of Aran, albeit one, the film argues, defined by 1400 years of devotion to the faith. It begins with geographical facts and a shot of men in currachs meeting the steamer from the mainland. Intertitles inform us that the islands have 2000 inhabitants, 'all of whom are Catholic'. Among the supplies and passengers which arrive are several priests, whose presence seems to verify the assertion. After briefly charting the exchange of imports and exports at the docks, the film cuts to scenes of islanders attending Mass. The film keeps this rhythm throughout, ensuring that scenes of religious devotion follow more general details. It is filmed mostly in wide and long shots. There are almost no close ups. This is reminiscent of *Eucharistic Congress 1932*, and again preserves a sense of ethnographic distance which makes the audience observers rather than analysts. The film does evince a greater variety of images though, and its makers were obviously less restricted in their positioning of the camera and their choice of scenery than Fr Browne.

In contrast with the later *Man of Aran*, the film does not focus on one particular family or group, or even on one island. One sequence even shows a priest travelling by currach between islands. Large crowds are featured in the religious scenes, including Mass and a service at the grave of St Enda. Like *Eucharistic Congress 1932*, there is no exploration of the beliefs of individuals or the nature of their faith, let alone a true exploration of its history. It is a generic, unquestioned obedience to religious authority seen in their attendance at events, and embodied in the landscape as portrayed by the film. Ruins of monastic huts, churches and gravestones are prominent, and intertitles explain the religious heritage of the islands as these are pictured.

The film does portray other institutions, including education. Following a title card which asks us to marvel at 'Green fields where boys may romp' followed by images of children, the film shows young islanders at school. That the activities filmed should primarily consist of saying prayers, communion day and a visit by Cardinal McRory (presumably there to promote and celebrate the Eucharistic Congress) comes as no surprise. This is not so much a question of distortion, though it demonstrates filmic and behavioural alterations, as it is another case of predetermination based upon unacknowledged subjectivity. There is no question but that monastic ruins exist upon the Aran Islands, or that locals attended religious events. Just as with *Eucharistic Congress 1932*, the documentary record attests to that on the level of the profilmic, even if it chooses to omit detailed history. It is by inflecting the commercial and educational life of the island with religion that the film becomes rhetorical.

The effect of the constant deferral and referral to religious events and rituals serves to make the religious life of the island its most important dimension, even when it features other elements of Aran's culture and economy. A sequence portraying the saying of the Angelus is particularly interesting in this regard. It begins with some islanders standing on a road in conversation with a policeman (an indication of the presence of law and order). It then cuts to a boy ringing the Angelus bell. It next returns to the men, who cease their banter, bless themselves and stoop in prayer. Though reconstructed, the sequence vividly illustrates the argument of the film.

In terms of the physical geography of the Aran Islands, both land and sea are present, as are the familiar vistas of cottages, currachs and stone-walled fields. These were the images which the Catholic Film Society, regardless of its other agendas, would have realised its audience expected. The fact that documentary film was part of a continuity of multi-media representation is again clear. The writings of Synge and the drawings and paintings of Yeats had already crafted an indelible impression of the islands, and though it was not universally romantic (many of Yeats's portraits of islanders were suggestive of psychological enclosure), it was rural. Norris Davidson, visiting Aran to assist Flaherty, also directed a documentary short entitled *Dancers of Aran* (1934) which emphasised the island's picturesque qualities. *Aran of the Saints* inflects rurality with a religious ethos, but otherwise portrays the island much as it was as a physical location.

In terms of economy, the film also features footage of cattle, sheep and pigs to indicate agricultural industry, and there is evidence of trade with the mainland. One shot features a kicking and squealing pig being loaded onto the steamer for the mainland. The title card informs us that the animal dislikes leaving the island – one presumes that its journey was to be only one way anyway. The film does not, however, portray the activity of farming, which would be more characteristic of an ethnographic film and was even featured in *Man of Aran*. In contrast to Flaherty's film though, it portrays the islands as an active community with modern economic and educational structures. This economic dimension alone is interesting in terms of how it demonstrates the *realpolitik* influence of the British documentary movement.

Films such as *Eucharistic Congress 1932*, *Aran of the Saints* and others documenting the activities of Irish missionaries abroad were distributed nationally, sometimes via cinemas, but also through a network of schoolrooms and parish halls. Indeed, this local distribution was a vital part of the development of cinema in Ireland. It provided the communal entertainment of a supervised gathering, and also highlighted amateur and semi-professional films which might not otherwise reach audiences. A significant number of these films were actually made by priests or other religious, whose access to equipment and ability to turn up anywhere to shoot without being questioned made them among the most thorough of amateur documentarists of the period (though obviously, the subject matter tended to be fairly repetitive).

While this does not quite reach the level of folklore, it is a twentieth-century version of the shared experience and interactivity which contributes to the development of a sense of placelore and folk memory. George Stoney's *How the Myth Was Made* (1979) explores this concept in relation to the people of Aran and the making of *Man of Aran*. One sequence features a discussion among islanders following a screening of Flaherty's film. Their observations on how the film represented and has defined their community illustrates how much a part of their lives it has become regardless of its referential shortcomings. According to Sherman, this practice, which may be traced to Jean Rouch's work in Africa and to the climax of *Chronicle of a Summer* where the participants are filmed viewing an unfinished rough cut of the film in which they appear, is integral to the methodology of modern ethnodocumentary and folkloric film. She observes that 'films that satisfy community or individual needs at the same time that they fulfil the film-maker's purposes demonstrate the filmmaker's respect for the people in the film' (Sherman, 1998: 239).

Though in Stoney's case the film they discuss is not the one in which they appear, the film under scrutiny is part of the fabric of their lives, and it serves the community by provoking debate. The dialogue among islanders illustrates tensions between individuals and groups, and between the community on the whole and the world's perception of them. Some argue, as do most cultural historians, that Flaherty's reductive interpretation of life on Aran outweighs the film's benefit to the tourist economy. Others have less difficulty with it, including original cast member Maggie Dirrane, who seems amused and flattered by the changes the film brought to her world. In raising the issue at all, Stoney provides a momentary glimpse of the process which takes place when a community sees itself represented.[9]

Poetry for progress: Harvest

Harvest was a 16 mm 100 ft amateur film about wheat harvesting shot with Kodachrome colour stock, made the same year that *Man of Aran* was premièred. Though footage from the film has been used repeatedly as filler material, the original is itself a striking example of directing and editing as well as a poetic evocation of the physical and social landscape of rural Ireland. It is strongly reminiscent of Soviet Naturalism in its evocation of the rhythms of farming and in its undercurrents of the need for change. The film draws attention to the antiquated methods and technologies still used on Irish farms and combines images of crops and farmers with an illustration of a typical harvest. In the manner of Alexander Dovzhenko's *Earth* (1930), its points are made through its depiction of rural labour and its evocation of the landscape.

Kepley, writing on Dovzhenko, takes issue with the reading of Soviet Naturalism as romantic pastoralism. He points out that despite the beauty with which nature is represented, the films are informed by Soviet politics. They depict a relationship between man and nature which, while harmonious, is not passive. He argues, 'in neither case will Soviet progress submit to some immutable ideal of the natural realm . . . Even when Dovzhenko employs motifs from ancient folkloristic sources, he is not so much baring his "peasant's soul" as rationalizing twentieth-century phenomena' (Kepley,

1986: 159–60). This same conception informs *Harvest*. While the film is obviously not linked to the ideal of a Soviet state, it is nonetheless concerned with the need to harness the forces of nature rather than coexist with them in leisured resplendence.

The film follows the standard 'day in the life' structure and divides the action into stages in a process which leads from work in the fields to the operation of machines in the mill. It begins with a shot of wheat fields, then proceeds to images of men with scythes accompanied by horse-drawn machinery stepping nervously into shot and commencing work. It vigorously intercuts a series of close ups of specific actions of men and machine cutting, tying and wrapping the wheat with establishing shots which allow a sense of place and time to evolve. It contrasts the actions of the machine with those of the men, at one point presenting a bill hook for our inspection with a title card which explains that it is the oldest known harvesting tool, followed by a demonstration of its continuing, backbreaking use. Curiously, the instrument is also visually reminiscent of the blade used in the flag of the Soviet Union to signify agriculture. Scenes of the use of the bill hook are juxtaposed with the turning wheels of a cart and the blades of a machine, and with images of a man sharpening a scythe.

These scenes of labour, while filmed attractively, are nonetheless far from the image of the peasant lolling in bucolic splendour which characterised many of the picturesque and romantic paintings of the preceding century. Writing on these depictions, McCurtain observes:

Nineteenth-century artists saw the peasant as a subject associated with a receding but passionately remembered scene: the haywagon, the communal harvesting of the crops, the patient figures with bowed heads reciting the Angelus–all the romantic evocations of a countryside before the railways swept peasants into the noisome, crowded ghettos and factories of the Industrial Revolution. (McCurtain, 1993: 11)

Egan features one of these scenes – the harvesting of crops (and the next of McCurtain's images, of 'patient figures with bowed heads reciting the Angelus' is featured in *Aran of the Saints*) – but the contrasts between tools and hands, men and machines, and wheat and human bodies is informed by an awareness of the relationship between labour and the sustenance of a rural community.

The film does indulge in moments which are purely 'poetic' though, in the sense that they evoke feelings and ideas beyond the direct references of the text which reflect upon their meaning. For example, a sequence of grain falling from a sieve shot in extreme close up makes the grain look like orange raindrops. It is an abstraction of the colour and texture of the grain rather than data on the process of sifting. One of Heider's criteria for good ethnographic film is that the camera should portray whole acts and whole bodies for maximum authenticity. Scenes such as this violate this precept for visual pleasure, shifting from scientific observation to aesthetic evocation. Though we do see the farmer holding the sieve in an establishing medium shot, the image of falling grain does not even show the sieve itself, let alone the hands holding it. It is pure movement and colour, like Promio's photography of train station hedgerows. Other such images occur throughout the film. The impression of movement from the top to bottom of the frame is repeated in a sequence featuring the water wheel which powers the mill. Though we are given the obligatory establishing shot, the images of rushing torrents are edited together more in the manner of a poem than an instructional film – its rhythm and repetitions suggesting reflections upon the effect of these congruences on visual pleasure. Egan also frequently fragments the human body. He portrays hands and feet alone, or the faces of farmers at work, again violating the precepts of ethnographic film for poetic effect.

It is curious that the use of footage from the film in later television documentaries should be in such marked counterpoint to the organisation of the original. Where it is merely treated as stock footage in programmes on history or illustrations of 'lost' traditions, Egan's film was more contemporary and more socially self-conscious. It is a depiction of a particular set of relationships between the Irish and the landscape which reaches beyond the physical and into the conceptual – in short, a poem, but one which understands poetry's relationship to the social and political world.

Renov reminds us that the popular conception of poetry as a form alien to documentary is a misleading one. Seen within a romantic tradition of rarefied, personal and interior art, poetry represents the exact opposite of documentary's engagement with 'real life'. When a documentary is seen to possess 'poetic' characteristics, it is sometimes dismissed as less than 'true'. Yet documentary discourse has, he remarks, 'occupied an unstable position at the juncture of science and aesthetics, structure and value, truth and beauty' (Renov (ed.), 1993: 13). Renov observes, citing Smadar Lavie (1990), that the impulse to separate poetry from politics is characteristic of western modes of thought descended from the Platonic ideal. According to Lavie, marginalised or colonised cultures, such as, in her case, the Bedouin tribes, more readily accommodate a poetic tradition in their conception of the social and political world because they are more dependent on oral traditions to record and disseminate cultural identities. She observes that 'the Mzeina culture, being under the continual threat of effacement, tells itself in an allegorical way that it exists, metonymizing private experiences for the history of the collectivity, and conjoining the local poetics of storytelling with the global political realities of neocolonialism' (Lavie, cited in Renov (ed.), 1993: 19).

It is not difficult to see how these general principles may be applied to the study of the relationship between poetry, poetics and politics in a study of Ireland, especially in the period in question where the struggle between colonial and indigenous culture continued even after independence had been achieved. Kiberd examines this impulse for a conjoined political and aesthetic self-definition which he terms 'the national longing for form' (Kiberd, 1995: 115). Though he argues, for example, that the work of W. B. Yeats is as internalised as that of any romantic poet, he points out that there is a strong political dimension to it. According to Kiberd, the search for a national form is first and foremost a personal one: 'the project of inventing a unitary Ireland is the attempt to achieve at a political level a reconciliation of opposed qualities which must first be fused in the self. In other words, personal liberation must precede national recovery, being in fact its very condition' (124). In this way the project of self-exploration embodied in poetry (and arguably visible in amateur filmmaking if we are to accept Sherman's framework as the corollary to this theorem) assumes political significance. It plays a role in defining ideas of the self which fuel the desire to redefine society.

Though written poetry and literature are freely discussed in such terms, little has been done in relation to the visual arts. Brian McAvera (1990), surveying attitudes to the production and reception of the visual arts in Ireland, concludes that Irish political art exists only insofar as art inherently reflects political conditions, a sentiment which calls to mind the thought of John Berger and Marshall McLuhan. As McAvera notes, there is no 'school' of Irish political art and the subject is often considered too serious for treatment in 'artistic' or 'poetic' form. Yet *Harvest* and *Aran of the Saints* both rationalise twentieth-century phenomena, to employ Kepley's terminology, through the use of what was still a relatively new medium. Even Fr Browne had sought to advance the representational parameters of painting and illustration through photography and cinema. Films of this type attempt to configure a set of relations between physical beings and physical spaces which engage questions of how they and their country may be defined through the moving image and the use of 'actuality'. Later in this chapter it will be shown how this conception of non-fiction affected the representation of the country as a whole, but the debate is complicated by the intervention of *Man of Aran*, so it is appropriate at this point to turn to a discussion of Flaherty's film.

Man of Aran

Much has been written about *Man of Aran*, and more has been said. It has been at the centre of debates on Irish cinema since its production, even though the film is more properly understood when viewed in the context of the life and vision of Robert Flaherty.[10] One of the key figures in the history of non-fiction film, this explorer and accidental filmmaker visited Ireland in the early 1930s to make another of his poetic meditations on the relationship between man and nature. All of Flaherty's films say more about him than they do about the places in which they were filmed. As Barsam explains:

All of Flaherty's films are variations on one ideal: happiness exists when man is free and lives simply and harmoniously with nature. Inevitably, however, there must be conflict and, in order to affirm the ascendancy of the human spirit, Flaherty concentrates on conflicts between man and nature rather than those between men. Nature thus serves both as a central motif and as a main character, symbolized by the animal and natural forces that co-exist with man but are also his antagonists. Almost every film has such an antagonist, expressed as a controlling metaphor: *Nanook* (snow, the sea and storms, wild animals); *White Shadows of the South Seas* and *Tabu: A Story of the South Seas* (the sea); *Man of Aran* (the sea and storms); *The Land* (drought, wind, dust storms); *Louisiana Story* (alligators and oil). (Barsam, 1988: 7)

Man of Aran is a poetic homage to the sea, the nurturer and would-be destroyer of the fishermen who live by its natural rhythms. Though it is a powerful document of the elemental power of the ocean, most of its other documentary elements are of questionable veracity. The congruence between Flaherty's view of Aran and the traditional romantic representation of the Irish landscape is striking. Corresponding with eighteenth- and nineteenth-century picturesque and primitivist representations, the film looks backward in a way in which none of the indigenous documentaries discussed so far did at the same time.

The making of the film came about after Flaherty's unsuccessful flirtation with Hollywood following the success of *Nanook of the North* and his subsequent journey to Britain to work with John Grierson on *Industrial Britain* (1933). Flaherty became interested in Aran after it was suggested to him that he read Synge's *The Aran Islands* (1907), a book already a quarter of a century out of date. Enthused by the prospect of making a film about the islands, Flaherty approached the British production pioneer Michael Balcon, then head of Gaumont-British, for backing. Balcon agreed, hoping that a prestige documentary by the legendary director would increase the profile of his fledgling company, Gainsborough Pictures.

The film was the largest production of its time in Ireland, but it was a wholly foreign venture, financed by British companies and directed by an American. Flaherty eventually raised a budget of about £30,000 and was supplied with state-of-the-art equipment, including a new lightweight camera and a number of long lenses, the longest being seventeen inches (twice the length of the camera itself). He researched the film in his usual manner, moving to Inismore in 1932 to live among the people and read more books. He was assisted by local researchers and amateur filmmakers, including Norris Davidson and Pat Mullen, the latter of whom wrote his own book about his experiences in its making. The size and scale of the production alone remains a point of some contention. Rockett summarises:

It is a bitter testimony to the history of film production in Ireland that even in the relatively inexpensive category of documentaries, the best known film, *Man of Aran* (1934) should be foreign-produced. Superficially, at least, Irish economies of scale explain why this should be. In the stringent economic reality of 1930s Ireland, Robert Flaherty's British-produced *Man of Aran* had a budget, as an originally conceived *silent* film, far greater than any indigenous *fiction sound* film until the late 1950s. With £30,000 to £40,000, Flaherty had the luxury of shooting 37 hours of film over two years on the Aran Islands to make the 74-minute film. Not only did he have a flexible time schedule and an indulgent budget but his lifestyle on Aran contrasted rather severely with the island primitivism depicted in this 'poetic documentary'. (Rockett et al., 1988: 71)

There is discernible ire in this observation, and it is representative of continuing indigenous scholarly reactions to the film. McLoone (2000) even explores certain congruences between Flaherty's neo-Rousseauian vision of Irish peasants and themes in European fascism, damning Flaherty with the faint praise that he was probably oblivious to the connection.

The action in the film takes place on the Aran Islands, where a small fishing family face the perils of the sea when the son spots a basking shark and the local men go off in pursuit. Though their boat is lost in a storm, the men swim safely to shore. The film ends with the family making their way home in exhausted defiance of the sea. It is a story film, like *Nanook* and *Moana* before it, and illustrates elements of ethnographic practice including details of farming and fishing. Strikingly filmed, painstakingly designed to evoke the drama of the relationship between man and water, it features, without doubt, some of the most stunning seascapes ever committed to film. Flaherty's long lenses allowed him to get the incredible shots of the boats being tossed by angry waves and the faces of the islanders filmed from the shore which made them appear more natural and less inhibited by the presence of the camera. They also allowed him to create a unique, painterly texture which still gives the film the elusive 'poetic' quality that is somewhere between scientific inscription and mythology. Using careful composition, edited with a steadier rhythm than his earlier films (perhaps as much the result of his working with editors John Goldman and John Monck as a fundamental change in approach), and stripping back his 'story' to the point of myth, he constructed a work of film which still inspires both hatred and admiration where others have disappeared into obscurity.

While *Man of Aran* certainly was Robert Flaherty at his most poetic, it was also him at his most removed from reality. In making the film, he took extreme measures to evade questions of the social and political context of the events and circumstances he portrayed. The film reconstructed a historical world which no longer (or perhaps never) existed, altering the profilmic until it fit the director's vision of what it should be like to live on an island. As a vision of the physical and psychic landscape of Ireland, it should be noted that Flaherty's conception of the environment inhabited by these people was not really of the land at all. This is not the story of man and Aran, but of man and the Atlantic. This allows Flaherty to sidestep consideration of the Aran Islands as an actual community, particularly a social and political one within the overall demesne of the newly founded Irish Free State. It leaves him free to explore another of his characteristic natural battlegrounds, pitting human beings against the elements in order to explore what Barsam terms 'the ascendancy of the human spirit' (Barsam, 1988: 7).

This also, of course, gave free rein to his delusion that he was capturing the 'true spirit' of life on the islands. Flaherty famously remarked, 'Sometimes you have to lie. One often has to distort a thing to catch its true spirit' (cited in Calder-Marshall, 1963: 97). The problems this approach raises are both of ethics and form, and of the degree of distortion acceptable before the documentary qualities are invalidated. As Sherman observes: 'whereas those who "play with" form are overtly providing viewers with their vision, other filmmakers still present their own stamp of authority while deluding themselves into thinking they are allowing their subjects to shape the film. Although one might suppose that because Flaherty tried to include his subjects' input, he was reproducing the natives' attitudes, his methods for *Man of Aran* and *Moana* indicate otherwise' (Sherman, 1998: 13).

Of all of Flaherty's films, *Man of Aran* is the one which is most loose with the realities of human experience. In order to obtain the desired rugged heroism in his characters, Flaherty cast three unrelated individuals as his mythical family. His star, 'Tiger' King, was not even a native of the islands, but had the square-jawed look that Flaherty sought for his leading man and so was cast as the father of this curiously small Irish nuclear family. The two most important factual documentary sequences in the film – the farming and the shark hunt – were both reconstructed from practices which had long ceased; shark hunting had not taken place on the islands in over one hundred years. Flaherty also violated ethnographic and ethical standards by significantly altering the rhythms of his subjects' lives and putting them in unnecessary physical danger. The fishermen's unfamiliarity with shark-hunting techniques meant that there was a genuine risk of their boat being capsized, and during the dramatic rescue of the boat from the sea in the opening scenes, 'mother' Maggie Dirrane was almost swept out to sea while Flaherty filmed from a quarter of a mile away.

Man of Aran was probably the most Rousseauian of all of the director's films and was proof of his continuing distance from those whose work he had inspired, including John Grierson. Documentary had outgrown Flaherty by the time he made it. Even his admirers made remarks to that effect at the time. Now, as previously noted, *Man of Aran* is more valuable as a documentary of Flaherty's vision of life than it is of life itself. On some level, even this is instructive. It reminds us of the essential subjectivity of documentary form, and of the necessary tension between the documentarist, the subject and the audience which is at the core of the encounter between them. It shows that the text is 'open' in the sense that, armed with external knowledge and an awareness of the authoring conventions of the medium, it is as rich a text for analysis both of the vision of Ireland it offers and of the relationship between that vision and the sensibility of the artist who produced it. As Eliot Weinberger remarks, 'the essential and largely hidden "conflict," of course, of any ethnographic film – one that, over the decades, was long denied and then debated – is between the filmmaker and the subject matter' (Weinberger, 1996: 143). Just as Kiberd noted with the 'political' poetry of W. B. Yeats, the internal project often precedes the external one, and just as with Yeats, the external project would have far-reaching consequences.

At the time of its making, the film was enthusiastically received by the Irish government, who saw it as a confirmation of their economic and social

3 Maggie Dirrane proudly holds a photo of herself as the idealised mother in Flaherty's *Man of Aran*. A scene from George C. Stoney's *How the Myth Was Made* (1978)

policies. Eager to prove Ireland's lack of necessity for aid of any kind in forging its own independent destiny, the Fianna Fáil government had encouraged an image of Ireland which was fiercely traditional, definitively rural and above all resilient in the face of hardship. *Man of Aran* might as well have been commissioned by Éamon de Valera, so close did it come to an idealised image of the 'mythic humanism' (Rockett et al., 1988: 72) favoured by his party. It is therefore no surprise that the première in May 1934 was attended by prominent politicians eager to see their dreams come to life. The fact that the film represents two separate dreams which happen to have coincided has not been missed by subsequent commentators. Ironically, *Man of Aran* was, in Nichols's terms, more a documentary of wish fulfilment than of social reality. Yet, as Pettitt points out, the film was marketed internationally as an unproblematic social realist documentary of life in contemporary Ireland, thereby fuelling perception and interpretation of the country for generations (Pettitt, 2000: 80). Since then it has been the whipping boy for indigenous scholarly analysis and has been the subject of numerous academic studies and several deconstructive documentaries, including *How the Myth Was Made* and *Looking for the Man of Aran* (1995).

The only other matter to arise from the production of *Man of Aran* worth noting here was the making of a short at the behest of the Irish Department of Education described by Pat Mullen but otherwise not recorded in Flaherty's filmography. Shot in Gaumont Studios during the post-synch recording sessions which provided the otherwise silent *Man of Aran* with its 'dialogue' in London in 1934, the film *Oidhche Sheanachais* was an Irish-language docudrama featuring members of the cast of *Man of Aran* as an audience listening to a tale narrated by *seanchaí* Tomás Ó Díorain. Flaherty served as producer. The ultimate irony is that the film, to which Rockett claims the Dáil voted a grant of £200, was the first 'non-fiction' film financed by the Irish government in the 1930s.

The country and the city

The cinematic figuration of Ireland as a landscape of the imagination, a physical and conceptual space onto which extraneous ideals could be projected, was consolidated by other international filmmakers. *Gem of the Sea* (1933) was a US-produced travelogue, one of the Father Hubbard educational films distributed in the 1930s. This ten-minute silent profile of Ireland shares the religious emphasis of *Aran of the Saints* and *Eucharistic Congress 1932*, and as such presents views of monastic and other ecclesiastical sights, though it also depicts a busy Dublin city and correctly observes the political existence of the Irish Free State. The city imagery is particularly interesting in that unlike films which would follow as late as thirty years after, it features copious amounts of motorised traffic; vans and cars instead of either empty roads or donkey carts. *Irish Pastoral* (1936), made only three years later but after the release of *Man of Aran*, is very different. Also distributed by Movietone, this film begins with rugged imagery of the Irish coastline, and speaks of mournfully of 'cold Erin'. In this film Dublin is 'a thriving world metropolis that was settled before the dawn of history', but the film tends towards an evocation of that dawn rather than the metropolis. One scene even features 'a fair colleen' in full peasant garb singing a love song surrounded by a group of clearly sceptical onlookers. 'Happy and contented are those who own and till a bit of the old sod', we are told, and the film concludes with children kneeling at a religious statue as darkness falls. Between these two films, Robert Flaherty had seemingly indelibly altered the complexion of Ireland on film.

Even in the twenty-first century, the touristic gaze is far from investigative. In contrast to amateur films, however primitive, or films which otherwise attempt to engage with and explore the natural habitat of the filmmaker, both domestic and foreign-produced tourist documentaries are concerned with the pleasurable arrangement of preconceptions of the land for the consumption of a prospective visitor. This represents a movement from investigation to projection, from geophany to marketing. It is also more characteristic of films produced later than the ones in question here, which is not to say that touristic films were not made in Ireland during this period. On the contrary, they were the dominant output. Many of them, including Norris Davison's *The Dancers of Aran*, fit within the travelogue category and this one in particular can easily be seen to be jumping on the *Man of Aran* bandwagon. Indigenous travelogues had not yet evolved to the level of professional tourist films. Films like *Aran of the Saints* and *Harvest* may have promoted a vision of the Irish landscape suitable for tourist consumption, but, as we have seen, their inward gaze is more compelling than their outward.

Tourist films made abroad about Ireland, like *Man of Aran*, say more about their country of origin than their subject. As Gibbons observes, such idealisations are the result of an urban culture, and speak less about the realities of life on the island than they do about the disenchantment with life elsewhere. He notes that:

idealizations of rural existence, the longing for community and primitive simplicity, are the product of an *urban* sensibility, and are cultural fictions imposed on the lives of those they purport to represent. In the United States, for example, it was not cowboys who sang the praises of the Old West but rather writers and ideologues from the East, intent on establishing a mythology of the last frontier. By the same token, it was urban-based writers, intellectuals and political leaders who created romantic Ireland and perpetrated the myth that the further west you go, the more you come into contact with the real Ireland. (Gibbons, 1996: 85)

A good example of this trend is James A. Fitzpatrick's *Glimpses of Erin*, made the same year as *Man of Aran*. The film was one of a number of 'postcard' movies used as fillers in American theatres throughout the 1930s and 1940s, cheerfully condescending 'travel talks' introduced by Fitzpatrick, whose characteristic address to the audience always concluded with the phrase 'and so we say farewell to . . .'.[11] In this film, the romantic portrayal of poverty and backwardism against a lush rural setting is posited as a spiritual panacea to audiences in depression-era America, where its lush rurality would have struck a contrast with the images of poverty and destruction filtering out of the drought-infested regions of the Dust Bowl.

Fitzpatrick's appeal to sentimentality and distortion of the profilmic is all the more telling given the modern country filmed by both the Lumières and the Horgans decades before and reinforces the notion that visiting film-makers were now working in the shadow of Robert Flaherty. Ireland is a 'purely agricultural country', the narrator informs us. The chosen footage is exclusively of the thatched cottages, donkeys and elderly women wearing shawls which constitute the soft primitivist fantasy discussed by Gibbons. The term 'Emerald Isle' is used liberally and the commentary concludes by mentioning 'the establishment of the new republic' which demonstrates a basic ignorance even of political reality understood by *Gem of the Sea*. The film's one concession to modernity is the inclusion of footage of Galway and Dublin. Galway is dismissed as a 'little town' though, and Dublin, whilst referred to as a 'cosmopolitan city', is posited as a gateway to history rather than an actual place in the modern world. Fitzpatrick lovingly explains that when you pass through the gates of Trinity College, you pass into the seventeenth century, and the viewer is treated to images of the statues and buildings which belie urban progress for the sake of a comfortable evocation of the dead hand of history.

Few films were made during the period in question about life in Irish cities. As Rockett notes, following Raymond Williams, the terms 'country' and 'city' are, in the Irish context, treated as binary oppositions, 'their ideological resonance is even more pronounced than elsewhere' (Rockett, 2001: 217). Sufficient attention has already been paid to the Lumière and Horgan films to allow us to discuss the *absence* rather than the presence of urban imagery in early twentieth-century Irish non-fiction film. There may be a number of reasons for this. The majority of urban-based non-fiction in Ireland from the turn of the century to the 1930s was in newsreels. Footage from the 'primitive' period such as that of Queen Victoria's visit to Dublin in 1900 or the operations of the Dublin Fire Brigade discussed earlier were more an official colonial record of the efficient operation of the city than a document of the urban landscape. Later scenes of the destruction of public buildings during the 1916 Rising and the 1921–22 period told another story.

These did not become part of discourse until their arrangement in the compilation documentaries *Mise Éire* and its sequel *Saoirse?* (1961), both of which will be discussed later.

There is a deeper question of the place of modernity in early twentieth-century Ireland. Gibbons discusses the relationship between the city and modernism with the observation that 'cinema is recreated in the image of the city, its emergence as a cultural form coinciding with the growth of the modern metropolis' (Gibbons, 1996: 165). The article in which he writes this is concerned with the use of cinematic imagery in the novel *Ulysses*. This encapsulates the dilemma of studies of the Irish city in film. While the conceptualisation of the modern metropolis as modernist experimentation was being undertaken worldwide in films such as *Rien que les heures*, *Moscow*, *Berlin* (1927), *Man With a Movie Camera* and *A propos de Nice* (1930), the equivalent, and indeed precedent, in Ireland was literary. While the sensibility of the urban intellectual may have informed the developing conception of the rural landscape, it was not subject to the kind of scrutiny on film as elsewhere. Even Joyce had frozen his Dublin of *Ulysses* in 1904 and held it up as a fractured mirror to the tempestuous present. The Irish city evaded the camera's eye except as a postcard view or a painting. While these forms themselves offer interesting possibilities, as discussed earlier, by the 1920s and 1930s, a documentary portrait was long overdue. It may have been partly a question of resources. Cavalcanti, Kaufman, Ruttman, Vertov and Vigo each embarked on their projects with financial backing unavailable in Ireland. There is also a matter of size: Dublin simply did not offer the same scale and variety of events and people as Paris, Moscow, Berlin, Kiev and Nice.

The absence of images of the city, or perhaps more correctly, of a *vision* of the city in Irish non-fiction film in this period may be conceived within philosophical terms as part of a general state of ambivalence about modernity. Kiberd describes this as the result of Ireland's suffering from 'a homeless mind' (Kiberd, 1995: 329) as a consequence of the country's social and economic decline throughout the nineteenth century. He concludes that 'the Irish wished to be modern and counter-modern in one and the same gesture' (330). This counter-modernity is arguably embodied in the Celtic revival and general pastoralism of the period. Yet, as Terence Brown points out, the revival can also be seen as contiguous with modernism, sharing many of its basic impulses while exhibiting less stylistic and formal radicalism. He argues that given the literary revival's association with nationalism (which advocated a certain type of revolution), 'The nationalist and the modernist can it seems share, as well as convictions about a historic fall from some previously existing state of European grace, a nostalgic, evasive vision of an integrated way of life (neither admits industrialism or the city to his thumbnail sketch of the national culture). They thereby indicate, in this precise conjunction of preoccupations, how parallels could exist between the two movements which can seem entirely antithetical' (Brown, 1995: 41).

Brown argues that Irish writers and cultural commentators tended to 'absorb and discharge the energies of the most original modernist texts and techniques' (28), reworking the radical ideas and formal strategies evinced in modernist works to suit quasi-traditional attitudes. He discusses, for example, Thomas MacGreevy's critique of T. S. Eliot's *The Waste Land* as an orthodox Christian fable of death and resurrection, and concludes that this tendency to neutralise the problematic aspects of modernism is 'an oddly Olympian conception of tradition which may in fact be the symptom of a certain self-protective provincialism of mind before the arresting challenge of true and threatening originality' (29).

It is arguable in similar terms that, in the impulse towards self-definition, the collective effect of 'geographic montage', and the grasping with the mechanics and representational capacities of the new medium, the pastoral and amateur films of this period represent a significant step towards the formation of a documentary practice which is both modern and progressive. They at least demonstrates a willingness to use the new medium to record the moment of hesitation between an unstable, shifting self-image of Ireland and the one which would soon emerge. As Leo Charney points out, such moments are usually recognised only after they have passed. He summarises the condition of modernity by identifying the two concepts which defined the study of modernity for writers such as Heidegger and Benjamin: movement and cognition. The basic position is thus: modern life is an unstable series of intense but ephemeral moments. The understanding of these moments is only possible after the fact and with the benefit of cognition, a fixed process of knowing or perceiving. Thus, the two axes of experience are both inextricably intertwined and mutually exclusive, a moment only having significance when it is clearly understood to have been a moment, yet only capable of providing an experience of reality when it is present. As Charney puts it, 'this dilemma led these writers [Pater, Benjamin, Heidegger and Epstein] towards the two interlocking concepts that defined their investigation of the modern as momentary: the evacuation of stable presence by movement and the resulting split between sensation, which feels the moment in the moment, and cognition, which recognizes the moment only after the moment' (Charney et al., 1995: 279).

People in this position found themselves reaching for forms of representation which would allow them to organise their own concept of reality. Writing in 1924, Jean Epstein remarked that cinema offered a convenient structure for doing this. With its emphasis on image, movement and editing, it was a perfect expression of the demise of actual experience, capturing the fleeting moment and then arranging it in a meaningful pattern for subsequent and repeated viewing. It is no surprise then that the 'city film' of the 1920s and 1930s should have emerged, nor that it should have assumed such a definitively modernist form. All of the films were informed by the practice of montage, the juxtaposition of scenes and images to create a sense of meaning beyond the individual moment.

Though Irish films of this period were not concerned with the city, they did nonetheless embody the conditions of modern life in Ireland. In terms not only of the world they portray, but of the manner in which they do so, films such as *Aran of the Saints*, *Harvest* and *Eucharistic Congress 1932*, demonstrate how non-fiction filmmakers responded to the challenge of representing Ireland during this period in political history. To compress the terminology introduced earlier in this chapter from Robinson, Nietschmann and Evans, such films are geophantic 'geographic montages' which contributed to (and arguably facilitated) the relationship between the inhabitants of the island and their habitat. That the imagery was predominantly rural does not necessarily mean that it was atavistic. As Brown points out, it represents a refiguration of the basic terms of modernism to reflect the conservative ideology of the period, but it shares inspiration and even certain techniques with the more nominally 'progressive' works of modernist art.

Significantly though, the chronology of the development of Irish documentary remains out of step with that of other places in the world. While economies of scale and political instability were significant factors, the wish to avoid the undesirable aspects of modernity was evident. The reassertion of what were perceived as traditional values by the government of the era was rather too geophantic, 'fixing' Irish identity rather than celebrating a moment of uncertainty. The unfortunate result was that the more speculative aspects of this approach to the relationship between internal and external self-definition and between the Irish man and his habitat soon became formalised as quaint, pastoral and touristic. The search for 'Ireland' became an assertion of a preconceived notion of 'Irishness', which included a self-depreciating willingness to evade philosophical conceptions of film in favour of the more rational and pragmatic model now offered by the social problem film developed by John Grierson and Paré Lorentz. Rather than exploring the lie of the land in order to see and understand what Ireland was or might be, films about the Irish landscape now followed a set of predetermined ideals. This made it easier to establish the country's credentials as a nation in its own right, replete with a politically expedient cultural identity. The results and consequences of this will be discussed in the following chapter.

Notes

1 See Rockett et al., 1988: 198.
2 Readings on all of these artists and surveyors may be found in Dalsimer (ed.), 1993.
3 There may have been other filmmakers, but Promio is the only Lumière cineaste whose name has been identified by the Irish Film Archive in connection with its Lumière collection. Promio is one of the few Lumière employees specifically remembered by history, primarily because he was noted in the memoirs of Louis Lumière, written some years after the fire which destroyed most of the company records. Promio was also active in Spain, Italy, Switzerland and Turkey.
4 The films were originally received by the Irish Film Archive on nitrate film, then copied on sixteen millimetre, then telecined to VHS videotape for viewing purposes. Stock dating is therefore not particularly helpful. Visual evidence in the films themselves includes the appearance of a steam ship which halted operations circa 1912 and therefore must have been filmed before that date, and a reference to 'Feis Day, 1920' in one intertitle and to a 'Veterans of the Great War' parade in another.
5 This film surfaced in 1998 when a Mr Hugh Taylor of Jersey contacted Fr O'Donnell and the Irish Film Archive. Mr Taylor possessed a 1935 copy of the 1931 film and his family were eager to date it because Taylor featured in it briefly as a child.
6 This film has been extensively written about. See (for example) Jacobs (ed.), 1979: 138–40; Welch, 1983; Barsam, 1992: 122–33; Barnouw, 1993: 100–5, and Grant and Sloniowski (eds), 1998: 99–118.
7 See Lee, 1989: 178–82.
8 See Barnouw, 1993: 50.
9 A much later film, *Spré Rosy Ryan* (1997), explored some of the same questions in relation to the making of *Ryan's Daughter* in Co. Kerry.
10 See Calder-Marshall, 1963 and Barsam, 1988.
11 See O'Brien, 2003.

2

Projecting the present:
Irish society and social documentary

The 1930s and 1940s saw the worldwide development of state and semi-state involvement in the finance and production of films representing social or political problems. Though they varied in style and tone, the films were predominantly made in what Nichols terms 'voice of God' or expository mode, or what Bordwell and Thompson call 'rhetorical form'. They were primarily informational rather than analytical, and usually followed the pattern of outlining a problem or issue and then presenting a sponsor-approved solution (tpically in accord with particular aspects of social policy). During this period, the conception of documentary shifted to accommodate the *realpolitik* ideals of the second quarter of the twentieth century, arguably at the expense of the more meditative, poetic mode which had preceded it. The debate continues as to how negative or positive this moment in history has been for documentary on the whole, with Brian Winston in particular an opponent of what is often termed the 'Griersonian' documentary.

In Ireland the particulars were different, though the questions asked of both society and documentary were the same. Writing in the Jesuit journal *Studies*, John Grierson remarked that Ireland was behind the rest of the world in developing production and distribution infrastructures. He noted, 'like all small countries, I imagine that it [Ireland] is finding it difficult to face up to the full implications of the use of the film for national purposes. It is an expensive medium; it requires special technical skills; and I have no doubt that Ireland is divided too as to whether or not it will develop the film on a governmental or on a commercial basis' (Grierson, 1948: 283).[1] His bias towards social documentary is obvious in his choice of phrase. He identifies the necessity to use film for national purposes, drawing upon former Empire Marketing Board secretary Sir Stephen Tallents's assertion that documentary was 'the art of national projection' (Tallents, 1932: 41). Writing in 1947, Grierson had said, 'the documentary film was conceived and developed as an instrument of public use. It was conceived, moreover as an instrument to be used *systematically* in all the fields of public instruction and enlightenment' (Grierson, 1947: 4). This gives a very clear summation of the aims of the

Griersonian social documentary, and in his later address, Grierson was clearly advocating the development of such a system in Ireland.

Grierson identifies four functions of film in the national service. Firstly, he argues that 'it can give other people a proper sight of Ireland' (Grierson, 1948: 286). He refers here in large part to the production of promotional and tourist documentaries, which will be discussed later. Secondly, he says that 'it can give the Irish people a proper sight of themselves' (286) by which he identifies the form's capacity for spreading information. Thirdly, he notes 'it can become a positive instrument of self-examination' (286). He frames this self-examination within the context of a national film service, giving it definable and pragmatic goals. This is nowhere more clear than in his state-ment of the fourth function of film in the national service, where he con-cludes, 'it can become a positive instrument for the co-ordination of the national effort and a directive instrument of educational and cultural lead-ership' (286). Here he specifically roots documentary production within the governmental rather than commercial sphere, despite noting that Ireland was at a crossroads in deciding which type of infrastructure to develop.

In the same article he also offered specific suggestions for the establish-ment of a film unit which would draw upon the financial support both of government and of industries such as textiles, motor manufacture and fuel. He claimed that with an initial £30,000 of investment from the government and combined sponsorship of £50,000 per annum from the departments of Health, Agriculture, Education and Labour, with an equivalent figure coming from private industry, 'a very considerable service' (291) could be successfully set up and run. This suggestion was ignored in practice, proba-bly because an alternative (and less demanding) infrastructure already existed. Yet ironically, he had identified the bodies who would later be most involved with the production of documentary films, albeit not necessarily within the demesne of a single film unit of the kind he had envisaged. Throughout the period in question in this chapter, government departments such as Health, Agriculture and Education, though primarily External Affairs (later Foreign Affairs), would become sponsors of a large number of films, and indeed textile and fuel companies would be among the major private investors.

The extent to which Grierson's pronouncements directly affected doc-umentary practice in Ireland is debatable. By 1948 limited government sponsorship of informational documentaries had already begun, and *Our Country* (1948), the first independently produced political documentary, was about to be released. The establishment of the National Film Institute of Ireland (NFI) in 1943 had marked the moment of official, organised inter-vention, but this was a nominally independent body formed with the approval, cooperation and even the participation of the Catholic church.

This was a case of delegation rather than hands-on involvement, the implications of which will be examined later. The majority of films produced during this era nonetheless projected approved images of the country. Many, such as *W. B. Yeats – A Tribute* (1950) and *Irish Gossamer* (1957), were of a promotional or touristic variety. Others were politically triumphalist accounts of Ireland's recent ascension to independence, such as *A Nation Once Again* (1946). Before discussing the specifics, it is useful to examine issues relative to understanding the social role of documentary in this period, and to explore some questions of the relationship between church and state in Ireland which will define the frames of reference.

Rhetorical form and national projection

The nature of a rhetorical documentary is that its argument may be located within social practice. It articulates ideas about the ordering of society which are understood by those who view it to represent 'reality' or 'things as they are'. As Bordwell and Thompson note, rhetorical form persuades the viewer not only of the problem-centred argument itself, but of the political and social parameters within which it is being made. Nichols observes that expository films are particularly suited to this task as the use of the didactic voice over and the presentation of ontological arguments as indisputable fact eliminates questions of the process by which knowledge is socially determined. He notes that the expository mode 'emphasises the impression of objectivity and of well-sustained judgment' (Nichols, 1991: 35). Rather than commenting upon society, or the social structures which sustain it, social documentaries take place *within* society. The veneer of 'objectivity' focuses attention on the subject matter and discourages the viewer from examining the mechanisms by which the information itself has been gathered, distilled and disseminated.

A precondition for the existence of this mode of representation is that there is an identifiable, recognised and generally acknowledged ordering presence. In the US and UK in this period, government involvement (or the response of governments to the films produced) determined both the content and the form of the films made. Grierson in the UK and Paré Lorentz in the US found themselves in a position where their films reinforced the official conception of public interest. Grierson operated within the domain of bodies such as the Empire Marketing Board and the GPO Film Unit, both with the duty to disseminate information on subjects of public interest. In the United States, Paré Lorentz operated initially with the support of the Resettlement Administration in the making of *The Plow That Broke the Plains* (1936) and *The River* (1937), the sucessses of which led to the foundation of the shortlived US Film Service. As William Guynn notes of the British documentary movement, 'on one hand the British documentarists defined themselves as socialists with a "socially progressive outlook"; on the other hand they worked within a conservative state bureaucracy that demanded restraint and self-censorship' (Guynn, 1998: 84).

The overriding social influence in Ireland throughout the period in question was that of the Catholic church and the Fianna Fáil government of Éamon de Valera. As Lee and Ó Tuathaigh (1982) note, questions of the role of the church in national affairs from Independence onward should refer not only to the precise mechanisms of control or particular interventions on the part of the church in social legislation, but to the more subtle form of influence exerted over the Irish people in the form of ethical, moral and social teaching. J. H. Whyte (1980) and Tom Inglis (1998) both discuss how the Catholic church came to have a pervasive influence over almost every aspect of Irish society throughout the nineteenth and most of the twentieth centuries. Though both Whyte and Inglis take issue with the supposed devotion of the ordinary people, given that it is difficult to ascertain the exact state of a person's inner belief at any time, all writers acknowledge that a high degree of collusion existed between church and state, and this projected a united front to the citizenry that helped to sustain what Inglis terms the 'moral monopoly' (the title of his book).

In practice this took the form less of direct intervention by the church in political affairs and more of an awareness of their policies which guided the decisions made by Irish governments. It is also evident in the Irish constitution, which even after several referenda maintains the tone of obedience to the higher authority of God and the church that it was founded upon in 1937. The church also had a firm hold over education dating back to Penal times and consolidated during the Great Famine. Even the 1922 Constitution had tentatively recognised that fact that the church had a 'special relationship' with education, and acknowledged that the state would not interfere with their running of schools. Educational institutions were considered to be privately owned and operated, and the state was to treat each one equally. In practice the majority of schools were run by religious orders until the introduction of vocational education, where more practical subjects were to be taught so as not to impinge upon the 'academic' programmes of the religious-run institutions. Church and state were thus subtly intertwined despite an official position of aloofness. It is clear that in terms of an ordering presence, the combined front presented by this collusion was a major contributing factor to the readiness of the Irish people to accept whatever ontological, spiritual or judicial argument was presented to them in the form of both documentaries and other forms of cultural expression. It was literally what they had been taught to do.

The state's authority to moderate the media was the final and most important factor in determining precisely how this ordering presence came to directly affect the practice of Irish documentary. Under the 1937 Constitution, Article 40:

1° The State guarantees liberty for the exercise of the following rights, subject to public order and morality: –

   i. The right of the citizens to express freely their convictions and opinions.

The education of public opinion being, however, a matter of such grave import to the common good, the State shall endeavour to ensure that the organs of public opinion, such as the radio, the press, the cinema, while preserving their rightful liberty of expression, including criticism of Government policy, shall not be used to undermine public order or morality or the authority of the State. (Bunreacht na hÉireann / The Constitution of Ireland)

Freedom of expression is hereby qualified subject to the state's definition of 'public order or morality' and of its own authority. No guidelines are given as to how these precepts are determined except that it is implicit that the criteria would be in line with the teachings of the Catholic church on matters of morality. This, coupled with explicit, specific statutes such as Acts covering the censorship of films (1923), publications (1929), offences against the state (1939, 1972) and official secrets (1963), accorded a high degree of power to the government and its delegated authorities to control the expression of ideas.

The implications of all this are that a system of social order was imposed upon Irish society in both subtle and obvious ways. Habitual church attendance and the presence of the religious in the education system meant that Catholic dogma was learned and reinforced throughout a person's life. Though Whyte notes the Irish propensity to separate religious and political beliefs when it suits them,[2] the presence of the church in everyday life was inescapable. The fact that this presence was then often legitimised by the state both in legislation[3] and in the outward display of respect and piety by Irish politicians (de Valera began inviting bishops to bless public buildings and attend major functions) meant that an attitudinal pattern was also established. This gave further force to the state's ability to act in a patrimonial capacity. The state benefited from the legitimation provided by linking its authority with that of God. It created a situation where the state was entrusted with defining what it meant to be Irish in practical and legal terms. Coupled with the church's definition of what it meant in moral and spiritual terms, this left only the question of how representation would define it in terms of human experience.

Church and state and film

In 1936 Pope Pius XI promulgated an encyclical on the subject of motion pictures entitled *Vigilanti Cura*.[4] In it he exhorted: 'entertainments of this kind should use their influence for healthy upbringing and education, and not for the ruin and perdition of souls' (Pius XI, 1936: 1). He argued that because films were imagistic in nature, unsophisticated minds could be more easily influenced than by literature or other forms of entertainment. He was aware that the production and distribution of films could not be prevented, and so recommended measures on two fronts. Firstly he urged the faithful to encourage the makers of films to ensure high moral standards by attempting to control them at source, but secondly he called for good Catholics to avoid films which did not attain these standards, knowing full well that the former was a hopeless task (he chided American filmmakers for failing to obey the infamous production code). To this latter end he advised bishops to obtain annual pledges from their communities not to attend films which offended Catholic morality, and recommended the establishment of a body which would keep people informed of the moral character of cinema releases. He also ordered bishops to ensure that only approved films were in places where Catholics congregated under the demesne of the church.

The Pope's suggestions would have far-reaching implications for the development of the Irish film industry, not least of all this final measure. By ensuring that even the venues were 'properly' regulated by Catholic authorities, the church could control the flow of representation even more efficiently than by relying upon state-approved censorship. The most direct effect of the encyclical in Ireland was the establishment of the National Film Institute of Ireland in 1943. The most prominent filmmaking and promoting body prior to this had been the Irish Film Society, founded in 1936 by Edward Toner, Seán O'Meadhra, Patrick Fitzsimons and Liam O'Leary. This was a secular organisation which specialised in arranging for screenings of films (especially foreign ones), setting up workshops for amateur filmmakers and bringing international guest speakers to address its members.[5] The IFS represented an attempt to centrally coordinate the activities of amateur filmmakers and to raise awareness of the potential use of film in education. Under its banner, several short fictions and documentaries were made, including some directed by O'Leary which will be discussed later. In 1940 the IFS held the first Conference on Film Education in Ireland (at which O'Leary delivered a paper on the social responsibility of film later reprinted in his book *Invitation to the Film*), and in 1943 it established Comhairle na nÓg, a special committee which arranged for countrywide screenings of films for children.[6]

The National Film Institute of Ireland was a very different organisation. Taking its cue directly from *Vigilanti Cura*, it was established with the specific aim of harnessing the power of the cinema for the good of the Irish people as they saw it. It was established under the patronage of Dr John Charles McQuaid, archbishop of Dublin, and constituted as a non-profit organisation limited by guarantee. It secured an initial grant of £2,000 from the Department of Education towards the cost of establishing a library of 'suitable' educational films, including films in Irish, and was granted a further £250 by the archbishop towards the cost of purchasing three film projectors which would be used to set up mobile exhibition units which would tour parish halls and other approved venues to show them. Some indication of the philosophical ideals of the Institute can be found in writings in *National Film Quarterly*.[7] In this publication, Rev. Reginald Walker wrote 'the Institute should address itself to the most important task of all: the education of public opinion' (Walker, 1950: 6), directly employing the phraseology of Article 40 of the 1937 Constitution. He goes on to state, 'if we want to indoctrinate the public with the teachings of *Vigilanti Cura*, let us once again take a leaf out of the enemy's book by concentrating on the young' (6). Another author, identified only as 'Sacerdos' (the Latin term for 'priest'), noted 'once people develop a critical approach to the film, then they will be relatively immune from the possibilities of contagion' (Sacerdos, 1950: 25). The language alone is telling. The word 'indoctrinate' is used unselfconsciously, as are the terms 'enemy' and 'contagion'. Such vehemence is a testament to the mental entrenchment of the self-appointed guardians of morality.

The Institute saw itself as more than just a moral guardian though. In contrast to what was possible in the United States (upon which the Pope had evidently given up), it presumed to be an actual *producer* of cultural values. It considered itself to be in a position to do so, assured by the legal foundations of the state. The films produced by the NFI were usually commissioned by government departments, who, given the institute's avowedly Catholic principles, were assured of their adherence to expected conventions. Writing on a more practical but equally definitive note as his religious colleagues, James C. Fagan, chairman of the Institute, claimed that 'there is no branch of film activity . . . and no aspect of its control and operation which does not come within the ambit of a National Film Institute' (Fagan, 1950: 15). The Institute's determination to exert an absolute influence over film in Ireland is clear. In the same article, Fagan states that the Institute is not a film society, with the 'not' emphasised in bold type, a not very thinly veiled reference to the fact that the Institute intended to replace the Irish Film Society as the most important film-related body in the country. NFI officials saw the IFS as a liberal organisation and disapproved of their importation of films which, according to strict Catholic principles, would not be acceptable.

The NFI also set out to coordinate the efforts at film education which had been initiated by The Film Society's seminars and guest speakers. Áine Ní

Chanainn (1992), a former member of the IFS who joined the NFI, outlines some of the programmes developed under the auspices of the NFI, including the training of school teachers in the practical and theoretical use of film as a teaching aid, film appreciation courses offered to the general public, and an extensive effort to distribute 'approved' films to schools around Ireland through a regional network of schools and parish halls controlled by religious organisations. Extensive writings on these courses and on the ideas behind them may be found in *National Film Quarterly* and its successors.

A Nation Once Again

It was through the NFI that the government was able to become involved in the sponsorship of documentary films. The government did not become direct producers, or provide substantial finance, but films were made by the NFI at the request of various government departments and finance was sought for individual film projects with the knowledge that the state had given its tacit approval. It was a circumspect method of state patronage, but the end result was the same. Informational and promotional films had been made before this, mostly by members of the Irish Film Society or other amateur enthusiasts, but in 1946 the government sponsored the historical documentary *A Nation Once Again*. The film was produced through the auspices of the National Film Institute, celebrating the life and ideas of nineteenth-century nationalist Thomas Davis. The investment of £3,000 was the first significant indication of official interest in the production of documentary films, though as noted in the previous chapter, the Dáil had approved the allocation of £200 towards the production of *Oidhche Sheanachais* in 1934.

The film begins with a parade held in Dublin in 1945 to commemorate the anniversary of Davis's death. Taoiseach Éamon de Valera and other members of the government are present, as is a large crowd. The marchers are mostly military personnel – a point worth noting because the film also ends with military scenes, specifically soldiers and armoured cars on manoeuvres in the Curragh. It is interesting that this emphasis on Ireland's military capability should follow the end of the Second World War, in which Ireland had been nominally neutral. The military presence reinforces one of the underlying themes of the film, that Davis's ideas represented one of the cornerstones of the struggle for Irish independence, a much more important conflict from the government's point of view. The film places Davis, as the voice over explains, on a continuum between 1798 leader Wolfe Tone and his 1916 counterpart Padraig Pearse, and attempts to illustrate through readings from his works how these ideas have come to fruition in the new Ireland. It argues that Davis's life story is 'not just the story of a man, but the story of a nation' and proceeds both to chart the details of Davis's life and provide a documentary overview of contemporary Ireland.

The film is notable for the comparatively modern image of the country which it portrays. It features many urban scenes and images of schools, hospitals and other institutions denoting social progress. People are very much in evidence, with almost every shot of Dublin featuring pedestrians and motorists. The gleaming white terminal building at Dublin airport is 'a symbol of the new Ireland', reflecting a modern architectural presence. The film is notably free of touristic vistas of the rural landscape, with the exceptions of some brief footage of wheat harvesting and some dramatised sequences. The first of these features a nineteenth-century peasant digging dirt with her hands. She signifies the toil and hardship associated with the Great Famine, about which the narrator is speaking as she is seen. A later sequence depicts a group of archetypal peasants reading Davis's nationalist newspaper *The Nation*. In both cases, stereotypical images of the land and rural peasantry are used to indicate the past, which contrasts with the generally progressive representation of the country in the present. Other reconstructed sequences depict Davis himself and some of his colleagues (actors dressed in the period garb of gentlemen) in discussion at Trinity College and walking through the Phoenix Park, over which the narrator reads excerpts from Davis's writings.

Despite the relatively progressive image of contemporary Ireland it presents, the film establishes a paradox in its referral to the past as the moral, social and political centre of the nation. The voice over tells us that Davis was a visionary because 'in Ireland's past he saw Ireland's future' and so foretold the success that is modern Ireland through issues such as the call for the revival of the Irish language and the idea of 'Irishness' as a lost racial heritage which had to be rediscovered and fought for against the forces of repression. This exemplifies the struggle between the outright rejection of the colonialist view of the past and the necessity to harness 'tradition' in a newly independent Ireland. As Kiberd observes, 'though it was quite understandable that people, in their anxiety to modernize, should dream of creating themselves *ex nihilo*, free of degrading past links, this was not to be absolute: the task rather was to show the interdependence of past and future in attempting to restore history's openness' (Kiberd, 1995: 292). The deferral to the past is therefore indicative of the ethical, moral and educational bias towards traditionalism rather than modernity, but not necessarily one which is antithetical to progress *per se*. Progress is good, but it only comes through obedience to the establishment and adherence to its ideological values.

A Nation Once Again is ultimately a reassertion of the patrimonial principle. It argues that the state, representative of the same strain of philosophical thought as Davis, embodies the ideals of 'God and the dead generations' invoked in the 1916 proclamation, and is thus best able to determine Ireland's destiny. The film's final sequence is particularly illustrative of this. De Valera reads a speech about Davis over the radio to groups of avid listeners clustered around their family radio sets, an idealised image of the populace hanging on the word of the state. This is followed by footage of military manoeuvres as described earlier. As the title song plays, Irish soldiers are shown raising the tricolour to a military salute. The camera tilts upwards along the flagpole and focuses on the flag fluttering in the breeze for some seconds before several army aeroplanes stream into view overhead. It is an image which echoes American propaganda films, and is quite dynamic. The camera then tilts to the clouds, excluding all sight of man with the suggestion perhaps that God himself is a part of this idea of Ireland which includes man, nation and a 'higher power'. This interpretation is sustainable when you consider that in the opening scenes of *Triumph of the Will*, Leni Riefenstahl accomplished something similar with her depiction of Hitler's descent into Nuremberg. His aeroplane was visualised in the abstract, with images of white clouds against the sky and shots of the city taken from overhead suggesting a great and powerful (almost mythic) figure looking down from on high upon the ordinary people. It is a visual argument which is echoed in reverse in *A Nation Once Again* as the camera looks up, deferring ultimate authority and the film's final image to God himself.

Written by John D. Sheridan, photographed and directed by Brendan Stafford, *A Nation Once Again* was a springboard for subsequent NFI production. It introduced personnel and established a template, amply demonstrating how informational films could easily be turned to articulate political ideas under the guise of a history lesson. Its assistant director, Colm Ó Laoghaire, would go on to become an important producer/director of Irish-language films. Sheridan later penned the award-winning *W. B. Yeats – A Tribute* (1950) while Stafford would serve as a cameraman on Liam O'Leary's films *Our Country* and *Portrait of Dublin* and later as director on a number of informational films before leaving to work in Britain. *A Nation Once Again* proved that the state had finally begun to appreciate the significance of a documentary film industry, and even if governments did little to encourage indigenous fiction film production, their involvement in nonfiction would continue.

Rhetoric, propaganda and *Our Country*

A Nation Once Again was followed by calls for similar films on more immediate topics. In *Irish Cinema Quarterly* in 1948, Brendan O'Shea wrote:

We are not short of problems that call for immediate treatment. Now is the time to flash Partition across the screens of the world while our representatives at home and abroad are denouncing it before audiences who are not utterly convinced because they cannot see it before their eyes in all its most hideous aspects.

Now is the time to declare screen warfare on the national scourge, TB, by short health films which will not only show how to attack the germ at its source but will destroy the barriers of fear and ignorance which are its most potent breeding grounds. (O'Shea, 1948: 22)

In 1952 the second of his wishes was granted with the production of the docudrama *Voyage to Recovery* (1952), and *Housing Discrimination* (1953) partially addressed the first. Instructional films sponsored by various government departments and civil authorities followed throughout the next decades, including films made for the Department of Health, the Marine Service, the Army, the Department of Local Government and of course Bord Fáilte, the Irish Tourist Board, established in 1955. Some of these will be discussed in more detail later. All were nominally concerned only with the presentation of information and did not interrogate the social infrastructure of modern Ireland. They were intended to reinforce the impression that the mechanisms of the state functioned efficiently and that all was well in de Valera's Ireland.

It is worth noting some points on the subject of propaganda here, as the term is perhaps too easily applied. Reacting to the release of *A Nation Once Again* in 1946, Liam O'Leary wrote 'one can see the easy primrose path to ballyhoo propaganda, chauvinistic and false but geared to the machinery of the Party' (cited in Rockett et al., 1988: 74). While his reaction is valid given the film's self-congratulatory tone, it is ironic that only two years later, O'Leary himself would be accused of being the propagandist following *Our Country*, a film specifically made to promote a political party and therefore no more or less 'geared to the machinery of the Party' (albeit not Fianna Fáil) than Stafford's.

The determination as to what constitutes propaganda is subjective, and has been the subject of several books in its own right. Given that our perception of the 'truth claims' of any given documentary film depends upon the ontological argument endorsed by the society in which we live, it is not difficult to come to the conclusion, as Nicholas Reeves puts it, that 'one person's "truth" is all too often another's "propaganda"' (Reeves, 1999: 11). It is possible therefore, as Barnouw observes, to argue that 'one can hardly imagine a documentary, or a film, or any kind of communication, that is *not* propaganda' (Barnouw, 1993: 345), in that all films represent discourse, an attempt to articulate a point of view and share it with other people. David Welch (1983) observes that the environment and context in which a propagandistic item is received are as important as the characteristics of the piece itself, an argument also favoured by Reeves. The point is that the dominant cultural and ideological discourse defines the context in which communication is received and understood. Welch specifically examines the case of Nazi Germany, where a film produced by the Nazi party for distribution to German theatres was merely part of an overall culture in which indoctrination was ubiquitous in the cinema, in newspapers, on radio, on advertising hoardings and in public rallies. Taylor (1998) argues likewise in studying the agit-props of the early Soviet Union.

In this respect, *Our Country* (1948) is perhaps the most important Irish documentary of this or any period. It is not an example of the 'official' propagation of an image of Ireland. In fact it was an aggressive attempt to debunk the official mythology of the state which, interestingly, had thus far barely found its way into films but was long understood to be in place in all other respects. Its significance stems not from its particular excellence, or even its formal or narrative conceits, but from its conception of the role and function of the documentary in modern Ireland.

The film was sponsored by Clann na Poblachta (under the banner of 'Irish Civic Films'), a newly formed political party, launched only in July 1946. The party itself represented the first chink in the republican armour of Fianna Fáil. Its leader, Sean MacBride, had impeccable republican credentials in that his father, Major John MacBride, had fought in 1916 and been executed. His mother was Maud Gonne, herself an important figure in Irish revolutionary mythology, immortalised in the work of W. B. Yeats. The Clann emerged out of committees formed to help republican prisoners during the war, and won its first victories in the by-elections of 1947, when MacBride himself entered the Dáil.[8] With the benefit of MacBride's singular personality and the radical health policies of Dr Noel Browne, the Clann piqued the public's interest. *Our Country* may have given them an additional edge. In the general election of 1948, they won ten seats in the Dáil, then formed part of a coalition government by teaming up with Fianna Fáil's largest competitor, Fine Gael.

Liam O'Leary, the director of *Our Country*, had been active as a pioneer in Irish filmmaking for over a decade by this time, and was, as noted earlier, one of the founders of the Irish Film Society. Born in 1910 in Youghal, Co. Cork (home of the Horgan brothers), he worked on amateur and semi-professional films throughout the 1930s and early 1940s, including *Scannán Scéala Éireann* (1943), a film now housed by the Irish Film Archive. Like Fr Browne's *Castle Rising*, *Scannán Scéala Éireann* is more of a curiosity than anything else. It is a loose assemblage of scenes filmed by O'Leary around Youghal while on holiday, including footage of a Gaelic League Rally and some of his sister, harpist Margaret O'Leary. These are of archive interest only, other than for the fact that they are shot in vivid colour. Other titles

4 Archivist, actor, writer and outspoken commentator on the development of cinema in Ireland, Liam O'Leary was a pioneer filmmaker whose *Our Country* (1948) was the most shattering documentary of its day. This film portrayed Ireland as a country ravaged by economic underdevelopment, emigration and import-fuelled inflation. It showed scenes of barefoot children playing in the slums of Dublin and featured political statements by members of Clann na Poblachta

which he discusses in his book *Invitation to the Film* include *Campa* (1942), on the Irish Boy Scouts, *Fishing Village* (date unknown) and *Aiséirghe* (1941).

Aiséirghe was his first overtly political film, a critique of the stasis in Irish life 'Forty-seven years after the foundation of the Gaelic League, Twenty-four Years after the 1916 insurrection', as title cards inform us. The connection to *Triumph of the Will* is unmissable here, a film which also began with title cards summarising recent German history in political terms which in Riefenstahl's case built up to the Nuremberg Rally. O'Leary was well versed in film history, and had read Pudovkin and other commentators upon the art of cinema. In *Invitation to the Film* he describes in detail how the opening scenes of *Aiséirghe* (the film itself is now lost) use montage to confront the mythology of the Irish state with its own contradictions. By juxtaposing the title cards which suggest nationalistic triumphs with images of the Nelson pillar and the Custom House, he counterpoints Irish rhetoric with icons of British power still evident in Dublin city. Ironically, his later film *Portrait of Dublin* would celebrate this same architecture as part of the historical fabric of the city.

Like Grierson, whom he referred to as 'the brilliant Scot' (O'Leary, 1945: 87), O'Leary was convinced of the rhetorical power of film, and of its value as a form of social progress. He saw the few films produced to date as having little real rhetorical value, and drew attention to the fact that the state had the (dangerous) power to begin making films (via the NFI, though he does not name it in his critique). This power, he argued, needed to be harnessed not to support an 'official' interpretation of Irish life, but to ask questions of contemporary society which would encourage progress.

Our people need the assurance of an inner freedom which we have not yet won. We want to realise our own potentialities and to seek the ways and means of adequately expressing them. Our rulers, if they would only acknowledge it, have the instrument of the film at their hand to clear the issues that bar our progress, to disseminate a knowledge and love of our countryside which alone can provide the stimulus to national action. Somebody must have the courage to disturb the rubble that lies about us and to clear the way. (102–3)

It is fair to speculate that O'Leary was speaking of himself, for not only would he later make government-sponsored public information films such as *Safe Cycling* (1949) and *Mr Careless Goes to Town* (1949), he may also have been the director of two short agit-props presented by an anti-partition organisation calling itself 'Aiséirge' made some years after O'Leary's film of that title. The films, *Partition Protest Parade* (1946), and *Treasna an Teorann* (1946) are fairly well photographed and not entirely without some sense of rudimentary structure, yet are little more than records of the activities of the Aiséirge group, particularly speaker Gearoid Ó Cuinnegán, whose grand-daughter donated the films to the Irish Film Archive in 2003. Tellingly though, an inflammatory title card at the conclusion of *Treasna an Teorann* reads, 'Somehow, sometime, by somebody, a begining must be made'.

When the opportunity to make *Our Country* presented itself, O'Leary rose to it with a strong sense of purpose. On the most basic level, the film presented Irish audiences with an image of themselves hithertofore unseen on the big screen. Like *Aiséirghe* it used counterpoint and juxtaposition to debunk commonly accepted images of the country. O'Leary was aided in this case by the words of three Irish politicians whose views the film is supposed to represent. It began with a welcoming introduction from Noel Hartnett, MacBride's main advisor within Clann na Poblachta, who asked, 'Do you ever think as much as you should about things here in Ireland?' Hartnett was filmed sitting at a desk and turned to face the camera as he spoke. His tone was matter-of-fact and his gaze directly at the audience. This was a lecture, not an entertainment.

Hartnett continued by noting, 'We've had twenty five years of native government in this part of the country. How have we utilised it?' This question was immediately followed by an image of rolling hills with sheep grazing in the foreground. It was an instantly recognisable Irish scene, yet the fact of its following the comment about 'utilising' self-government implies criticism.

The scene is devoid of people and certainly contains no evidence of industry. There is not even a suggestion of a farm, and the land seems barren in a way which is firmly anti-pastoral. As the voice over continues to drive home its points, explaining 'this is your country, our country, we have to live in it', the image changes to an establishing shot of O'Connell Street and O'Connell Bridge taken from Westmoreland Street. It is the signature image of the city in direct continuation of those discussed previously and already used by O'Leary in *Aiséirghe*. The film then shows the lines of people outside the UK permit office to obtain travel documents, and the voice over informs us that options are limited at home 'unless like so many of our sons and daughters we emigrate to a land which offers more opportunity to earn a living than does our own country; an emigration which should not be necessary'.

The entire film follows this pattern of imagistic and aural counterpoint, reinforcing the voice over with illustrative shots whose shock value alone was sufficient to gain people's attention. This demonstrates O'Leary's familiarity with the Russian agit-props of the 1920s and his awareness of montage. Images which should be comforting and touristic turn out to be used either for irony or to portray what was obviously being suggested to be a 'true' image of Ireland. The film does not appeal to pride and satisfaction, but actively encourages dissent and dismay. It even attacks the authority of the state in a way that must have given constitutional experts a moment's pause. An image of the Dáil buildings is followed by the comment that public affairs are not the sole responsibility of elected officials. The film follows this with images of children playing in puddles of water amid ruined buildings in Dublin city accompanied by the exhortation 'public affairs are the responsibility of all of us. They are your affair and they will be the affair of your children.'

Our Country is an emotive and aggressive attempt to demythologise the triumphalist conception of the nation. It could not but succeed, relying as it did upon the evidentiary primacy of the image, and it shocked contemporary audiences. As a piece of propaganda, it achieves the necessary aims of spreading its ideas and of presenting a call to action. As Taylor has argued, one of the defining characteristics of propaganda is its need to encourage action. Propaganda is propaganda partly because of its intention to produce specific social effects. It is, as he puts it, 'the attempt to influence the public opinions of an audience through transmission of ideas and values' (Taylor, 1998: 15). The continual message of *Our Country* is that the people of Ireland must do something to change the situation in which they have found themselves. 'The need is vision, enthusiasm and a plan for the future,' says MacBride in the closing scenes. He does not discuss specific solutions or articulate the particular mechanisms through which Clann na Poblachta will achieve them. (Nor, for that matter, does the film actually mention the Clann or identify its speakers as members of the party.) This may be related to the unkind but not untrue observation that Clann na Poblachta did not have any policies to articulate. It merely represented a growing frustration with Fianna Fáil and capitalised upon its errors in overestimating public support. *Our Country* encourages its audience only to see and to believe that change is necessary, and therefore, by implication, to elect MacBride in order to do 'something' about it. The action required is a vote for the Clann, and while the film obviously could not have a 'hypodermic' effect on voters, it undoubtedly contributed to the Clann's public profile.

Our Country proved to Irish observers that the documentary film could be used to present a political position which would be then accepted not as rhetoric, but as fact. The film seeks to elude ideological complexity and create the sense that it is an objective appraisal of the modern Irish condition: an appeal to 'reality' rather than rhetoric. The direct address style used by O'Leary was sufficient at that time to establish the film's 'objectivity' in the eyes of the general public, which is why the film's opponents were so quick to respond and draw attention to its political bias. It is also why it becomes propagandistic, because this alone makes a specific argument which is implicit rather than stated and which audiences will absorb without being conscious of it as discourse. This strategy echoes Daniel Boorstin's analysis of the speeches of the American founding fathers, discussed by Richard Kearney. Boorstin argued that the use of images of American geography in political speeches represented an attempt to assure American citizens that, as Kearney puts it, 'in spite of differences of colour and creed, there was a basic *givenness* which bound them all together' (Kearney, 1997: 52). In this conception of America, the political system was natural rather than constructed, as if it had sprung fully formed from the landscape rather than being the result of ideological choices and political decisions. *Our Country* operates within the same paradigm. As the new republic dawns (the coalition of which the Clann was a part would be the one to officially declare the Republic in 1949), the film calls for a reappraisal of the image of the country and changes in its social order. Without proposing any definite path to the goal (or even identifying its sponsors), the film offers a new type of national unity. It purports to demonstrate that the preceding political order, based upon what, in the film, MacBride terms 'flag waving . . . national records and personalities' (i.e. old-style political divisions based on the comparatively recent war of independence and civil war), must give way to 'a policy based upon realities, instead of recriminations and self glorifications based on past events'.

The invocation of 'realities' is itself interesting, suggesting again that the film was making a deliberate attempt to argue that this was 'the real Ireland' and that that represented by de Valera was not. Paradoxically, MacBride is repudiating dominant political loyalties by purporting to be apolitical. He claims instead to be interested in the reality of modern Ireland reflected in the film's hard-edged images. As with American republicanism, the call to a homogeneous national identity transcending traditional divisions (not of race, but certainly of creed) depends upon the evocation of a common heritage based on the landscape of town and country. By implication the poverty, deprivation and immigration we see in the film affect all levels of society equally. The film requires only that the audience accept that these organic images of Ireland are incontestable fact, devoid of interpretation extraneous to the profilmic – they speak for themselves.

Ironically, as would be pointed out by its detractors, not all of the images were quite what they appeared to be. A shot of a barefoot news boy standing on a street corner, for example, was later revealed to have been set up by O'Leary, who asked the boy to remove his shoes so the image would be more dramatic. This recalls the work on the streets of New York in 1888 of Jacob A. Riis, whose genuine concern for the conditions of emigrants living in tenements and slums was not above a degree of distortion, such as posing his subjects to create greater drama. Arguably, slight deceptions do not detract from the realities of the situation being portrayed. If we dare to invoke the words of Robert Flaherty, 'one often has to distort a thing to catch its true spirit' (cited in Calder-Marshall, 1963: 97). The conditions photographed by O'Leary did exist, though he was attempting to make the point with a degree of force which compelled him to cheat a little.

The reason this works is that O'Leary's conception of reality is firmly within the interpretative mode. He believes reality to be malleable to the extent that minor distortions make no difference to the authenticity of the vision of reality the film represents. He therefore assumes both an access to the external, knowable reality of contemporary Ireland and a right to shape images taken from it into a rhetorical structure without tainting the referentiality of the profilmic itself. Ironically, the fact that the film demonstrably manipulates the profilmic in order to alter the political structures which maintain it paradoxically implies that reality is fluid, ambiguous and changeable, but this is a point beyond the sophistication of the makers at that time. Yet the film is open to serious criticism for its choices. It does not examine its own political bias, or draw attention to the political process on the whole and the role the film plays in affecting change. *Our Country* does not problematise the veracity of the images of barefoot children (were all Irish children barefoot? or some? or just those in Dublin? etc.[9]) or the nature of truth (what is 'our country' given the ongoing political and social divisions and the spectre of a divided Ireland?), or even of the political philosophy which underlies the production of the film (it is a paid political announcement, after all), nor, importantly, does it mention or question the financial structures which facilitated its own production and distribution.

Eithne MacDermott (1998) reports that Rank distributors initially refused to deal with the film because they did not want to get involved in politics. The film's writer, Maura Laverty, travelled to Rank headquarters in London to appeal the decision, and there was also a local campaign of bill posting. However, Rockett notes that film distributors and exhibitors had a good reason to support the film's release in order to affect the outcome of the election, as they objected to an increase in entertainment tax introduced by Fianna Fáil two weeks before the film opened.[10] This is relevant because it again represents an attack upon the infrastructure established by the dominant order in which films produced by the NFI and distributed via parish halls and other venues were only those of the 'approved' type, as we have seen. For Irish cinema owners to exhibit an 'unapproved' film which actively opposed the government was a political act, albeit one motivated by self-interest.

Adding fuel to the proverbial fire, *Our Country* was produced outside of Ireland (in Elstree Studios in London), opening itself to attack from political opponents who could, and did, argue that it was foreign-made propaganda (Rockett, 1988: 78–9). Detractors also drew attention to the fact that O'Leary appears in the film in a dramatised sequence, playing the role of a grocer. Seán MacEntee, Fianna Fáil's Minister for Health, cited this as an example of disingenuousness which negated the film on the whole. He also, as Rockett notes, attempted to use the film to tie Clann na Poblachta to the IRA, to communism and to England, suggesting also that the Irish Film Society was a subversive organisation.[11] Rockett documents the reaction to the film in some detail in *Cinema and Ireland* and I will not repeat that material here. Suffice to note that it became such a centre of contention that like its descendant *Rocky Road to Dublin* (1968), it became the subject of household debate.

In the final analysis *Our Country* is a typical direct address documentary film, strongly influenced by the British documentary cinema of the 1930s, although also related to the wartime propaganda films which had evolved from that movement. It was also, despite its apparent radicalism, ultimately a reassertion of the same ideas of Irish culture which it seemed on the surface to oppose, and was equally dependent upon the social consensus that the Ireland it represented was a homogeneous and unproblematic one. Though it offered an alternative political party with policies (unstated) which would help the Irish people to more directly confront the problems which beset them, the film did not necessarily empower the citizenry to which it so directly appealed. The mechanisms of state control continued, and the supremacy of the church was not even tangentially challenged: Indeed MacBride was as respectful of the Catholic hierarchy as de Valera, as was demonstrated by the infamous 'mother and child' controversy in 1951

5 The son of 1916 rebel Major John MacBride and of Maude Gonne, Seán MacBride emerged as a political force in Ireland with the foundation of Clann na Poblachta, the first party to challenge the Republican mandate of Éamon de Valera's Fianna Fáil. He is pictured here in Liam O'Laoghaire's *Our Country* (1948), the controversial document of the problems faced by mid-twentieth-century Ireland in respect of which MacBride was offering himself as a solution

when he supported the calls for Dr Noel Browne's resignation after Browne had run afoul of church authorities.[12]

    Our Country was ultimately a reassertion of the principle of patrimony. MacBride, with his peculiar accent and fierce countenance, was merely setting himself up to replace de Valera, not change the underlying social structure. *Our Country* is not an example of radical cinema, but it was proof that a film could change the world at least to the extent that it could make things happen. Film's intervention in social process was perceived not in terms of genuine subversion (despite what Sean MacEntee might have feared), but as a powerful tool with which to transmit ideas, values and specific arguments. This revelation had come long before in both the United States and Britain, but it was *Our Country* which brought it home to Ireland, nearly twenty years after *Drifters* (1929).

Docudramas and informational films

Aware now of just how powerful a documentary film could be, government departments involved in the sponsorship of films through the National Film Institute began to demand the same level of effectiveness as *Our Country* and *A Nation Once Again*. Though, as Rockett warns, 'it would be a great mistake to assume that the government had a major commitment to these smaller scale indigenous projects' (Rockett et al., 1988: 84), most non-fiction films produced during this era bore the mark of the NFI, which itself had the tacit approval of the state, if not in the form of finance, at least to the extent that it was permitted to go about its business unhindered. Satisfied that the mark of Catholic authority which always hung over NFI productions guaranteed the vision of Ireland endorsed by the state, the government did not need to intervene or supervise directly other than to initiate the projects and lend their endorsement. There was a conviction that what was said on film would be believed. This, coupled with the formal simplicity of the social documentary, resulted in politically uncontroversial films which assumed authority over the realities of Irish life and which did not stretch the formal boundaries of the medium.

Initially there was a lateral step towards docudrama, which offered the benefits of direct address with the capacity to reinvent the physical environment for 'dramatic' purposes. The form is still frequently used for 'public information' films, a troubling fact given that the 'truth claims' of such films rely heavily upon the ethical standards applied during production. As Michael Rabiger notes, 'the dividing line seems to be one of good faith' (Rabiger, 1992: 303). Derek Paget identifies three areas of potential dispute where such 'good faith' becomes subject to ethical behaviour. The first is 'the nature and status of the factual material used in the programme' (Paget, 1998: 1); the second is 'the kinds of dramatic representation the programme employs' (2); the third is 'the overarching worry that "dramatic licence" might mean that liberties are taken, and gross simplifications made, by programme makers' (2). These formualtions echo John Corner's identification of key issues affecting perceptions of the form, which he lists as (1) referentiality, (2) representation, (3) manipulation and (4) thematic issues (Corner, 1996: 42–3). The difficulty is that docudramas rely upon several of the same elements as documentaries, including evidence, argument and the fair and accurate representation of reality. Docudramas however must recreate or reconstruct that reality for the purposes of unfolding not events or situations themselves, but re-enactments thereof usually designed to draw in the viewer on an emotional level. They also characteristically use the conventions of dramatic storytelling and employ actors, which makes the audience more attuned to the expectations of passive narrative pleasure.

As Dirk Eitzen notes, documentary is a mode of reception which relies on the audience's willing participation in the discourse *as* discourse. Audiences must be engaged on a level which makes them active and aware in order for the argument (or, to use Nichols's term, the 'voice') to be evident. The distinction is partly on the level of raw materials; the physical difference between a world as 'recreated' or 'restaged' for the drama, and where the drama transpires in the profilmic world. This places additional weight upon the docudramatist to ensure that, in the areas identified by Paget and Corner, the highest standards of research and ethics are applied in the production of their reconstructed world ('evidence' must be weighed against 'motivation', the profilmic must be weighed against the level of referentiality, etc.).

It is also, Eitzen notes, a distinction on the level of reception, where the audience assumes the documentary to represent reality and is aware that its arguments are drawn from the historical world rather than the imagination of the fiction artist. Docudramas therefore tread ethically problematic ground because their reference to 'fact' and 'truth' ('This film is based on a true story', etc.) asks the audience to offer the same level of trust as to a documentary, yet their world is as malleable and dramatically convenient as their makers need it to be. He observes, 'viewers seem to assume that the scene is telling the truth, even though they do not pay attention to its particular truth claims. This assumptions is precisely what makes it possible for viewers to ignore the truth claims. It is what makes it possible for them to focus on the melodrama in the scene rather than on its historical arguments. The assumption that the film is telling the truth also serves to validate their emotional responses to the scene' (Eitzen, 1995: 88). There is therefore an inherent risk that docudrama's 'truth claims' go unchallenged in terms of an ontological argument. As in Goebbels's favoured propaganda films, or arguably the world as represented by classical narrative, a 'natural' state of constructed and ideologically weighted 'reality' is in place before the argument itself begins, which would not be true of documentary drawn from actuality. In documentary the ideology exists in the social world in which the text is constructed, and the nature of the medium should, ideally, ensure that audiences respond to the argument *as* argument. In docudrama, the danger is that they will respond emotionally to character and situation and assume the truth claims to be valid and the ontology authentic even though both are artificial, fictive and dramatically contrived.

Following *Our Country*, Liam O'Leary's next major undertaking was the direction of several docudramas on behalf of the newly elected government. The Department of Local Government commissioned a series of road safety films in the late 1940s, including *Next Please* (1948), *Mr. Careless Goes to Town* (1949) and *Safe Cycling* (1949). O'Leary's films were similar to US and UK films from the war and postwar periods. Comic in tone, they usually featured a character behaving foolishly contrary to the 'obvious' laws or rules under discussion. Using disapproving voice overs and even indulging in some slapstick, they provided information in an entertaining form, advising people on road safety in an increasingly modern Ireland. *Safe Cycling* plays in particular upon what was then a traditional mode of transport. It highlights the fact that bicycles are no longer alone on the road. One scene depicts cyclists weaving through vehicular traffic, another demonstrates the hazards of driving along tram lines (the wheel gets caught, the cyclist is thrown off). Other sequences illustrate the dangers of carrying loads: one person drops a pile of books into a puddle to the observation 'Won't the librarian be pleased?', another rides with a ladder protruding in front and behind which threatens to topple him over. The condescending tone is not unusual; on the contrary, it is the norm for this type of film. It reinforces the idea that there is a higher power who condemns or condones the behaviour of the ordinary citizen, in this case the government. The element of humour is also characteristic: it helps to ensure that the audience is drawn to the side of the authority and shares their disapproval of the errant individual.

Another errant character was at the centre of the most high-profile docudrama of the period, *The Promise of Barty O'Brien* (1951), written by Irish dissident author Seán Ó Faoláin but otherwise demonstrating a strong international influence. Not only was the film funded by the Marshall Aid Programme's Economic Cooperation Administration, but its director, George Freedland, was Russian. In its own way, *The Promise of Barty O'Brien* was little different from the Kalem one-reeler *The Lad From Old Ireland* (1910), noted in the history of cinema as the first indigenously produced Irish fiction film, which told the tale of a young man forced to flee his homeland only to return at the end to save his girlfriend's family from eviction with the money he has earned in America. *The Promise of Barty O'Brien* followed the adventures of a frustrated farmer's son whose fascination with electricity has him first collude with his mother and sister to have power routed to their rural home and then, after a clash with his conservative father, flee to America to train as an electrical engineer. He eventually returns to find that in his absence things have improved and there is a future for him and for Ireland after all. The narrative dynamics are fairly similar to the melodramas of forty years earlier, and the message is not substantially different. Its appeals for modernisation, specifically rural electrification, are obviously particular to this era, but this of course represents the official policy of both the Marshall Aid Administration and the Irish government. Its attitude to emigration is still the same as that of *The Lad From Old Ireland*, where the ultimate goal is always to return to the homeland, regardless of how bright the lights of America may seem.

This nostalgic fantasy may have been made for consumption by a domestic audience, but it bears all the hallmarks of an immigrant saga designed to please foreign sponsors. Bernadette Whelan notes this in her appraisal of the film as part of the Marshal Aid Economic Cooperation Administration's campaign in postwar Europe. She observes that 'the Americans wanted the participant states to increase production, expand foreign trade by lowering or removing barriers to free trade, achieve financial stability and realise European unity. In other words, to create a United States of Europe. The promise of the Marshall Planners was encapsulated in one ERP [European Recovery Programme] slogan – You Too Can Be Like US' (Whelan, 1999: 33). It was a vision of Ireland filtered through a generic vision of Europe seen through the eyes of the Marshall Plan, and despite Ó Faoláin's input, it subscribed to a romantic, agrarian interpretation of Ireland which not only failed to challenge received views of the country (though it did include a dispute between father and son over the importance of 1916), but reinforced them in the name of 'progress'. Only one year later *The Quiet Man* (1952) would open itself to charges of stereotyping and cliché for doing the same thing. Yet, as Rockett has documented, *The Promise of Barty O'Brien* was largely well received. Kevin O'Kelly enthusiastically claimed that it was 'the first Irish propaganda movie worth serious consideration *as* a movie' (1951). He did not stop there, but went on to comment that 'The documentaries sponsored by the Irish Government have either had incompetent direction or bad scripts dictated to the unfortunate by civil servants', and while he seemed happy with the film, he did note that he felt the story was contrived and thought that Eric Doyle was unhappy in the lead.

The Marshall Plan was the subject of a separate film photographed by Brendan Stafford and Liam O'Leary under the banner of 'Editorial Film Productions'. *The Marshall Plan at Work in Ireland* (year unknown) provided viewers with an equally generic overview of the Irish economy, largely focused on agriculture and tourism. It told viewers that 'newcomers are enchanted by the magic' of Ireland, and despite attempting to argue that $200 million in Marshal Aid investment would help to bolster Ireland's economy, spent a notable amount of time visiting tourist locations, including Blarney, Co. Cork. It was among the earliest films to feature what would become an emblematic image of Irish agricultural industry, namely peat harvesting machines ploughing their way across the dark landscape of the midland turf bogs. This blend of modern machinery and traditional scenery would become an icon of progress in Ireland for years after, not least of all because of the sponsorship of films on the subject by Bord na Móna, the state authority responsible for harvesting and exporting peat.

Other informational films followed, with the approval of other government departments. *Lifeline* (1949) was sponsored by the Marine Services. It deals with the importance of shipping and features some scenes of dramatic reconstruction which bookended an otherwise ordinary documentary. It argues that the shortages plaguing Ireland in the postwar period are partly the result of the loss of ships during the Second World War. It encourages the development of indigenous industry rather than the importation of goods to ease pressure on the Irish economy and on shipping itself. This was a direct statement of the still prevalent protectionist policies of the Irish government, and the film even includes footage of a Catholic priest launching a new Irish ship. Its bombastic voice over is reminiscent of *The March of Time* (which had visited Ireland in 1944), but its heavy emphasis on statistics is more typical of the British documentary school.

In contrast to *Lifeline*, *Éire* (1955) was a British-produced overview of the trade relationship between the new republic and the UK. Though it argues that Irish agriculture is an important contributor to the welfare of British citizens, its portrayal of Ireland as a purely agrarian economy contrasts with the urban/industrial one seen in *Lifeline* and *A Nation Once Again*. The first image of Dublin in the film is not the signature scene of O'Connell Street traffic featured in most films, but following narrator Liam O'Leary's introduction, 'Dublin is the capital of Ireland', we are treated to a shot of a farmer driving his cattle to market. Only then do we find our way to O'Connell Street. The implications are obvious.

Independent indigenous production continued throughout this period. Hibernia Films was a small company established by architect Michael Scott, solicitor Roger Greene and Austrian émigré George Fleischmann. Desmond Egan, director of *Harvest* (1934), was one of their executive producers. Their film *The Silent Order* (1948) on the lives of Cistercian monks in Co. Tipperary was photographed and directed by Fleischmann, who was to become an important figure throughout the next decade. *The Silent Order* demonstrated his ability to capture the essence of his subject with crisp photography and professionally structured sequences depicting monks at work, prayer, rest and recreation. It was a very serene and respectful image of the religious life, but an uncritical insight into a largely hidden world.

Born in 1912 in Austria, Fleischmann trained at the Berlin Film Academy and worked on documentaries in Germany before the war, including *Olympia* (1936). During the war he crash landed in Ireland while on a surveying mission and was interned along with his comrades and other foreign military personnel. He remained in Ireland after his release to work with Hibernia Films, but his talent was quickly noticed and he obtained independent assignments on projects including *Who Fears to Speak of '98?*, *Next Please*, *Lifeline*, *W. B. Yeats – A Tribute*, *Voyage to Recovery* and *Housing Discrimination*, most of which were key films of the period. He was also hired by US and UK newsreel companies to make their Irish-themed specials such as Rank's *Look at Life* series and *Movietone News*. He later became a producer and was behind a large number of informational films made throughout the 1960s. Inevitably, with a filmography like that, we will return to his work again later.

As noted in the previous chapter, Fr Browne continued making films at this time with *The Waters of Providence* (1949). Like *Eucharistic Congress*

1932 and *The Silent Order*, the film is visibly and purposely informed by the (positive) influence of the Catholic church and features religious rituals alongside scenes of industry, progress and unity. It demonstrates a much greater command of rhythm and structure than Browne's previous work. Like the similar and roughly contemporaneous *Convoy Mills* (1955), it is what Rabiger terms a 'process film' (Rabiger, 1992: 289). It focuses on the various stages in the processing of wool, from sorting and washing to carding and spinning. As with all films of this genre, it is designed to highlight the efficiency of the industry. It emphasises the relentless, repetitive actions of machinery and worker contributing to the impression of a steady, reliable production line.

Where *The Waters of Providence* differs from *Convoy Mills* is in its portrayal of the human rhythms. *Convoy Mills* is strongly reminiscent of its American counterparts on American industry, portraying the production of Donegal Tweed as a streamlined and modern mechanical process, almost totally ignoring its workforce in favour of a constructivist emphasis on the patterns of movement of gears and fibres. Its voice over is clear and informative and does not draw attention to details of economy or culture extraneous to the production process, unlike its US equivalent, *Flaxen Heritage* (1953), which generalised about 'Irish colleens' and 'gentle rolling hills', featuring copious imagery of the latter which had little to do with the nominal subject.

The Waters of Providence is also coloured by social, historical and religious awareness. The mill was established by Sister Mary Arsenius, a member of the order of the Irish Sisters of Charity, to alleviate poverty in the area. The film argues that her work has been central to the development of the area to the extent that a young couple are shown building a new house in preference to emigrating. The film's aims are to integrate the needs of the then troubled Irish economy with those of the Catholic church: sustaining indigenous structures and maintaining traditional patterns of community fidelity in order to construct a self-sufficient and independent country. This was seen in a relatively limited capacity in *Lifeline*, but here it is an important thematic concern. Scenes of workers taking time for prayer during their lunch break and of them dipping their fingers respectfully in a convenient holy water font on entering the workspace ensure that the endeavours of the workers are not perceived within the kind of social democratic terms favoured by John Grierson and the British documentary movement or the anonymous capitalism of the US equivalent seen in *Convoy Mills*.

The film is careful to portray Irish industry as integral to the continued evolution of a Catholic country and Catholicism as integral to the development of Irish industry, replete with its notions of community. The final section of the film is almost exclusively concerned with documenting the social lives of the Providence workers. Their labour is seen not in isolation, but as part of the fabric of community life. They attend public music recitals and religious retreats, participate in the rosary and in a lively dance to harp and piano. The religious dimension is extremely strong, and the film concludes with a reconstruction featuring the aforementioned young couple (who are clearly amateurs) kneeling in prayer at the grave of Sister Mary Arsenius on the completion of their new house, simultaneously cementing the bonds of community, family morality, the physical and spiritual continuity of the work-force, and an awareness of the past and role of the church in building a new and prosperous Ireland.

The Waters of Providence is a notably more polished and purposeful film than any of Browne's other work, so much so that it may be incorrectly cred-ited to him. There is no evidence to suggest any other hands though, and Browne is known to have made a film on Foxford Mills. In the absence of an alternative possibility or proof to the contrary, *The Waters of Providence* has been presumed to be that film. It bears interesting similarities to the earlier work in its strong sense of basic composition and in its continual assertion of a religious context. The use of reconstruction is consistent with Browne's willingness to use amateur actors in *Castle Rising* and of course the growing prevalence of their use in other documentaries at the time. Its somewhat uncritical endorsement of religious ritual suggests merely a more accom-plished version of the director of the early 1930s, and also reflects the absence of a critical paradigm for the examination of the church in Irish doc-umentary on the whole. Yet its formal organisation demonstrates a much greater awareness of the requirements of documentary narrative, possibly resultant from the director's exposure to British and American films, or even those now coming out of Ireland via the NFI.

Probably the most important of the public information films were those sponsored by the Departments of External Affairs and of Health, both of which were headed by men with good reason to support the film industry. On the strength of their electoral performance in 1949, Seán MacBride and Dr Noel Browne both became ministers in the coalition government. MacBride became Minister for External Affairs and Browne, naturally, took the health portfolio. Both men played a significant part in solidifying the relationship between filmmakers and the state through the sponsorship of documentary films. The year 1949 saw the establishment of the Industrial Development Authority (IDA), a semi-state body which took over some of the functions of the Department of Industry and Commerce. One of the aims of the IDA was to encourage the development of Irish industry, includ-ing the film industry, and though it did little as far as fiction films were con-cerned, it would later become one of many co-sponsors of informational documentaries. Rockett even notes that in 1950 the Minister for Industry and Commerce, Liam Cosgrave, reported that he had instructed the IDA to investigate the possibility of establishing a film industry (Rockett et al., 1988: 81).

In 1950 MacBride established the Cultural Relations Committee, a body designed to encourage the fostering of Irish culture through informational films and other types of Irish-centred events both at home and abroad. It served as a liaison between filmmakers and the Department of External Affairs, and Liam O'Leary was invited to sit on the board. He did so briefly, but retired from it to continue making films. He began work on *A Portrait of Dublin*, a documentary sponsored by the Cultural Relations Committee which sought to examine Dublin's culture and history with a view to marketing the city abroad for tourist purposes as well as being seen by indigenous audiences. When the government of which MacBride and Browne were part collapsed, an unsympathetic Fianna Fáil regime ascended to power. The new Minister for External Affairs, Frank Aiken, withheld O'Leary's film from distribution, presumably in an act of revenge for *Our Country*. O'Leary became disillusioned with Ireland and left to become an acquisitions officer for the British Film Institute's film archive in London. His legacy remained in the form of the new and now thriving industry in non-fiction public informational films and in his individualism, to which subsequent Irish directors would look for inspiration. Though he would never direct a film there again, he did later return to Ireland to work as a viewing officer for RTÉ and became a pioneer archivist as well as a long-time campaigner for a secular and independent film industry until his death in 1992.[13]

On being awarded his health portfolio in the coalition government of 1948, Dr Noel Browne encouraged the Department of Education and the NFI to distribute a series of health education films to Irish schools. From 1948 to 1951 he sponsored a series of these screenings throughout the country. In 1951 he wrote, 'I have come to the conclusion that the only means of procuring health films really suitable for our people is to have them produced in this country' (Browne, 1951: 11–12) and noted that he had put the matter 'in hands'. The most immediate results were docudramas including *Everybody's Business* (1951) and *Voyage to Recovery*. The first was directed by Tony Inglis, the set designer of *The Promise of Barty O'Brien*, and concerned itself with the benefits of proper hygiene in Irish shops and restaurants. The second and better-known film was on Browne's special subject, tuberculosis (of which three of his own family had died and on which he had been a vigorous campaigner). The film was released under the newly reappointed Fianna Fáil Minister for Health, Dr James Ryan, who, unlike Frank Aiken, did not attempt to rescind his predecessor's promises.

Voyage to Recovery is formally simple and generally straightforward in its argument in favour of the state-funded sanatoria. It is a problem–solution film which presents the Irish health service as efficient, modern and friendly.

It initially presents the problem in the form of the protagonist's illness, and, combining the frames of reference of drama and documentary, offers a series of both dramatic and practical complications which are eventually overcome. The central character's own reluctance to accept treatment is the first of these, which is solved by his wife's insistence that he do something about it. She is portrayed as a typical 1950s homemaker, firmly defined within the domestic sphere and yet possessed of enough power to compel her husband to act regardless of his own doubts. The second dramatic complication is represented by the figure of his conservative aunt (Maire Kean), who, the voice over tells us, 'is rather old fashioned'. She represents the widespread social prejudice against the disease and its victims. Her character is set up for ridicule, dressed in fussy clothes of the previous generation, and seen driving an old-style jalopy. The hero (Joe Lynch) overcomes this prejudice by refusing to be ashamed of his illness.

Once inside the sanatorium the difficulties are all practical. Particularly insistent on the point that the protagonist does not have to pay for any of his treatment, the film focuses on the various tests he undergoes and the

6 A scene from *Voyage to Recovery* (1952). In this docudrama directed by Abbey Theatre veteran Gerard Healy, a man suffering from tuberculosis (Joe Lynch – pictured right) challenges the ignorance and prejudice of his aunt (Marie Kean – pictured left). With the help of a government-sponsored sanatorium and his own personal courage, he overcomes both the social and physical obstacles put before him

questions he asks. The final third of the film veers away from the dramatic story into conventional documentary exposition of statistics which are intended to provide 'factual' evidence to back up its claims. The fictional drama is resolved in the final minutes when the protagonist's wife and aunt collect him from the sanatorium. The last scene features his son playing with a model sailboat, an image introduced at the beginning of the film as a prelude, which now becomes a metaphor for a free and healthy life and brings the visual narrative full circle.

As an informational film, it serves its sponsors well. It subtly combines the purely practical demands of presenting the facts about the treatment of TB to Irish audiences with a definite vision of Ireland with which these correspond. The tightlyknit nuclear family living in well-appointed surroundings was meant, on one level, to demonstrate, as the protagonist informs his aunt, that 'TB can occur even in the most respectable of families'. It was intended to attack assumptions about the disease and allay fears about how it was being dealt with by the authorities. Its protagonist's resistance to peer pressure suggests a 'progressive' society in which such prejudices were no longer prevalent. Its comforting vision of a middle-class man spending a brief spell in a clean and restful state-run institution was an assertion of the state's ability on the one hand to manage the immediate crisis, and on the other to look out for the welfare of its citizens on the whole. The film is crisply directed by Gerard Healy and beautifully shot by George Fleischmann. It makes clever use of the environment, depicting the hospitals as orderly but not institutional, sanitary but not cold. One particularly effective moment has the central character dance down a long white corridor which would otherwise have a rather chilling and desolate quality. The film subverts expectation, and in that way, like *Our Country*, attempts to debunk myths. Yet also, like *Our Country*, it is ultimately a reassertion of the dominant value system, a homage to the marriage of state and citizen in which the former always looks out for the latter.

Tourism

Projecting images of the country designed to achieve specific ends, tourist films give perhaps the strongest indication not necessarily of what a country thinks of itself, but of what its cultural industries believe is expected of it.[14] Such films tread some of the ground explored in the previous chapter regarding the relationship between habitat and inhabitants, but as T. J. M. Sheehy observed, 'sponsors of tourist films are not philanthropists. Their interest is tourist publicity. In the films they sponsor they want quality and artistic integrity, but in their approach art, desirable as it may be, takes second place to publicity needs' (Sheehy, 1967: 5). Tourist films are promotional, and engage a different set of expectations from those which attempt to understand the identity of a place and its people. As Terry Lovell observes, such films are interested in the creation of desire: 'The cultural producer is keenly interested in the proliferation of wants which will lead consumers to seek out the commodities sold to satisfy those wants' (Lovell, 1983: 58).

Lovell here identifies the paradox which is at the centre of the tourism industry. Tourism is not merely the result of a capitalist conspiracy. The desire to travel and visit places of which we have no direct experience has always been central to human behaviour. As discussed in the previous chapter, the exploitation of this desire has been organised within a capitalist infrastructure since the nineteenth century. Tourism capitalises upon that which already exists: on one hand the desire for experience and on the other the existing qualities of the place in question. Lovell notes that consumers must seek out 'the commodities sold', not the commodities created to meet the wants. It is what is being sold and how that is in question in our assessment of the tourist film, which is itself a cultural object which may in turn be sold as a film or video. While there are grains of truth and elements of reality contained within this object, it requires closer analysis to separate form from content and understand what wants are being satisfied and how.

Derek Paget identifies another paradox. While he acknowledges that tourism is an expression of economic supremacy, and draws attention to its colonialist origins, he is not so naive as to suggest that countries which are popular tourist destinations are wholly victims; 'who, exactly, is exploiting whom in the Greek taverna on Rhodes or Corfu (intertextual with the film *Zorba the Greek*)? It is difficult to say but quite likely that both tourists and "ethnic entertainment" understand each other' (Paget, 1999: 48). He observes that in Britain, the recourse for a nation whose economic outlook is less salubrious than it was is to fall back upon its past. So-called 'heritage industries' are a significant contributor to the economies of most European countries in the late twentieth century, Ireland included. Paget's paradox does not imply the absence of exploitation, however, and his point about the retreat into the heritage industries is well taken, especially in Ireland.

Exploitation is a common theme in writing about postcolonial societies, as is the labelling of touristic self-caricature as a symptom of colonialism. Kiberd, whose work follows and often cites Fanon and Said in this regard, takes such a view. He discusses, for example, how Synge portrayed the Aran Islands as a living tableau of cultural stereotype, where 'every man and woman becomes a sort of artist' (Kiberd, 1995: 288). He notes of Synge's writing on the Aran Islands that 'English typology has encouraged this stage Irishman to mimic a stock type – with no saving sense of irony – and to confuse this type with "personality"' (288). The comment about irony may be unjust, or at least unduly restrictive. The Irish have long been aware of the necessity to commodify their culture. Though it may represent a colonial stain upon national identity in general terms, a point contended by Howe (2000) which I will not debate here, this awareness deepened over time into a form of counter-exploitation, as evinced in Micheál Ó Siochfhradha's short story 'An Corp', in which Irish villagers stage a phony wake to defraud a visiting author eager to document Irish customs and rituals. Problems ensue when the 'corpse' is tormented by his drunken friends, who eventually light matches and stick them between his fingers. He jumps 'to life' and terrifies the author. The character of the author is most probably modelled on Seán Ó Súilleabháin, whose researches into the customs of Irish wakes from 1921 eventually resulted in the book *Irish Wake Amusements*.

In film, among the earlier examples of parodic counter-myth may have been the short parody *Pathetic Gazette* (1930), which dealt with characters in Irish mythology, but which obviously referred to the contemporary newsreel even in its title.[15] A much later television series called *Incognitus* (2002), produced for the Irish-language station TG4, did much the same thing, inventing 'lost' characters from Irish history whose stories ran the gamut of stage Irish cliché in a 'realistic' context. While it may not have been elevated to the level of an articulated concept of self, this approach is at least evident in the schism between the image of Ireland promoted by the tourist industry from the 1950s such as *Irish Gossamer* (1957), which actively proposed a romantic, pastoral ideal, and informational films made for distribution within Ireland such as *Lifeline* and *Convoy Mills*, which emphasised industry and progress. It may be argued of course that this is indicative of ongoing cultural schizophrenia rather than an authentic attitude towards cultural representation. There is nonetheless a consistency in the vision of Ireland proposed by both tourist films and informational films throughout this period, not only visually, but in terms of theme and argument (echoing Jameson's idea of the interrelationship between representability and form).

The most high-profile promotional/informational film of this era was *W. B. Yeats – A Tribute*, an NFI film made in conjunction with the Cultural Relations Committee and the Department of External Affairs, which neatly combined the process of cultural commodification and marketing under the banner of celebrating the life and work of the poet and statesman, who had died in 1939. It was written and co-directed by John D. Sheridan, who wrote about the film's production in *National Film Quarterly*. Though giving himself a great deal of the credit for the film, he acknowledged that its sponsors were important in determining its message:

The making of a sponsored documentary has this in common with the building of a ship or the making of a suit – that both customer and craftsmen are involved. The customer knows roughly the kind of finished product he has in

7 This image from *W. B. Yeats – A Tribute* (1950) shows the solemnity with which the burial of the great poet was treated. His naval honour guard stand with heads bowed as the ship sails towards open waters. The film was the first of many tributes which would posit Yeats as a symbol of Irish creativity

mind. He has certain ideas about the shape and material. But he does not know *exactly* what he wants, any more than an editor looking for a new cover design knows exactly what he wants. He says 'what I had in mind was something like this'; and the director and script writer get to work. (Sheridan, 1950: 11).

He also noted that his co-director, George Fleischmann, had been helpful, but subtly dismissed him by noting that while Fleischmann thought in pictures, he (Sheridan) was 'the man of words' (11). The much-touted script is substantially a compilation of extracts from Yeats' work read with great dignity and effect by distinguished thespians Micheál MacLiammóir and Siobhán McKenna. If words are important to the film's effect, they are Yeats's, not Sheridan's. Fleischmann, in contrast, worked with characteristic professionalism. The film has a measured pace which matches the delivery and lends great weight to what are otherwise fairly generic, if beautifully composed, images of the Sligo countryside and of various buildings connected with Yeats. The very fact that they *are* generic belies how thematically important they are to the film overall.

A film so heavily backed by state and semi-state bodies would obviously carry a much greater weight of responsibility than a casual or independent production. Being sponsored by the Cultural Relations Committee, the film was intended for foreign distribution. It was to be an exemplar not so much of Irish filmmaking, but of Ireland itself, specifically the Ireland represented by the poetry of Yeats and the landscape of Sligo which the film argues inspired him. Paradoxically, while it therefore presents an interrelationship between man and landscape, the film demonstrates the capacity evinced by the majority of Irish tourist films to strip the geographical space of its actual inhabitants. It envisions, as Robert Ballagh noted of such films in general, 'a country nobody lives in' (cited in Gibbons, 1996: 86). The sole inhabitant of this landscape of mountains, waterfalls, trees, lakes and even urban edifices is a dead man: the disembodied presence of W. B. Yeats.

The film was nonetheless (or perhaps consequently) a considerable success abroad. It was awarded a certificate of merit at the Venice Film Festival in 1950, and it was also shown at the Edinburgh Film Festival that year. These awards represent an important step forward for Irish documentaries in terms of having an international profile. Prior to this few enough Irish films had had such exposure, let alone ever won any kind of recognition. The distribution of the film to festivals of this kind may be seen as part of the project of giving people 'a proper sight of Ireland', as Grierson had urged two years before. We might take issue with the idea of 'proper', however, as *W. B. Yeats – A Tribute* exhibits the same paradoxical fascination with Ireland's achievements in the past as a means of promoting its future (tourism) that *A Nation Once Again* had. It also completely denies the modernity evinced in *Lifeline*, *Convoy Mills* and in the government-sponsored docudramas. Though Yeats was not long dead, his status as an icon of Irish cultural heritage was already assured, central as he was to ideas both of the romantic and mythic past and the mythology of more recent history. The film was part of an attempt to present Yeats as a paragon of Irish identity, an appeal ironically undermined by the unproblematic aesthetic and literary approach it takes. It charts only his artistic career and his inspiration by the places being shown. These are obviously offered as a site where prospective tourists might find their own inspirations endowed with similar profundity simply by being there, as if it were characteristic of the Irish landscape to produce great poetry. The film lacked a sense of his political status, not only in terms of 1916 and the search for national form, but even as a statesman in his latter years.

As Gibbons notes of the image of Ireland proffered by Bord Fáilte and the IDA in the 1980s, this has little to do with a preexisting historical or cultural fact, but was largely an invention of a burgeoning heritage industry learning how to exploit its representability through the distillation of the raw material of the profilmic and the psychic conception of Ireland long established by the poetic films of the early twentieth century. He says:

This is not a reassertion of vestigial ideology, as if 'prehistoric planning' was part of an ancient cultural legacy which survived into the contemporary world. It is instead an invented tradition, a recourse to the past which exceeds even the most imaginative flights of nationalist history in its desire to confer an aura of permanence on the new information order. The facility with which distant aeons are collapsed into the present has more in common with the ersatz history of American wax museums than with the lingering traces of rural values. Traditionalism looks to history for continuity: neo-traditionalism abolishes not only continuity but history itself. (Gibbons, 1996: 89)

Gibbons identifies the dichotomy of traditionalism and neo-traditionalism which Kiberd elaborated upon regarding the project of cultural self-determination in the early Free State and upon which the paradox at the centre of *A Nation Once Again* rests. In the case of the tourist film, however, as Gibbons notes of the publicity materials distributed in the 1980s in Ireland, it falls on the side of what he terms 'neo-traditionalism', 'a fabricated relationship to the past' (89) resultant from the underdevelopment of smaller nations in the late twentieth century. This returns us to Paget's assessment of the heritage industry in Britain and to the 'proliferation of wants', where we begin to see that, whether deliberate and conspiratorial or part of a process of evolution, Irish documentary sponsorship at the behest of the state had begun to endorse a representation of the country amenable to the need to generate revenue through tourism.

This project continued in subsequent films. Independent, government-sponsored and foreign-produced films followed this lead and seized upon the willing reduction of the landscape to romantic metaphor in *W. B. Yeats – A Tribute*, an 'official' film. For example, *The Irish in Me* (1959), produced by Universal International, featured a young American girl travelling to Ireland to visit her grandfather. She finds herself at one with Irish culture because of her ability to commune with the landscape (on what was evidently a whirlwind one-day tour of all the major sites between Dublin and the West of Ireland). She is left with 'a feeling of belonging in her heart' as she leaves 'The Emerald Isle', or so her grandfather claims in the film's patronising voice over.

A variant on this formula originating in the UK was *Charm of Ulster* (date unknown). This 1950s promotional travelogue distributed by the British Embassy fits in with the standard view of Northern Ireland in promoting its industry and world-famous landscape (the Giant's Causeway, the Glens of Antrim). Its most peculiar aspect though is a half-realised attempt to cash in on the popularity of Irish religious mythology by constantly referring to 'St Patrick's Ulster'. It is almost as if, not quite sure that the lure of thriving industry would attract visitors to the country, the makers felt the need to mystify the very 'charms' they were trying to capture. After some political clarification early on that Northern Ireland is a 'self-governing province' and a clear presentation of other basic factual detail, the film concludes with a vague, mystic attempt to define the 'magic' of the landscape in mythological terms. The film closes with the summation that it is 'something to do with the atmosphere, something to do with the light, something to do with St Patrick's Ulster'.

Domestic productions were little different. The Irish Linen Guild sponsored *Irish and Elegant* (1957), a profile of Irish clothing designer Cybil Connolly. It begins by appropriately asking 'How do you think of Ireland?' over images of green fields and rolling hills which eventually lead us to flax harvesting and the production of clothing, as did *Flaxen Heritage*. What follows is a series of artificial and uncomfortable juxtapositions as overdressed models wearing clothes designed by Connolly stand awkwardly posed against the landscape which supposedly inspired her. The bright yellows and purples featured in some of the dresses seem more likely to frighten the livestock who pepper the scenes than demonstrate any inspiration from them, and the film's 1950s glamour is totally at odds with the unchanging pastoral Ireland it pictures with its crumbling ruins and free-roaming horses. Again personality and landscape are collapsed in what is ultimately a contrived attempt to promote an idea of Ireland which commodifies not only the product on sale (the clothing), but the land itself. Colm O'Laoghaire's *Irish Gossamer* follows the same route by using images of the landscape which, as in *Irish and Elegant*, are supposed to represent the inspiration for the textures and patterns of Irish clothing products.

Obviously, the large number of films produced from this era to the present defeats comprehensive cataloguing here, though details may be found in the appendices of several titles viewed in the course of this research. Their production and proliferation may also be seen in relation to the establishment of Bord Fáilte in 1955, a body charged with the specific responsibility of promoting Ireland as a tourist destination and of maintaining standards in the tourist industry and its related culture and heritage projects. A brief statistical review of figures provided by Bord Fáilte demonstrates the centrality of this organisation to the development of the Irish economy. In 1960 £41million in foreign-exchange earnings came from tourism. By 1998 the figure had risen to a total of £2.281 billion.[16] With this kind of revenue at stake, it was and is obviously vital that the image of Ireland projected in films sponsored or otherwise endorsed by this organisation continues to encourage visitors, regardless of the cost in cultural terms – as Sheehy remarked, 'sponsors of tourist films are not philanthropists' (Sheehy, 1967: 5).

Dublin

As discussed in the previous chapter, Dublin's urban landscape had been shaped under colonial authority. Representations of the city changed little despite the shift in power after 1921. The signature image was still O'Connell Street dominated by the Nelson pillar. Though the GPO in front of which the pillar stood had taken on a new nationalist history thanks to the events of 1916, as had several other public buildings, it was impossible for Dublin to rest comfortably upon its colonial icons for the purposes of tourism. Documentaries produced during this period found themselves trapped between the necessity to represent the profilmic, which included buildings and sites whose associations with colonial history were indisputable even after the rebellion (e.g. Trinity College, the Four Courts, the Customs House, the Bank of Ireland), and to create a nationalistic context from which to view them. Unsure as of yet precisely what qualities the city offered in terms of housing, employment and industry (most of which were in crisis), they were left with little option but to compromise.

In 1946 David Barry had produced the silent 16 mm colour short *Dublin – Capital City of Ireland* (1946) which established the template for most subsequent representations of the city. Its title card tells us the city is 'a progressive metropolis with a strange mixture of the mediaeval and modern, its glamour heightened by memories of famous personalities in Irish history, literature and art'. Many subsequent films took this position. Rather like *Glimpses of Erin* (1932), they argued that while Dublin was a modern centre of industry and trade, it was also steeped in safe, apolitical 'cultural' history which will help the tourist to avoid the former. Barry's film depicted the achievements of Irish writers and artists in some way associated with Dublin, and in addition shifted to sporting activities, specifically cricket and polo (both colonial remnants) as well as hurling and Irish dancing (both strongly nationalist). Sport was often a feature of Irish tourist documentaries in its own right. It was the subject of an entire film in 1959: *Ireland – Isle of Sport* (1959/60), which began with an image of a priest tossing a ball in the air to a child. It featured prominently in many others, including *Cork Draws the Sportsmen* (1965), which was a promotional film sponsored by cigarette manufacturers Carrolls advertising their golf tournament (featuring numerous hoardings for the company's product).

Dublin – Capital City of Ireland also included scenes of the seaside and 'a little bit of Holland' in Rush, where horticulture was presented as a pictorial fantasy rather than an agricultural activity. This is curious but not unexpected as a depiction of the urban centre. Fearful perhaps that viewers might not find the subject appealing in itself, and unsure quite how to 'sell' a site of squalor, crime and deprivation, the maker ensured that the film presented possibilities for escape from the urban landscape. The questions raised by the pressures of contemporary life were sidestepped not only by the inclusion of images of horticulture and sport, but by the references to its literary heritage and 'cultural' history rather than the type of *realpolitik* situations pictured in *Our Country* or the historical issues which would be addressed in later films such as *Mise Éire* (1959).

In 1950 Liam O'Leary began *A Portrait of Dublin* with the support of the Cultural Relations Committee. As noted earlier in this chapter, the film, though completed in 1951, was never released. Despite O'Leary's pedigree and his obvious hope that the film would be an important one, it is a tame touristic exercise which adds nothing in particular to what Barry and his amateur predecessors had already done apart from the tentative incorporation of the nationalist past through fleeting reference to figures such as Grattan, Emmet, Wolfe Tone and Daniel O'Connell. For the most part it conforms to the previous pattern of non-threatening cultural advertisement. The film begins with images of the pages of a book of photographs turning, as if to suggest that a new and superior method of documenting Ireland had emerged and was about to be turned on its capital. This is interesting because a similar self-referential sequence would later open *Mise Éire*. Shot in black and white (photographed by Brendan Stafford), and less obviously concerned with the romantic ruralism which had found its way into Barry's film, it still took the same route away from 'issues' and on to less tangible qualities associated with nostalgia and the desire for 'contact' with an alternative Ireland steeped in memory and heritage.

It attempts to follow a 'day in the life' format of the kind popularised in the city films of the 1920s and 1930s. While European directors attempted to match form to content and comment upon the madness of modern life, O'Leary's film was a sedate meander through a single day (obviously the footage was shot over some weeks, but it is presumed to represent a 'typical' day) in a relaxing, comfortable place in which the chaos of modernity is answered by the gentle whispers of the past. It begins by reinforcing the church/state hegemony by explaining that 'the day begins with prayer' over shots of a Catholic church and images of old men praying at a shrine. As in *Aran of the Saints* (1932), the casual depiction of ordinary people at prayer reinforces the idea of Ireland as a religious country, regardless of how much or little debate existed in practice. It then features shoppers in the city centre with no suggestion of the kind of consumerist insanity captured in European films twenty years earlier. Though this is partly because the level of consumerism was undoubtedly lower in Dublin than in Paris, Berlin or Nice, the fact is that O'Leary did not attempt to represent the city in these terms. As in Barry's film, O'Leary also gives prominence to sporting activity, in this case linked to the natural environment. The voice over explains that 'sports and recreations of all kinds spring from the natural environments of sea and hills' over scenes of boating and of Gaelic games. It is as if Ireland is literally a 'natural' playground. We may also infer from this that the Gaelic games, whose nationalist heritage is underlined simply because of their 'exotic' nature relative to the games played in the home countries of prospective visitors, also emerge 'naturally' from the land. This is a significant if subtle political argument.

A Portrait of Dublin is more detailed in its portrayal of literary heritage than *Dublin – Capital City of Ireland*. O'Leary reminds us of the 'golden age' of Dublin culture, with references to Swift, Edmund Burke, the première of Handel's *Messiah* and the Abbey Theatre. The Abbey was of course the national Theatre of Ireland, and took on an enhanced 'heritage' role after independence.[17] From its foundation in 1904 as part of the Anglo-Irish Gaelic Revival, it had been the site of much controversy and staged many of the nationalistic dramas which fuelled the mythology of 1916. As the most important artistic institution in the Free State and the new republic, it bore the responsibility of 'representing Ireland' far more than the cinema. The theatre and its heritage was the subject of a documentary in its own right, the Oscar-nominated *Cradle of Genius* (1958), directed by Paul Rotha. Made as part of the efforts to raise funds to rebuild the theatre after it was destroyed by fire, the film, narrated by Siobhán McKenna, appealed to nostalgia and national pride by naming all of the major personalities associated with the theatre through its history. It was most notable for featuring a reunion between the hitherto estranged Sean O'Casey and Barry Fitzgerald, both of whom had contributed greatly to its international fame. The Abbey was also directly linked to documentary production by Gerard Healy, who had worked there as an actor before turning to the direction of public information films like *Voyage to Recovery* and *Power for Progress* (1956).

While there is no question that the Abbey, and indeed the literary heritage of Dublin city, constitute an important part of its past, *A Portrait of Dublin* and, to a lesser extent, *Dublin – Capital City of Ireland*, are nonetheless culpable as promotional films in their contraction, simplification and ultimate reduction of historically and politically specific people and moments to the generalities of cultural tourism. This would later find fuller exploitation in *Mise Éire*, where the art of W. B. Yeats and the politics of Padraig Pearse would be collapsed into one another without distinction through referral to their 'mutual' artistic project (see next chapter). *A Portrait of Dublin* also retreads the metaphorical propaganda of *W. B. Yeats – A Tribute* in its suggestion that dead literary figures constitute the character of the living city, an even more troublesome fact here because so many subsequent films would do exactly the same with less deference.

Peter Bayliss's *See You at the Pillar* (1967) was an Associated British Pathé film featuring quotes from Thomas Davis, Oliver Goldsmith, Sean O'Casey, James Joyce, G. B. Shaw, Jonathan Swift and Oscar Wilde read with exaggerated comical flourish by Anthony Quale and Norman Rodway as they discussed the pleasures of the city in 'conversation'. In one extraordinary moment, the destruction of the Nelson pillar by the IRA the previous year is dismissed as 'a detail: worthy neither of examination nor discussion'. The film suggests that Dublin remains frozen in some pre-Independence wonderland of Anglo-Irish culture and ironic self-depreciation. It freely quotes a variety of commentators upon the city while showing places such as O'Connell Street, Trinity College and Phoenix Park whose historical context is made to seem more interesting than the proflimic reality on display. The film also demonstrates the presence of its sponsors, again Carrolls cigarette manufacturers, whose golf tournament is also promoted. It goes so far as to invoke the myth of Cúchulainn and argue he was a golfer at heart, appropriating what was already a nationalist appropriation for capitalist ends. The film is an extension of the project of its earlier counterparts to plunder the cultural resources of the city for ends other than developing an understanding of its history and character. Instead that character is fixed within a familiar stage-Irish mould where the works of these writers are reduced to the quaint and colourful ramblings of picture-postcard caricatures.

Dublin was frequently featured as a stop on a general tour of the country, and would often serve as a fleeting proof that there were modern conveniences there. Films such *Autumn in Dublin* (1962) treated it so. This film was partly financed by Joe Malone Self Drive Ltd., and featured scenes of a 'typical family' driving around the suspiciously empty roads of Dublin County and environs experiencing the expected touristic pleasures. The former was nominally centred on newly naturalised citizen John Huston and his family, but was really another promotional look at the sights of rural Ireland ('a country of farmers and fishermen', says Huston) produced by George Grafton Green of *Cork Draws the Sportsmen*.

Films like *Lifeline* and *An tAirgead ag Obair* (1957) made similar use of the city, but for entirely different ends. Intended for domestic consumption, these featured scenes of industry and commerce in Dublin as part of a general fabric of industrial activity and progress in which few specifics and little sustained focus were necessary to make the point. *An tAirgead ag Obair* was not exclusively concerned with Dublin and portrayed industry throughout the country. Sponsored by the Department of Posts and Telegraphs' national Savings Committee, the film was, like *Lifeline*, an argument for investment in Ireland's future through labour and industry which claimed 'we are all of us shareholders' in Ireland's economy. It was interesting in its endorsement of foreign trade, however, with its explicit statement that 'no country is entirely self-sufficient'. This reflected the changing economic policies of the Fianna Fáil government under de Valera's successor Seán Lemass, which will be discussed later. Yet it too drew its authority from the past, featuring footage of Free State officials taking responsibility for the control of the banks in 1922 to remind audiences of their responsibility to live up to the ideals of the previous generation.

Parting ways: Northern Ireland, *Housing Discrimination* and documentary intervention

Amid the nostalgic, propagandistic and generally superficial cajoling of the population, it might be assumed that the defiant political spirit of *Our Country* had been entirely lost to the expedience of rhetorical form in advertising an agreeable image of Ireland both at home and abroad. Only one subsequent film produced during this era attempted to match the vehemence of the earlier film, and to directly tackle pertinent questions about the current political and social state of Ireland. Sponsored by the Department of External Affairs under Fianna Fáil minister Frank Aiken (who had withheld O'Leary's *Portrait of Dublin*), *Housing Discrimination* was a direct assault upon the allegedly discriminatory housing policies of the Omagh Rural District Council in Fintona, County Tyrone, where large nationalist families were being ghettoised while elderly loyalists with small families or living alone were being provided with new houses in order to affect the numbers of potential voters in key electoral districts. Aware of the possibilities of political documentary after *Our Country*, Aiken hoped that a series of films highlighting social injustices within Northern Ireland would increase sympathy for Fianna Fáil's position and gain support abroad for the removal of partition.

The film was photographed partly with a hidden camera by George Fleischmann, who obtained permission to shoot under the pretence that he was making a tourist documentary. Its purpose is clear from the outset though, and its arguments are plainly stated. The majority of images in the film are purely evidentiary, serving the extremely rhetorical voice over. Only the repeated use of a number of cosmetic, touristic images of a horse-drawn omnibus seems out of place, but one presumes these were the scenes which sold the project to the local authorities. The film is not otherwise stylistically radical. The spoken narration carries the bulk of the argument, and the film is entirely unselfconscious about the rhetoric which it presents. It uses emotive language to make anti-partitionist statements on the political situation in Northern Ireland using the situation in Fintona as a starting point and as a form of evidence more compelling than the images themselves. Without attempting to present an alternative interpretation of the situation, it portrays Northern Ireland as a territory, 'held under British rule' (emphasis added). It loftily claims at its conclusion that 'only an informed public opinion can destroy the structure of injustice which here in Fintona and throughout the partitioned territory sustains the *unnatural* division of Ireland' (emphasis added).

The film shows scenes of families living in unsanitary conditions in dilapidated houses and notes that poor drainage and disrepair constituted health risks not uncommon elsewhere in the world. The film then seems to offer a solution to this problem, noting that the Omagh Rural District Council had provided ample numbers of clean, modern houses for those in need in different parts of the town. Images of these houses were shown to contrast with those of the 'miserable dwellings' shown earlier. But a new problem is then introduced. The viewer is informed that two thirds of the population of Fintona are nationalists who 'long for unity with the rest of Ireland'. Without feeling the need to substantiate this claim, or to point out that, given the number of these people under voting age, the statistics are misleading, it then argues, purely verbally, that the town is unfairly controlled by a unionist minority. Houses are allocated on this basis, it tells us, because this will increase the percentage of unionist voters in key electoral districts.

The film proffers Fintona as a symbol of Northern Ireland as it is seen by the anti-partitionist government of the Republic. It uses title cards and drawings to illustrate how large areas within the six counties are 'largely nationalist' and claims that discriminatory policies were rife not only in housing, but also in employment. The film does not provide any examples or statistics other than those given for Fintona, but presumes that what little point it has made with Fintona may be applied across the country without condition or qualification. It does not attempt to discuss cultural heritage, philosophical differences between the loyalist and nationalist communities there, or even the history of Ulster relative to the nationalist movement in the South. These are not of interest to the film, which instead directly embraces 'things as they are' and contextualises its evidentiary material within a political argument which is substantiated simply because it has been made with the cooperation, approval and direct sponsorship of the Irish government. It also makes the implicit argument that all nationalists are Catholic, and, as a corollary, all loyalists are Protestant. This is said without direct reference to religion simply by the fact that, as the film highlights, the nationalist families are larger (they are shown standing outside their squalid homes, whereas only the dwellings of the loyalists in question are filmed). This again demonstrates the degree of confluence between church and state because, as in the constitution, it need not be specified for it to be known. Despite no evidence of church involvement with the production of the film and no quotation from religious authorities (as there was in *Our Country*), the spectre of the spiritual ideal of large families and a united community looms large in the conception of the nationalist 'majority'.

The film breaks the boundaries of informational documentary and applies the problem–solution framework as a rhetorical bludgeon by arguing that the 'larger' problem was ongoing and required 'an informed public opinion' to which, of course, the film itself was contributing. It laid the blame not so much with the Omagh Rural District Council as with the British government which had 'imposed' itself upon this 'nationalist' community. It was not surprising therefore that the film produced heated debate about propaganda, and not merely within the Republic this time. The Department of External Affairs successfully distributed the film abroad through the auspices of sympathetic organisations such as the Anti-Partition League, and this provoked angry reaction from the Northern Ireland cabinet. Rockett describes how a protest was lodged about the film with the secretary of the Department of External Affairs following an appeal by the cabinet to the British government to take action. The film was without doubt an outrageous intrusion by the government of the Republic into the internal affairs of what was legally a separate country. It was nonetheless a natural step for state-sponsored Irish documentary in terms of contributing to the evolution of an idea of Ireland. Having begun to establish dominion over its own territory through public information films, the state assumed it could flex its muscles over Northern Ireland, which was, as far as many of its officials were concerned, part of the country anyway.

There had been films about Northern Ireland made in the North during the preceding years, including *Ulster* (1940) and *A Letter from Ulster* (1943), both wartime morale-raisers discussing the synergy between 'loyal Ulster' and the Allied forces at that time involved in the Second World War. These were significant statements of the difference between North and South, stressing the natural affinities between Northern Ireland and the wider world beyond (the US in the case of *A Letter from Ulster* and the UK in the case of *Ulster*). Given the Republic's continued self-imposed political isolation, the films have a strong polemical centre which is unstated but not unclear. *Ulster* begins with images of Belfast harbour, a port so large, we are told, that it is ideal for battleships. Belfast itself is described as 'the largest industrial city in Ireland', a significant reference to the whole island rather than the province alone. The film emphasises the industrial strength of Northern Ireland throughout, and makes explicit links between the labour and economy of the country and the continuing war effort; 'out of these high, dark hills is dug the granite for the pavements and palaces of the great cities across the sea', we are told at one point, and the film concludes with images of the Royal Ulster Rifles who 'share the burdens of their kith and kin in every part of the empire'.

Of interest in the postwar years was *Ulster Heritage* (1949), produced by Ronald H. Riley in association with the Film Producers Guild, a UK organisation. This film, like its Southern equivalents of the era, did not directly describe the immediate political situation which determined its titular 'heritage'. Instead its recourse was, as with its predecessors in the South, to the land. It concerned itself with the life of 'A typical Ulster farming family', and charted their lives as part of a tradition handed down 'from father to son' for generations. Its images of Belfast, like those of Dublin in some tourist films, were symbolic rather than descriptive. An impressive image of Stormont established the film's political allegiance without any reference to loyalism or government. In contrast to some of the films previously discussed, it restricted its depiction of sporting activities to ballroom dancing, and though it also featured some scenes of the family enjoying the seaside, it was mainly concerned with harvesting on the family farm. The familiar images of Irish films are absent. There are no Celtic crosses, no round towers, no working horses, and little time is spent on scenic advertisement. The family picnic which accompanies the harvest is almost American in character, featuring an open-air barbecue and children drinking bottles of Coca-Cola. Without needing to say what it implied, the film suggested a separate set of nonetheless traditional values from those of the South which defined the 'character' of Northern Ireland.

Housing Discrimination made no such argument, at least insofar as it applied to loyalists. It did maintain that Northern nationalists subscribed to the same set of values as their Southern equivalents, but described their culture in terms of a colonial siege rather than as being exemplary of a community divided by different and often but not always oppositional experiences of life. It is not my intention to debate the culture of Northern Ireland here. It is sufficient to note that the attitude of the Irish government, as depicted in *Housing Discrimination*, was one of extreme sectarianism exemplifying the nationalist attitude that regardless of the political realities, Northern Ireland was still within the demesne of the Republic (a claim made by the 1937 Constitution). The rebuff they received from the British authorities resulted in the end of the proposed series of films on Northern Ireland and a greater measure of care to avoid direct representation of the political situation within or around the country in Irish-made documentaries. While the rest of the world would later become fascinated with representing Ireland's troubled relationship with its Northern neighbour, indigenous filmmakers tended to avoid it.

The same sense of caution applied to political documentary in general. While American-sponsored films such as *Ireland – The Tear and the Smile* (1959) and *Look Up and Live – Ireland in Transition* (1965) would subsequently begin to examine more general political and social questions about Ireland using interviews with contemporary politicians and commentators upon Irish culture, Irish filmmakers remained locked within a pattern of representation which deferred ultimate authority to the past. For many years subsequently, few political films were produced in the Republic which did not employ history in making their arguments. The production of informational films continued, and examples will be discussed as they become relevant, but after *Housing Discrimination*, the sponsors of Irish documentaries turned to the model provided by *A Nation Once Again*. They presumed to give people 'a proper sight of Ireland' (Grierson, 1948: 286) by ensuring that that sight was filtered through an ideology which prescribed even the limits of cultural expression. Interestingly though, it would no longer be the government which provided the finance, but independent or semi-state organisations empowered by the state and liberated by the period of direct state involvement to continue the project of determining not only what the Irish saw of themselves and their country, but how they saw it. While Walter Kronkite would observe in *Ireland – The Tear and the Smile* that 'today Ireland cares more about live men than dead heroes', that same year George Morrison's *Mise Éire* would prove him wrong.

Notes

1 This paper was a published version of a lecture delivered under the auspices of the National Film Institute of Ireland on 11 May 1948 in the Gresham Hotel, Dublin.

2 Citing the example of the Fenians and later the IRA, both of whom the church condemned as murderous and illegitimate organisations but whose members traditionally counted themselves amount the most devout of Catholics. See Whyte, 1980: 8–12.

3 Though Whyte points out that only sixteen of the 1,800 statutes enacted by the Irish government from 1923 to 1970 came about only after direct representation from church authorities, a quick glance at the list (Whyte, 1980: 363–4) shows that these were fundamental pieces of legislation, e.g. Censorship of Films Act, Censorship of Publications Act, Legitimacy Act, Vocational Education Act, Health Act, Intoxicating Liquor Amendment, Adoption Act, Succession Act, etc.

4 Translated literally as 'with vigilant care' but subtitled 'on motion pictures' in English.

5 Their most famous event was their inaugural one, a 'private' club screening of *Battleship Potemkin* (1925), a film which had as yet not been shown in Ireland (ten years after its release). When word of the screening got out, many people were eager to attend, including a district court justice who promised that in exchange for admission he would not to send the organisers down if they were brought before him. The screening was labelled a scandal by the reactionary press and the film was quietly returned to its international distributor after only one showing.

6 See Ní Chanainn, 1992: 10–12.

7 *National Film Quarterly Bulletin of the National Film Institute of Ireland* was latterly renamed *Irish Film Quarterly Bulletin of the National Film Institute of Ireland*. It may sometimes be referred to as *National Film Quarterly* or *Irish Film Quarterly*.

8 See Lee, 1989: 293–321 and MacDermott, 1998.

9 An interesting counterpoint here is the Encyclopedia Brittanica film *Irish Children (Rural Life in Western Ireland)*, made the same year, which presents a documentary

profile of a relatively cheerful pair of children living in Clare and going about their business in a fiercely traditional but certainly not impoverished environment. Is it a more 'true' picture? Of course not, but it illustrates how two different filmmakers with two different agendas produce entirely different representations of approximately the same subject.

10 See Rockett et al., 1988: 80. He also notes that within six months of taking office the coalition government rescinded these taxes in what must be interpreted as some measure of acknowledgement.

11 An accusation which dates back to the 'scandalous' screening of *Battleship Potemkin* in 1936.

12 In 1946 de Valera announced the subdivision of the Department of Local Government and Public Health into two departments with separate ministers. In 1947 he appointed Dr James Ryan Minister for Health. Ryan attempted to redraft and reintroduce a controversial health bill first proposed in 1945, which would restructure Ireland's health services. Among its proposals were the extension of free medical care for ante- and post-natal mothers and free medical care for all children under 16. There was opposition from both the medical profession (who feared an end to private practice) and the church hierarchy (who disliked the idea of Catholic mothers being exposed to the advice of non-Catholic doctors on matters relating to family life), but the matter was complicated by other objections from within the Dáil which delayed the full implementation of the act (see Whyte, 1980: 120–55). In 1950 Browne decided to reactivate the so-called 'Mother and Child Scheme', and briefly consulted with the hierarchy to obtain approval. He mistakenly believed that he had obtained it, and compounded his error by failing to ensure the support of his cabinet colleagues before going public. This he did in March 1951 only to find himself alone and facing church objections on the grounds that the scheme conflicted with Catholic social teachings (see Lee, 1989: 317). Ironically the crisis arose because the state actually aligned itself with the church, with both Taoiseach John A. Costello and Seán MacBride condemning his actions and forcing his resignation in April. This, coupled with the withdrawal of support for the government by three other deputies over an unrelated matter, resulted in the fall of the coalition. In the general election which followed, the Clann lost eight of its ten seats and MacBride himself only barely won his. Browne ran as an independent and polled well, but he remained outside the circle of power. The consequences of this affair ran deeper than a mere shift of leadership. For many people the entire fiasco represented an unwelcome encroachment by the church into social affairs. They had denied many families the opportunity to obtain services and support they felt they deserved. Despite their faith and continuing obedience to the church, the seeds of resentment had been sown. Though it would not have any immediate effects upon the moral monopoly, both Inglis (1998) and Whyte trace the eventual fall of the church's authority to this moment.

13 His life story was told in the film *At the Cinema Palace: Liam O'Leary* (1983).

14 Elements of this material were previously published. See O'Brien, 2003.

15 Both Rockett and McIlroy mention this film, which was screened as an accompanying short with Norris Davidson's drama *By Accident* in 1930. It was not viewed in the course of this research.

16 Excluding domestic travel expenditure. Total revenue from tourism in 1998 was £3.032 billion. However, total expenditure by Irish visitors abroad amounted to £1.665 billion, resulting in a net inflow of £616 million. Source: Central Statistics Office and Bord Fáilte.

17 See Morash, 2002.

3

Projecting the past: history and ideology[1]

Writing in *Scannán* in 1959, Leon O'Kennedy exhorted the teaching of Irish history through film. He argued that such a rich and exciting narrative, from Celtic times to the establishment of the Free State, deserved dramatic exposition and wide distribution: 'Ireland has been a land of sieges and battles and lost causes; of music and culture and folklore; strong religious belief and a very superstitious cult; of strong conservatism in manners, habits, and customs; of political complexities and heroic idealism; of National failures and gallant resurgence' (O'Kennedy, 1959: 12–13). It is not surprising then that the official history of the Irish state was filmed at that time, or that that history was blinkered by ideological constructions of the then present conception of the nation. The archival compilation *Mise Éire* (1959) and its sequel *Saoirse?* (1961) did indeed document the history of Ireland from ancient times to the Free State, ending ominously with the outbreak of the civil war. A third film in the planned trilogy, intended to bring events up to date, was never commissioned. As Pierre Sorlin writes, 'We know that history is a society's memory of its past, and that the functioning of this memory depends on the situation in which the society finds itself' (Sorlin, 1980: 16). The situation in which Ireland found itself was that the nominally liberating political and intellectual force of anti-colonial nationalism had itself become an inert ideology, inhibiting rather than stimulating the desire for change. This would inform both the history recounted in these films and the manner in which it was related, with notable consequences for historical documentary in general.

Historiography and ideology

Documentary became one of the standard media of historiography in the twentieth century; sometimes the only one with any degree of popular penetration. Robert A. Rosenstone (1996) writes of a 'postliterate' age, where people *can* read written historical texts, but choose not to. It is certainly true, as Jerry Kuehl (1988) points out, that television documentaries are often the only form of exposure to history people have after completing formal education. Their understanding of historiography is therefore often framed by the structuring conventions of cinema, which are not subject to the kinds of interpretative strategies available to readers of print. As Donald Watt observed, 'there can be no recall, no flipping back of the page, no elaboration of parallel themes by footnotes or parenthesis' (cited in Kuehl, 1988: 436).

It important to be able to identify the culturally and politically determinate forces at work in historical documentary not so that we may revise history itself, but so that we may elucidate how that history has been represented. It is necessary therefore to introduce the concept of ideology, a much maligned term which nonetheless has its uses. Raymond Williams (1983) tells us that the term was originally intended to distinguish rational, scholarly enquiry into the science of ideas from traditional metaphysics, and came into use in English in this context in the eighteenth century. Today the word is more commonly understood to refer to the system of ideas at the basis of an economic or political theory, though it may also be invoked in describing the manner of thinking characteristic of a class or individual. Like the term 'propaganda', 'ideology' is usually employed in the pejorative as a synonym for 'false consciousness' (a usage which owes its roots to Marxism), though as we have seen with the term 'propaganda', this is probably ill advised without some qualification.

The difficulty with the term is in defining how 'ideology' manifests itself and explaining its relationship with social reality. Eagleton suggests several analytical approaches in his distinction between ideology as a type of ontology and as an effect of the conventions of language. The recourse to language as subject and object brings us back to Heidegger, who notes, 'it is language that tells us about the nature of a thing, provided that we respect language's own nature' (Heidegger, 1971: 146). He further observes that 'man acts as though *he* were the shaper and master of language, while in fact *language* remains the master of man' (146). Eagleton points out that ideology is not a language system in that it is not concerned with a system of signification *per se*. Instead, he argues, it is concerned with the articulation of an idea of political and social reality *within* language.

[Ideology] represents the points where power impacts upon certain utterances and inscribes itself tacitly within them. But it is not therefore to be equated with just any form of discursive partisanship, 'interested' speech or rhetorical bias; rather, the concept of ideology aims to disclose something of the relation between an utterance and its material conditions of possibility, when those conditions of possibility are viewed in the light of certain power-struggles central to the reproduction (or also, for some theories, contestation) of a whole form of social life. (Eagleton, 1991: 223)

Ideology can thus be located within the realm of representation as defined by Nichols where documentaries 'represent' reality in terms of *standing for* the beliefs of a person or society (Nichols, 1991: 111–12). Documentaries fulfil a social and political purpose, and often play a role in the political process as information, promotion or propaganda. Yet they cannot themselves be incorporated within the discourses of sobriety insofar as the term denotes the specific power structures (or, as Eagleton would put it, power-struggles) which order and sustain a society, or which, as Nichols says, 'have instrumental power' (Nichols, 1991: 3). This raises again the question of the role historical documentary plays in 'social reality' as chronicler or activist. It is not mere 'signification', but is often an active agent within a given set of social relations, at least insofar as history itself is considered to be a determining factor in a concept of the world. While the exact impact of a particular film upon society is difficult to establish with any certainty, its *role* is not. The place occupied by the documentary in our conception of social process (as the authoritative 'record' of profilmic reality) allows it to occupy an ideological position, 'impacting' upon 'certain utterances' relevant to 'the reproduction of a whole form of social life', especially in relation to the historical genre as an inscription of history itself. In Eagleton's terms it 'discloses something of the relation between an utterance and its material conditions of possibility' (Eagleton, 1991: 223). A documentary provides an articulation, on some level, of the approach to 'truth' and 'fact' at the time of its making, and as such allows access to the possible interpretations of 'reality' prescribed by the structures of knowledge prevalent at the time of its production. Knowing this allows certain conclusions to be made about the ideological conception of history defining a society at a given time. It is on these terms that we will approach Irish historical documentary.

The shape of history: Gael-Linn and Seán Lemass

Though historical dramas abounded in the early years of Irish cinema and the theme of history and its place in contemporary Irish life was prominent in the films examined in the previous chapter, few non-fiction films specifically assigned themselves the task of documenting Irish history. *Who Fears to Speak of '98?* (1948) and *A Nation Once Again* (1946) might claim to have done so, but in both cases the film was tied to newsworthy events occurring at the time of making, and history was more an object than a subject. The latter film was discussed in the previous chapter, the former was a record of the parade held in Dublin to commemorate the one hundred and fiftieth anniversary of the 1798 rebellion. The rebellion was a failed uprising against the British Crown supported by factions from both the north and south of the country, the failure of which led directly to the Act of Union of 1800 (the basis of the continuing link between Northern Ireland and the United Kingdom). With no evident sense of historical irony, the one hundred and fiftieth anniversary celebrations were held within the demense of Catholic nationalism. The parade featured marchers from the old IRA and floats marking the 1916 rising and the war of independence. Banners calling for an end to partition are plainly visible, thereby linking a politically and socially specific moment in Irish history with contemporary issues. The film itself was a 'neutral' record of a colourful day out, not an actual historical documentary. Yet in it we see the process by which history had already been refigured in the wake of independence, a process also seen in *A Nation Once Again*.

The historical documentary as it is commonly understood begins in Ireland with *Mise Éire* and *Saoirse?*, both directed by George Morrison. The films chart the evolution of the modern Irish state through the 1916 Rising, the war of independence and the civil war, using archival footage of the events, newspaper headlines and extracts from official documents. To this day they are considered definitive records of the period they purport to document and are successfully distributed on video both domestically and internationally. Both films were sponsored by Gael-Linn, an independent body established in 1953 with the aim of using the modern media to promote and expand the use of the Irish language. The organisation was a spin-off from Comhdáil Náisúnta na Gaelige (the National Gaelic Congress), founded a decade earlier to coordindate large-scale educational and entertainment-based efforts to revive the language, and grew out of a football pool used to raise funds.[2]

Gael-Linn became involved with filmmaking in 1956, when it began producing a series of three-minute short documentaries under the title *Amharc Éireann*. Colm O'Laoghaire was the series director, assisted by a team of people whose names would become well known thereafter, including Vincent Corcoran, Jim Mulkerns, Val Ennis, Nick O'Neill and Morgan O'Sullivan. The films were initially made with the intention of establishing the Irish language as a natural medium of modern communications. They were considered 'vest pocket' documentaries by their director, who intended each of the items to exist as an individual, informative study of the particular subject in question. They tended to be anecdotal and expository in the manner of the British newsreels of the time. In an article published in the *Irish Film Quarterly*, O'Laoghaire explained:

The purpose of the true Documentary is to explain a viewpoint or put forward an argument on some topic of interest. It is given the required 'slant' in production by careful choice of scenes, selection of camera angles, control of lighting and so on. In the case of the Gael-Linn films, there are certain difficulties in achieving this. Their primary purpose is to encourage the public to accept Irish

8 Colm O'Laoghaire (producer) and Vincent Corcoran (camera) filming 'Cursai Ostain', an episode of *Amharc Éireann* in 1957. This Irish-language newsreel ran between 1956 and 1964 and remains a valuable archival resource for images of the period in contemporary documentary production. Both O'Laoghaire and Corcoran would go on to become independent producer/directors

in the cinema as something normal and everyday (no more: not even to teach a few words). (O'Laoghaire, 1957: 9)

It is clear even from this short summary that a culturally defined project informed the making of the films (the propagation of the Irish language), and, to a certain extent, affected their intended level of interrogation (without the full complexities of a detailed voice over to interact with the visuals, little critical argument was possible). The comment also indicates that the makers of these films were aware of such issues and were familiar with the capacities of the medium to interpret and argue rather than simply to record.

Amharc Éireann was initially a small-scale enterprise based on individual film items as described by O'Laoghaire. Rank Film Distributors agreed to rent the films for limited distribution in Ireland in 1957, attached to their own regular newsreel service, and they were shown in several Irish cinemas, where they were seen by an estimated three quarters of a million people each month. In 1958 Rank ended its newsreel, leaving a gap which was quickly filled by Universal, who also featured *Amharc Éireann* items. The latter became a full-blown weekly newsreel from 1962 until 1964 after Universal ended its own service. The success of *Amharc Éireann* encouraged Gael-Linn to continue its sponsorship of documentaries, beginning with *Mise Éire*, previewed in the Cork Film Festival programme with the comment that 'the most important achievement of this film is that as a visual record it *confirms and supplements* written history in a way that is unique' (uncredited, 1959: 40) [emphasis added]. As befits the aims of Gael-Linn, both *Mise Éire* and *Saoirse?* are narrated exclusively in Irish. To this day they have not been issued with subtitles by the sponsors, who remain adamant that they should be seen in their original form. The emotive effects of an Irish-language narration and a majestic score by Seán Ó Riada (which will be discussed later) supplemented the films' reading of history, which, reflecting and contributing to the ethos of the time, was largely nationalist. These were 'Irish' documentaries on every level.

Mise Éire and *Saoirse?* were released at a significant juncture in Irish social and political history. Éamon de Valera retired as Taoiseach in 1959, thereby essentially ending the direct connection between the 1916 generation and the reins of power. Though he would move on to assume the office of President of the Republic and thereby remain a figurehead of Irish history until his death, his ability to direct policy and effect legislation was over. This represented a challenge for Fianna Fáil, a party whose republican credentials were still its mainstay, even though they had missed out on declaring the Republic in 1949. The subsequent reign of pragmatic politician Seán Lemass as leader of the party which had so dominated the post-independence political landscape was characterised by a shift, however slight, from relying on the certainties of past achievement to an attempt to build on economic and social realities. *Mise Éire* and *Saoirse?* amplified the obsession with recent history which had featured in the films of the preceding decades, and provided a credible mythology of Ireland's past which would shield the Irish people from the effects of change during the subsequent period of social and economic redefinition.

Released the year de Valera retired, *Mise Éire* provided a sense of continuity, and reassured the public that the age of Lemass would offer the same ideological comforts as that of de Valera. This is something of a paradox given that Lemass was about to reverse many of de Valera's policies, including bringing about an end to the culture of self-sufficiency. It is also paradoxical because both of the films seem to be about historical evolution – the path from colonisation to independence – yet their focus on the formation of the state ironically serves to reinforce satisfaction with its achievement. Rather than investigate and problematise historical events in a manner which would stimulate the desire for further progress, the films enshrined the past and ensured that the discourse of history remained within the frames of reference set by the preceding decades of nationalist rhetoric. It was as if political (and ideological) events had reached their apex with the end of British rule, and subsequent history would build on the certainty that the past had been a triumphant ascension to political independence, which represented an 'end of history'. This may be one reason why *Saoirse?* was never the success that *Mise Éire* was, because by 1961, the benefits of Lemass's economic policies were being felt, and the film's focus on the events of forty years before seemed increasingly anachronistic.

An 'Irish' documentary?

Though Irish documentarists had exposure to certain international films though the auspices of the Cork Film Festival and the activities of the Irish Film Society, there seems to have been an attempt, or at least an ambition, to develop an Irish documentary school, along the lines suggested by fiction filmmakers at the same time, which would express Irish individuality free from foreign constraints. As Brendan O'Shea asserted, 'for continuity of effort, for economy in production, for truthful representation on the screens of the world, we must establish our own industry in the long run and bring the documentary movement into line with our national efforts' (O'Shea, 1948: 23). This can be seen of course as part of the ongoing campaign undertaken by the National Film Institute and the Irish Film Society to do just that, but the exclusive dimension of O'Shea's comment is worth noting: evidently 'truthful representation' was only possible with 'our own industry.'

Mise Éire actually has two major precedents. Soviet documentarist Esfir Shub's work with archival material scrounged from a variety of sources and fashioned into the compilation documentary *Fall of the Romanov Dynasty* (1927) was a similar project, both ideologically and physically, to that under-taken by Morrison. Shub's film clearly demonstrates the principles of then contemporary dialectical theory in practice. It employs the intercutting tech-niques of Soviet montage to draw comparisons between its series of cross-correlated images of wealth with poverty, nobility with peasantry, and pomp and circumstance with suffering. Shub builds upon a series of associations which problematise the legitimacy of the tsarist state which lead to the patri-otic climax composed of footage of the masses celebrating Lenin's ascen-dance to power. The use of contradictory images to produce mental associations on the part of the audience is typical of other Soviet modernists such as Dziga Vertov and Sergei Eisenstein. Graham Roberts summarises: 'a particularly effective technique of Shub's is her ability to take footage shot in order to promote the activities of individuals and groups but transform them into sequences which criticise their subject's decadence or complacency. This is often achieved by the juxtaposition of contrasting shots to create bitter ironies' (Roberts, 1991: 150).

Shub's film posits that Russian history was inexorably drawn to a 'natural' revolution in response to untenable conditions, an argument which would be reprised in *Mise Éire* in an Irish context. The logic of this historical argument is entirely dependent upon the political context in which the film was made, in Shub's case the post-revolutionary Soviet need to affirm its accomplishments through what Lenin called 'the most important of all arts'. But unlike *Mise Éire* (though it is arguably true of *Saoirse?*), *Fall of the Romanov Dynasty* is critically engaged with both the historical events themselves and the political circumstances which define them. As Shub herself wrote, her aim in utilising archival footage was not simply to record a narrative of history, but to produce 'works which agitate and propagandize the struggle with our class enemies, works which reveal the failures and successes of the only country in the world which is building socialism. Here is our task . . . Nothing is more convincing than the fact which is scientifically verifiable and inventively subjected to the clear aim of serving a social goal' (cited in Roberts, 1991: 155).

Morrison has always maintained that his films were based on the principles of the dialectic, and purported to critically examine the failure of what he termed the 'bourgeois revolution' of 1916. The impression one takes from them both, however, is of an attempt to fashion a mythology of the state integral to the ideology of the time. If Morrison's intention was that the political tragedies detailed in *Saoirse?* (the treaty debates, the civil war) would contrast with the triumphs of *Mise Éire* (the 1916 Rising, the war of independence) and thus operate within a dialectical mode, he was at best admirably ambitious and at worst naive in his estimate of the public's engagement with the texts. The films do not evince a dialectical mode of interpretation or offer cross-correlations and criticisms as Shub does. On the contrary, Morrison presents an orthodox history of the struggle for independence which may, given factors overly dependent on the circumstances of viewer reception (educational background, level of visual literacy, the amount of contradictory information they possess), raise certain questions about the nature of that history, but which does not evince such goals in itself.

The second methodological precedent was more contemporaneous. The Canadian film *City of Gold* (1957), shown at the Cork Film Festival in 1957, detailed the American gold rush of the late nineteenth century entirely through the use of still photographs. Using a collection of recently discovered photographs by the American photographer A. E. Haig, the filmmakers reconstructed the history of the period with a feeling for the human drama purely by their technique of focusing on details from the photographs and moving the camera around them to highlight different elements. The stills were intercut with maps and voice over, which reconstructed a lost past from

an 'impartial' archival source, or at least a visual record which was more concerned with capturing reality than describing it. It was considered the pioneer
in this particular form of historical reconstruction, and won an Oscar. *Mise
Éire* would repeat these reconstructive techniques two years later (albeit
using photographs *and* moving images) with the claim that it had not been
done before.

These facts speak more of the determination of Irish documentarists to
provide self-definition on their own terms than of a conspiracy to claim
exclusivity of innovation. Indeed, Colm O'Laoghaire remarked: 'having
seen a great number of British, American and Continental films over a
number of years, I feel strongly that our documentary style, if such ever
develops, will be much closer to the Continental than British' (O'Laoghaire,
1957: 10). O'Laoghaire makes the extraordinary argument that because
British documentaries are inherently 'rational' and scientific and embrace
the principles of humanism, they are anathema to the Catholic beliefs of the
Irish documentarist. He argues that because the Irish are more emotional
than the English, Irish documentaries should operate on a more emotional
level. *Mise Éire* does precisely this. In fact, one could easily apply Shawn
Rosenheim's critique of the American PBS documentary series *The Civil
War* (1990) to the film. He states that 'in its manipulative way, *The Civil War*
presents a romantic history that demands a continual empathy from its viewers. Caught in the trap of Burns's nostalgia, viewers feel, rather than think,
the meaning of the war, experiencing pity, fear, but above all, a self-congratulatory affirmation of loss and redemptive nationhood than ennobles North-
erner and Southerner alike' (Rosenheim, 1996: 220).

Mise Éire's lack of structural or stylistic innovation on an international
scale does not disaffirm its importance in Ireland. These things may have
been done abroad, but they had not been done here, and this contributed
greatly to its success at that time. When the film was released, it was a
national event. The première was attended by members of the government,
some of whom were survivors of the events it chronicled, and it remains, to
this day, one of the best-known documentaries produced in Ireland. A poster
from the film still adorns one of the lobby displays at the Irish Film Institute
in Dublin and copies of the film are still sold both in Ireland and abroad. The
film's rapturous reception in 1959 was sufficient inspiration for Gael-Linn to
continue their sponsorship of documentaries to an even greater degree
throughout most of the subsequent decades, and it inspired the work of
other documentarists such as Louis Marcus (who worked on the film as an
assistant editor) and Kieran Hickey.

Shaping history: *Mise Éire* and *Saoirse?*

Morrison began work on the project which would become *Mise Éire* in 1952 (at the age of thirty) following a meeting at the congress of the International Federation of Film Archives at Amsterdam where he became aware of the level of archival material available on Irish history. He had, in fact, submitted a proposal for a similar venture on Victorian Britain to the BBC in 1949 but was turned down on grounds that, in the estimation of the BBC, such material was not suitable for television. As with Shub, Morrison's work is important for its contribution to archival development. During the six years of preparation for the film, he catalogued up to 300,000 ft of material, much of it sourced abroad. His labours established the same precedent for storing and recording stocks of filmed material in Ireland that the work of Shub had done in Europe since the 1920s.[3]

Morrison cut this material together with newspaper headlines and photographs into first one, then two compilation documentaries organised in roughly the same way. The two films are divided into six sections in all, bookended Irish-language title cards framed by images of crests and statues on important municipal buildings of historical importance such as GPO, the Customs House, the Four Courts and Grattan's Parliament. The use of these edifices emphasises the importance of the material, evoking the sense that like the statues themselves, whose power is iconographic, transcendent and eternal, this film is a document beyond 'mere' history. It also recalls the use of monuments in colonial-era representations of the kind explored in Chapter 1, and demonstrates how the Irish state had now apparently unproblematically appropriated these places as icons of its own ascendance. The appropriation was assisted by the historical events portrayed in these films, of course, and was now being reinforced by the films themselves.

The opening scenes of *Mise Éire* also demonstrate a formal and aesthetic concern with the methodology of historical record. The film begins by describing how the Irish have sought to record their impressions of things in the past, first using the familiar icons of early Christian Ireland – crosses, statues, etc. – moving on to drawings and illustrations, then to photography and finally to film. This brief overview of the evolution of visual recording establishes that film and photography have now liberated the filmmakers from the constraints of subjectivity – the camera has arrived and cannot lie. Indeed, despite Colm O'Laoghaire's assertions that documentaries put forward arguments, *Mise Éire* was largely accepted in 1959 as an unfiltered record of 'absolute' history.

Mise Éire concerns itself largely with the build up to, events during, and the immediate aftermath of the Easter Rising of 1916, climaxing with a newspaper headline of 11 January 1919 which declares 'Saoirse' (the Irish word for 'freedom'), signifying Sinn Féin's victory in the general election. *Saoirse?* then charts the war of independence, the electoral battle between Michael Collins and Éamon de Valera over the Anglo-Irish Treaty, and ends with the beginning of the civil war. The opening image of *Mise Éire* is a flag with the words 'Irish Republic' on it, which runs throughout the credits. It is quickly followed by the sound of waves breaking against the shore and an image of footprints in the sand being washed away by the tide. If any proof of the film's ambition to articulate an interpretation of history were necessary, this alone would suffice. The symbolic associations with erasing the stain of colonial occupation are unmissable. The film then puts this process in motion by charting highlights in Irish history, centred on images of struggle against oppression. Depictions of the battle of the Boyne and the execution of Robert Emmet are juxtaposed with photographs from the 1880s charting the hated evictions and the land war, with haggard Irish peasants staring in horror as their neighbours are forcibly ejected from their homes by policemen and landlords. Such scenes remain the mainstay of school texts on the subject, and exert emotional pressure on an Irish viewer through recognition and association, 'everyday life apotheosized', as Susan Sontag put it (Sontag, 1977: 90). Likewise the footage of the shattered city in the wake of the rising is moving, but when juxtaposed with a montage sequence which dramatises the execution of the rebel leaders, probably the film's most dramatic scene, it takes on mythic proportions.

The execution sequence is in some ways reminiscent of Alain Resnais' *Night and Fog* (1955) in its intercutting between past and present to create disjunctive effects. Resnais' juxtaposition of the placid, empty sites of former concentration camps now overgrown with grass and overwhelmingly silent were an eerie counterpoint to stark black and white images and footage from the time when they were active.[4] In Morrison's film, images of the now abandoned cells at Kilmainham Gaol are juxtaposed with stills of the men once imprisoned there, the cut between them signified by the sounds of a firing squad taking aim and the crack of a barrage of rifles. Like Resnais, Morrison also shifts between still and moving cameras. The present-day footage is shot with a moving camera, which glides up to the eerie grey door of the cell and its screen-centred peephole. Just as our attention is focused on its details, the sound of the gun snaps us to the montage of still photographs, portraits of dead men now becoming martyrs. Each of these photomontages is followed by newspaper listings of the names of the men who have been shot, simultaneously identifying them for an audience unfamiliar with the faces and drawing attention to the coverage in the popular press of the day of events which were changing the sympathies of the city in favour of the rebels.[5] It is a dynamic sequence given even greater force by the hammer-blows of the music score which accompanies it.

In scenes such as this and those which open the film, *Mise Éire* establishes the concept that the history of Ireland has been one of political struggle against colonial domination, devoid of any nuances of economics, culture or society. A telling example of this lack of nuance (or perhaps of the deliberate simplification of nuanced historical facts) comes shortly after the opening and during the account of the build up to the 1916 Rising. An image of W. B. Yeats is displayed without commentary or identification, presuming that his significance in the Literary Revival is automatically understood. This is followed by one of Padraig Pearse, which segues into scenes of the establishment of the Irish Citizens' Army and the events preceding the rising itself. The juxtaposition seems to suggest an unproblematic link between the two men, as if they were fellow travellers on the road to revolution. In one sense they were, yet the discord between them on a number of key points of cultural identity was well documented at the time, both in *An Claideamh Soluis* (of which Pearse was editor) and in the national press. The film does not discuss their differences, or suggest in the commentary that they were diametrically opposed on many issues, especially, significantly, the Irish language.

The juxtaposition also establishes a pedigree for the cultural dimensions of the rising, linking Irish politics to Irish art in a way which can only be described as ideological. The linkage perpetuates the myth of 'blood sacrifice', a romantic notion of deliberate martyrdom which became the official mythology of the struggle for Irish independence.[6] Kiberd sums it up thus:

The invention that was the Irish Republic was initially visible only to those who were the agents of freedom glimpsed as an abstract vision before it could be realised in history . . . From that vantage-point, many texts by Wilde, Shaw, Yeats, Synge and dozens of others might be seen to have represented, years earlier, a complex of ideas which found their fullest expression in the Rising of 1916. Yeats was the first knowingly to divine that connection when he told the young George Russell 'absorb Ireland and her tragedy and you will be the poet of the people, perhaps the poet of a new insurrection,' . . . The Rising, when it came, was therefore seen by many as a foredoomed classical tragedy, whose *dénouement* was both inevitable and unpredictable, prophesied and yet surprising. Though it remained mysterious to many, the event was long in the gestation. (Kiberd, 1995: 200)

By linking Pearse to Yeats, the film legitimises and aggrandises Pearse's own poetry, and supports the romantic belief that the rising was as much the act of poets and dreamers (read: saints and scholars) as of political revolutionaries. The reverse is also true in that Yeats's relationship with Irish politics is solidified by the association with Pearse, a political martyr who had died fighting for his ideals. Having linked Yeats to the landscape in 1950 in *W. B. Yeats – A Tribute*, Irish documentary now linked him to history, and for much the same reasons. Just as the landscape was mythically endowed with greatness by its association with the poet, so history was now aggrandised though the same juxtaposition. The fact that Yeats not only survived the rising but turned his back on many of its ideals is not only ignored; it is erased by the unproblematic suturing of these two images.

This is pure grand narrative, and the approach to history throughout the film is consistent. Morrison cuts a clear line through complex and nuanced historical events, charting a linear path to revolution devoid of metahistory, even the concurrently evolving history of Northern Ireland. Violence seems inevitable under these circumstances, patriotic anger is understandable given these frames of reference established by this reading of events; Irish history now has a 'natural' trajectory towards insurrection which, as noted, echoes Shub's representation of tsarist Russian history in *Fall of the Romanov Dynasty*. Predictably, given the nationalist ethos of the Irish state in the 1950s, the film was a massive success. It was described in *Scannán* as 'a national document' (uncredited, 1959: 7). Schoolchildren were brought in groups to see it, because of both the history it recounted and the fact that it was narrated exclusively in Irish. Premièred in the presence of veterans and others who had lived through the events it portrayed, it was hailed as a triumph for Irish cinema and for Ireland itself.

By the time *Saoirse?* was released in 1961, the mood seems to have shifted. Though premièred with as great a level of ceremony as its predecessor, the film was not a commercial or critical success. Morrison contends that '*Saoirse?* illustrates how the bourgeois revolution of 1916 (hence the lace curtain in the main title background of *Mise Éire*) could not sustain itself and deteriorated, ultimately, into civil war and neo-colonialism. This is also a reason why *Saoirse?* has never been as popular a film, in Ireland, as its predecessor. *Saoirse?* makes no concessions to romantic nationalism' (cited in Harris and Freyer (eds), 1981: 69). This claim is not supported by the film itself. Though the events portrayed in the film are more politically nuanced than in *Mise Éire*, the underlying project of historical enshrinement is continued without ideological contradiction, the question mark in the title notwithstanding. The film details the growing discord between factions of Sinn Féin during the treaty negotiations by juxtaposing footage of de Valera and Collins stating their positions on the subject at mass meetings. The film stops short of Morrison's claims of a critique of 'neo-colonialism' though, signalling, in contrast, that while the civil war with which the film ends was indeed tragic, it was as inevitable as the 1916 Rising. A movement towards liberation is still in question. While the events in *Saoirse?* are darker in tone, they remain unquestioned within a view of Irish history as a progression of violent political struggles leading to a state of ultimate independence from the 'other', be it the British empire or, in this case, the anti-treaty forces.

9 Free State troops engage anti-treaty forces during the Irish civil war. This original newsreel scene was used by George Morrison in the compilation documentary *Saoirse?* (1961), a commercially unsuccessful sequel to the massively popular *Mise Éire* (1959). At the time of *Saoirse?*'s release, the civil war was still a contentious subject with many painful memories for those who had lived through it only forty years before

The second film begins on safer ground with a graphic account of the war of independence, using a variety of colourful newspaper headlines such as 'Hope for Ireland. Truth and justice must triumph in the new world: failure of coercion' and 'Victims of empire – Ireland, Egypt, India and South Africa'. Its treatment of Bloody Sunday, 1920, evokes the montage sequence of the execution of the 1916 rebels in *Mise Éire*, crosscutting still images and newspaper headlines while Ó Riada pours on the anxious, sad, tragic music. These sections of the film reinforce the assertion that Irish nationalism was an anti-colonial movement. There is no question of the validity of the conflict or the respective heroism and villainy of the belligerents. Though emphatic images of the wounded civilians are displayed to suitable musical accompaniment, the assassination of fourteen British military personnel which preceded the massacre is summarised in the somewhat cheerful headline, 'Fourteen Killed: Amazing Deadly round-up of Military and Auxiliary officers in Dublin'. There is virtually no account of republican activity other than as a response to the build-up of hostile British forces and images of the police-state measures employed for the repression of the citizenry.

The political complexity and sensitivity of the events which followed the war of independence were, perhaps, daunting material for any filmmaker. The topic had certainly been avoided thus far by both fiction and non-fiction filmmakers, and after the failure of *Saoirse?* it was not tackled again for forty years. Morrison simplifies matters by a focus on images of de Valera and Collins throughout the section concerning the treaty debate. This person-alises the issue, and has the not accidental side effect of presenting a plethora of images of the Republic's current president. This again meets with the ideological project of establishing the history of the state within memo-rable, non-complex (non party political) terms without reference to the intri-cacies of economic or social policy.

The footage of both men speaking at mass rallies evokes memories of similar footage of Lenin and Hitler in the films which had accompanied their respective rises to power. Notably, de Valera is seen with more crowds than Collins. The latter is often pictured as a sad, lonely man seated by a lakeside, or in the cabinet room away from the public. When there is footage of Collins with large crowds, they are often juxtaposed with scenes of arguing or protesting individuals. For example, footage of him addressing a meeting outside the GPO contains visible, menacing men in heavy overcoats holding back the crowd, whereas de Valera seems to hold the audience in his sway with ease. Fiction director Neil Jordan made use of this difference in his biopic *Michael Collins* (1996) which reconstructed these scenes with remarkable fidelity to the original newsreels. Seán Ó Riada's score is again decisive in the film's emotional effect. He makes use of a fractured, percus-sive harpsichord piece signifying confusion and disharmony, and hints at the oncoming military engagement by the recurrent use of snare drums. The last scene of the film detailing the siege of Sackville Street concludes with images of dark smoke billowing around burning buildings in the nation's capital as a sad trumpet plays the final refrain. The emotional, rather than the histori-cal (let alone the intellectualism implied by Morrison's conviction that the film was a critique of neo-colonialism), is the note sounded both musically and visually at the end.

Music and nationalism: the role of Seán Ó Riada

One aspect of both films singled out for particular praise then and thereafter, and equally important to their ideological project, is the musical score. Even a preliminary viewing of *Mise Éire* testifies to Ó Riada's contribution to the film's emotional and nationalistic dimensions. The music reflects a particular conception of Irishness, one with which Ó Riada himself was subsequently identified for the rest of his life. Mostly unknown until his work for Radio Éireann in the late 1950s, and then as John Reidy, it was his association with

Mise Éire (and the consequent Gaelicisation of his name) which established his reputation and his identity in the public eye at the vanguard of the Irish music revival. His best-known works are his arrangements of traditional Irish music which rekindled widespread interest in the subject in the 1960s (during which he founded the group Ceoltóri Cualann). He was a serious musician though (later subject of a documentary in his own right, *A Vertical Man* (1998)), and his identification with revivalism was something he did not always enjoy. During the production of Louis Marcus's *An Tine Bheo* (1966), commemorating the fiftieth anniversary of the events he scored in *Mise Éire*, he remarked, 'This is the hardest job I have ever had to do – to try and bring a fresh mind to this subject – my mind was already overexposed to 1916 before I started. I know now what my hell will be' (cited in Harris and Freyer (eds), 1981: 23). In his study of music and cultural history in Ireland from 1770 to 1970 Harry White sees Ó Riada as a melancholic figure, an incompletely realised artist struggling with the urge to embrace modernism yet unable to find his way past revivalism. He notes, 'Ó Riada's huge gifts forced a degree of recognition and repudiation which profoundly affected not only his own ability (and inability) to compose, but the understanding of music in the cultural fabric of modern Ireland' (White, 1998: 50).

Ó Riada was employed to work on *Mise Éire* by Gael-Linn representatives Dónal Ó Móráin and Bob Mac Góráin. Morrison had been strongly in favour of a European model of film scoring inspired by Benjamin Britten's work on *Night Mail* (1936). He discussed this with Ó Riada, whose affinities were also with European musical styles, before showing him any of the actual footage, and the two men collaborated on the final details. The score was the first major orchestral composition exclusively produced for an Irish-made documentary film. It was composed for fifty-one-piece orchestra and recorded with the Radio Éireann Symphony Orchestra. The arrangements of both traditional Irish songs, many with roots in resistance struggles, and a more general classical style reminiscent of the European romantics (of which Ireland had none of its own to draw upon) within a traditional idiom (embellishments of basic themes which are repeated with increasing complexity in the manner of *sean nós*) provided the film with a rich Gaelic texture. White observes that because Ó Riada referred to traditional folk music in these scores, he legitimised and aggrandised the visual history in a way that folk music was traditionally used to enhance verbal art forms such as bardic storytelling, which also recounted and commented upon historical events.

Though the era of musical nationalism has traditionally been fixed in the nineteenth and early twentieth centuries, the precedent nonetheless exists from which to study the ideological significance of Ó Riada's composition in nationalist terms. In his consideration of music as propaganda, Perris points out that the struggle for political independence throughout Europe in the nineteenth century often found musical expression not least of all because its political realisation was crushed by military force. He notes that many artists were themselves subject to imprisonment or banishment, and sought to articulate what he terms 'their longing for national identification' (Perris, 1985: 27) (a phrase which echoes Kiberd) through art. He tell us that 'their methods and materials were the subtle ethnic elements of music: melody, rhythm, dance forms, and peculiar instrumental preferences' (27) and observes that for some composers and songwriters, the use of native language was an act of cultural and political resistance. Thus while the Irish tradition of rebel music has a long history both in the Irish language and in English, the kind of musical nationalism in question here is rooted more in classical composition of a kind largely unknown in Ireland until the twentieth century.

Ó Riada's achievement was to integrate the project of musical nationalism with that of reconstituting an Irish classical tradition. His simultaneous revival and expansion of the traditional music forms therefore assumes a particular cultural significance of its own, one easily applied to the ideological project of *Mise Éire* and *Saoirse?* Apart from any individual effect achieved in conjunction with the visuals, the score for *Mise Éire* received high praise for its own pervasive quality and emotional affect, achieving an ideological significance of the kind outlined by Perris as follows:

The works which we might easily label as political music – and there are many – endure because of the eloquence of the composer's skill . . . If the composition is effective and expressive, *the non musical message will endure with it,* and continue to be restated to succeeding generations . . . A classic with such a moral or social or political meaning is restated again and again to later generations, even when the referential aspect is diluted or perverted by performers or concert organizers. (Perris, 1985: 8)

This musical achievement corresponds with the film's larger cultural project of fostering a sense of Irishness founded not only on the history it enshrined, but on the widely publicised fact that it was the first major film to be made in the Irish language. It was hoped that it would be the embodiment of a significant moment in contemporary Irish culture, the celebration of Ireland's recent past as part of the living present.

The legacy of *Mise Éire*

Together, *Mise Éire* and *Saoirse?* form an important part of the history of Irish documentary. In terms of production economics, they established the necessary link to non-state funding and proved that financial return on investment was possible for private enterprise (although, of course, it must be remembered that Gael-Linn was in receipt of government grants). Though the government's involvement in documentary production had been relatively steady, there remained a strong case for non-state-funded films, and, more importantly, for the development of the mechanisms of independent production. Ironically, however, it was evident from these films that while the state did not necessarily exert direct influence upon production, the interpretation of history and the idea of Ireland embodied in them was entirely in accordance with that seen in state-sponsored films in the previous decade. Despite the rise of the private sector facilitated by Lemass's economic strategies, the political and philosophical beliefs which 'represented' Ireland had not changed.

In terms of logistics and personnel, Gael-Linn's subsequent involvement in documentary production was to become the backbone of the industry for a decade, providing both finance and experience for young producers and directors such as Colm O'Laoghaire, Vincent Corcoran, Jim Mulkerns and Louis Marcus and a number of other technical personnel, some of whom would later work abroad. It would also encourage other private sponsors to become involved in independent production, and while for the moment this represented merely an enforcement of the idea of documentary as a rhetorical tool and an expository communicator of 'facts', in time it would produce a generation of filmmakers with the freedom and facility to question these notions. These will be examined in more detail in the next chapter.

In terms of history and ideology, *Mise Éire* and *Saoirse?* established the template for many subsequent representations of Irish history. Problematic political questions were greatly simplified: projecting the past, not exploring how its currents and patterns affected the shape of the present. It was an unproblematised Irish history where each moment had been a natural progression to the homogeneous, seemingly classless, certainly united, Irish society of 1959. No reference was made to Northern Ireland as a place with a separate history of its own. After *Housing Discrimination* (1953), it seemed that it was best simply to ignore the north of the island entirely, or at least not to draw attention to it. By presenting such a seemingly definitive account of recent history and by using its archival footage so judiciously, *Mise Éire* suggested that even the historical documents themselves were now closed off. The raw footage had been shaped into its 'rightful' pattern and found perfect expression in the romantic nationalism of the period.

This was given further force by the fact that Gael-Linn themselves were the sponsors of *Amharc Éireann*, which remained the only indigenous newsreel made during this period. This ensured that their document of then contemporary society would, in time, further feed subsequent representations of the period in which the films were made, thus securing past, present and future (the arrival of state television in 1961 raises new issues which will be discussed in the next chapter). Within this conceptual model, the historical referent becomes a usable commodity, a saleable, arrangeable object (rendered tangible on the physical, archivable strips of film), easily stripped of ambiguities of production and contemporaneity. Though it has the ability to dredge up memories of the past and invoke emotional responses and associations, the historical moment captured by 'pure' documentary footage (or *actualités*) becomes incontestable fact.

In *Mythologies* Roland Barthes discusses the process through which this occurs. He observes that history may be reduced to mythology when the historical object denies its signification. He posits that it is possible to naturalise an actively connotative cultural product produced within a given historical framework through a purification of its contextual ambiguities. The object becomes not a product of a time or place or cultural tradition, but an eternal signifier devoid of history yet assuming the character of an incontrovertible reality.

What the world supplies to myth is an historical reality, defined, even if this goes back quite a while, by the way in which men have produced or used it; and what myth gives in return is a *natural* image of this reality. And just as bourgeois ideology is defined by the abandonment of the name 'bourgeois', myth is constituted by the loss of the historical quality of things: in it, these things lose the memory that they once were made. The world enters language as a dialectical relation between activities, between human actions; it comes out of myth as a harmonious display of essences. (Barthes, 1989: 155)

Ironically, according to Barthes, this leads to a process of depoliticisation, where bourgeois ideology becomes the natural order rather than a specific set of interpretations. His most famous example is of the Negro soldier saluting the French flag, which denies the problematic elements of French colonial identity. But there is an important distinction between the process of naturalisation of an ideological interpretation and an outright denial of history, and he elaborates on this as follows:

In the case of the soldier-Negro, for instance, what it got rid of is certainly not French imperiality (on the contrary, since what must be actualized is its presence); it is the contingent, historical, in one word: *fabricated*, quality of colonialism. Myth does not deny things, on the contrary, its function is to talk about them; simply it purifies them, it makes them innocent, it gives them a natural and eternal justification, it gives them a clarity which is not that of an explanation but that of a statement of fact. If I *state the fact* of French imperiality without explaining it, I am very near to finding that it is natural and *goes without saying*: I am reassured. In passing from history to nature, myth acts economically: it abolishes the complexity of human acts, it gives them the simplicity of essences, it does away with all dialectics, with any going back beyond what is immediately visible, it organises a world which is without contradictions because it is without depth, a world wide open and wallowing in the evident, it establishes a blissful clarity: things appear to mean something in themselves. (Barthes, 1989: 156)

This model may clearly be applied to the project of *Mise Éire* and *Saoirse?*, where this process of naturalisation is precisely as Barthes describes. The films do not deny Irish history; on the contrary, they present it directly. Morrison, as noted, even claimed that they retained a dialectical relationship designed to criticise the failure of bourgeois revolution. Yet when the facts are presented as incontestable documentary images of the period, the internal contradictions and meta-narratives of the history itself are ignored, and the only conflicts presented are those between Ireland and England. This results in a depoliticised political history, built solely upon the construction of an image of the nation amenable to received nationalist mythology.

The consequence is a bourgeois ideology which, as Barthes observes, abandons the word 'bourgeois'. The Ireland of *Mise Éire* and *Saoirse?* is a classless homogenate of 'Irish' people, whose history is predicated upon the revolutionary upheaval which brought about their political independence rather than the specifics of cultural and social (or even economic) history which defined the society of the 1920s or which then defined the society of the late 1950s. It is a *reassurance*, to use Barthes's term, that without saying it, all who see the film will know that the truth is that Ireland fought for independence, and now, even though economic problems are rife, it was important to remember what it fought for. *Mise Éire* and *Saoirse?* present a tamed and moribund history predicated upon monumentalist idolatry which denies the social processes by which history becomes history and within which even the faces of Éamon de Valera and Michael Collins become objects stripped of specificity, commodities for archival reconstruction within proscribed ideological parameters.

Continuity and nostalgia

The lesson of *Mise Éire* was well learned, and subsequent films reinforced this use of history to sustain slight shifts in the political climate. The most direct was Morrison's own *The Irish Rising 1916* (1966), a sixteen-minute documentary produced by the Department of External Affairs to mark the fiftieth anniversary of the rising. The film was supplied to some eighty networks and independent television stations worldwide, and came with a written script which could be read by a local narrator. By this time the emphasis was on an exportable mythology of Ireland, and to this end the film concludes with some images of contemporary Dublin: factories, power stations, generators, buses, suburban houses and other signifiers of modernity. In a sense this was a repetition of *A Nation Once Again*, although its use of contemporary imagery was less integrated with the historical footage.

The bulk of the film consists of a distillation of *Mise Éire*, using the same footage and some of the same structure (the sequence portraying the execution of the rebels is identical). Given that the film was made with the specific, stated purpose of celebrating the events of fifty years before, there is no question as to the place it occupies in an ideological construction of the state. Many members of the government and opposition were still of the 1916 generation, with de Valera himself now president. The appearance of public figures at the celebrations as veterans gave a renewed sense of the integral continuity of the ethos. The widespread sponsorship of such programs in that year for film and television was characterised by a pride and euphoria about Ireland's Catholic and nationalist traditions which was unquestioned, and would not be challenged until the events of 1968 and 1969 in Northern Ireland made clear the potential adverse effects of uncritical jingoism.

Another example of this is Louis Marcus's *An Tine Bheo* (1966) released for the same reasons but with a more explicitly internal focus. The film documents the 'living flame' that is the continuing legacy of 1916 in 1960s Ireland. Rather more directly than *The Irish Rising 1916*, the film establishes the link between then and now by intercutting sequences from the newsreels which featured in the former film and other photographic records of 1916 with shots of the locations and personalities still in existence. It cuts, for example, from a photograph of Éamon de Valera under arrest in his Volunteer uniform to a sequence of the elderly president working in his office in Áras an Uachtaráin, and from shots of 1916 locations such as the GPO and Boland's Bakery in a state of ruin to the buildings as they stand now.

The film begins with a funeral dirge over shots of Irish soldiers standing in a respectful pose at a monument to 1916 martyrs. The camera pans along the faces of elderly men wearing medals, and then provides some English-language interview material in which one of them says, 'I feel 1916 is part of my life.' The interrelatedness of the past and the present and a glossing over of the factors of class, profession and life experience since 1916 are typical of the kind of ideological simplification discussed by Barthes. Like *Who Fears to Speak of '98?* and *Mise Éire* (but unlike Marcus's own later *1798 Agus Ó Shin* (1998)), the film implies an unproblematic relationship between 1798 and 1916 by beginning with details of the former rebellion and shots of Catholic monuments and statues commemorating it, then moving on through Thomas Davis and O'Donovan Rossa to arrive at Padraig Pearse and other figures directly involved in the 1916 insurrection. The voice over, in Irish, does not suggest the broadness of this movement across religious and political divides, but merely suggests an unbroken historical narrative which leads to 1916, and, by inference and direct suggestion via its images, to 1966.

While less emotive than its predecessors and more concentrated on images of statues and monuments than images of the actual events and people, the film serves the same ideological purpose. It articulates a conception of Irish society and Irish history which specifically ties the infrastructure of 1966 Ireland with the acts of fifty years before: shots of Dublin's docklands are juxtaposed with discussion of James Larkin; shots of devastated Dublin are intercut with a vital and thriving city full of traffic; buildings which have changed their function are identified as having once been part of that important and living past. The film endeavours to ensure that Ireland's sense of its present is rooted in an awareness of its past, and that the political beliefs which underlie it are consistent with those of its spiritual founders. Given that the purpose of the film was to celebrate the fiftieth anniversary of the rising, it is unfair to criticise it for not addressing the contemporary political world through contemporary politics, but even on its own terms, the film's omission of the subtleties of that moment in the past demonstrates its ideological preformation.

Marcus would himself remark only a year later:

We are a highly diverse people which does not fully understand itself, and our community awareness must be accelerated to meet pressures which can no longer be postponed. As a further handicap, we are caught between two culturally powerful countries for whose mass media productions we are a receptive audience. This is a classic situation for the documentary film which excels in interpreting a community to itself as well as others, and which can invest the life of its audience with the drama and significance which they otherwise find only vicariously in the star-studded imported features. (Marcus, 1967: 18)

It is worth noting that this particular interpretation of the community was consistent with the one posited seven years earlier in *Mise Éire*, a film on which he had worked, and which he described as 'truly an event of the most shattering consequence, not only for Irish cinema, but in the general life of the country' (Marcus, cited in Rockett et al., 1988: 86). It neither presents diversity nor encourages community awareness beyond that of the living past, and in no way subjects history to question. Marcus would also later direct the six-part series *The Heritage of Ireland* (1978) interrelating Ireland's past and present through comparisons drawn between history and contemporary events. Presented by historian and journalist Douglas Gageby, the programme was as much intended for export as it was produced for domestic consumption, and as such provided the expected themes and imagery (religion, the landscape, political violence) while adding some sense of reflection through its direct-to-camera editorial content. In spite of the acclaim with which the series was met at the time (it even received funding from the Arts Council), it was retreading familiar territory in all respects.

While it would be unfair to say that all Irish documentary films bear the mark of *Mise Éire* and *Saoirse?* it is fair to observe that the compilation genre never developed the ironic, dialectical counterpoint which made it flourish elsewhere. No archive-based Irish documentary has ever attempted a subversion of the referent in the manner of Shub, or Rafferty and Loader's *The Atomic Café* (1982). Though the intervention of foreign-made documentary series such as *Ireland – A Television History* (1981) and *The Troubles* (1981) may be linked to the gradual development of more critical historical films following the events of the late 1960s and early 1970s, the belief in the absolute referentiality of archival images continues. Even examples of compilation documentaries made in the late twentieth century retained the respect for the raw material which only comes through a denial of its potential ambiguity and the assurance that it has been 'purified', as Barthes would put it.

The television series *The Years of Change* (1997), for example, directed by Louis Marcus, examines the period between 1956 and 1964, using *Amharc Éireann* footage. It is a compilation documentary in the traditional style, and though produced nearly forty years after *Mise Éire*, embarks on an identical project of using archival sources to fashion an unproblematic record of a particular historical moment. What is interesting here, though, is that that particular moment is suggested to be a pivot of change rather than continuity. Though the commentary draws attention to the fact that the original footage has been drawn from a politically and culturally specific source (a brief explanation of Gael-Linn's purpose), and is self-consciously limited to the years during which the newsreel was produced, it nonetheless posits that these years represent the most important period in the foundation of the modern Irish state. The opening narration observes, 'For some this was the making of modern Ireland, an awakening after a decade of stagnation. For others it signalled the decline of traditional values and beliefs. But, for better or for worse, these were the years that made us what we are today.'

There is a wealth of material featuring the leaders of church and state attending public functions, which was obviously newsworthy at the time of shooting. But now, stripped of its original news value, it has become simply a record of people and places, presented as information that they were there. This then becomes subject to reconstruction, and the resultant series therefore becomes merely a further enshrinement of the monuments of Irish history without critical engagement of the meaning of that history. It does not study the processes through which this footage has become historical, or assess the context in which it was originally filmed. It is robbed of its specificity by historical distance, and has been commodified and repackaged in a sanitised form as tamed history.

Little of the material featured charts the internal dissensions of the period mentioned in the opening narration (although footage of Unionist marches and the Northern Irish elections of the early 1960s is presented with a cheerful explanation that nationalist candidates only ran in constituencies where they had some chance of winning), and without the benefit of footage from the preceding period of 'stagnation' with which to compare it, the presentation is merely an undifferentiated history of a period which may or may not represent the changes it purports to show. It also seems to suggest that those changes have directly led to the Irish society of 1997, which it does not argue through the presentation of evidence regarding the contemporary state, but through its statement of purpose.

It is arguable that the series assumes an inherent critique of the 1950s, and presumably argues that the 1960s represents a period of significant change for the television viewer of the 1990s. But firstly, this assumes that the Ireland of the 1990s owes its moral and ideological foundations to the presumed radicalism of the 1960s, a radicalism which did not seem to exist in *The Irish Rising 1916* and *An Tine Bheo*, and secondly, this very radicalism is highly questionable given the manner in which the film chooses to present these 'years of change'. For example, the first episode, 'Faith and Fatherland', recounts events such as the election of Eamon de Valera as president, the celebrations for the Patrician Year (1961), commemorations at the grave of Wolfe Tone and the Fianna Fáil and Fine Gael Ard Fheiseanna. It is significant that the series should begin by charting the ascension of de Valera to the presidency, the sponsors of *Mise Éire*, *Saoirse?* and *Amharc Éireann* itself having left off in 1921 with his evident sway over the populace during the treaty negotiations. The years in between have been omitted by the circumstances of historical record: insufficient archival footage exists. Thus de Valera's significance as nominal head of the Irish state and symbolic domination of the period in question is assumed without any serious consideration of how or why he got there. While his successor as head of Fianna Fáil, Seán Lemass, would then spearhead significant changes to the economic structure of the state, he is seen here attending the same public functions and paying the same obeisances to the same events and persons as the president. This suggests continuity, not change; which is precisely what *Mise Éire* established and this series consolidates using footage sponsored by the same organisation.

In addition, the prejudices of the period are presented without serious question within a contemporary context. In fact, there is an implicit assumption that these things are beyond question, 'common sense'. No comment is needed because these are facts of history, complete with footage to prove it. Hence, like *Mise Éire* and *Saoirse?* before it, this archival compilation represents a reinforcement of ideology rather than a reconsideration of history.

For example, in the section dealing with the commemoration of the Patrician Year, the commentary notes that the heads of the Protestant communities were not invited to the celebrations, but there is no further attempt to engage this issue or its implications. It then moves swiftly on to state, 'for many of the faithful, the Patrician year was a reminder of how the Island of saints and scholars had saved Christianity in the Europe of the Dark Ages, and later spread its message through missionaries around the world'. This sectarian observation is accompanied by footage of a black bishop walking past the camera precisely at the point where the words 'Dark Ages' are spoken. This is no accident of editing, it is an unapologetic assumption that the figure of a Catholic Negro represents a religious and moral victory for 'the faithful' and 'the island of saints and scholars'. It is a direct transposition of Barthes's soldier-Negro to an Irish context, where instead of saluting the flag of the coloniser, a black man dressed in the garb of Catholic orthodoxy represents a purification of the process of missionary conquest.[7] There is even a notable absence of irony in the use of language, given further *gravitas* by the fact that the narrator is RTÉ newsreader Eamon Lawlor, a figure Irish audiences will automatically associate with the 'facts' and 'reportage' of RTÉ's news programmes. Phrases like 'the island of saints and scholars' and 'the faithful' are used liberally, and the music which accompanies the entire series is the type of upbeat newsreel music used in the period in question rather than today, further removing the footage from the modern milieu. This renders the material distant, unproblematic and nostalgic, a statement of simple historical fact. The absence of interview material or contemporary discussion compounds the reduction of history to myth yet again.

Ironically, a superior record of the changes taking place in Ireland in this period is to be found in a two-part CBS news documentary, *Look Up and Live: Ireland in Transition* (1965). While it suffers from a milder form of the cultural schizophrenia which affected many foreign-produced documentaries about Ireland in that era (denying modernity while attempting to chart it: 'Ireland as an idea . . . has existed for centuries. Ireland as a nation is a recent development', the opening narration states), it manages to incorporate contemporary discussion of the government and politics of Ireland. Individuals such as then Senator Garret Fitzgerald and members of the general public assess the issues in an interview format. This film follows the style and approach of the earlier *Ireland – The Tear and the Smile* (1959).

The difference between these foreign films and indigenous ones is the inherent ideological project of Irish historical documentary. Films made for domestic consumption which address Irish history inevitably avoid the taint of 'revisionism' in an effort to posit the 'natural' ideological foundation of Irish political and social identity. Whatever value archival material may have in its original context, it is easily pressed into the service of mythology because the tradition of dialectical historical critique pioneered in the Soviet Union by Dziga Vertov and Esfir Shub and continued elsewhere never developed in Ireland. Films made for foreign consumption by international filmmakers have the potential advantage of emotional distance, but are, of course, subject to other dangers of romanticism and sentimentalism which also result from the distance between observer and observed.

There is even an argument that nostalgia is the dominant discourse in Irish-made documentary films, especially on television. It represents a form of historical amnesia, where events in the past become neutralised by their distance from the present, and thus are malleable and may be used not only for ideological advertisement, but for entertainment. The turn of the millennium brought a rash of these superficial 'wallpaper'-type programmes. The RTÉ series *100 Years* (2000) was one example, a daily one-minute series charting significant events on each day throughout the century. A massive undertaking in terms of research for those involved, it was nonetheless, as presenter Brian Farrell remarked in the hefty coffee-table book which followed the series, 'translating the whole sweep of this century of change into 10-second television sound bites, as it was transcribing the rich fabric of a whole people's experience into a set of postcards' (Farrell, 2001: v–vi). In a similar vein, the compilation series *Reeling in the Years* (1999) featured footage from RTÉ's news archives from each year of the 1980s (ten episodes) overlaid with popular music. Scrolling subtitles provided some contextual data, and though the images were of a particularly unhappy period in Irish economic and social history, the emphasis was on cheerfully indicating how far the country had come since then, given that the series was broadcast at a time of record-breaking economic prosperity. It was followed by sequels dealing with the 1970s (2000) and 1990s (2001).

Archival rebroadcasting was also popular around the turn of the millennium, including episodes of television news and magazine programmes such as *Radharc* (which will be discussed in the next chapter) and *Féach*, an Irish-language news magazine from the 1970s and 1980s. The music retrospective *Come West Along the Road* began in 1998 and ran for several years thereafter, a comedy review featuring skits and stage performances from the past (*Make 'Em Laugh*) ran in 1999, and in 2001 RTÉ ran a large number of retrospectives to celebrate their fortieth anniversary, many of them presented by both past and current television personalities, all of them recycling material for which RTÉ needed to pay no rebroadcast fee because it was theirs to begin with.

The stand-alone documentary *A State of Crisis* (1995) is a good example of how the superficial use of archive material can be culpable in not merely reducing history to an entertainment, but using the past to escape having to address the present. The film examined the arms crisis of the late 1960s when members of the Irish government (including later Taoiseach Charles J.

Haughey) were accused of attempting to supply arms to the IRA. The film, which was an adequate account of the events using archival footage, was produced during a period of political crisis in the 1990s (when a series of financial scandals had begun to lead back to prominent politicians, including Haughey) as if to distract the public from what was going on around them. The crisis in the past seemed remote and non-threatening, and thus again a tamed history which fulfilled an uncritical role in current ideological formulation.

The film is nominally investigative in that it explores a crisis in modern Ireland and therefore offers the viewer the opportunity to explore a problematic moment in Ireland's past. But it retains no sense of the contemporary and makes no suggestion that, for example, the actions of Charles J. Haughey in the 1960s might be an indicator of his possible guilt in the 1990s (except, as usual, by inference). Part of the reason for this, of course, may be the fact that Irish libel laws are notoriously stringent (and, indeed, at that same time a prominent member of the Oireachtas was involved in a libel action with a British newspaper), but it is nonetheless testament to the tendency of Irish documentaries to shy away from employing the past as a means to make greater sense of the present. Instead, *A State of Crisis* represents a bizarre inversion of historical interrogation. A sort of allegorical elaboration on the potential cracks in Irish ideology, it documents a moment where state and terrorist nationalism retained uncomfortable congruities which almost spilled over into a direct relationship between ideology and the mechanisms of political power.

It is perhaps all the more surprising then that a series marketed with the intention of establishing its radicalism and motivated by strong metahistorical convictions such as Trish McAdam's *Hoodwinked* (1997) should reprise the same methods of historical whitewash. The series was a professed feminist 'herstory' of Irish women produced with the intention of asking, as the press release publicising the series asks, 'were Irish women "hoodwinked" in the past into believing in an idealised image of a pure, mother homemaker or are they equally "hoodwinked" into believing that legislative equality will solve all their problems?' With such a strong polemical base, extensive archival sources and access to a range of interviewees from various women's movements and historians, the film promised and professed to offer a radical reconsideration of the processes and omissions of official historiography.

It begins by arguing that archives offer insufficient documentary material with which to explore the questions it seeks to address. The series is therefore largely composed of interview material. In his critique of *Ireland – A Television History* John Pym remarks:

The oral tradition, with roots in Gaelic Ireland, remains a powerful influence on, and contributory factor to, the course of Irish history . . . Kee's is, above all, 'spoken' history – his listeners, like the poet's, are gathered at the hearth; and, while a modern television audience has not the patience for the intellectually warming delights of an epic tale wrapped in a skein of conventions and internal rhythms, it does expect another, modern sort of wizardry; that the teller of the tale appears not only to hold in his head, but also actually to *know* – like Lord Kenneth Clark and Dr. J. Bronowski – what he is talking about. The act of listening to this kind of 'prestige' storyteller, and of watching him as well, requires for it to work a certain sense of audience wonderment, an unconscious submission to the story and the authority of the teller. (Pym, 1988: 480)

This, curiously, accurately describes the project undertaken in *Hoodwinked*, where, in the absence of a written or recorded history of women in Ireland, McAdam purports to build one based not upon the voice of one man, but on those of many women. This film will be examined again later in the context of a feminist project and feminist documentary in general, but for the moment it is important to note that in this attempt, it merely becomes another grand narrative. It dispels its own potential internal contradictions and merely restates what is already 'common sense' and 'well known', omitting the male rather than inserting the female. Its authority, such as it is, derives from the voices of its interviewees, veterans of the women's movements in Ireland.

Yet there are detectable tensions within the histories as related by different organisations, for example between the Irish Countrywomen's Association and the Irish Housewives Association, between the academicised feminism of university lecturers and the experiences of female TDs.[8] The film does not address these, but attempts to fashion a totalising 'herstory' of Irish feminism. As in the standard Irish historical documentary, projection is more important than exploration, the purpose overrides the potential, the polemic dictates the conception of reality presented on screen. Internal contradictions and metahistories within the metahistory of Irish women are left for the viewer to detect (there is little discussion of the experience of working-class women, for example). They are not addressed by the voice over or even by the interviewees, except in one or two remarks in which a strong hint of mutual disregard between subgroups may be heard (particularly between older pioneers and younger radicals). This brings the film back within Pym's conception of the 'oral tradition' of storytelling, asking the audience to submit to the story and the authority of the teller – in short, presenting a 'closed' 'herstory' not dissimilar in intention from the mythological aims of *Mise Éire*.

It is arguable that this 'oral tradition' is somehow central to Ireland's conception of history. We will examine this idea again when we discuss the growth of television talk shows. It is also arguable that the process of historical mythology growing out of such an 'oral tradition' is characteristic of the state. It is certainly enshrined in the Constitution that the government occupies a paternal role in relation to all public utterances and acts of journalism, as established in the oft-cited Article 40, discussed in the previous chapter. Therefore, even given the (qualified) freedom of the press, the state becomes like Pym's storyteller or poet, the instrument of Barthes's mythology and the articulation of Eagleton's discourse, a conceptual presence within which any elaboration or exploration of the lapses and contradictions of the state itself are subject to a measure of proscription which often inhibits true investigation. History and ideology are inextricably intertwined at a constitutional level, at least for those filmmakers who are not willing to use the freedoms granted to them by law. The constitutional presence of the idea of statutory authority is merely an outward manifestation of the conviction that Ireland (embodied by the state) knows what is best for itself, and that the forces which record and document its history are benevolent and objective, interested in the well being of its citizens and therefore not subject to question.

Revisionism and resurrection: historical documentary at the turn of the millennium

A tradition of interrogative historical documentary did eventually emerge in Ireland, and there is an ever-growing sense of the past as a realm of investigation which attests that, as Jeffrey Youdelman puts it, 'the importance of having a clear view of the past is, of course, to know how to interpret the present, act upon it, and thereby influence the future. If we fail to be discriminating about what we think happened in the past, we're likely to be equally imprecise about the present' (Youdelman, 1988: 463–4). This is not to imply that the present must be moulded to fit the past, but that the past may offer suggestions as to why the present has assumed its current shape, and how both may help us to move towards a future which offers progress, not repetition. The dread tag of 'revisionism' is often attached to those who challenge the received notions of nationhood and nationality offered by a study of history and of the present, and it is worth briefly expanding on this notion. Stephen Howe summarises:

It has sometimes been argued that some versions of at least academic social science and historiography have simply been unable to perceive the significance of colonial and neocolonial influences on Ireland, because of their own ideology or methodological blinkers. This is especially often alleged of what has been labelled revisionist historical writing. Here disputes over interpretations of the past have become associated, not only in the intellectual community, but to some considerable extent in the popular mind, with political agendas and even social class. Thus critics have identified historical revisionism with 'Dublin 4' – shorthand for a nexus of politicians, broadcasters, media commentators and academics who are claimed, by those like Desmond Fennell who believe themselves unfairly excluded by it, to form a kind of anti-national mafia. (Howe, 2000: 76–7)

Eagleton also addresses questions of the role of revisionism in debates upon history in contemporary Ireland, concluding that the argument is less between traditionalism and modernism than between modernity and post-modernity: a somewhat redundant grappling with identity in an age where even the ideas of self and nation upon which these arguments rest are in a state of flux. He observes that there is an essential difference between those for whom the past is a site of a particularly Catholic source of comfort (a time of hardship in which 'things were better') and those for whom such ideas represent outmoded ideological constructs which must be debunked before progress can occur. He notes the tendency for historians and those who debate history to entrench themselves in research and argument which supports whatever theory of the past they choose to endorse, but notes, as we would expect given the material discussed earlier in this chapter, that both sides are engaging in discourse within an unmistakable ideological context. He argues that the difficulty is that neither side in the 'revisionist' debate is able to acknowledge that the frames of reference commonly assumed (nationalist vs. anti-nationalist) are in fact merely an overlay for a deeper debate within an overall discourse upon human history.

It is not in the end a matter of nationalists versus anti-nationalists, but of two divergent readings of human history – the one liberal-rationalist, generously trusting to the civilising forces of modernity, the other materialist, reading the record of humanity to date as largely one of scarcity, exploitation and injustice. It is, in effect, a distinction between what Walter Benjamin termed 'history' – the fable recounted by the governors – and 'tradition' – the narrative of the dispossessed. (Eagleton, 1998: 317).

Interestingly, as we have seen throughout this and the previous chapter, the treatment of history in Irish historical documentaries has been a combination of what Eagleton defines as 'history' and what he labels 'tradition': an official 'fable' which recounts the 'narrative of the dispossessed' that is Irish colonial history. If, as he concludes, 'all history-writing is revisionist, just as all poetry-writing is. It is simply a question of which ideological label a particular revisionist current comes under' (320), then it might be interesting, by way of concluding the present chapter and leading into some of the films of the subsequent decades during which these patterns began to break down, to examine the case of 'history' which has itself been 'dispossessed', in that it was not recorded or examined during the period in question but is now in the light of a developing idea of Ireland.

Mise Éire was not supplanted as the official visual history of the Irish state until the much-vaunted *Seven Ages* (2000), a seven-part television series directed by Seán Ó Mórdha. There had been pretenders to the throne including the previously mentioned *The Heritage of Ireland* and the British-produced *Ireland – A Television History*, but *Seven Ages*, subtitled 'The Story of the Irish State', focused specifically on Irish history since 1922 (with due reference to the struggle for independence in its first episode) and was launched at the turn on the millennium with as much aplomb as *Mise Éire* in 1959. It was marketed nationally and internationally, and available both on videocassette and DVD after the initial broadcast period, during which the series was shown twice by RTÉ and also by BBC Northern Ireland, who were associate producers. *The Heritage of Ireland* and *Ireland – A Television History* had been major events in their own time, and, as noted, Marcus's series was even intended for export, but however much of a stir they may have created, neither was publicised with such a level of saturation nor were they distributed for 'home use' (neither of these series is available today, whereas, as noted, *Mise Éire* and *Saoirse?* are). *The Seven Ages* videocassette and DVD packs gave consumers the ability to add these 'texts' to their bookshelves and enabled educational institutions to offer students the same opportunities that the groups of schoolchildren were compelled to appreciate in 1959.

Another significant difference between *Seven Ages* and those programmes which had gone before it was one of format. In spite of the observed tendency towards 'oral history' through the use of interview techniques marked in *Ireland – A Television History* and other historical documentaries from the 1970s onwards, both *The Heritage of Ireland* and the latter series were very specifically 'presented' by noted historical commentators (Douglas Gageby and Robert Kee respectively). The presence of these 'authorities' fulfilled a pedagogical or even authorial function in the programmes' constructions of historical narratives. It also, to some extent, disengaged the spectator from the notion of a 'neutral' reading of history because they were able to identify the words, gestures and facial expressions of the person relating 'the story' to them. *Seven Ages* took the less formally explicit route of illustrating its points through interview material interspersed with archival footage. Some of the interviews were culled from other historical documentaries and most of the archive footage had been seen before. The series incorporated scenes from *Eucharistic Congress 1932*, *Our Country* and other films previously discussed, while also conducting extensive new interviews with important figures in Irish history including several former Taoisaigh. All of this contributed to the sense that it was very much the definitive document of twentieth-century Irish history on film, an impression reinforced by the fact of its initial broadcast near the end of the year 2000.

The years leading to and following the turn of the millennium saw an increase in the number of historical documentaries in general. In Ireland, where the history of the state did not even cover the span of the century, the level of self-scrutiny seemed very intense. Individual films or television series exploring aspects of Ireand's past hitherto not examined in any detail were broadcast amid debates about 'revisionism', and *Seven Ages* took many of these into account in its 'redrawing' of the patterns and currents of Irish history. The year 1998 was an important one, itself a time of significant constitutional revision. A referendum held on 22 May successfully carried the motion to revise the controversial Articles 2 and 3 of the Irish Constitution which claimed dominion over 'the Island of Ireland.' The actual constitutional change was not enacted until 2 December 1999, at which time political power was devolved to the Northern Ireland Assembly led by First Minister David Trimble (unionist) and Deputy Minister Seamus Mallon (nationalist). The proposed change to the official idea of Ireland embodied in the constitutional amendment would have far-reaching consequences for the future of the island. The year 1998 was also, by curious coincidence, the bicentennial of the 1798 rebellion in which factions from both north and south had united against crown forces for the liberation of Ireland. Though it would fall to the BBC to produce a documentary series chronicling current events in the series *Endgame in Ireland* (2001), the events of two hundred years previously were marked by several films and television programmes made within Ireland, just as the 1916 Rising had been celebrated in 1966.

1798 Agus Ó Shin (1998) was first broadcast on the new Irish-language television station Telefís na Gaelige (TnaG) in April. *Rebellion* (1998) was a three-hour, three-part RTÉ production broadcast in May. Both were in part financed by contributions from the government's 1798 Commemorative Committee, but funding came from several sources. Though different in their approach to the subject, both shared the ideological proposition that the events of 1798 represented a shared heritage for the people of Northern Ireland and those of the Republic. On one level this has progressive implications, and the films represent the first significant attempt to incorporate questions of the unique history of Northern Ireland into a film about that of the Republic. Yet this is a double-edged sword which also implies, as *Mise Éire* did, that complex historical and political developments may be subsumed by a 'neutral' reading of history which charts a 'natural' affinity between diverse social and political traditions. They argue ultimately from a nationalist position that a united Ireland is not only possible, but with historical precedent. Though neither film does so on the level of voice over or even in their presentation of data, it is not difficult to read beyond the ostensible (re)conciliation offered by such films between the unionist and nationalist traditions. They do not so much celebrate the differences between

traditions as suggest that the past two hundred years represent a tragic mis-
understanding given the cooperation between the sides in 1798.

1798 Agus Ó Shin is the more direct of the two in attempting to redress
some of the myths of 1798 seen in films like Marcus's own *An Tine Bheo* and
the even earlier *Who Fears to Speak of '98?* The 1998 film features interviews
with historians and commentators from both northern and southern institutions who often have different interpretations of the same happenings. This
was part of Marcus's rationale in the making of the film. He hoped that
incorporating the voices of Presbyterian historians would acknowledge their
reading of events traditionally seen within the narrative of Catholic and
nationalist history in the Republic. He remarked, 'the mythology was simplistic, it has to be, because that's what gives people comfort, but this is not
comfortable . . . The reaction against nationalism was a reaction against a
very simplistic idea of Irish history, and it is probably no harm that that simplistic myth was thrown out' (cited in O'Donoghue, 1998a: 14). It is clear
that Marcus considered his film a contribution to the rewriting of history
necessitated by the accommodations being made in Irish politics at the time
of broadcast. The film fits within the 'new Ireland' being forged by the
Belfast/Good Friday Agreement as a direct reappraisal of traditional nationalist historiography. It is interesting that he would arrive at this juncture
some thirty years after *An Tine Bheo*, but not necessarily surprising if we
think of it in the context of developments in Irish politics which had shifted
the parameters within which historical documentary could operate.

Rebellion was less concerned with current events. It presented the details
of the rebellion in three hour-long episodes featuring extensive reconstruction, 3D graphical illustrations and a variety of written and visual records
(paintings, drawings). The elaborate series was accompanied by an RTÉ
Commercial Enterprises publication *Rebellion: A Television History*, and was
later retailed on videocassette. It was designed not to problematise notions of
history, but to 'document' them. The history recorded by *Rebellion* was
nonetheless in accord with its predecessor. It represented a moment in which
all peoples of the island of Ireland shared a common goal. The interesting difference between the two documentaries was that in *1798 Agus Ó Shin* this was
the subject of argument whereas in *Rebellion* it was a statement of fact. *Rebellion* therefore represents the continuity inherent in the project of Irish historical documentary regardless of the nuances of the political climate which
surrounds the production of individual films. Like *Mise Éire* it is a large-scale,
highly public assertion of a concept of history which appears unproblematic.
That it represents a political reading suited to the times in which it has been
made is incidental to the process which underlies its production.

The civil war had been a problematic subject since the failure of *Saoirse?*
and had not been the subject of a documentary treatment in its own right

until *The Madness from Within*, also broadcast in 1998. This film included footage of the modern IRA on manoeuvres and constantly reinforced the point that the political divisions which define contemporary Ireland are still descended from the events of seventy-five years earlier, though it argued that this represented a form of 'madness' as the title stated. The film did not suggest that the political positions maintained by the two main parties are identical to their 1920s counterparts, but it illustrated that the divisions still exist, and run deeper than mere policy or party-political loyalties. Through interviews with veterans of the conflict and a careful portrayal of both sides as equally gripped by a postcolonial rage, the film was able to suggest quite subtly that fidelity to the parties among members of the older generation remains divided along traditional lines even though Ireland has nominally progressed. It concluded with one interviewee noting that upon the cessation of hostilities 'De Valera told us to bury the guns', not destroy them, because they might be needed yet. This legacy is seen to be very much alive in the bitterness with which many interviewees spoke of their experiences. Overlaid by its interpretation of the war as tragedy rather than triumph, however, the film successfully redressed the enshrinement of this situation for the purposes of nationalist propaganda.

Significant historical repositioning also took place in two films on the First World War, namely *Sown in Tears and Blood* (1999) and *The Green Fields of France* (1999). Both were screened as part of a general commemoration of the end of the war, which was marked worldwide by similar projects. The production of these films at this time in Ireland conforms to the pattern we have seen throughout this chapter. The presentation of a vision of history inevitably coincides with a wider preexisting interest in the subject area into which Irish documentarists enter armed with whatever interpretation is most relevant to the needs of the time. Ireland's participation in the First World War was a troublesome one from the point of view of traditional nationalism, representing as it did collaboration with Britain at a time when the 1916 insurrection had nominally established a pedigree for republicanism. In spite of the many films and series made throughout the century, these were the first to examine Ireland's involvement in this significant moment in world history.

Sown in Tears and Blood was written and presented by RTÉ radio personality Myles Dungan in an attempt at, as Vincent Browne put it, 'reclaiming the memory of the war from the ordinary soldier who fought and died in it' (Browne, 1999: 41). Though the programme was orthodox in style and approach within a traditional news/journalism mode, the very fact that it addressed this previously sensitive topic was worthy of note, and indeed it successfully reincorporated Ireland into the history of the First World War as if it had never been wilfully excluded. Alan Gilsenan's film was also traditional as a depiction of the war, though not made in the same style. This was a more reflective, poetic study of men at war using poetry and letters home from writers Francis Ledwidge, Tom Kettle and Patrick McGill, a model familiar from many documents of the First World War from other countries, but again, hithertofore unseen in Ireland. Gilsenan also made use of images from Fr Browne's collection of photographs from the conflict as well as deliberately grainy, out-of-focus and abstract images of the French landscape to create a sense of otherworldliness which drew attention to the distance over which the events were being perceived. *The Green Fields of France* also draws attention to this element of oral history, identified by Pym, which continues to define such films and provide them with an evidentiary quality stemming as much from an emotional response to the spoken word as from the information they present.

The existence of documentaries such as these which gave exposure to new aspects of the history of Ireland is significant, not least of all because when Ó Mórdha put the seal on the process with *Seven Ages*, especially in conjunction with the kinds of investigative and social documentaries which had begun to emerge at the same time (which will be discussed later), it seemed as if a new conception of Ireland and its past had definitely emerged. Yet these were only some of the many films produced, and there was a considerable proportion of less critical attempts to revisit Ireland's past. One example worth singling out is the heavily publicised docudrama *Ballyseedy* (1997), whose approach signifies the continuing belief within Irish documentary that facts still speak for themselves and that reality is not subject to a process of negotiation between ideology and ontology. This was perhaps distressing in the late twentieth century, but understandable given the context in which history had been perceived at the time, as evinced even in *The Madness from Within* (which was at least critical of such attitudes).

Ballyseedy reinforced the traditional stereotypical interpretation of the civil war from a vehemently anti-treaty point of view. It charted the story of an atrocity which took place during the war where Free State troops summarily executed several members of the anti-treaty forces by tying them to a mined barricade and exploding it. The film presented much historical data to substantiate its claims, and as a documentary investigation of a specific moment in history, it was relatively straightforward. The inclusion of docudrama segments, however, gave the film an emotional register which frequently threatened to overwhelm the veneer of investigative objectivity . The portrayal of Free State troops as inhuman monsters and the anti-treaty IRA as heroic young volunteers was simplistic and morally indefensible forty years after *Mise Éire*.

Writing in *Film Ireland* in defence of the film, writer, researcher and presenter Pat Butler claimed he just wanted 'to tell a story', arguing that 'it is not the historian's job to justify the present by reinventing the past' (Butler, 1998: 46). This observation places him firmly within the revisionist debate on the traditionalist side. He denies the capacity of docudrama to verify its truth claims by recourse to melodrama, as discussed by Paget:

Viewers seem to assume that the scene is telling the truth, even though they do not pay attention to its particular truth claims. This assumptions is precisely what makes it possible for viewers to ignore the truth claims. It is what makes it possible for them to focus on the melodrama in the scene rather than on its historical arguments. The assumption that the film is telling the truth also serves to validate their emotional responses to the scene. (Paget, 1998: 88)

Butler's failure to realise this is akin to the failure of many historical documentarists and docudramatists to address their subjectivity in a way which makes it less 'reinventing the past' than being responsible for its representation. It is more a question of form than content, specifically the use of a form which excludes alternative readings of the content, arguing, by inference and also directly, that this 'rediscovered' history is incontestable in veracity because the facts speak for themselves. The larger and more important question of context is not addressed.

The debate is further complicated by the lack of formal innovation in all but a few of even those films which expanded the palette of historical subjects. Though *1798 Agus Ó Shin* showed some reflexivity in its use of reconstruction (as *Ballyseedy* did not) and *The Green Fields of France* had foregrounded style in a way which drew attention to its relationship with content, even *Seven Ages* remained stylistically conventional. Its director, Seán Ó Mórdha, was best known for a series of arts and literature documentaries including *Samuel Beckett: Silence to Silence* (1984) and *W. B. Yeats: Cast a Cold Eye* (1989). These films were marked by thorough research and the ability to both get inside these writers and stand apart from them, achieved by mixing reconstruction and readings with solid, discursive analysis which did not attempt to close off the subjects from further investigation.

Seven Ages constituted a 'revision' of history in including problematic subjects and raising significant questions about Ireland's chequered past. It certainly questioned the nationalist ethos which had informed so many of its predecessors, but was also balanced enough to present an unproblematic nationalist point of view through selected interviews with those who continued to endorse it. The use of interviews in general reflected Ó Mórdha's attention to detail and his eye and ear for information which was more than purely expositional. Observations by political commentators from opposing sides in various historical debates, or even with political rivals from the same generation, created a sense of an ongoing dialogue with the past which worked to its advantage. Yet, overwhelmed by a musical score by Bill Whelan (best known for *Riverdance*) which clearly hoped to emulate the emotional charge of Ó Riada, the subtlety of some of the points being made was lost. Almost every sequence seemed to be accompanied by the same overbearing musical theme, which rose and fell on its internal harmonies seemingly oblivious to the relationship between the music and the images. This worked against the otherwise restrained tone characteristic of the director and was more distracting than ennobling.

In spite of its thoroughness and its ability to draw a range of opinions about history into one series, *Seven Ages* did not encourage viewers to engage with history as an open subject. The overall style was conventional, and the series lacked the sense of epistemological space created by the use of enigmatic reconstruction in Ó Mórdha's literary films. This had the effect of closing off many of the debates it raised in a way which hearkens back to *Mise Éire*. *Seven Ages* exemplifies the paradox identified earlier, whereby Irish history in documentary becomes both an official history and a traditional narrative of the dispossessed. Its sense of the arguments which surround interpretations of events in Irish history allows the series to engage with the subject in a balanced way, but it is never quite able to bring the discourse of history itself into focus. As historiography, it offers as unproblematic a presentation of 'the story of the Irish state' (now with pro- and anti-nationalist perspectives) as any of its predecessors.

One film produced during the millennial years proved a notable exception. *Harvest Emergency* (1998) successfully combined the projects of historical reconstruction and archiving in dealing with a moment in Irish history little recorded in textbooks. It charted the events which transpired in 1946 when the grain crops threatened to rot in the fields following bad weather. Given the food shortages throughout Europe in this period and Ireland's continuing isolationist policy, this was a potential disaster. Up to 125,000 people from the cities volunteered to work on the 'Harvest Army', including old rivals from the not too distant civil war. City dwellers and farmers who traditionally thought little of each other worked side by side and the harvest was saved. The peculiar fact about this story was that when the emergency was over, the spirit of cooperation and comradeship between people disappeared. The Harvest Army disbanded and the incident was more or less forgotten. It does not appear in any of the standard history books published before the film was made, though it later featured in *Seven Ages* as if it had never been excluded in the first place.

Harvest Emergency becomes fascinating on its second level of documentary, since it is also a film about how history is recorded, and about how the process of exclusion works on the most mundane level. At the time of the events in question, Colm O'Laoghaire and fellow amateur filmmaker Kevin O'Kelly travelled with the volunteers and filmed the events. They planned to assemble and release the footage and thereby provide an important document of what seemed a significant moment in post-war Ireland. However, they were unable to raise the mere £500 needed to complete the project and the film was lost to posterity, until fifty years later when Liam Wylie restored the footage and combined it with interviews with some of the people who took part in the harvest in 1946. Wylie's film cannily combined a commentary upon the way in which both history and the efforts of amateur film-makers were ignored because they did not necessarily subscribe to an interpretation of Irish life endorsed by the authorities in 1946. It explored history and historiography all at once, combining form and content in a way which invigorated its process of historical interrogation.

Without shying away from pointing out that there were political and gender divisions between those who worked on the harvest, Wylie nonetheless managed to argue that there was a spirit of genuine collectivity about the Harvest Army which was sadly lost afterwards. Interviewees described how injuries received during the harvest were never compensated for by the state, and how people who spoke to one another as comrades for that short time never did so again. Wylie also uses an interview with O'Laoghaire to draw attention to the way in which the film itself was quietly ignored until it went away, which in turn raises questions about the role played by documentarists not just in reconstructing or revisioning history, but simply in recording it. Had O'Laoghaire's film been made in 1946, it might have contributed to a sense of a new present and a new future for Ireland and for Irish documentary. Instead, as we saw in the last chapter, that year saw the release of *A Nation Once Again* and an appeal to the (quasi-mythic) past, with all its consequent effects.

The existence of Wylie's film is proof enough of a change in attitudes. Where the past is not necessarily reinvented to serve the present, but is reconsidered (and indeed, restored) within a view of Irish history which does not propose an uninterrupted continuum of patriotic nationalism. Without needing to argue the point relative to the events of the 1910s and 1920s, it nonetheless suggests that there is a 'lost' history which waits to be discovered and reappraised in terms of what it implies about Ireland and the Irish. In an attempt to put some of this argument to rest, Terry Eagleton notes, 'it is thus, by sublations rather than once-and-for-all subversions, that intellectual development usually comes about' (Eagleton, 1998: 311), and while he observes that change is not possible through intellect alone, he concludes that the debate on revisionism within Irish society is only resolvable with history itself, where events will continue to transpire which will alter people's perception of themselves and of other countries to the point where traditional debates become less important. It is also worth nothing that Eagleton observes that 'revisionism' itself is an ideology, and thus it too is subject to the specific contextual positioning which allows scholars and readers to question the values upon which the 'revisionist' project is based. It is an unfortunately circular and unresolvable issue which, perhaps, as Eagleton himself notes, should be left to history itself.

The question remains though as to how Irish documentary and the idea of Ireland embodied therein progressed from the earlier to the later state. What shifts in perception occurred which allowed documentarists to finally question the basis of Irish society and history so firmly enshrined throughout the period we have examined thus far? This can only be answered by examining developments during the years in between, including the establishment of RTÉ, the expansion of the independent sector and the eventual production of films whose challenge to the dominant orthodoxy would call to mind *Our Country* in their audacity, especially Peter Lennon's *Rocky Road to Dublin* (1968). To suggest that a change did occur is not to deny the presence or effect of ideology, or any other form of cultural or political argument or determination. It does imply that, as the production of films like *Harvest Emergency* and *1798 Agus Ó Shin* suggests, these conceptual precepts have at least become subjects, which means that a more complex understanding of the relationship between documentary, history and ideology is possible.

Notes

1 Portions of this chapter were previously published. See O'Brien, 2000.

2 See Lyons, 1973: 664. The organisation's name is a play on words, meaning 'Irish Pool', but it can also mean 'Irish is with us' in the sense of both the language and the culture.

3 Although there was a fully operational archive section of the National Film Institute, it would be forty years before it was given its own building and resources (in 1992).

4 See Barnouw, 1993; Barsam, 1992; Rothman, 1997, etc.

5 There is some historical dispute about the actual nature of public sympathy for the rebels. The traditional reading, such as that advanced by Lyons (1973), has been that the general public did not approve of the rebellion, but the courts martial and executions turned the tide of support in their favour. But Lee (1989) has argued that the exact mood of the public is impossible to decipher given the blanket of press silence around the rising and the difficulty of finding eyewitness accounts of public feeling. What is clear is that the style and structure of *Mise Éire suggests* that the executions were at the crest of a wave of public outrage, signifying that support for insurrection is an intrinsic part of the Irish consciousness.

6 This long-held reading of events has been recently reassessed by Lee (1989). According to Lee, the insurrection would not have been undertaken unless the rebels felt reasonably confident of victory. Though their failure has been fuel for a romantic image of revolutionary sacrifice, it may have been more the result of a combination of circumstances than a deliberate plan for martyrdom.

7 The same transposition occurs in an *Amharc Éireann* item from the era not featured in the compilation, where footage of a 12 July Orange Order parade in Northern

Ireland features a black man who is singled out by the camera and commented upon in the voice over with evident amusement: 'and here is the first black Orangeman!' (in Irish: 'seo é an céad Oraiste dubh!'). The colour-specific pun is made more cutting by the fact that in the Irish language, the word 'dubh', meaning 'black' is not usually used to describe the colour of a person's skin. The phrase 'Fear Dubh' (literally 'black man') is a term for the devil. The phrase 'duine gorm' (literally 'blue person') is the correct form. By referring to this unionist as a 'black' Orangeman using the word 'dubh', the speaker links unionism with diabolism on a linguistic level.

8 TD is the acronym for 'Teachta Dála', which is the official term for members of the Irish parliament, Dáil Éireann.

4

The rocky road to change

The founding of Telefís Éireann under the Broadcasting Act of 1960 was preceded by a decade of political wrangling and mostly secret debate between senior civil servants in the Departments of Finance and Posts and Telegraphs. Radio broadcasting had existed under the demense of the state since 1926, when Radio Éireann was inaugurated by President Douglas Hyde. Radio Éireann was, as its television equivalent would later be, a public service broadcaster and not a commercial enterprise. The station was funded by licence fees set by the state and also by revenue from advertising. This was an interim position between the state-funded BBC and the commercial American radio networks.[1] The debate around the foundation of the television service has been detailed by Robert J. Savage (1996), whose book this account will draw upon.

In 1950 Leon O'Broin, secretary of the Department of Posts and Telegraphs, began what would become a ten-year campaign for the development of television in Ireland. Beginning with his request to purchase a television set (which was turned down), his struggle was primarily with the Department of Finance, whose scepticism was fuelled by the commercially unremarkable performance of Radio Éireann and also by cultural and political concerns. Many feared the introduction of television would augur an end to indigenous culture and the lowering of moral standards not only with the importing of foreign-produced programmes, but because sets would be able to receive signals from the UK. Indeed it is arguable, as Savage does argue, that it was the establishment in Northern Ireland in 1953 of a BBC transmitter capable of sending television signals into the Republic which alarmed reactionary elements enough to encourage debate on an Irish service despite their reservations.

In 1957 then Tánaiste Seán Lemass inaugurated a series of exploratory committees which eventually resulted in the high-profile Television Commission. The commission submitted an interim report to Minister for Posts and Telegraphs Sean Ormonde in 1958, consisting of proposals from both Irish and non-Irish organisations willing to undertake the running of Irish

10 Though Telefís Éireann did not go on air until New Year's Eve 1961, tests of television broadcasting equipment were carried out before that date. This image shows one such test, with camera operator George Fleischmann pictured right. Fleischmann was one of the most important documentarists of the era, a former German army surveillance expert who was interned during the war after a crash landing and remained on afterwards

television, including one from Gael-Linn, obviously inspired by their success with *Amharc Éireann* and *Mise Éire*. These schemes were ignored in favour of O'Broin's conviction that television should operate like the radio service: controlled indirectly by the state through the supervision of a nominally independent body. These were the terms set down in the Broadcasting Authority Act of 1960, which established the bureaucratic basis from which Irish television would operate. It would be a semi-state body, allowed to seek advertising revenue and generate limited profits (called an 'operating surplus') which were to be used only in the continuing operation of the service or as the government saw fit, but it was also funded by compulsory television licence fees paid by Irish citizens. The company would be run by directors and executives as normal, but it was to be supervised by a Television Authority, a board of political appointees answerable to the state.

As a public service broadcaster, Telefís Éireann (as it was first known) was required to contribute to the well being of the citizenry. It was expected to foster and develop national culture and public discourse, and was thereby significantly placed to define the terms within which subsequent debates on the realities of Irish life would take place. Writing on public service broadcasting in the United States, Barry Dornfield observes that PBS documentary series are considered part of public discourse and are therefore 'designed, adjudicated, legitimated, and received as representations of and contributions to public understanding' (Dornfield, 1988: 11). He argues that they are inevitably treated with more weight relative to the discourses of sobriety than documentaries produced for commercial television even by scholarly institutions and government agencies. In the absence of an indigenous commercial competitor, it would seem that all television in Ireland was to be treated with such gravity.

When the station went on air on New Year's Eve 1961, it was clear that despite the celebrations which were broadcast to the nation, sobriety and caution were the watchwords. Broadcasting began with an address by President Éamon de Valera, who admitted, 'sometimes when I think of television and radio and their immense power, I feel somewhat afraid'.[2] He urged people to use television to seek what was good in man, not what was depraved; a sentiment which echoes Pius XI's pronouncements in *Vigilanti Cura*. The president also remarked, 'I have great hopes in this new service. I am confident that those who are in charge will do everything in their power to make it useful for the nation, that they will bear in mind that we are an old nation and that we have our own distinctive characteristics and that it is desirable that these be preserved.' It is clear that even with the veneer of independence provided by semi-commercial operation, Telefís Éireann was subject to supervision under the constitution. Standards of public order and morality and the authority of the state would remain protected by the same terms as other forms of expression in the preceding decades.

De Valera may have hoped that television would be 'useful for the nation' but it is unsurprising that the terms of that usage should be so contentious. This chapter will see the development of a pattern of struggle, representing the fostering of a culture of interrogation which would emerge more fully in the 1980s and 1990s. The 1960s and 1970s saw a great deal of development in terms of how Irish fiction and non-fiction practitioners approached and thought about their art, but it was also a period in which the prevailing political and social currents were still wavering between progress and traditionalism. Lemass's economic policies had begun an irreversible transformation of the infrastructure, but, as argued in the previous chapter, he was also careful to foster an impression of ideological continuity. Church and state continued to exert a strong measure of influence over documentary production both on television and in cinemas, and though the 1960s saw the gradual emergence of an independent filmmaking community, the breakthroughs did not come until much later.

Irish society was nonetheless beginning to change. With that change came new ideas and, perhaps more importantly, new attitudes to the mode of discourse which had defined the expression of ideas. Television was still important to the development of non-fiction in Ireland, as it was in America and Europe. In the United States, it was under the auspices of television that Robert Drew Associates began the direct cinema/*cinéma vérité* revolution which changed the way in which people thought about reality and its relationship to film. The shift from the rhetorical or expository modes was characterised by a movement away from overt pedantry towards a seemingly more 'neutral' or observational approach, characterised by techniques such as handheld photography, wildtrack sound and a lack of explicit commentary. This re-energised documentary as a medium and gave rise to a new strain of polemical filmmaking in which 'reality' seemed to be speaking for itself.[3] As Barsam notes, these changes were not necessarily causal. There was widespread social and political transformation at a time when television happened to be at its most dominant. He observes that the revival in political filmmaking resulted 'partly from the rise of revolutionary politics throughout the western world and partly from the dominant youth culture that understood and embraced cinema as the most political of art forms' (Barsam, 1992: 300). Though similar change was in progress in Ireland, the effects were less dramatic. The new medium was greeted more cautiously, and the spirit of liberation which fuelled the pioneers of *cinéma vérité* was muted by cautious and lingering obedience to authority, at least in public. In Ireland the drive was towards not innovation, but the consolidation of position. The 1960s was a time of struggle between the protection of the traditional image of the nation and an attempt to articulate an emergent, oppositional sensibility.

The control of television was still firmly in the hands of the state, and rather than encouraging investigation, RTÉ tended to uphold the status quo with programming policies which did not invite challenges to orthodoxy. As Mary Kelly has observed, the reporting of current affairs on Irish television emphasised avuncular and paternal broadcasting – what she terms 'the personality system' (Kelly, 1984: 91). There was even a perception among certain politicians that television was a personal utility with which to make statements without being subject to question or analysis. This perception was at the heart of several clashes between Telefís Éireann and the government, one resulting in a pronouncement by Seán Lemass that 'The Government reject the view that RTÉ should be, either generally or in regard to its current affairs programmes and news programmes, completely independent of Government supervision' (cited in Dowling et al., 1969: 91).

Frustrated by the constant interference by management, RTÉ producers Jack Dowling and Lelia Doolan tendered their resignations in 1969 and co-authored (with contributions from Bob Quinn and Raymond Williams) a polemical book entitled *Sit Down and Be Counted* (1969), attacking the station for its conservatism. They argued that its obedience to the twin authorities of the state and advertising was at the expense of true 'public service' broadcasting. Irish television, they maintained, was not giving people a true sight of Ireland. There was, they said, an unwillingness to confront important current events in any detail because of fears which echoed de Valera's. They wrote:

It was soon discovered, too, that the frontiers of debate were tightly constricted. Subjects that could be freely discussed in a pub were regarded as shocking or unsuitable on the screen. The Producers quickly learned that the nation had little stomach for satire, irony or criticism of revered institutions or personalities. It had two standards. In private anything could be said and often was. In public – on television particularly – wit flagged, ideas evaporated, humour became pawky and gauche. The new Irish, apparently, were determined to be terribly, terribly respectable. They were, to a depressing extent, terribly, terribly dull. (Dowling et al., 1969: 27)

In spite of well-founded reservations like these, television still represented a new market for non-fiction, and with the demand for material to fill schedules, greater numbers of films were produced. Unfortunately, the formal and thematic conservatism of most of them further reinforced the prevalence of the Griersonian tradition. There were counter-effects though, which produced some radical and innovative films in the late 1960s, including the contentious *Rocky Road to Dublin* (1968) and the docudrama *Insurrection* (1966), as shall be shown.

Old chestnuts, new growth

Many of the films of the 1960s were essentially continuations of the project begun under the sponsorship of the Department of External Affairs, very often on the same subjects. One of the more high-profile examples was *Yeats Country* (1965), another tribute to W. B. Yeats, again partly sponsored by the Department of External Affairs. The film was virtually a remake of *W. B. Yeats – A Tribute* (1950), and achieved even greater international recognition. It eventually won a Golden Bear at the Berlin Film Festival, a diploma of merit at the Edinburgh Film Festival, first prize at the Chicago Film Festival, first prize for best colour short at the Barcelona International Film Festival, and was nominated for an American Academy of Motion Picture Arts and Sciences Award in 1966. This level of attention brought its maker, Patrick Carey, into the first rank of Irish documentarists, where he remained until his death in 1994 without ever making a film on a social or political subject.

Observing the landscape: the films of Patrick Carey

Patrick Carey was born in London in 1916.[4] His family moved to Dublin in 1923 as the new state was taking shape, and there he attended art school before returning to London to work as a photographer and freelance film director. He honed his craft under the auspices of the British documentary movement, then came to the attention of Columbia Pictures, who hired him to work on their *The World of Life* series of nature films. The nature genre had evolved world-wide in the 1940s, progressing from the imperialist triumphalism of the pre-war years towards a more observational style. In what would amount to a foreshadowing of the emergence of direct cinema, the emphasis on 'allowing nature to take its course' and recording the results shifted the focus from man's relationship with nature to the study of nature's relationship with itself. This approach suited Carey's own personal affinity with the natural world and his desire to film it with the eye of a practised artist. He received his first Oscar nomination in 1958 for the Edgar Anstey-produced *Journey into Spring* (1957), a film which also won him a BAFTA award.

Seeming to follow the trail of the classical Griersonian documentary, Carey moved to Canada and began working for the National Film Board, where he photographed the again Oscar-nominated Inuit film *The Living Stone* (1958) and also *Arctic Outpost* (1960). His work continued to fall into the category of pictorial documentary, a paradox given that because of the constraints of the genre, his films were also subject to the continuing influence of voice over. Though direct cinema had begun to dispense with the device, the perceived necessity to narrate and explain the action in nature films left them stranded in a half-life between the visual techniques of the observational mode and the aural explication of the expository. This tension is very evident in Carey's films, where his poet's eye was continually upstaged by the primacy of the spoken word, a situation which always frustrated him.

He returned to Ireland in the early 1960s and in 1964 established an independent production company, Aengus Films, in partnership with his wife Vivien. His first commission was *Yeats Country*. This film restated the correlation between landscape and poetry employed by *W. B. Yeats – A Tribute*, adding only colour photography to its predecessor's weaponry of nostalgic evocation. Essentially it is the same in style, content and approach as its predecessor, with the exception of some sequences which abandon voice overs of any kind to linger on the natural beauty of the landscape. These are the moments which come closest to the poetical musings of the pre-NFI amateur films, and they are the signature of its director. The beautiful colour cinematography and use of natural sound are evocative and lyrical, and at times almost seem to constitute another film altogether. Yet as in *W. B. Yeats*

– A Tribute, the level of poetic contemplation of the profilmic is limited by the constant referral to Yeats's life and work, and literal, specific imagery of his home and workplaces. Though Carey longed to make a film without words, this particular film could not be made without recourse to some of the most showstealing verbiage of all, and in spite of again stunning cinematography the film essentially retrod territory thoroughly covered fifteen years earlier.

The success of *Yeats Country* triggered a new phase in Carey's career. After seeing it, veteran Hollywood director Fred Zinneman engaged Carey as second unit director on *A Man for All Seasons* (1966). The opening scenes of this film depict a twilight landscape populated by swooping birds and natural sounds. For those who know his work, the scene is evidently all Carey's. The success of the film gave him the opportunity to continue to work internationally as a second unit director for much of his subsequent life. Documentary remained his first love, however, and he directed *The Mists of Time* (1968) for RTÉ, a visual portrait of Ireland's megalithic tombs and standing stones. In this film Carey's by now characteristic imagery was placed in juxtaposition with a commentary which referred to Irish mythology. As the words of Yeats were a slim but powerful linkage between the visual and the aural in *Yeats Country*, so the fairy tales and legends of Ireland's pagan Halloween festivals drew the viewer into the haunted spaces created by the images of incongruous and enigmatic rock in the otherwise seemingly uninterrupted countryside.

Carey finally succeeded in making his film without words with *Oisín* (1970). Sponsored by the Department of External Affairs as part of the celebrations for the European Year of Conservation, the film is notable for its lack of either voice over or music to accompany its images of Irish flora and fauna. The very appearance of such naturalism does nonetheless indicate its prefabrication. Nichols identifies this paradox in his analysis of the observational mode. He notes that in observational documentaries, the filmmaker is 'an absent presence' (1991: 43) which invites us to treat the reality we see on screen as we would the reality we experience. In appearing as unmediated as it does, *Oisín* reveals the presence of its filmmaker all the more clearly. The viewer is asked to participate in a procedure of fictive engagement, whereby the filmmaker's presence is acknowledged, but coded as absence, rather like the classical third-person narrator in written fiction. It is still clear what the film is trying to say: 'Ireland is beautiful. Let's keep it that way', a message communicated purely through reference to the profilmic.

As a documentary sponsored to celebrate the Year of Conservation, *Oisín* had to serve a rhetorical purpose and fulfil the needs of its sponsors. But though it deliberately excludes a human presence and does not make explicit statements, viewers are given enough information with which to make the necessary associations. Even the title provides direction. In Irish mythology, Oisín was the son of Fionn MacCumhaill, the legendary Celtic warrior whose exploits were invoked by Yeats. The film makes no explicit reference to myth (unlike *The Mists of Time*), or to human habitation. It is concerned exclusively with the 'natural' landscape and the 'living presence' of flora and fauna. But it is not difficult to infer a concern with the relationship between the people and the land in myth from this juxtaposition. The mythical Fianna were respectful of the natural environment and lived in harmony with it. This was obviously intended to be an exemplar of behaviour which should be followed in the Year of Conservation, and hence the film carries a weight of documentary analysis despite its (in)formal structure. This almost pantheistic appeal to man's place in the ecosystem was advanced for its time, and quite a radical departure from the specificity of *Yeats Country*.

Voice over returned in *Errigal* (1970), a film also commissioned by the Department of External Affairs. Announcing the commission in *Vision* one commentator noted, 'as is to be expected, this will be in the nature of *landscape painting*, as was his beautiful *Yeats Country* for the same sponsors' (uncredited, 1967: 12; emphasis added). In what on the surface appears a strange decision given his penchant for non-interference but on another seems a response to such expectation, Carey opted not only to include a voice over, but to impose a fantastical narrative upon his footage. A portrait of the mountains of County Donegal, specifically Mount Errigal, the film is framed like a fairy tale. It introduces a 'hero' and a 'villain' in the forms of Errigal and nearby Mount Muckish. The latter is described in the voice over as 'brooding, humpbacked: ranging a sombre army of storm and shadows against the peace of Errigal', making the image of an otherwise relatively inoffensive mountain appear like something from Tolkien. Its narration reinforced through the use of dramatic footage of storms and lightning accompanied by a thunderous score by composer Brian Boydell, the film told the 'story' of how these mountains battled with one another with the weapon of weather. Errigal, the 'hero', emerges as victor in the end. On one hand this represents a kind of classical anthropomorphism not untypical of nature documentaries from the 1930s onwards, but on another the film represents Carey's continuing frustration with the schism between word and image and is almost partly a parody of the form which nonetheless helps him to give shape to a 'story' drawn from the environment as he had filmed and observed it. In this respect it is the most Flahertyesque of his films, which is interesting given that it was followed by the BBC-commissioned *Waves* (1973), shot on the Aran Islands.

The islands had been revisited before this, not least of all by Jim Mulkerns, the former *Amharc Éireann* camera operator and director. In *An tOileanach a d'Fhill* (1970), a film sponsored by the Department of the

Gaeltacht, Mulkerns presented the framework of a fictional story in which a native islander now working in the noisy building sites of London longs for the simple pleasure of home. This all-too-common story was a feature of many tourist documentaries in the preceding decades, but Mulkerns presented it here without discernible irony. The film was very clearly intended as a homage to Flaherty. Not only did Mulkerns emulate specific scenes and images from the earlier film (including the cliff fishing), he and his family moved to the islands for the duration of the shoot and lived in the cottage Flaherty had built for himself in the 1930s. Mulkerns also cast Maggie Dirrane's granddaughter in a small role in the film. Though beautifully shot in vivid colour, the film is a tepid attempt to fuse the romanticism of *Man of Aran* with the pragmatism of *Drifters* (certain shots of fishermen, now working on an industrial rather than an artisanal basis and using trawlers, resemble key shots in Grierson's film).

Carey approached *Waves* from quite a different perspective. He visited the Aran Islands accompanied by veteran producer and close friend John Taylor, who shared directing and photographic duties on the film. If *Man of Aran* was the ultimate document of the sea as man's greatest challenge, *Waves*, a film made again without voice over, sought to visualise its rhythms and patterns by absenting 'man' altogether. As in *Oisín*, humanity is excluded in favour of a depiction of the eternal presence of the living world which, apart from the assumed presence of the camera's eye, is unaware of our existence, or even of our observation. Carey filmed waves breaking on the Aran rocks, water swirling in tide pools, sea spray forming delicate patterns in the air before crashing on the shoreline without ever referring to the geographical specificity of the scenes. Though the *Man of Aran* controversy has been largely focused on its omissions, *Waves*, like Joris Iven's *Rain* (1929), makes all referentiality an irrelevance in the face of breathtaking aesthetics.

The implicit environmentalism of *Oisín* (and indeed most of his work) notwithstanding, Carey's films never specifically engaged with political or social issues. He continued to work in Ireland, Canada, Britain and the United States for the remainder of his life, including on projects for RTÉ and Radharc Films. An unquestioned artist, he seemed content to operate within the boundaries of the poetic. It is perhaps for this reason that his work falls under a continuum of pictorial evocation in spite of the technical and aesthetic advances it demonstrates. Indeed, without the extratextual labelling which comes with either voice over or a knowledge of the production details, it would be difficult to distinguish between scenes from *Yeats Country* or *Oisín* and those filmed elsewhere. This globalist eye is a mark of Carey's work, and makes it different from the specifically local focus of the nature documentarist Éamon de Buitléar, to whom we will return later.

Seeing and selling the 'new' Ireland

Though Carey's work foreground the 'natural beauty' of the Irish landscape which Bord Fáilte had always been eager to advertise, and the film fit relatively easily into the category of promotional film, the Irish Tourist Board sponsored several films in this era which did not share Carey's subtlety, including *Ireland – The New Convention Country* (1966) and *Ireland Invites You* (1965). These films again embraced the paradox of progress vs. traditionalism so prevalent in the previous decade. Even in the light of an open appeal to internationalisation and expansion (which made Lemass's economic policies its manifest inspiration), these films were not reluctant to appeal to the romantic projection of a peaceful, bucolic county inherited from its predecessors; on the contrary, they found ways to employ that imagery aggressively.

Ireland – The New Convention Country, directed by camera operator Robert Monks, depicted 'modern' Ireland by showing its hotels and airports (which were, evidently, the trappings of civilisation conference delegates could most identify with). It also foregrounded the many leisure activities and sightseeing possibilities. 'Take a day off from your conference, you won't be missed,' says the voice over conspiratorially while the film extols the virtues of golfing, horse racing and medieval banqueting in Bunratty Castle. In this context, Ireland was being promoted as a potential site for pleasure. It was a theme park to be exploited and enjoyed rather than appreciated or understood. As a convention centre, it was obviously less concerned with international affairs than it was with entertaining guests. Far from the pre-NFI films which tentatively probed the meaning of the Irish landscape to its people, this film and others like it were concerned with specific and direct projections of a land stripped of culture except to the extent that culture itself may be seen and enjoyed in museums, art galleries and theatres in between speeches and lunches at well-appointed, modern hotels. The film thus encapsulates the paradoxes of Lemass's Ireland, where modernisation remained subject to a lingering traditionalism modified to meet the demands of the expanding economy.

Gibbons describes this condition in his consideration of the postcard art of John Hinde, where, as he points out, 'traditional or vernacular is relegated, quite literally, to the level of a cottage industry, to pave the way for industrialisation and progress' (Gibbons, 1996: 43). He argues that the nostalgia of Hinde's late 1950s postcards was a new type, where the process of modernisation and industrialisation was laid alongside traditional 'village' values to appeal to visitors in the same manner as *Ireland – The New Convention Country*. The film was very much an old-school expository documentary which focused upon aspects of Irish culture that lent themselves to pleasurable exploitation while also assuring potential visitors (and, in general terms, investors and industrial concerns) that the country was changing. The irony is that these values (and images) were being commodified and stratified within an economic infrastructure where 'the tourism industry' was itself a capitalist cultural and political entity concerned with the manufacture and distribution of 'Ireland'.

Ireland Invites You was even more explicit in its appeal to capitalism. Intended as a guide for travel agents, the film not only promoted particular aspects of Ireland's countryside and city pleasures for the consumption of international visitors, it gave prices. The film was commissioned by Bord Fáilte and directed by Jim Mulkerns. Advertising a range of prepackaged tours and accommodation deals from which travel agents might select in promoting the country as a holiday destination, the voice over, spoken by Bart Bastable, breathlessly detailed the deals most likely to appeal to clients. Beginning relatively gently with references to Ireland as a 'gem of rare beauty' and familiar sentiments such as 'Ireland of the soft-spoken, friendly people. Ireland of the one hundred thousand welcomes', accompanied by the expected rural imagery and vaguely Irish music, the film becomes an assault on the ears as Bastable launches into a listing of prices, options and packages at a speed which virtually overwhelms all attempts to record them.

Other promotional films advanced different causes, but with no less of a sense that a new Ireland was emerging, one in which progress was the watchword. The themes were the same, but the tone was changing. *Gold in the Grass* (1964) was an unusually scientific argument in favour of the modernisation of Irish agriculture. *Life for the Soil* (1966) was a less detailed variant on the same theme with an emphasis on peat production, sponsored by Bord na Móna. *The Harvest is Rich* (1966) dealt with the commercial fishing industry, and was sponsored by an Bord Iascaigh Mhara. The land, though evidently a site of touristic pleasure, was also a centre for industrial production, and films such as these made that explicit. Other films blended culture and history with the needs of the evolving infrastructure. *Celtic Gold* (1966) was a film with some docudrama sequences showcasing the National Museum of Ireland's collection of jewellery and other objects of Celtic origin. *Crystal Clear* (date uncertain – 1960s), meanwhile, was among the first films to showcase Waterford Glass as an exemplar of the fusion of traditional crafts and modern industry. The film recounted the history of the company, but also detailed the production process by which glass is skilfully blown and crafted into exportable art objects. One film even made use of one of Irish documentary's most hallowed subjects – the missionary role of the church – to promote the cause of pro-European investment. *Saints Went Marching Out* (1967), sponsored by the Department of Foreign Affairs and partly produced by George Fleischmann, made the unashamedly neo-colonial argument that because Irish missionaries had traditionally played an important part in civil-ising the world and had always had close connections with Europe (where Irish priests were often trained, and of course the Vatican was located), Irish people should not be afraid of doing business with Europe or of becoming part of the European Union.

There were also Dublin films, as there had always been, but in the 1960s they began to take on a new theme – James Joyce as a guide to the city. Several Joyce-themed films, including *The City of James Joyce* (1963) and *James Joyce's Dublin* (1968), were made during this period. The foregrounding of Joyce was an indication of change because Joyce was formerly such a controversial figure that he did not previously feature in films of this kind. Only one of these films is worth singling out. *Faithful Departed* (1967) was a portrait of the city as depicted in the writings of Joyce and seen by turn-of-the-century photographer Robert French. Combining French's images of the period in which *Ulysses* (1922) was set with extracts from the book read by actor Jack MacGowran, the film attempted to give a sense of the time, place and people now passed into the realm of the 'faithful departed'. Though not uninteresting in its attempts to give a sense of context for the appreciation of Joyce's Dublin through reference to important world events in 1904 and some nods to social conditions, the film was still quite touristic. It was notable however for its elegance and economy, and for introducing the talents of director Kieran Hickey, who would become a significant figure in the subsequent emergence of an independent indigenous Irish fiction film industry in the 1970s and early 1980s before his death in 1993.

Faithful Departed was financed by Hickey's own production company, BAC Films, which he established with partners Sean Corcoran and Pat Duffner upon returning to Ireland after training at the London Film School. In this he, like Carey, was among the first of the new generation of young, professionally educated filmmakers who began to work in Ireland at this time (though Hickey was one of the few to attend an actual film school). Hickey would go on to other documentaries including *Jonathan Swift* (1967), *The Heritage of Ireland* (1974), a Bord Fáilte-sponsored film on historical architecture not to be confused with Louis Marcus's series of the same name, and a fifty-minute extension of *Faithful Departed*, *The Light of Other Days* (1971), which tackled the same era of Irish history and again used the work of Robert French and other photographs from the William Lawrence Collection at the National Library of Ireland. Stylistically, both *Faithful Departed* and *The Light of Other Days* are similar to *City of Gold* (1957), using pans and zooms to heighten the drama of static scenes and drawing attention to details. Many critics singled this out for praise, though it had been done in *Mise Éire* (1959) ten years earlier. Hickey was also hired to make promotional films, such as *Motorway to Ireland* (1969), sponsored by the ferry company B & I Line and intended for foreign distribution. This would become a pattern at this time, where a young and energetic filmmaker would produce work essentially as a means to get further employment. This consolidated the basis of the independent sector, though it did not necessarily evince stylistic or thematic evolution.

One of the genuine oddities of the early 1960s, but one which also grew out of familiar subject matter and gave a fascinating insight into the 'new' Ireland, was *The One-Nighters* (1963). The film followed the adventures of the popular Royal Showband on tour. Documentaries on musical performers were not uncommon at this time. Roman Kroitor and Wolf Koenig had already produced *Lonely Boy* (1961), a portrait of pop singer Paul Anka, and the late 1960s would see an explosion of similar films. What was interesting about *The One-Nighters* was its preempting of Richard Lester's *A Hard Day's Night* (1964) in its depiction of its subjects as a group of happy-go-lucky 'kids' with clearly defined semi-comic personae. The film played upon the relationship between the boys and their manager and featured scenes of hysterical fans hounding them as they attempt to secure hotel accommodation and other true-to-life but clearly 'fictionalised' incidents. It was photographed and edited by Robert Monks and directed by Peter Collinson, a British-born floor manager working at Telefís Éireann at the time. The film presented a very lively and contemporary portrait of the music scene in Ireland, which though later the subject of a nostalgic retrospective *Good Night, Safe Home and God Bless* (1998), was relatively contentious in its time.

Dance halls had been enormously controversial throughout the preceding decades, vehemently opposed by the church and the subject of many sermons and encyclicals decrying the lapse in moral standards they represented. A Dance Halls Act was passed in 1935 which introduced the supervision of dance venues in response to clerical pressure. That *The One-Nighters* would portray the world of the Irish dance hall was therefore interesting in and of itself. Even more interesting though is the way the film was careful to emphasise the 'traditional' values represented by the Royal Showband. The depiction of music in Irish documentaries to date had been limited to displays of rurality associated with tourist films, where 'lovely colleens' might burst into song at any moment. Traditional music had been represented also in terms of 'exotic' subject matter, remembering that it was only at this time that Seán Ó Riada had begun his serious attempts to organise and revitalise the genre.

The Royal Showband was representative of a more 'modern' type of Irish music, and yet its continuity with previous varieties was evident. Band members are shown going home to their families at night, and are 'captured' discussing the importance of family life over a friendly card game on their tour bus. The film was relatively challenging in its foregrounding of the music of Elvis Presley and other American performers still falling outside the

11 *The One-Nighters* (1963), Peter Collinson's playful documentary of the Royal Showband on tour, was one of the genuine oddities of the 1960s. Released one year before *A Hard Day's Night* (1964), it demonstrated some of Richard Lester's stylistic flair in depicting the lives of these 'ordinary' boys as a series of quasi-documentary adventures. Significantly though, these nice Irish boys showed deference to authority and family values at all times, even when performing 'risqué' music such as Elvis Presley hits

rubric of 'acceptable' entertainment for good Catholic boys and girls, but it was also careful to point out how the band incorporated more traditional songs like 'Danny Boy' into their routines, as well as their own original compositions. The film attempts to give a sense of the busy fun of the band's lifestyle, while curiously reminding audiences that this is a uniquely 'Irish' group of lads who perform in halls run by priests and who travel home at night to their wives and children.

It was nonetheless quite an iconoclastic film, and attempted to match form to content with an infectious and cheeky tone. It opens with an image of horses tied to a fence and of Irish fields and hills with a voice over commenting on how Ireland was the land of folklore and legend. It then abruptly cuts to images of the band in performance, replete with Dutch angles, rapid editing and loud music in deliberate contrast to the peaceful rural idyll previously shown. The film concludes with an equally emblematic image of cows being driven across the open road upon which the tour bus has been seen travelling, another commentary upon the traditional Ireland from which the film is eager to be seen to be breaking away. It seems initially like a cross between the type of films made in Britain as part of the Free Cinema movement and a more traditional musical biography. Sequences of the band preparing for their show in their dressing room and working their way to the stage through throngs of fans have the feeling of observational documentary. Later scenes of them travelling around the countryside on their tour bus and having difficulties registering at a rural hotel are more contrived, as are the scenes where the different members of the band go to different types of shops which delineate their 'personalities'. While they are clearly comfortable performing on stage and playing to the camera on the street, when the camera gets close to them during a stage performance several of them give it suspicious and vaguely irritated glances which give momentary insight into the sub *cinéma vérité* nature of at least some of the filming.

The One-Nighters was screened at the Cork Film Festival in 1963, where it received a certificate of merit. Collinson later went on to make fiction films including the comedy *Up the Junction* (1967) and the legendary *The Italian Job* (1969) with Michael Caine, before his death in 1980. Photographer and editor Robert Monks went on to become one of Ireland's leading camera operators and chairman of the Society of Independent Film Makers. He worked extensively with Louis Marcus and Gael-Linn, and also photographed the CBS documentary *Look Up and Live: Ireland in Transition* (1965) before directing *Ireland – The New Convention Country*. *The One-Nighters* was not quite the kind of penetrating social critique seen in British Free Cinema, nor was it the pure observation of direct cinema. It was not a modernist farce in the manner of *A Hard Day's Night*, nor was it a particularly revealing look at show business and its personalities like *Lonely Boy*. It was something of a hybrid of all of these things, and a lively and entertaining film of a kind not previously seen in Irish documentary. It is all the more remarkable for its uniqueness, as few subsequent films would attempt anything close to its sense of humour until *The Road to God Knows Where* (1988).

RTÉ and the winds of change

Telefís Éireann joined with its radio equivalent in 1967 and was renamed Radio Telefís Éireann (RTÉ). The organisation offered new opportunities for employment and for non-fiction film to reach a general audience. As a public service broadcaster it was required to have news and information programmes. A number of the films discussed above were screened on television, though many were also screened in cinemas and film societies and distributed internationally as educational aids or news items. Throughout its years of broadcasting, Irish television has been replete with news and current affairs programmes, and with many short journalistic reports which are used to illustrate issues in both formats. The majority of non-fiction material produced for television is either directly financed by RTÉ or produced in conjunction with British or other European broadcasters. In the 1960s, independent operators like Gael-Linn and Radharc Films did make contributions, but an organised system of commissioning independent production did not begin for some decades, and then only on direct orders from the state. As a result the environment which had fostered the growth of American direct cinema did not really exist in Ireland. Consequently, the type of non-fiction featured on Irish television throughout its first decades was limited largely to in-house informational material with little critical insight.

One of the few examples still extant is *Men for the Harvest* (1963), a profile of St Patrick's Seminary, Maynooth which dealt with the lives of postulants in training to become Catholic priests. Like *Silent Order* (1948) and the many films produced by religious orders on their missionary activities, *Men for the Harvest* was uncritical of the institution of the church. Directed by BBC veteran Chloe Gibson, who had been hired by RTÉ because of her experience in broadcasting, it charted in detail the daily rituals of prayer and study undergone by the students. The film emphasises history and tradition through footage of the paraphernalia of a long-established institution and the constant use of images of collectivity, showing students working in groups rather than as individuals. Like many of the films of its time, *Men for the Harvest* was more an exercise in documentary making than a film exhibiting genuine feeling for recording and exploring the historical world.

The lack of penetration of subjects became the defining feature of Irish television documentary, with some notable exceptions to which we will return later. As the political and religious scandals of the late 1990s illustrated, another Ireland lurked beneath the placid exterior. RTÉ nonetheless contributed to the climate of change simply by virtue of recording events that demonstrated change in progress. One of the places in which this was most evident was the television chat show *The Late Late Show*. Indicative perhaps of a culture which had grown out of a strong oral tradition, an idea we have already explored, most of the interrogation of the new Ireland on television took place on this programme. Originally pitched as a televisual update of the traditional fireside chat, *The Late Late Show* went on the air in July 1962. Always popular and frequently controversial, it became the centre of major public outcry three times in the space of a few months in 1966, not for what its presenter, Gay Byrne, said, or for any stance taken by the programme over any particular issue, but simply because controversial individuals appeared and expressed their views.

The first case surrounded Playboy executive Victor Lownes, who appeared on the show to promote the opening of Playboy clubs in Britain. The second was centred on an apparently innocent question asked about what colour nightdress a woman wore on her wedding night, to which her reply was that she had worn none at all. The bishop of Clonfert responded angrily to what he saw as objectionable and debasing television, and the entire affair became a major public scandal. The final *furor* was over college student Brian Trevaskis, who made a claim later taken up by Peter Lennon in *Rocky Road to Dublin* that the ideals of the 1916 proclamation had not been lived up to in the current, bourgeois Ireland. He also referred to the bishop of Galway as 'a moron' for insisting on spending money on Galway Cathedral instead of helping the poor.[5] In a sense though, the casual nature of this technologically refigured fireside chat reinforced Ireland's obsession with the 'talking cure' of 'oral history', and disabled more sustained and challenging documentary analysis of many of the same issues.

Trevaskis made his pronouncements on *The Late Late Show* as 1916 commemorations were in progress, and they ran contrary to the swell of patriotism evident in films such as *Irish Rising 1916* (1966) and *An Tine Bheo* (1966), both previously discussed. The most interesting film made by RTÉ during this period also questioned some of the more unproblematic assumptions about 1916 and its legacy. The docudrama *Insurrection* (1966) was originally broadcast as part of the celebrations, but while demonstrating the expected respect for the martyrs of the rising, the film attempted to deconstruct elements of its mythology. Taking its cue from Peter Watkins's *Culloden* (1964), this six-part series written by Irish author and playwright Hugh Leonard was a reconstruction of the events of 1916 which combined 'live' footage with commentary in a television studio by a news anchorman played by actor Ray McAnally. It charts events from just before the rising to the aftermath of the surrender, and encompasses a broad range of both famous and obscure moments. Scenes take place at various points throughout the city, and the participants are not always well-known historical figures. Dialogue is mostly in English, though there are snatches of Irish. The musical score by A. J. Potter again reflects the influence of Seán Ó Riada in applying traditional airs with lush orchestration, but the music is largely restricted to the credit sequence and some incidentals. The series was shot on a mixture of film and videotape, and use was made of RTÉ's Outside Broadcasting Unit for location scenes.

Though not as stylistically radical as *Culloden* (the series did not really use the conceit of being contemporaneous reportage as McAnally did not pretend that events were 'in progress'), it was groundbreaking for Irish television. *Insurrection* was also challenging on a political level as it reassessed many of the myths of 1916 and deglamourised the conflict with hard-edged realism. Its depiction of the bloody battles was not so much that of heroic warriors and poets yearning for a Free Ireland as of tired and frightened men, sometimes borderline psychopaths (on both sides), engaged in a violent struggle for supremacy. It did not perpetuate the myth of blood sacrifice, emphasising instead the misinformation which led the rebels to believe they had widespread support and that reinforcements were on the way as they held out under siege. Though it saluted the bravery of the Irish, it was unusually evenhanded in its portrayal of the British armed forces. It depicted, for example, a growing respect between a British medic trapped in the GPO and wounded rebel commander James Connolly. It even managed to include sequences depicting disapproval among ordinary Irish people of what the rebels were doing. One scene features actor Anna Manahan portraying a typical Irish mother, wearing a shawl, her children swarming at her feet, speaking to the camera as if she were being interviewed. She complains about the disturbance being caused, and the shocking disloyalty to the crown being displayed, and concludes by defiantly singing 'God Save the King'.

The series reflects a then rare willingness to question the prevailing attitudes to Irish history. It proved, along with Brian Trevaskis's comments on *The Late Late Show* and the later, more explicit assault upon the 1916 generation in *Rocky Road to Dublin*, that at least some voices of protest were being raised against orthodoxy, isolated though those voices may have been. Most importantly though *Insurrection* was also a reaction to the form with which the prevailing hegemony had been represented. Its shifts between conventional dramatic reconstruction and studio commentary demonstrated self-awareness and drew attention to the process of dramatic construction. This worked alongside the historical debate to problematise assumptions about both Irish history and its recording. *Insurrection* seemed to promise a development in non-fiction form which unfortunately did not continue.

Radharc

Television did begin to have an impact on the scope of social documentary, but under the auspices of independent producers. Probably the most important was Fr Joseph Dunn, the latest in a line of filmmaking priests contributing religious-themed documentaries to Irish non-fiction. We have already examined the work of Fr Browne, but there were many other amateur filmmaking clergy active throughout both the early years of Irish cinema and right through to the 1960s when the activities of Radharc Films set a new standard. Amateur enthusiasts like Fr Jackie Moran and Fr Tommy Doran became respected enough to earn commissions and prizes, and to use their work for fundraising or promotional purposes, while yet more like them simply recorded events and scenes from community life throughout the country.[6] In common with his predecessors, Dunn began making films on an amateur basis, but, like Kieran Hickey and others of the emerging generation, he also received professional training. His work on the *Radharc* television programme for more than thirty years was a significant contribution to the medium. Writing in *Film Ireland* following Fr Dunn's death, former colleague Peter Kelly observed:

Radharc played an important part in the Ireland of the 1960s, stimulating public debate as Ireland opened up to the outside world. And in that big open world, Joe Dunn was also there leading the Radharc Team. While the Irish TV audience watched documentaries about religious issues in far-flung places in the world, what Joe Dunn was actually showing them was religious issues about themselves. Joe often spoke about his foreign documentaries being parables and metaphors about the Irish church scene. (Kelly, 1996: 25)

This interpretation of the work of Radharc corresponds with the position adopted by the church leading up to the foundation of Telefís Éireann. Rather than making specific representation to the government regarding the direction Irish television should take, the hierarchy was notably silent during the public debate. They did tacitly support the application made by outspoken Catholic Charles Michelson to the Television Commission, and there was an extraordinary suggestion from the Vatican that Ireland should become the Catholic anti-communist propaganda centre for the whole of Europe if Michelson's pan-European radio broadcasting system was approved,[7] but by and large Archbishop John Charles McQuaid awaited the decision of the government in the knowledge that it was still to a large degree guided by instinctual deference to him and to the church.

McQuaid was nonetheless aware that television was coming. Even before the government had made its mind up on the issue he was prepared. In 1959 (a year before the Broadcasting Act, two years before Telefís Éireann began operations) he asked Dunn to attend a course on television production being run by the BBC in Manchester. His hope was that Dunn would be able to advise television producers on the religious content of potential programmes. Dunn later attended a more comprehensive course in New York along with another priest, Des Forristal, and when the two men returned they began making amateur films. Their first attempt, *Lá 'le Bríde* (celebrating St Brigid's Day, the first day of spring), won a National Film Institute of Ireland award for outstanding Irish-language film in 1960.

Radharc was the umbrella title given to a regular series of documentaries on disparate topics from homelessness (*Down and Out in Dublin*, 1964) to African missionaries (subject of five separate documentaries shot during one trip to Kenya in 1965) to prostitution (*Open Port*, 1968); the latter filmed partly with hidden cameras – a technique previously employed by George Fleischmann in response to conditions which also necessitated it. Despite the presence of secular current affairs programmes, *Radharc* was the series with the most pronounced ability to examine social institutions. This was probably as much because institutions and individuals were reluctant to be inhospitable towards a Catholic priest. Dunn was therefore able to examine aspects of the emerging new Irish society untouched by other broadcasters, including making the first film inside an Irish prison, *The Young Offender* (1963), in which he was able to put some telling questions to then Minister for Justice Charles J. Haughey, who agreed to appear on the programme only if shown their filmed report on the prison before he was interviewed. As Pettitt records, *Radharc* also broke the taboo on documentaries about Northern Ireland with a film on inequalities within politics in Derry city in 1964 (Pettitt, 2000: 84–5). RTÉ refused to broadcast the programme because the subject was deemed 'too sensitive'.

Radharc films were inevitably coloured by their insistence on a religious dimension and were largely less than critical of domestic social and political institutions than the exceptional individual titles above would suggest. Like the standard rhetorical documentary, these were problem–solution films in which the solution was inevitably some recourse to faith or Catholic social teaching and the problem was rarely the result of domestic social inequalities or government policy. It was more likely to be 'human' weakness which could be redressed through spiritual counsel. Yet the very fact that *Radharc* managed to touch upon sensitive topics at all (sometimes with a surprisingly humorous edge) meant that subsequent filmmakers would be less intimidated by them, and this is important. Writing in *Vision*, Antoinette T. Fortune observed that *Radharc* was singular among contemporary Irish documentary series for its ability to tackle meaningful subjects. She noted, 'it has apparently, simply, and certainly unpretentiously, evoked the real spirit of Ireland; Ireland past and present, Ireland urban and rural. Radharc has shown one half of Ireland how the other half lives' (Fortune, 1965: 26). Her use of the phrase made famous by Jacob Riis is a reminder of the position occupied by the public service broadcaster in society, and she was not alone in remarking that of all of RTÉ's output, this independently produced series was the most penetrative, and the one with the most conscience about its role in society. Pettitt concurs: 'Joe Dunn was a maverick and a humane priest who astutely helped to produce a body of films that niggled and probed Irish society' (Pettitt, 2000: 83).

Dunn was an unpretentious and humorous man. His book, *No Tigers in Africa!* (1986) is illustrated with his own witty cartoons and his writing reveals him to be both self-aware and self-effacing. Yet as with any of the filmmaking clergy active before him and since, all of his work was tempered by his devotion to religious principles. He saw documentary film as part of a project of enlightenment. Effectively, it was his pulpit from which he delivered sermons. He was an ordained priest and in good standing with the hierarchy, but he was not a parish priest and did not write academic theology. He was under no illusions about the role of television in society or his place as a maker of television programmes; as he remarked himself, 'one of my core beliefs is that television broadcasting – the area to which I have given most of my working life – has been a very significant agent of change; change to which society in general and the church in particular have so far found great difficulty in adapting. Radharc programmes have inevitably helped to chronicle some of these changes' (Dunn, 1994: 7). It is interesting that he saw himself in the role of chronicler rather than advocate, a mere observer shedding light on human experience to further the cause of human knowledge in the name of God.

Despite his sincerity, like Fr Browne before him, Fr Joseph Dunn was working within a set of determinates predefined by the church. Though Dunn's technical competence was vastly superior to Browne's, *Radharc* avowedly and unashamedly promoted Christian principles. Thus while its social conscience was evident and while the series did chronicle (and investigate) the changes taking place in Irish society, like the government-sponsored films before it, *Radharc* operated wholly within the domain of dominant discourse. Dunn could be critical of the church and of institutions, but his invective was always tempered by respect, and, as he said himself, 'so if I am sometimes critical of the captain and crew, it's my ship as well, and I am sticking with it' (Dunn, 1994: 9).

Gael-Linn and Louis Marcus

Having failed in its bid to run the national television service, Gael-Linn persisted in sponsoring documentaries throughout the 1960s and 1970s. The production of *Amharc Éireann* continued until 1964, at which time their support for one-off films intensified. These could be exhibited theatrically and also sold to RTÉ, making Gael-Linn an independent producer even though its work was partly grant-aided. The films it sponsored may be seen as something of a secular equivalent to *Radharc* (though the volume was considerably smaller), in this case promoting the values and virtues of speaking Irish (another long-held priority of de Valera's Ireland taking on a new complexion in the age of Lemass). Gael-Linn films inevitably turned to the Irish language as medium and message, and regardless of subject matter, they made it seem a 'natural' element of everyday Irish life (which, increasingly, it was not). Ironically, the organisation was itself the subject of a BBC Wales documentary in 1966 which held its activities up as a model for efforts to preserve and promote the Welsh language.

Louis Marcus was the most obvious beneficiary of Gael-Linn's activity during this period. Beginning with his work for this organisation, his career spanned the remainder of the twentieth century. Marcus was born in Cork in 1936 and became a member of the Irish Film Society while still in his teens. The experience of watching films quickly turned to a desire to make them, and he worked as an assistant to George Morrison on *Mise Éire*, and actually directed the film's theatrical trailer. Shortly thereafter Marcus directed his own first film, *The Silent Art* (1959), a profile of sculptor Seamus Murphy, also a member of the Cork Film Society with which Marcus was affiliated. Marcus concedes that the film was little more than a showreel, financed by his mother and shot on 16 mm film bought through a local pharmacy. It nonetheless succeeded in getting him attention. He worked as an editor on *Saoirse?* and was then hired by Gael-Linn to direct a series of films on different topics. These were usually distributed with both English-language and Irish-language soundtracks. The English version was intended for international distribution only. Most of the scripts were written by Brendán Ó hEithir, and though spoken English was allowed, it was to appear only as it did in the profilmic, as natural sound rather than as language. One of the earliest of these films was *Peil* (1962), a profile of Gaelic football which presented the sport as an integral part of indigenous Irish culture. This was immediately followed by *Christy Ring* (1963), a popular tribute to a much-loved Cork-born GAA star.

After a brief stint in Israel where he attended a course run by American filmmaker Carl Foreman (then living in exile following his refusal to cooperate with the House Un-American Activities Committee), Marcus returned to work for Gael-Linn on the government-sponsored *Rhapsody of a River* (1965), a portrait of Cork's River Lee and the industrial and agrarian life along its banks. Marcus was unhappy with *Rhapsody of a River* for various reasons. Though he was interested in making a film about Cork and particularly pleased with the musical score composed by Sean Ó Riada, he resented the interference by the Department of External Affairs. Speaking later about the film, Marcus observed, 'everyone had to have something: a bit of agriculture, a bit of electricity, a bit of industry, and so on. Technically it is a beautifully shot film, the music is gorgeous and it allowed me to improve my editing skills. But it is totally and absolutely without heart' (cited in McIlroy, 1988: 121). What might perhaps have been Ireland's equivalent to *The River* (1936) was eventually a tourist film virtually indistinguishable from countless others.

Despite his frustration, Marcus continued to collaborate with Gael-Linn. Following the 1916 commemoration film *An Tine Bheo*, he directed his most famous film, *Fleá* (1967).[8] The film documented a traditional music festival held in Kilrush, County Clare using observational techniques. It was closer to a true *cinéma vérité* film (as opposed to the faux *vérité* of *The One-Nighters* or the associational poetry of Patrick Carey). Though there was a voice over (written by Brendán Ó hEithir), the film communicated in visual terms through judicious selection of raw actuality and artful editing. In contrast to the artificial sense of culture used by previous and later tourist films, *Fleá* presented Irish music as a specific, living and vital element of everyday life. It managed to convey the impression that traditional music was a unifying force in contemporary Ireland, bringing crowds of people together in informal settings (mostly pubs) to celebrate things they enjoyed (both drinking and music – the film is not shy about establishing the relationship between them). The opening voice over informs us, 'it is the music which gathers the people', and this is the message reinforced throughout the film despite its veneer of observational objectivity.

The film was shot over the two and a half days of the festival. A mixture of synchronous and non-synchronous sound footage was shot by Marcus, Robert Monks, Nick O'Neill and Réne de Clercq. The activity in the town was clearly frenetic, and Marcus and his camera operators waded among the revellers (very much as their counterparts elsewhere in the world had been doing for most of the decade) in an attempt to get closer to the authentic experience of reality. Among the material shot were scenes of specific bands or groups playing organised events in the streets of Kilrush, but also the more informal, improvisational sessions which took place inside the town's many public houses. Handwritten signs on public and private house windows offered food and refreshments, pints of Guinness filled the countertops as eager hands grasped one only to have it replaced instantaneously by another. People young and old took part, famous and anonymous, and Marcus succeeded in capturing all of them with the most unselfconscious camera hitherto seen in Irish documentary.

There had already been *vox populi* pieces on RTÉ programmes like *Newsbeat*, where reporter Frank Hall (later film censor) would travel the country and casually interview ordinary passersby in the manner of the early French experiments in *cinéma vérité*. As noted in regard to the earliest filmed images of Irish people, there was also a level of awareness of the camera in Irish life which may have come from the extent to which Ireland and the Irish had been pictorially represented throughout the centuries. As Fr Joe Dunn remarked of filming the homeless for *Down and Out in Dublin*, 'when the novelty of seeing cameras and microphones had worn off and people understood what we were at, they tended to forget their inhibitions and say what they thought' (Dunn, 1986: 44–5). In spite of this, Hall's delivery style on *Newsbeat* was very self-conscious. He practically winked at the camera as he interviewed strange or interesting individuals about local or national affairs in an attempt to gauge the 'authentic' reaction of the 'ordinary' Irish person. Marcus eschewed this style of psuedo-altruistic journalism in *Fleá*, and through careful selection and editing created the desired *cinéma vérité* impression of invisibility while nonetheless obviously betraying a great deal of behind-the-scenes organisation.

One particular editing technique employed frequently was the extension of the moment through intercutting different individuals involved in the same act at different stages. For example, one sequence depicts the serving and drinking of pints by beginning with one image of a pint being pulled, another of it being placed, another of one person taking it, another of a different person drinking followed by a third person further along in their drink, and so on. There are several examples of this throughout the film. This accomplishes two things. Firstly it illustrates the ritual or event itself by representing it. Secondly it suggests both the uniformity and the universality of the activity in the town, linking disparate individuals taking part in the same act, just as the film on the whole depicts large numbers of people gathered together for a common event. This is quite a Vertovian idea, which is

12 *Fleá* (1967) was a *cinéma vérité*-style portrait of the traditional Irish music festival held that year in Kilrush, Co. Clare. This popular film won a number of international awards, including a Silver Bear at the Berlin Film Festival. Pictured here is singer Dolly MacMahon

entirely appropriate given *cinéma vérité*'s acknowledged debt to Vertov. It gives *Fleá* a very unified formal structure, as Marcus is able to link sequence after sequence in this manner and never creates a sense of disorder despite the impression of busyness. It is an embodiment of the technique observed by Barsam, 'the presentation of disparate material as if it were equivalent; the resultant ambiguity creates the illusion of reality itself' (Barsam, 1992: 304).

Fleá created a sense of the spontaneous through a careful arrangement of the profilmic, and thereby encapsulates the paradox of *cinéma vérité* perfectly. It managed to seem natural and unpremeditated, fluid and pacy, yet it was not only an organised structural text, but a specific (and even explicit) statement about the presence and importance of native culture (and the native tongue) in contemporary Ireland. It was clearly a step forward for both the form of Irish documentary and the potential reach of the medium as a method of both investigating and projecting an image of Ireland. It is interesting that music as a subject had brought about this change, and with *The One-Nighters* and *Fleá* representing two diverse musical styles in radical forms, it almost seems as though this was an unconscious response to the power of Ó Riada's score for *Mise Éire*, which had been such a voice for traditionalism.

Marcus completed a double blow in the name of the film industry in the same year when he wrote a series of polemical articles in *The Irish Times* later published in pamphlet form by the Irish Film Society. He was giving voice to the frustrations of a number of independent filmmakers, particularly in fiction, a situation amply discussed by Rockett, McLoone and Pettitt. Conditions were difficult for fiction filmmakers at this time in a market glutted by British and American films which represented an image of Ireland increasingly unacceptable to the younger generation. Few indigenous feature-length fiction films were being produced, and in spite of considerable government investment in an Irish film studio in County Wicklow in 1958, the situation was grim. Despite what was clearly quite an active documentary industry, the possibilities were limited for independent production. It was still difficult for a dissenting voice to be heard through the conservatism of both the form and subject matter of Irish documentary films.

Only one of Marcus's polemical articles was specifically focused on documentary, where he argued for much greater funding for educational and instructional films free of interference from the sponsors (obviously echoing his frustrations on *Rhapsody of a River*). To a certain extent his reading of the situation was idealistic (and not necessarily all that new), but on another level he was finally giving voice to the emergent generation of nonconforming filmmakers eager to test the boundaries of the medium and of Irish society itself. He did at least acknowledge that there were problems with finding a voice for Irish documentary, though he directed the blame towards the government and towards the system of sponsorship rather than questioning the sensibility of the filmmakers.

He was not alone in his pessimism. Alf MacLochlainn offered a critique of documentary form based upon a history of the Griersonian tradition and upon specific analysis of the films of Robert Flaherty entitled 'Documentary is Dead'. MacLochlainn seems to have been largely unaware of *cinéma vérité* and direct cinema in his condemnation of rhetorical form, which he considered to be the whole of documentary. He concluded by saying, 'let us not debase the word documentary by using it as catch-all, when it has a perfectly clear meaning in describing the exciting and beautiful products of a movement which was of great importance – but which is very dead' (MacLochlainn, 1966: 13). There was a general feeling that documentary films were a moribund relic of a form of communication which had lost its ability to participate in the ongoing development of the country. Despite the work of *Radharc*, which had, as noted, received high praise, non-fiction was being perceived as either a tool of advertisers or the domain of current affairs broadcasting. This latter was itself subject to criticism, as noted earlier because of the government's assumption that their mandate over the state broadcaster included their right to control its output.

In counterpoint to this view, Marcus argued, using points startlingly similar to those made by Grierson two decades earlier (and quoted in Chapter 3), that documentary was uniquely placed to advance the representation of Ireland as a medium of self-exploration as well as of self-promotion, allowing it both to give Ireland sight of itself and give others a sight of Ireland. His reading of the situation of Irish documentarists was obviously coloured by that of fiction film, as the culturally powerful countries to which he referred in the pejorative (the US and the UK) had only limited interest in non-fiction. Now that RTÉ was broadcasting regular news and public affairs programmes, Irish audiences were not dependent on weekly British newsreels or one-off CBS documentaries for their exposure to Irish documentary material. There was a point to his argument, however, insofar as he successfully identified the increasing tendency to entrust *all* non-fiction to RTÉ, turning documentary production into an offshoot of the tourist industry, making it, in Gibbons's words, 'a cottage industry' (Gibbons, 1996: 43) rather than an active and vital force in contemporary society.

As far as Marcus's career was concerned, *Fleá* was enormously successful both domestically and abroad. The film won the Silver Bear at the Berlin Film Festival in 1967, a diploma of honour at the Moscow Film Festival (where Marcus noted with irony how *Pravda* had held it up as an example to the Russian film industry of how to authentically represent the ordinary people), and the critics award at La Felguera Catholic Film Festival in Spain. Perhaps most significantly, the film was also nominated for an Oscar in

1968. While *Yeats Country* had also achieved this distinction, Carey had a previous pedigree from his UK and Canadian work. *Fleá* was also a more contemporary film than *Yeats Country*, both in style and content. Its recognition by so many international bodies validated its approach to its subject and promised a new intellectual and technical energy for Irish documentary cinema. Afterwards, however, Marcus became increasingly less critical and analytical and turned his skills instead to expositional and informational short subjects with little evident polemical value. He became among the first victims of careerism in Irish documentary, settling for less than his first efforts promised in the face of the necessity to keep working. Only *Capallology* (1968) evinced even a trace of the invective and political commitment promised by his written attack upon the forces of cultural production. The film gently lampooned the Irish attitude to the horse, particularly its fetishisation at the Royal Dublin Society's annual show (a regular feature of so many tourist documentaries).

Marcus directed one other noteworthy film for Gael-Linn: *Dubliners Sean agus Nua* (1971). This film also contained a trace of the critical voice of the author of *The Irish Film Industry*, though it was also a statement of Gael-Linn's own concern with the Irish language. It used the English language ironically to create a sense of contrast between 'traditional' and contemporary Dublin. The film juxtaposed old-fashioned images of the city and its denizens with contemporary ones and argued, in response to the Bord Fáilte films, that 'It is not a museum we have here, but a city which is motoring'. A voice actor portraying a 'typical' old Dubliner spoke in heavily accented, caricatured English about 'the good auld days' and the film attempted to present a modern image of the city which would liberate it from the clichés. It may be seen as something of a rejoinder to tourist pieces like *See You at the Pillar* (1967) in this respect, and it is certainly an improvement on that film, but in employing stereotypes and foregrounding its sense of humour rather than the anger we might expect from the author of *The Irish Film Industry*, Marcus's piece falls victim to its own subject and remains little more analytical than the average Irish historical documentary. It is unable to escape the mantle of the past, and by wallowing in it, even for the purposes of parody, it fails to advance the debate to a new level.

A sobering counterpoint to Marcus's efforts came in the form of *Capital City: Dublin 1974-1975* (1974), a striking film directed by Jim Mulkerns on behalf of the Labour party. Like *Our Country*, it was a self-conscious agit-prop, but it took a completely different form. Mulkerns began working with the Labour party in 1968, when he was approached to direct a twelve-minute promotional film. Noted for his thrift and efficiency, Mulkerns developed a close friendship with the party's general secretary, and made several more such films in the course of the next few years. *Capital City 1974–1975* was produced as part of Labour's election campaign, but it was not intended for public exhibition. It was to be shown to selected groups of people including members of the Dáil, Dublin City Council and Bord Fáilte, and was to be a rejoinder to the cheerfully vapid image of the city being preferred so widely at the time.

With footage scraped together from leftover stock from previous commissions, Mulkerns and his perennial collaborator Val Ennis shot this seventeen-minute film for about £50. It consists of a montage of images of urban decay: crumbling buildings, boarded-up shopfronts, filthy streets strewn with rubbish, temporary walls adorned with half-torn posters, glum, grainy, smoggy shots of well-known and obscure streets in the city not far from the paths usually trod by tourists. It made use of specific juxtaposition such as intercutting between advertising hoardings selling the more usual image of Ireland (alcohol, Aer Lingus, a 'discover Ireland' exhibition) and the broken windows, corroded statues and rotting woodwork which illustrated the current state of all too much of the Irish living space. Though silent, it was provided with a score by Joe Doherty, using excerpts from Jerry Goldsmith's *Planet of the Apes.* This gave the visuals an added dimension of otherworldliness and alienation. The film was edited at Radharc Films' facilities, which were given over for use free of charge by Fr Joe Dunn.

Though a social document in one sense of the term, *Capital City 1974–1975* is especially interesting as a work of landscape portraiture in that it, like the more romantic and rural images more usually discussed, absented human habitation. Of course the actual point of most of these images was that no one *could* live in these places, and, furthermore, that some people did, or at least lived nearby. It is ironic that this film never received theatrical exhibition at the time of its making, though it has been shown in retrospectives. While *Dubliners Sean agus Nua* was seen both at home and abroad (albeit with slightly different commentary tracks), this film, like *Portrait of Dublin*, *Radharc in Derry* and *Rocky Road to Dublin* before it, and later *The Family* (1978) and *Our Boys* (1981), would have to remain another example of the muted voice of genuine political radicalism in an age where 'progress' was a question of packaging.

For his part, Louis Marcus went on to become probably the most important commercial documentarist in Ireland in the 1970s. He made some other interesting films, even if they lacked a critical social voice. *Páistí ag Obair* (1973) was a fascinating insight into the thought processes of young children as they learn through play, and was also nominated for an Oscar. *Conquest of Light* (1975) was a beautifully photographed poem to the artisans of Waterford Crystal which influenced several others on the subject. Marcus remained the focus for a great deal of writing, and was named 'the Moses of

13 Louis Marcus (right) directs actor John Kavanagh (left) during the production of the docudrama *Revival* (1980). Leading sound operator Peter Hunt is also pictured (left rear). Considered revisionist at the time, Marcus's film delves more deeply into the psychology of the 1916 martyr than ever before

the Documentary' by *The Irish Times* in 1979. His docudrama on the life of Padraig Pearse, *Revival: Pearse's Concept of Ireland* (1979), was the impetus for much debate on historical revisionism, especially because his portrayal of Pearse was of an intellectual rather than a romantic poet. The much later four-part series *Famine* (1994) was embroiled in similar debate as it brought to light suggestions that the most famous crisis in Irish history had been as much a series of miscalculations and exaggerations as it was a classical tragedy. In 1985 he directed the GAA centenary commemoration *Sunday After Sunday* (1984), returning him to one of the subjects with which his career had begun. He continued to operate successfully throughout the 1980s and 1990s, and his name appears in the credits of a large number of films. However, while individual series such as *The Irish Condition* (1993) and one-offs such as *1798 agus Ó Shin* (1998) reached greater levels of analysis and self-reflection, much of his work remained disappointingly ordinary. By the late twentieth century Marcus had come to represent as institutional a voice of documentary as those which he seemed prepared to sweep away in 1967.

Rocky Road to Dublin

There was a ferment of anger in the 1960s which had to find true expression sooner or later. *Fleá*, probably the first evidence of new ways of seeing and thinking about Ireland on film, was followed by an even more explicit statement that a new cinematic sensibility was emerging. Peter Lennon's *Rocky Road to Dublin* was released in a storm of controversy in 1968 and to this day remains the standard bearer for the frustrations of a generation of Irish film-makers and citizens whose voices were never heard. It is an avowedly personal film, narrated by the director himself, which analyses and criticises the state of then contemporary Ireland through a combination of direct-address voice over and interviews with individuals such as writer Sean Ó Faolain, member of the censorship board Liam O'Briain, theatre director Jim Fitzgerald, and *Irish Times* editor Douglas Gageby (later the presenter of Marcus's *The Heritage of Ireland* (1978)). It also featured a substantial profile of the state of the church in Ireland through a lengthy sequence depicting the 'typical day' of young Fr Michael Cleary.

In many ways the film is a direct descendant of *Our Country*, an angry and rhetorical attack upon the institutions and attitudes which have, in the view of its director, brought the country to a social and cultural standstill. It argues, as *Our Country* did, and practically using the same language, thatafter over forty years of independence, the so-called Irish Republic is a stagnant continuation of outdated political and ideological values. It does this literally by speaking the director's mind and by using a combination of expository and observational techniques to portray the hypocrisies and prevailing conservatism of even the most supposedly liberal Irish people.

Lennon was working as the Paris correspondent for the *Guardian* in the mid to late 1960s and was witness to the changes taking place there, particularly among young people. He found himself disgusted with the lack of similar progress in Ireland, and even more so with the assumption made by many of his Irish friends that the country *was* changing.[9] He wrote a series of thoughtful and impassioned articles for the *Guardian* on the subject in 1964, but making the film gave him more latitude to explore his ideas. Inspired by the work of French *nouvelle vague* directors like Jean-Luc Godard and François Truffaut, he saw the making of the film as a natural extension of his writing – *caméra-stylo* in the parlance of the times.[10] It was produced by Victor Herbert, an independent American investor, and photographed by famous French New Wave camera operator Raoul Coutard. Herbert invested £15,000 in the film largely based upon the participation of Coutard, whom Lennon was able to engage via his contact as a journalist with *nouvelle vague* directors. Though professionally acquainted with people like Truffaut and Jean Rouch, Lennon had no experience as a director, and the film was largely improvised around particular subjects.

It begins with a startling and rather funny scene of a young boy at a Christian Brothers' school standing and reciting a line of doctrine which he has obviously learned by rote: 'Because of Adam's sin we are born without sanctifying grace, our intellect is darkened, our will is weakened and our passions incline us to evil and we are subject to suffering and death.' The film then abruptly cuts to an image of a winding country road and the credits run over the sound of the band The Dubliners singing 'The Rocky Road to Dublin'.[11] From this opening, Lennon establishes his satirical intention. The rapid cut from one thing to the other is jarring, and produces a sense of awareness of the mechanism of cinematic narration typical of French films of this era (but not of Irish ones). It also immediately establishes Lennon's intention to tackle institutions. The education system is here identified as the prime mechanism by which consensus is achieved in Irish society. Under the guidance of religious orders, Irish education has given rise to generations of individuals like this child, who blindly and without question recite and obey doctrinaire admonitions. This is one of the film's most compelling arguments, though it is never spoken in words (as it was in the second of Lennon's articles): that the education system feeds the conformity upon which the forces of the state rely in their attempt to keep the nation moribund in a homage to the 1916 generation.

One of the most important aspects of the film, regardless of its qualities or failings, is that, like Our Country before it, it draws attention to the social and political forces which shape Irish society. Rather than allow them to guide its discourse, the film reacts to them, thus shattering the conventions of expositional documentary and forcing viewers into a new relationship with the cinematic text. Lennon makes clear from the outset where the voice of this film is coming from with a voice over which states, 'this is a personal attempt to reconstruct with a camera the plight of an island community which survived more than seven hundred years of English occupation and then nearly sank under the weight of its own heroes and clergy'. Drawing negative attention to the forces of both state (heroes) and church (clergy), Lennon immediately establishes himself within a counter-cultural paradigm. He also reminds viewers that the film is 'personal', and thereby disengages from conventional documentary, certainly as it was understood in Ireland. He also then asks the question 'What do you do with your revolution once you've got it?' and describes (with the help of an interview with Seán Ó Faolain) the 'freezing of history' by the 1916 generation. This left the Irish people with the idea that independence had been the apex of the country's achievement, and that all events thereafter were subject to the patrimony of the state; as he puts it, 'We were told that we were the sons and daughters of revolutionary heroes and our role was to be one of gratitude.'

The film then expands on this contention, arguing that the 1916 Rising was an attempt at a socialist revolution which failed and collapsed into bourgeois self-glorification. Lennon shows images of the Royal Dublin Society's annual horse show (the target of Louis Marcus's gentle scorn in *Cappallogy*), describing it as a haven of tranquillity for the Anglo-Irish and the Irish middle class. Significantly, images of priests and other clergy in attendance are shown. Lennon then defers to an interview with diplomat Conor Cruise O'Brien, whose assessment of Irish foreign policy in recent years is that the country has relinquished what little independent identity it had to the United States. This again questions the basis of the independence which supposedly sustains the ideology of the nation.

Up to this point the film has been relatively swift and clearly focused. It now shifts pace and direction with a lengthy sequence of people drinking and singing in a pub. This presumably illustrates the behaviour of the typical Irish person taking refuge from the world of politics and political concerns, but it is inordinately long and consists largely of a recitation of 'The Rocky Road to Dublin' by one of the drinkers. It is filmed in typical *cinéma vérité* style, with lots of awkward, hand held photography and long takes. It uses synchronous sound, and the noises of low chatter and chinking glasses are audible under the singing. This gives a strong sense of the atmosphere of the moment, but unlike *Fleá*, which used dynamic editing to achieve the same effect, *Rocky Road to Dublin* allows the viewer to savour the moment as if they themselves were present in the manner of the more conventional observational film. This curious mixture of approaches gives the film its unique tone. After its highly personal introduction, it suddenly becomes impersonal and distant. The viewer oscillates between a type of raw realism hitherto largely unseen in Irish documentary and the kind of direct address which had *Our Country* branded 'propaganda' twenty years earlier. This rhythm persists as Lennon jumps between *cinéma vérité* and *camera-stylo* throughout.

Lennon next turns his attention to 'Gaelic culture', specifically the kind of cultural institutions central to the 1916 generation. He interviews a spokesperson from the GAA on the subject of the ban on members attending or participating in 'foreign' games (such as soccer, rugby and hockey). Again there is a shift in methodology as Lennon allows the speaker to subvert himself and observes the result. The interviewee attempts to appear progressive when in fact he is supporting an obviously repressive policy. As the man speaks of the ban being 'democratic' as it is voted upon by GAA members, he seems unable to appreciate the paradox that if only the membership can vote, it is hardly democratic. It is obvious that this narrow-minded sectarianism is symptomatic of prevailing attitudes towards Irish culture and 'democracy' in general. As Lennon wrote, 'it is a legacy of the fervent and hysterical attempts of our revolutionary fathers to force the people to take sides publicly against the foreign invader in all spheres of their activities' (Lennon, 1964b: 8). He finally gives way to satirical cross-cutting when his interviewee speaks proudly of the relationship of Gaelic games to Irish masculinity. Lennon intercuts his observations with an image of two athletes facing off in an unsportsmanlike manner on the field, followed by shots of children hitting bits of garbage on the street with their hurley sticks. The section concludes with yet another example of juxtapositional irony, as the sarcastic admonition 'while the diehard patriots were still modestly diverting their gaze from the game of hockey, the politicians, forced to industrialise, had to open up the country, tax free, to real foreigners', is made over an image of a Japanese factory.

This last observation feeds into the next section, where newly naturalised Irish citizen John Huston speaks briefly about the necessity for an indigenous Irish film industry on the set of his British-produced, Irish-shot comedy *Sinful Davey* (1969). It is not clear if Lennon is being ironic at this point, because Huston was an important member of the newly established Film Industry Committee (of which Louis Marcus was also a member), and his point is valid enough. However, given the context in which it appears and the obvious paradox of seeing such an identifiably American director as John Huston extolling the values of being Irish, there is an element of scepticism. A similar question of attitude confronts the next sequence, where Trinity College students discuss national affairs with Douglas Gageby. While their points are very much the stuff of counter-cultural concern – the influence of advertisers, the vested interests of capitalism in the culture industry, etc. – there is something faintly arrogant about them. The audience would be expected to associate Trinity College with a colonial legacy of intellectual snobbery, and this round-table discussion has more than a small element of self-importance to it. It is reminiscent of the scene in *Chronicle of a Summer* where the participants were placed in an artificial dinnertime scenario and conversed on political matters. Lennon approaches the subject with an 'objective' distance again, but follows it with a specific assault upon the education system by returning to the Christian Brothers' school from the pre-credit sequence and asking the question 'what will they grow up to be?'

Lennon then turns his attention to censorship, and the state of Irish literature and theatre. Again he criticises the cultural institutions for conservatism, referring to the Abbey Theatre as 'petit bourgeois' and scrolling a list of major Irish literary figures whose work has been banned by the censorship board over a black screen to the sound of church bells tolling. It is a deliberately provocative juxtaposition. By his own admission, however, Lennon encountered difficulties with the interview with Professor Liam O'Briain of the Censorship of Publications Appeals Board. While undoubtedly rigorous in his views about 'good' and 'bad' art, O'Briain comes across as quite human. He makes several poignant observations about his own childhood and even suggests that youth culture will eventually 'find its own style'. Lennon was genuinely surprised by O'Briain and noted that he was the only one of his interviewees who departed from their brief and said things that he did not expect him to say. The inclusion of these moments is testament to Lennon's ethical standards. Though the interview was edited as appropriate to the final cut, he chose to include comments which threatened to under-cut his own argument. Ultimately they do not, but they at least provide the audience with the kind of gap necessary for a truly interactive mode of representation to be effective.

The film then moves towards its final section with a study of the youth culture which perceived itself to be radical, but which Lennon approached with such disbelief. Young adults are seen dancing together in a typical Irish dance hall, 'the approved meeting ground of middle class men and women who have been separated all through their education'. The images are all too familiar: rows of single ladies waiting patiently for men on one side of the hall; a couple dancing who do not even make eye contact, but gaze vacantly over each other's shoulders or wave at their friends. Lennon juxtaposes this dance hall with a more 'underground' club where more up-to-date music plays and more bodies are packed inside. Though it certainly appears more contemporary, this club is being filmed in the same country and at the same time as the other, and Lennon concludes the latter sequence on an image of a girl dancing, wearing a tight sweater and short skirt but also a crucifix.

The final section is concerned with the clergy. It is focused substantially on the adventures of 'progressive' priest Fr Michael Cleary. Cleary was assigned to the project by Archbishop McQuaid, who evidently thought him a model young person's priest because he sings, dances and smokes. Again Lennon allows the subject to make a fool of himself by standing back. We watch in disbelief as Cleary, with no doubt the best of intentions, attempts to succour women in hospital by singing 'The Chattanooga Shoeshine Boy', makes bad jokes at a wedding banquet, and engages in stilted and awkward conversation with gravediggers before walking off into the sunset in an image which Lennon describes as being deliberately like a John Ford west-ern. To be fair to Cleary, there is a certain amount of contemporary scepti-cism about these sequences because, after his death, his housekeeper published a scandalous book in which she claimed to have been his long-term lover and to have had his child (which proved to be true). This revela-tion becomes particularly ironic when Cleary speaks in one sequence about his desire to have a family, but his choice to serve God preventing him from having one. He also observes, 'we're not against sex, that would be stupid'.

The section begins with a general introduction where Lennon notes, 'the close involvement of Irish politicians with the clergy is not so much a villainous conspiracy as it is a bad habit'. He features images of both de Valera and Lemass paying obeisance to bishops, suggesting the kind of continuity between their attitudes explored throughout this chapter. His assault upon the twin authorities of church and state is explicit, and sets the tone for his approach to Fr Cleary. The film was made some years after Vatican II, and Lennon does note that this event had sent shockwaves through the Irish hierarchy and that attitudes to the clergy were changing among young people. In the third of his 1964 articles in the *Guardian*, Lennon had noted the progressive potential of dissenting clergy to articulate the frustrations of those with different points of view from the orthodoxy. But it is clear from the sequences which follow, including Cleary officiating at a wedding, coaching children at amateur boxing and singing in the hospital, that the 'modern' church is not so different from the older one. It is also equally clear that Lennon views this with some anger, and that the film is his attempt to highlight the issue and address it.

The film is not openly critical of Cleary and his 'modern methods', but it is obvious that he is being treated in a tongue-in-cheek manner. Given the frames of reference established thus far in the film, and particularly the brief introduction referring to the 'bad habit', it is clear that the audience is positioned to view him in a negative and even absurd light. His final send-off in the graveyard is particularly parodic, and was, according to Lennon, the only moment when Cleary did anything Lennon asked him to do. Yet not a bad word is spoken on the commentary about him, and on the whole Lennon entrusts the more violent criticisms to visual juxtaposition and the audience's capacity to 'read between the lines'. This is not characteristic of the observational mode, though again, arguably, it is of what Nichols terms the interactive mode. It is also perhaps characteristic of a certain strand of Irish satire, where the joke need not be spoken to be understood.

The section closes out with a serious coda, which makes clear its criticism of the church. A young married woman (who is filmed in shadow) tells a story of how, after a number of successive pregnancies, she wanted to stop having children for a time and went to her local priest for guidance. She was told not to use artificial birth control methods, but to sleep in another room away from her husband. To her this was scant comfort and suggested the church's distance from the problems of real people. Her sense of despair was increased by the feeling of isolation from the kind of support the church professed to offer people in need. Images of empty beaches accompany parts of her testimony to emphasise the idea of abandonment and desolation.

The film ends with Liam O'Briain wishing the future well and hoping that modernisation does not dehumanise people, and a sequence of children chasing the van in which the crew are leaving a location shoot (improvised by Coutard when he noticed them). This latter image becomes a powerfully optimistic and poetic finale, suggesting the hope for the future through the excitement and enthusiasm of the children running happily after the van. Though it has reminded some observers of the end of Truffaut's *The 400 Blows* (1959), Lennon claims that the film's final freeze frame of a child standing on a beach was not intended as a homage to Truffaut, but it may well have been an unconscious nod to the movement which most clearly had influenced his direction.

Rocky Road to Dublin is a powerful document of the paradoxes of late 1960s Ireland. It is a compelling and often funny film, though it has many slower stretches which do not go down well with contemporary audiences. It is something of a puzzle though. Not only does it mix and blend documentary techniques to an extent that it becomes as guilty of manipulating the profilmic as any of its predecessors, but this supposedly radical document which is academically lauded and still held up as an example of the emergence of a new Ireland was in fact barely seen on its original release. It did not receive wide distribution, probably because the church's (unspoken) disapproval was well known. A private screening for the Christian Brothers resulted in a solicitor's letter claiming they would sue. Lennon then appeared on *The Late Late Show* only to be accused of having obtained communist funding (a criticism also levelled at *Our Country*, remember), and the press were almost uniformly hostile. *The Evening Herald* dubbed it 'an anti-everything film' (cited in Browne, 1996: 35) and Alf MacLochlainn attacked Lennon as, 'one of those sincere guys who make very bad films' (cited in Browne, 1996: 35). Lennon's response to these attacks was to observe that this was 'an interesting insight in what happens to a country where the establishment is too powerful and too suffocating, so what they do is they always want to please the establishment and anybody who's against the establishment, he's an easy victim, you know, and they can say anything: they don't have to do any research, they don't have to get their facts right – nothing' (public interview, 1998). Only Fergus Linehan of *The Irish Times* was supportive. He called it 'a breath of fresh air' (cited in Rockett et al., 1988: 85) and praised it both as a rejoinder to Bord Fáilte's vision of Ireland and as an example of what an indigenous Irish film should be.

Lennon then submitted the film for consideration at the Cannes Film Festival, where it was selected for a screening at Critics' Week. It was, in fact, the last film shown before the festival was abandoned in sympathy with the students who had come under fire by government troops during an anti-war protest. The students actually adopted the film as a revolutionary document, and it was screened in a Sorbonne theatre 'still rancid with CS gas', as Lennon describes it. It was hailed by *Cahiers du cinéma* as a masterpiece and by the time it came to be screened again in Ireland, it already had such a weight of political history upon it that it is perhaps unsurprising that it was being branded 'communist'. Screenings eventually took place at a small cinema venue at Earlsfort Terrace, Dublin, a situation which vaguely recalls the Irish Film Society's showing of *Battleship Potemkin*. Despite a successful seven-week run in the city, *Rocky Road to Dublin* never made it on the road itself. According to Lennon, it was reluctantly accepted for the Cork Film Festival simply because it had been shown at Cannes. It might have been distributed via local film societies as a 16 mm print, but none was never made, probably because Lennon was aware that few rural film societies would have been interested in the film given the church's disapproval. It was still a major public scandal and everyone knew of its existence, though few had seen it. Lennon noted that there were some positive notices during this second run, but the bulk of public and press opinion went against it. With the spectre of communism hovering over it, the film was bound to receive such a response, as the Catholic church had long-held and outspoken views on communism with which church congregations would have been well familiar. Ironically, the one 'communist' in the film was theatre director Jim Fitzgerald, who spoke of the Abbey's conservatism. But as Lennon notes, 'I don't think anyone took him very seriously as a communist except the *Catholic Standard*', and this man articulates personal grievances in the film, not political beliefs.

Whether communist or no, *Rocky Road to Dublin* is a key film of its era, but not for the reasons you might expect. It did not have much direct influence. Subsequent filmmakers did not take their cue from Lennon's vitriol, and the majority of Irish films remained pro-establishment and only very

14 *Rocky Road to Dublin* (1968) was one of the most important films of its era, yet it was seen by a relatively small number of people on its original release. This rare image of the original poster shows Fr Michael Cleary (top left) and director John Huston (bottom right). Picture copyright © Peter Lennon

mildly critical of authority. It was never even screened on television. According to Lennon, even those within RTÉ who considered themselves liberal and radical and who gave him their verbal support and assurances that he was a genius did not offer to run it. At the time of writing it has still not been screened, and Lennon insists that if they wanted it now, RTÉ would have to accompany it with a panel discussion to contextualise it for a contemporary audience. The film's style remains unique and Lennon never directed another. The eclectic mixture of observational, interactive and expositional documentary was not seen again until twenty years later in *The Road to God Knows Where* (which will be discussed in the next chapter), but even that film lacked the *cinéma vérité* elements which locate Lennon's film so firmly in its era. The film does remain a centre of academic analysis and it does, both in itself and its content and in the *furor* which surrounded it, encapsulate something of the state of flux in which Ireland found itself at that time. It was an important moment in Irish documentary, though it raises questions about exactly what role it plays in society. Like the arguments over propaganda which dogged *Our Country* and the swelling of national pride which accompanied *Mise Éire*, *Rocky Road to Dublin* and its peculiar lack of a legacy is testament to the evolution of Ireland in documentary. This is not something that can be seen in audience terms, or even in the medium, but which, in retrospect, we can analyse and understand within an overall historical framework.

Rather like *Rocky Road to Dublin*, the rebellion by RTÉ personnel which followed in 1969 did not so much directly affect non-fiction film in Ireland as signify that the outbreak of hostilities between 'independent' and state-sponsored sources of funding had begun in earnest. The incident itself resulted only in a few resignations and a polemical book about the events leading up to them (though it also affected some management policies within the organisation), but at least one of those who resigned (Lelia Doolan) would go on to become chairperson of the Irish Film Board and one of their supporters (Bob Quinn), who had already resigned, became one of the most important film practitioners of the 1970s and 1980s.

The 1970s saw the growth of independent production in Irish fiction film, as extensively documented in the standard histories of Irish film. This growth was fuelled by a sense of rebellion and a perceived need to address the misrepresentation of Ireland by foreign fiction films in the preceding three quarters of a century. While we will not concern ourselves with those developments here, it is important to note that much of the drive for an independent, indigenous Irish film industry came from documentarists and that one of the inciting incidents arose over the control of non-fiction broadcasting in the public arena. It is therefore worth briefly outlining some of the issues involved.

The RTÉ rebellion and its consequences for the film industry

The dispute arose over the rescheduling of programmes and the reorganisation of management structures within RTÉ. Over the space of some two years leading up to the resignations in 1969, a series of confrontations between management, producers and trades unions resulted eventually in the resignations of producer-director Jack Dowling and head of light entertainment Lelia Doolan.[12] The heart of the matter was less the specifics of which programme went where and under whose control than why any of it was happening. The producers resented management's attempts to transfer control of the programme 7 Days from current affairs to the news division, and saw it as a result of their continued attempts to investigate political events. They also objected to what they perceived as undue interference by the RTÉ Authority in the daily operation of the station, cancelling a proposed trip to Vietnam to film a documentary on the conflict there, among other things. Several current affairs documentaries produced by the programmes division had been objected to by prominent politicians and members of the government, including then Fianna Fáil Minister for Agriculture C. J. Haughey, already cautious enough of the media to have set preconditions on his appearance on Radharc in 1964. As Dowling et al. note, 'programmes which had sought to test the public's maturity inevitably increased the testiness of national leaders' (Dowling et al., 1969: 112).

The struggle was essentially the familiar one between the creative and administrative personalities which must work together to operate a television station, public or private. As Kilborn and Izod note regarding the determining impact of the television company or network on documentaries broadcast on television:

The institution in turn is shaped by, and continues to be exposed to, a series of different forces (economic, political and cultural), some internally generated, others externally enforced. And when the institutional priorities of the organisation change as a result of political intervention or in response to a new economic situation, then sooner or later these changes will have an impact on the programming strategies of that institution. (Kilborn and Izod: 1997: 170)

This was precisely the situation in RTÉ in the late 1960s. The rebels voiced objections to the institutional priorities which seemed more concerned with placating the government and ensuring advertising revenue than providing a public service. Management responded with appeals to follow procedure and obey the chain of command, itself answerable to the RTÉ Authority, and in turn, the state. Coming after decades of state intervention in the arena of documentary and at a time when attitudes had begun to shift, however slightly, this conflict came to assume greater significance than it merited on its own terms. Raymond Williams wrote an introduction to Dowling, Doolan

and Quinn's book which spoke loftily of 'the freedom of professional com-
municators' (Dowling et al., 1969: xi) and likened events in Dublin to those
in Paris where the pro-student members of the radio and television services
were later dismissed by the authorities.

The programmes and documentary series in dispute in RTÉ were not
necessarily so challenging or radical as to invite such comparisons.
Haughey's objections to the *Division* programme (a sister of the magazine
programme *7 Days*) in 1966 were based merely on the juxtaposition of his
recorded comments with those of members of the national Farmers' Association. Yet so minor a complaint eventually spiralled into statements in the
Dáil by Seán Lemass to the effect that RTÉ was 'responsible to the Government' (cited in Dowling et al., 1969: 90). It is clear that in this type of atmosphere, individuals whose social conscience demanded greater freedom to
explore and investigate political and social developments in their own country (and others) needed to abandon the mantle of state control. In the
absence of alternative sources of funding, or even an alternative medium
with a distribution infrastructure which would support them, a framework
for independent production needed to be established. From this, individual
filmmakers and documentarists might be able to negotiate terms with the
national broadcaster based upon the latter's need for programming and the
former's ability to supply it (on their own terms, of course).

Unfortunately for documentary, the shift was towards fiction. With
RTÉ closing ranks and *Rocky Road to Dublin* lingering in non-distribution
limbo, this is not surprising. While several independent documentary producing companies did emerge, not least of all those established by Kieran
Hickey, Louis Marcus and later Bob Quinn, the possibility of successfully
circumventing the political influences upon current affairs severely limited
the opportunities for independent documentarists. They could neither
obtain suitable footage (in the light of politicians' reluctance to appear on
anything over which they could not exert a measure of control and the
necessity for such access before any meaningful investigation of any public
affairs subject could begin), nor would they have been able to dictate terms
to RTÉ (where else could they go?). Therefore, as Gibbons observes of
serial drama on Irish television, the recourse was to different forms of representation with which issues of public concern could be problematised.
He states that 'one of the most interesting features of the early years of
Irish television is that it was not so much an emphasis on "the true" – if by
that we mean current affairs and documentary – which brought about its
departure from traditional cultural norms, but rather developments in such
marginal areas as light entertainment (as in the case of *The Late Late Show*),
and in some of the less prestigious forms of television drama' (Gibbons,
1984: 21–2).

Rocky Road to Dublin proved to be the only significant voice of opposition raised by Irish non-fiction film for some twenty years, and, as noted, it was a voice not heard by the majority of the population. Instead a large number of short fiction films began to emerge which questioned the basis of Irish 'official' culture and presented a harsh and unromantic interpretation of Irish life. These, as noted, have been examined and discussed many times. Rockett gathers them in a chapter entitled 'Breakthroughs' and they did indeed represent that. Unfortunately, they were breakthroughs for fiction. As McLoone (2000) notes, many of the issues introduced through these films were first broached in documentary, however tentatively, and many of the people who made these films had worked in documentary beforehand. Some of the most eagerly discussed films were directed by documentarists, including Bob Quinn, whose *Caoineadh Airt Ui Laoire* (1975) and *Poitín* (1977) remain two of the key films of the era, and Kieran Hickey, whose *Exposure* (1978) and *Criminal Conversation* (1980) moved the debate even further along towards the emergence of postmodernism. Along with Cathal Black's docudrama *Our Boys* (1981), Thaddeus O'Sullivan's experimental quasi-docudramas *A Pint of Plain* (1975) and *On a Paving Stone Mounted* (1978), and Joe Comerford's *Down the Corner* (1977) and *Withdrawal* (1979), these films did share a definite realist aesthetic which may be related to the directors' experience in non-fiction. Yet, as any of the many studies of this material reveal, these are universally bleak and almost hyperrealistically downbeat films, and are perhaps best understood relative to the history of Irish fiction film, which is not the concern here.

The quiet men

RTÉ continued to produce and broadcast documentaries and documentary series throughout the 1970s, some of which, in their own way, did chart the changes taking place in Irish society. Louis Marcus's *Paistí ag Obair*, produced by Gael-Linn, dealt with children in a Montessori School. In a country where education remained firmly within the rubric of the religious orders, the very fact of it being represented is noteworthy, even if the film did not address issues regarding education or even the rise of Montessori in Ireland. *Inis Fáil – Isle of Destiny* (1973), a joint BBC/RTÉ co-production, stretched the boundaries of the touristic landscape film slightly by allowing it to be guided by novelist and television writer James Plunkett. Though still full of romantic imagery of the green fields and rolling hills of Ireland, the film explicitly investigated the relationship between the landscape and people, with particular attention to Irish myth and history as befitted the interests of its presenter/narrator. Radharc's docudrama *The Late Dr. Plunkett* (1975) picked up the stylistic strain of *Insurrection* by 'interviewing' historical personages about the events which led to the death of Oliver Plunkett, archbishop of Armagh in 1681. It said nothing new, but the approach was interesting. Jim Mulkerns continued to work in public information films regardless of the polemics of his work for the Labour party, making the road safety docudrama *A Game of Chance* for the Department of Local Government. Meanwhile Bord Fáilte squared the circle of its particular brand of tourist film by promoting promotion itself in *Tourism is Everyone's Business* (1978), which encouraged the public to support its endeavours so that the economy on the whole could benefit from foreign visitors.

Among the more active filmmakers were producers and directors of long-running series such as Dutch director Gerrit van Gelderen, who made a series of wildlife films with cinematographer Éamon de Buitléar broadcast under the titles *Amuigh Faoin Speir* (1960s) and *To the Waters and the Wild* (1970s). De Buitléar was born in Wicklow, and began working in Radio Éireann on traditional music and children's programmes before moving over to television shortly after RTÉ went on air. *Amuigh Faoin Speir* was a shoestring operation reminiscent of many 1960s direct-cinema outfits. Filming on location with a pawnshop Bolex camera and other equipment built and improvised by van Gelderen in response to the needs of particular situations, many episodes were broadcast live from RTÉ's studios because the cost of film was too high. Obviously given the title, the series was both in English and Irish. It also frequently used scenes of members of de Buitléar's own family in various natural locations. This contributed to a sense of the living experience of the living world which was at the core of its philosophy. John Daly remarks: 'In a journey that moves between images of the last skilled hooker sailors ferrying turf from the Aran Islands to the river bed habitats of the Blackwater, the Suir and his native Dargle, the life of Éamon de Buitléar is as much a mirror to the wonders of nature as it is to the changed morals and mores of the territory he traversed during an almost half century of massive social change' (Daly, 2001: 24). De Buitléar went on to become an important freelance cinematographer, as did his son, Cian. The elder de Buitléar was also outspoken on environmental issues and the Irish language, and his filmmaking reflects this political concern not through rhetoric, but through a devotion to natural beauty which he brings out with a loving eye. He was eventually made a senator for his work in this political arena.

Van Gelderen, who also provided the lively drawings used to distinguish fine details the camera was incapable of recording, worked initially with the assistance of David Shaw-Smith, a freelance photographer influenced by Henri Cartier-Bresson. Smith was hired by Telefís Éireann as a trainee floor manager and later graduated to production and direction. He established his own production company in 1969 and produced and directed the documentary *Connemara and its Ponies* (1971). This detailed the breeding and training of the famous animals, and made associations between the hardiness of the creatures and that of the landscape and people who surrounded them. It was enormously successful when distributed internationally as a short subject, and Shaw-Smith was immediately hired by Aer Lingus to direct promotional documentaries on their behalf. He was later commissioned by RTÉ to produce the first of three major series, *A World of Houses* (1975). Produced to commemorate the European Year of Architectural Heritage (as was the Bord Fáilte-sponsored *The Great Houses of Ireland* (1975)), this series attempted to make the subject accessible to general audiences. This was followed by the hugely successful *Hands* (1978–88) (and later *Patterns* (1979-83)), profiling the traditional crafts of Irish artisans. The series was marked by its close-up observation of the techniques involved, and though lacking an explicit social commentary always gave the sense that these skills were gradually disappearing.

The Little People (1970) was a rather more direct speculation upon the subject. This film went so far as to suggest that 'traditional' styles and designs were in fact an invention of the craft workshops which had become so successful in the 1960s, such as the Kilkenny Design Centre. It nonetheless encouraged the development of small industries and attempted to incorporate some political discussion into a subject too easily treated lightly. As *Clothing and Donegal* (1999), an episode of RTÉ's *The Last Resource* series, showed, textiles were far from the colourful handicrafts envisioned by so many tourist-centred films in the past. Presenter Kathy Donaghy, a native of Donegal, discussed how closures of textile manufacturing plants in Donegal threatened to destroy not just some vague notion of 'tradition', but the local economy and the lives of those who depended upon it.

It is not that Smith did not share these concerns, but his approach was more in keeping with the non-confrontational nature of Irish documentary in the wake of *Rocky Road to Dublin*. What Renov terms the impulse to 'record, reveal and preserve' is in question, not to 'persuade or promote' (Renov (ed.), 1993: 25). Documentarists were content to allow the documentary process to perform a social function. Standing back and observing the changes without comment was a far safer attitude to adopt. Such films had a much greater chance of being broadcast and would, in time, prove a document of change if not an instrument. This is particularly true of *Hands*, which was later distributed on videocassette and rebroadcast as late as in the year 2003, when its careful documentation of the work of skilled artisans created a poignant counterpoint to the latter-day collapse of manufacturing concerns that had grown out of traditional crafts.

Fleadh '73 (1973) was another good example of the 'preservation' trend. After *Fleá* this was a disappointingly tame and stylistically ordinary account of the Fleadh Ceoil held that year in Listowel, Co. Kerry. Though it opens with an image of a hippy girl with exposed midriff, beads dangling and large earrings, the world it portrays is not of an Irish culture of music in transition, but of tradition sold on street corners to foreign tourists. The film emphasises the unusual, the quaint and the international. It focuses on eccentric figures, such as a man seated on a Garda motorbike playing Uileann pipes, a cigarette drooping from his lips, a crucifix hanging from his neck; a female beggar wandering around the town amid the tourists laden with cameras; two drunks dancing on top of a phone booth, encouraged by the attention of the crowd and of the camera, and finally a drunk fiddle player who informs us of his intoxication with pride before launching into an impromptu recitation. There is a rapid montage of foreign visitors speaking their names and where they come from, an English concertina seller shows off his wares, the voice over informs us that this is 'an international festival'. It is almost grotesque, a parade of eccentrics and drunkards which is apparently intended to demonstrate how 'open' Ireland has become. Though it certainly demonstrates that, the film makes no attempt to contextualise anything that is happening. The camera wanders around with little evident purpose except to record, and the voice over does not comment upon the meaning of any of it. If this is an attempt at observational form, then it could only be understood in terms of criticism. Yet there is a tone of celebration, and the film has been made with the evident intention of encouraging viewers (and tourists) to join the party.

By contrast *The Family*, filmed in 1978 but not broadcast until the early 1990s, dealt with a world of eccentrics for quite different ends. Filmed as part of RTÉ's *The Other Ways* series (produced by later director general Bob Collins), which was intended to examine alternative lifestyles in contemporary Ireland, *The Family* focused on a commune in Donegal named 'Atlantis' where English expatriate Jenny James lived with an extended 'family' of hippies, drop-outs and other seekers of alternative living. Through role play and scream therapy sessions, James counselled her charges through a series of emotional crises as director Bob Quinn filmed. Shot over one week, the film captured, without exaggeration, the intensity of these people's lives. Interviews with individuals are contrasted with their hysterical group sessions. The philosophy of love and understanding is revealed to have its dark and turbulent underside for which James makes no apology. As the avowed matriarch of the family, she exerts a strong presence both in the commune and on the film. She acts as our guide to the personalities and events within, and Quinn is careful to represent Atlantis as a world unto itself. The film begins with establishing images of an elderly man in drab clothes cycling on an old bicycle staring at the colourful murals which adorn the building, including the yin/yang symbol, which acts as a kind of counterpoint to the

Christian imagery usually so dominant in Irish films. As it progresses, the world becomes increasingly claustrophobic, with the narrow halls and cluttered rooms of the commune echoing the state of mental siege under which most of its residents seem to live. Its distance from 'ordinary' life is signalled clearly. Only one of her 'family' is Irish, a Dubliner named Jim, who at one point observes, 'I'm just a visitor here, I don't have anything to do with what's going on.'

The Family is a provocative interrogation of the role and nature of the family in society. Though there is an element of grotesquerie to it, like *Fleadh '73*, *The Family* at least raises such questions and draws attention to its contrasts and challenges to convention. Indeed, it is precisely with these that the film is concerned. Contrasting this commune's attitudes to life, love and each other with a docudrama sequence depicting a 'typical' nuclear family, Quinn makes clear that despite his own (or the audience's) personal reaction (apparently he found the experience 'frightening'[13]), the film is asking questions of Irish society. Forcing viewers to examine their own feelings about open displays of emotion in a usually reserved culture, it asks them to take stock of their own situation relative to what they see and attempt to understand why these people behave as they do. Quinn was hired to make the film on a freelance basis, having resigned from RTÉ and established his own production company, Cinegael. It was completed and ready for broadcast in 1978, but RTÉ did not transmit it. The reasons were vague, but it was obvious that they felt this particular alternative lifestyle was simply too shocking. Jenny James and her family seemed too radical a revision of an institution enshrined in the constitution as the cornerstone of Irish life.

A more traditional view of Irish motherhood and family values was evinced in *ICA: 60 Years a Growing* (1970), a promotional film made on behalf of the Irish Countrywomen's Association (ICA). At a time when widespread cultural changes in the arena of women's issues had begun to be evident even in Ireland, this film advocated the rather traditional activities of the ICA. It would be almost two decades before a genuine feminist documentary was produced in Ireland (this will be discussed in the next chapter). The film emphasised how the ICA provided a focus for Irish women through 'learning skills for improving domestic life' and highlighted activities including crafts, selling farm produce, the preservation of historical landmarks and the beautification of the landscape through planting flowers on grass verges and other activities. The film does not reflect upon these in terms of a more general discussion of how women are therefore positioned and defined within Irish society. Images of de Valera greeting the leaders of the organisation and an overall sense of traditionalism are testament to the documentarist's unwillingness to move beyond the parameters set by her sponsors.

The decade concluded with Louis Marcus's docudrama *Revival* and his six-part series *The Heritage of Ireland*, both of which re-engaged issues of Irish history in a manner which raised questions in their time, but which now seem not all that different from their predecessors. *Revival* did reassess the mindset of Padraig Pearse at the time of the 1916 insurrection, and attempted to understand his motivations with readings from his commentaries upon Irish culture, education and language. As an insight into his life it is revealing, and it debunks the myth of blood sacrifice by portraying him as an intellectual instead of a windswept poet. Yet the film never satisfactorily resolves the question of why he chose to turn to violence, and his death is mourned in a manner not far distant from the nationalistic canonisation. The film was commissioned by the Department of the Taoiseach, and despite the debate it sparked in the Irish film industry journals, it subscribed quite heavily to traditional notions of Irish history as discussed in the previous chapter. Marcus himself admitted as much in an interview with Kevin Rockett in *IFT News*: 'I don't see the value of trying to destroy Irish nationalism which I don't think can be done in the long run anyway. The value I see is in trying to give it the maturity and the unprovincialism with which Pearse invested it' (cited in Rockett, 1980: 11). It was again a subtle distinction between investigation and mere projection, and to his credit Marcus had attempted at least to address the issue of mythology through his docudrama. But it is arguable that a more vigorous approach was needed if Irish documentary was ever to subvert the influence of orthodoxy, and ten years after *Rocky Road to Dublin* it did not seem to have managed it.

Writing in 1969, Bob Quinn aptly summed up the position:

When confronted by a monolith which proposes to eat you, even in the nicest possible manner, you must do something. The worst thing to do is allow the monolith to define the terms of the battle. Ignore its pleas for logic, because it uses logic to obscure the truth; ignore its calls for reasonableness, the assumptions and premises of which are entirely questionable; query its sacred cows, its gods and its liturgies, its systems, its impeccable phrases imported from the respectable corruption of business management. Ignore above all its offers of a comfortable place in the technocratic womb; its bribes of security status and free burial service.

Having ignored all of these expressions you will find yourself out of a job. And you can't afford this because you have a mortgage, an overdraft, a hire-purchase agreement and a realisation that you were never free. So you will not follow the advice in the preceding paragraph. That is when the organisation laughs.

What all this amounts to is that you can do absolutely nothing. You are completely trapped. You must now enter a period of despair, in which you will fulfil your functions in a perfect mechanical, unthinking, organisational manner. And this is all that is required by the system of organisation in which you work. And that is why the organisation decays and becomes a bloated and swelling corpse, feeding the increasing number of parasites but incapable of directing itself because there is no life, no human spirit to quicken it. (Dowling et al., 1969: xxxiv–v)

Quinn's dark assessment of the position of the documentarist in Irish society is in contrast to his own eventual response to the situation. Peculiar as it was in the Ireland of the 1970s, Quinn's answer was to abandon the system and strike out on his own. Founding Cinegael in 1973 and establishing his base of operations in the west of Ireland instead of Dublin, he successfully shifted the goalposts of the relationship between the documentarist and the sponsor. As an independent producer/director, he was in large part responsible for the turn in fortune of the Irish fiction film industry insofar as the films he directed helped Irish cinema to find its own voice for the first time. We will examine his work in more detail in the next chapter.

Unquiet times

The most glaring omission from this period in Irish documentary history, from the point of view of the outside observer, must be commentary upon, analysis of and reaction to events in Northern Ireland from the late 1960s onwards. The startling and shameful truth of the matter is, as Rockett notes, that RTÉ largely ignored Northern Ireland except for news items: 'this policy has led to the downgrading of Northern Ireland as a subject of documentaries and dramas' (Rockett et al., 1988: 91). Though Rockett here refers directly to the policy by RTÉ to exclude members of politically subversive organisations from speaking on television under the terms of Section 31 of the Broadcasting Act, which was subsequently rescinded, the attitude of exclusion is more widespread. Since *Housing Discrimination*, Irish documentarists had been extremely cautious when approaching Northern Ireland, to the extent that they barely approached it at all. As noted, Radharc's film from Derry in 1964 was essentially banned and though there was a wealth of international interest in Northern Ireland, very little of it demonstrated anything above morbid curiosity.

The most important of these international films is probably Marcel Ophüls's *A Sense of Loss* (1972), directed by a German-born French-American for US and Swiss Television. The film followed the stories of families damaged by violence on the streets and attempted to give audiences an insight into the 'losses' they had suffered as individuals and as a culture. Released between *The Sorrow and the Pity* (1969) and *The Memory of Justice* (1976), *A Sense of Loss* is one of Ophüls's least-discussed films. When written about, usually in reviews rather than scholarly texts, the film is often damned with faint praise. Again interview-based and running to some two hours, it is distinguished by what Peter Biskind termed a 'paralysed humanism' (Biskind, 1979: 556). The director's sympathy with the nationalist community is evident throughout the film, but as McIlroy (1998), points out, this is really a transposition of Ophüls's experiences chronicling the lives of Jewish people under Nazism in *The Sorrow and the Pity*.

However, the partisanship of *A Sense of Loss* was presented in terms of a liberal-humanist empathy with human tragedy rather than as a political perspective, as if Ophüls was hoping his so-called 'film report' would side-step the requirements of an historical 'chronicle' like *The Sorrow and the Pity*. The film's stated thematic preoccupation with loss raised larger questions about the 'loss' of Northern Ireland itself in broader historical terms which the film did not fully vocalise. Although he presented the stated views of nationalists and loyalists of varying degrees of extremity, Ophüls's questions led his interviewees to use religious designations rather than political ones. This semantic distinction had the effect of portraying the conflict in Northern Ireland as a relatively clear-cut sectarian antagonism which had been instigated by colonial and imperialist Britain imposing its religious values on the native Irish. This provided safe grounds for an empathetic response to the losses represented in the film – loss of family, loss of peace, loss of innocence – without ever needing to fully understand the historical, political and cultural context of the events and social categories.

The same problem, if not the same attitude to the subject, arises when considering the plethora of British- and American-produced documentaries and documentary series emerging out of 'the troubles'. Though Pettitt singles out the UK-produced *Ireland: Behind the Wire* (1974) for particular praise for 'attempting to create real social cinema' (Pettitt, 2000: 90), most of these programmes were incapable of getting inside their subject. It would be some time before either Irish or Northern Irish directors began to take stock of their situation in a meaningful way, and, as shall be seen in the next chapter, some of the responses have been peculiar. With developments in the province in the late 1990s, some films began to appear which tentatively probed the past in search of answers, but as Pym, writing on *Ireland – A Television History* and *The Troubles*, concludes, 'the past, on television, can be marshalled with some success, can be made manageable; but the present remains, for all its vividness, a largely unknown country' (Pym, 1988: 487).

When we review the output of Irish documentarists during the 1960s and 1970s, we can perhaps see this observation in a broader context. Not only were there appeals to the past in terms of the many films which drew upon or otherwise dealt with Irish history, but in tourist documentaries history itself became commodified and purified into a nostalgic idyll with a manufactured 'heritage' which could be easily pressed into the service of commercial productions. Even *Rocky Road to Dublin* was obsessed with the past. Though in its case (and arguably an undercurrent in many others), the question was not so much of what the past can teach us as what we can learn from its mistakes, Irish documentarists remained unable to examine, explore or otherwise envision the present in the kinds of terms which observational documentaries had done and were doing in the United States and elsewhere.

The sense of contemporaneity and of a political role which might be played by the medium and its practitioners noted by Barsam was absent. Apart from *Fleá* and *The One-Nighters*, few Irish documentaries from the *cinéma vérité* period evinced a sense of the here and now. *Rocky Road to Dublin* demonstrated an awareness of the need for such a sense, but was itself subject to the same frames of reference which it sought to deconstruct and found itself trapped by its own objects. Other films, like *Capital City 1974–1975*, were not even seen by the public until the here and now was here and now no more. Yet the roots of change were visible in the work of this period and the personalities of the directors who struggled to establish the beginnings of an independent sector. There was an interrogation, at least on some level, of many of the social and political ideas which had influenced the lives of Irish people since the foundation of the state. Fissures had begun to appear in the monolith (which extended much further than the management structures of RTÉ), and in time Bob Quinn's fears about its ability to rob Irish people of their sense of life would become moot in the face of work which finally began to understand the capacity of the medium to do more than simply hold up a mirror to Irish life without truly understanding what it saw.

Notes

1 See Gorham, 1967; also Pine, 2002.

2 De Valera's address is reprinted in full in McLoone and MacMahon (eds), 1984.

3 This has been the subject of several volumes in its own right apart from being featured in the standard textbooks on documentary cinema. See, for example, Macorelles, 1971; Rosenthal, 1971, and Mamber, 1974.

4 Carey was the subject of an informative documentary, *Paddy Carey: Film Maker* (1999), from which many of the factual details in this section are drawn.

5 These incidents are discussed in more detail in Dowling et al., 1969 and McLoone and MacMahon (eds), 1984. The 'Bishop and the Nightie' affair is also featured in Corless, 1998.

6 The work of the filmmaking clergy has been spoken about in a paper by Irish Film Archive curator Sunniva O'Flynn entitled 'Black and White Collar Films' (Irish Film Centre, 2002), from which some of this information is drawn. It is scheduled to appear in R. Barton and H. O'Brien (eds), *Keeping it Real: Issues and Directions in Irish Film and Television* (London: Wallflower Press, forthcoming, 2004).

7 For more details on this particular proposal, rejected at the time, see Savage, 1996: 154–7.

8 The title card on the print viewed in the course of this research is simply *Fleá*. The film is often known by the longer Irish-language title *Fleadh Ceoil*. Both may be translated as 'music festival', as the Fleá or Fleadh Ceoil is just that, an annual festival of traditional Irish music held in different towns throughout the country.

9 Much of the material which follows is derived from a public interview given by Lennon at the Irish Film Centre on 16 April 1998 conducted by Fergus Linehan, formerly of *The Irish Times*. The author was in attendance and possesses a complete transcript of the interview. At Lennon's request, this transcript is not available for reproduction, though I will quote from extracts.

10 This is the term coined by Alexandre Austruc in 1948 which became a cornerstone of radical French film criticism in *Cahiers du cinéma* in the 1950s and then the basis of the techniques behind *nouvelle vague* filmmaking in the 1960s. It referred to the capacity of the camera to act literally as a pen with which the director could 'write' what they felt personally and creatively about a subject.

11 The Dubliners were themselves controversial and very popular figures at the time, having been the subject of public scandal when their single 'Seven Drunken Nights' was released and subsequently banned from the airwaves by RTÉ. They had appeared on the *Ed Sullivan Show* on St Patrick's Day in 1968 and were therefore well recognised internationally.

12 For a full description of the convoluted chain of events, see Dowling et al., 1969.

13 According to his old friend, Lelia Doolan, who introduced the programme when it was eventually screened on television in the early 1990s as part of the series *First View*, which Doolan presented.

5

Uncertain spaces: postmodern, postcolonial, postnationalist Ireland?

Writing in 1998, Frederic Jameson noted that one difficulty with defining the postmodern was the impulse to assign dates and identify key moments when it began. He argued that certain stylistic elements within high modernism were characteristic of postmodern preoccupations, and, conversely, that the recurrence of such elements or motifs within postmodernism might suggest a continuity of the project of modernism. His solution is one which has obvious implications for the present study. He maintains that rather than representing a true 'break' with modernism, postmodernism represents a period of unstable or shifting frames of reference in which the dominance of particular ideas, styles or material contents fluctuates. He concludes:

I must limit myself to the suggestion that radical breaks between periods do not generally involve complete changes of content but rather the restructuring of a certain number of elements already given: features that in an earlier period or system were subordinate now become dominant, and features that had been dominant again become secondary ... My point is that until the present day those things have been secondary or minor features of modernist art, marginal rather than central, and that we have something new when they become the central features of cultural production. (Jameson, 1998: 18)

Irish documentary demonstrated this kind of 'restructuring of elements' in the 1980s and 1990s. While in some cases new themes, ideas and arenas of debate emerged, for the most part films reflect the same concerns as their predecessors. The difference is that, as Jameson points out, issues regarding ideology, landscape and the schism between modernity and tradition became 'central features of cultural production' (18) embodied in the texts rather than part of a strategy of interpretation in academic discourse. This chapter will demonstrate how what Nichols might term a self-reflexive mode of documentary representation gradually found expression in Irish documentaries despite the noted relative absence of the observational and interactive modes which preceded its introduction elsewhere. The difference is characterised by subtle shifts in emphasis and in the balance of content rather than in an obvious, radical break with tradition or a wholesale change in practices, pointing towards what has been termed 'evolution' rather than 'revolution' throughout this book.

This notion of 'instability' is also an important point for Homi K. Bhabha in his discussion of otherness and difference in the colonial novel. Though postcolonialism is concerned with breaks with the (colonial) past and separation from orthodoxy (which suggests revolution, a model not entirely appropriate in an Irish context), Bhabha notes that the space within which the discourse of otherness takes place is not as clearly defined as is generally assumed. He argues that the condition of colonial separation pre-dates the (re)discovery of the 'authentic' which often defines postcolonial debate. The aboriginal is always defined in terms opposite to the colonial, which necessarily are terms in turn defined only by the act and conditions of colonialism itself. The backward gaze of nostalgia (or of nationalism, though he does not discuss it here) is through the filter of the colonial experience. This paradox makes, to use his example, Conrad's *Heart of Darkness* not merely a work of orientalism or colonial plunder, but a complex discourse on the shifting boundaries of antagonism between authority and resistance.

The place of difference and otherness, or the space of the adversarial, within such a system of 'disposal' as I've proposed, is never entirely on the outside or implacably oppositional. It is a pressure, a presence, that acts constantly, if unevenly, along the entire boundary of authorization . . . The contour of difference is agonistic, shifting, splitting, rather like Freud's description of the system of consciousness which occupies a position in space lying on the borderline between outside and inside, a surface of protection, reception, and projection. (Bhabha, 1995: 32)

Both Bhabha and Jameson arrive at the conclusion that transition and transgression are in question in their respective arenas: in Jameson's case, the culture of late capitalism, and, in Bhabha's, the Third World. Though late twentieth-century Ireland could not be said to exemplify either, it has often been discussed in terms of both. During the 1980s, when emigration, unemployment and national debt were the most pressing social and economic difficulties, analyses tended to draw parallels with the experiences of the Third World. In the 1990s, a period of economic prosperity, they inclined to the late capitalist model, making a nonsense of the earlier paradigm. In both cases the perception was of an Ireland gradually emerging from the period of colonial mimicry and towards a 'post-postcolonial' phase of self-definition which Kearney has termed 'postnationalist'.

Kearney proposes a model which, rather than denying nationalism or subscribing to anti-nationalism, attempts to locate the nationalist impulse in Irish (and European) history within both progressive and retrogressive paradigms.

He acknowledges the role played by nationalism in the emergence of Ireland as a nation-state, and argues that though it lacked the philosophical discipline of European nationalisms and was thereby an 'arrested' form (Kearney, 1997: 186), it contributed to the discourse of nationality, which remains relevant even in a postnationalist context. Like Jameson, his impulse is towards a concept of inclusion and contemporaneity (though their reasons are very different) which does not so much reject the past as incorporate it into a different concept of the present. It is, in Bhabha's terms, a kind of pressure along the boundaries of authorisation rather than a complete break. This is characteristic of several of the documentaries we will examine in this chapter. For example, unlike *Rocky Road to Dublin* (1968) Bob Quinn's *Atlantean* (1984) does not reject outright the culture about which it speculates and which it subtly criticises, though it repudiates many of the tribal and racial myths upon which the ideology of the state had been founded. Similarly, although many of the films of the 1980s and 1990s reflect the shifting frames of reference of contemporary culture, few of them are reactive or oppositional. Rather, like the much-vaunted *States of Fear* (1999) which will be discussed later, they reflect a public acknowledgement that the frames of reference have changed.

Stephen Howe (2000) has also investigated many of the notions of postcolonialism and colonialism presumed to have been central to the conception of Ireland in the twentieth century. Taking writers such as Kiberd to task, he asks to what degree such factors as colonial history are determinating upon a country which, while its history may reflect superficial similarities with other postcolonial nations, never occupied the same cultural, racial or economic spaces as the nations discussed by the likes of Bhabha and Fanon. Howe's is not a unique argument. Pettitt and McLoone also devote some time to repudiating the mechanistic view of these relationships, especially when they are applied to film interpretation. McLoone, following Colin Graham, notes: 'the way out of the impasse is to recognise the complexity of the relationship between coloniser and colonised and to explore the "liminal spaces" of this encounter. This requires rethinking concepts of irony, hybridity, mimicry, and transculturation. It requires at the same time being sensitive to the history of colonial repression as well as to the narrowness of essentialist nationalism that resulted' (McLoone, 2000: 121). This perfectly describes the project of a self-reflexive mode of documentary, one which though not fully developed in the period in question, certainly became the ideal aspired to by individual films and filmmakers eager to engage with the 'liminal spaces' forming around the emerging Ireland.

As specific, identifiable historical events provided evidence of both progress and conservatism (the 'Kerry Babies' case, the first divorce and abortion referenda, the peace process, the second divorce referendum, the tribunals of inquiry into corruption, the Bishop Casey affair, the elections of

Mary Robinson and Mary McAleese as president, the revelations of clerical abuse, etc.), so Irish documentary provided evidence of instability in the concept of 'the real Ireland'. Some films entered the arena of public discourse armed with 'facts' which 'proved' their arguments. Others stood back and speculated about what any of it meant. Viewers of Irish non-fiction films of this period thus find themselves in an oscillation between the axes of postmodernism, postcolonialism and postnationalism within which documentary film is ideally placed, in Grierson's words, to 'give other people a proper sight of Ireland' and 'give the Irish people a proper sight of themselves' (Grierson, 1948: 286), or, in those of Louis Marcus, help in 'interpreting a community to itself as well as others' (Marcus, 1967: 18).

The fringes of Irishness: *Atlantean*

In *Deconstructing Ireland* (2001) Colin Graham devotes some time to exploring the crackpot theories of nineteenth-century Irish-American author Ignatius Donnelly, particularly his 1882 book *Atlantis: The Antediluvian World*. Donnelly endeavoured to prove that Plato's lost continent could be found somewhere west of Ireland but east of America, and argued that Ireland was most likely one of its surviving colonies. This, he mused, could explain Ireland's sense of cultural and social dislocation. Graham points out that crank though he may have been, Donnelly had hit upon an interesting core idea:

It may be at the edges of logic, and at the margins of the logocentrism of nationalism, but Donnelly's *Atlantis* is an overblown exemplification of the dislocations of Irishness throughout its history. In its 'excess' of logic, its 'phantasms' of 'scientific' evidence and its vision of an Ireland which is not Ireland but a remnant of Atlantis, Donnelly's Ireland is the apotheosis of the utopianism which this chapter has discussed – Ireland is everywhere and nowhere, 'broken in pieces', enveloped in a story in which its particularity and therefore its definition will never be resolved. (Graham, 2001: 22–3)

Graham's speculations make an interesting prelude to a study of the work of Bob Quinn, particularly his epic television 'history' *Atlantean*. As mentioned in the previous chapter, Quinn became an important figure in the Irish film industry in the 1970s and 1980s. Born in Dublin, he worked in a variety of jobs before joining RTÉ in 1961 as a trainee studio operator. Working initially in current affairs and then religious programming, he directed several films for RTÉ, including a series on the psychological development of children. After a leave of absence studying sociology in Nova Scotia, he returned to Ireland in 1968 and found the atmosphere stifling. He resigned from RTÉ along with

Lelia Doolan and Jack Dowling, then moved to the west of Ireland where he established the company Cinegael. He continued to contribute on an independent basis to Irish film and television for the remainder of his career, refusing to resign himself to the position of being a member of any 'staff' or even to ascribe to any one notion of history, culture or Irishness.

His most important fictional work was the Irish-language, low-budget experimental drama *Caoineadh Airt Uí Laoire* (1975). This was an aesthetically radical statement that the medium could be employed to articulate political ideas. Sponsored by Sinn Féin, the Workers' Party (and thereby the first publicly distributed film to be financed by a political party which was not in government since *Our Country*), the film blended a reconstruction of the events told in an eighteenth-century poem with contemporary scenes of the poem being staged in the Conamara Gaeltacht by a troupe of native-speaking actors under an English director. Embracing paradox, juxtaposition and montage techniques, it was a clarion call for an indigenous, engaged and independent Irish cinema. Though fiction, and thus not really our concern here, this film was also an example of a reflexive mode of representation. McLoone notes that it 'raises issues of cultural representation in general and presents history in particular, not as a given set of irrefutable facts, but as a question of representation itself, a matter of interpretation which it used to meet the ideological needs of the present' (McLoone, 2000: 132). This is significant because this cultural, historical and ideological reflexivity would be seen again in *Atlantean*, his documentary *magnum opus*.

Atlantean was a Cinegael production made with the cooperation of cultural and historical institutions and filmmaking bodies including the Irish Film Board and RTÉ. Though broadcast as a three-episode television series, it is often referred to as a trilogy of films. It was an attempt to explore the possibility that the Irish were not Celtic in origin but 'part of an ignored culture of maritime peoples who stretch all the way to North Africa' which Quinn terms 'Atlantean'. The intriguing premise had several obvious motivations. Apart from whatever ethnographic and anthropological interests Quinn explicitly discussed in the programme, it was clearly part of an overall project of revisionism begun with *Caoineadh Airt Uí Laoire* and *Poitín* (1978). Directly entering the arena of postcolonial and postmodern debate, it was an attempt to debunk the ideas of Irish history and culture expounded upon by programmes as recent as *The Heritage of Ireland* (1978). It critiqued the project of historical revival and the obsession with cultural nationalism characteristic of postcolonial nations.

Quinn was aware of these issues. Within minutes of its opening, he has established the arena of debate with specific verbal reference to orientalism, colonialism and multiculturalism. The narration, spoken by actor Alan Stanford, is written in a third-person form which Quinn frequently employs when referring to himself. It is playful, ironic and self-effacing, acknowledging Quinn's eccentricity and preempting the scepticism with which his thesis will be received. Though this has led some to argue that the film works as parody rather than as rhetoric, and while this may be a valid reading, especially within a postmodern context (though Jameson, of course, claims parody to be a feature of modernism and pastiche its postmodern equivalent), it is in fact part of a strategy of self-reflexivity which is best understood in Nichols's terms rather than those of Irish Studies.

According to Nichols the reflexive mode of representation is evident when filmmakers foreground their own subjectivity. Some directors, like Quinn, even signal their presence as an authoring agent by appearing in the film. The concerns of such filmmakers is as much with the process of representation itself as with that which is being represented. While a reflexive documentary presents information and makes arguments, it constantly draws attention to the means by which the information has been gathered and by which the arguments are made. As Nichols observes, 'the reflexive mode emphasizes epistemological doubt' (Nichols, 1991: 61). The purpose of such films is often twofold, on one hand a 'poetic' meditation upon form and structure which increases the viewer's awareness of discourse and disengages them from the expectations of rhetorical, observational and/or interactive types, and on the other to raise political consciousness insofar as the phrase denotes an increased awareness of society and social issues. In questioning their own epistemological basis, reflexive documentaries ultimately aim to restore a measure of rhetorical engagement with social discourse by destroying myths of their 'objectivity'.

This is why the reading of *Atlantean* as parody fails. Rather than undermining documentary form, Quinn is reinvigorating the medium's capacity to engage with the 'reality' of Irish life by problematising not only notions of Irish culture, but the forms by which it has been represented. *Atlantean* draws attention to the schemata by which knowledge about Irish culture is accumulated and presented to the Irish people. It criticises the process of mythological reconstruction by which the nation has defined itself in the preceding half century and asks that the Irish people at least open their minds to alternatives. It is ironic in approach, but serious in intention. Its reflexivity prompts uncertainty in the viewer about how to approach it. The result, in some cases, is to fall back on traditional positions and assume the entire series to be a joke. This is an inadequate response.

The opening minutes of the first episode illustrate the film's many concerns. It begins in Cairo, where two Egyptian men perform a traditional dance. Quinn himself steps into shot and takes over from one of the dancers. He is dressed in everyday clothing, apart from some native headgear, and strikes a deliberate contrast with the remaining Egyptian. The narration then begins:

This Irishman, making an exhibition of himself in a public park in Cairo, imagines that he has something in common with these Egyptians. He believes that this dance is the antecedent of a dance in Ireland. In the nineteenth-century, he would have been called, among other things, an orientalist. These eccentrics looked at the abject remnants of the Irish nation, compared them to the Arabs, and came to the conclusion that the Irish were Arabs. This was meant as a compliment to neither.

A series of juxtapositions of images of Irish farmers and native Egyptians follows. Guided by what we have just heard, the viewer sees remarkable similarities between them. Distancing himself from the project of orientalism, Quinn then describes, in third person, how this 'odd fellow' (himself) embarked on a project of exploring the commonalities between Irish and North African cultures, and 'at the risk of spoiling the story' came to the conclusion that the Irish were not Arabs. The narration then notes, over images of both Irish and Egyptian subjects laughing, 'his friends, and also possibly the Arabs, were relieved. But then he alarmed them by saying the Irish were not Celts either.' The playful, self-depreciating narration is complimented by Stanford's delivery which, in a rich Anglophone accent, mimics the traditional classic expositional voice over.

Quinn establishes himself at the centre of the film, not only as a physical presence, but as an epistemological presence (as the researcher), and an authoring presence (as the author of the narration), and hereby casts himself as an eccentric, an 'odd fellow' and indeed, 'an Irishman'. Following the titles we go to the west of Ireland, where Quinn lives. The film discusses his relationship with this part of the country, which he explains he had fled to in search of the 'real' centre of the 'Irish identity' he had been seeking. This personalisation was largely unprecedented in Irish documentary. Though James Plunkett had been central to *Inis Fáil – Isle of Destiny* (1972) and Douglas Gageby has presented *The Heritage of Ireland*, these documentaries did probe their presenters' actual motivations or attempt to explore their personalities relative to the subject. Robert Kee was likewise an important presence in *Ireland – A Television History* (1981), as noted by Pym and as previously discussed, in terms of exemplifying an oral tradition of the authoritative 'storyteller'. But this kind of presence was not an element of reflexive self-interrogation; on the contrary, such participation reinforced the authority of the text.

In *Atlantean*, Quinn makes himself central to the film's argument and to its methodology. It is about one man's journey to the heart of his own sense of Irishness, an exploratory and speculative journey which eventually dismantles all that he has been taught and deconstructs his ideas of the 'reality' of Ireland's distant past. Though it is not strictly autobiographical, it does intertwine the filmmaker's 'making an exhibition of himself' with an exhibition of the subject matter. As we are introduced to Quinn's home and his neighbours, the voice over describes the sense of cultural dislocation which has driven him to live 'as far west as you can go' in the centre of 'Celtic Ireland': 'being reared on English comics, American movies, a Roman version of a Palestinian religion in Dublin, a city founded by Vikings, overrun by Normans and developed by Anglo-Saxons, how could Ireland possibly make sense? Particularly because in school he was told he was something called a Celt.' We are then informed that he later realised he was a victim of 'a colonised mind', thereby again fore-grounding the postcolonial discourse within this personal journey to the roots of Irishness upon which he has embarked.

Inside Quinn's home, located in what is evidently a rural setting, the first images are of film reels and other technological paraphernalia. Quinn sits beside a projector and runs footage of a man singing, which turns out to have been the inspiration for his research. The programme later demonstrates the similarities between the forms of traditional Irish singing and those of North Africa. It points out that the *sean nós*, one of the oldest forms of song known in Ireland, is similar to the elaborate, wailing ritual songs (often religious) in North Africa and even the Indian subcontinent. Quinn even backs up his claims by invoking the writings of Seán Ó Riada, an authority with noted ambiguities of his own, which Quinn uses to subvert the 'Celtic' ideals he was presumed to symbolise.

As the narration continues, Quinn alternates between images of himself screening the film in his home to the film itself occupying the entire field of vision. As with similar scenes in *Caoineadh Airt Uí Laoire*, this serves to rein-force the awareness that film is a form of representation rather than 'reality' *per se*. It emphasises the artificiality of the conventions of documentary by contrasting the 'observational' material on the film he is watching with images of himself observing the observed. He also further inscribes himself within the text of the film here as 'director' – the man who made the film. He reminds us that all that what we are about to see must be understood in context. *Atlantean* is an attempt to articulate on film an idea of culture which is of personal importance to its maker but which is not fixed. On the con-trary, the entire purpose of the film is to throw open the questions of cultural nationalism. Quinn's 'solution' is not that the Irish are Arabs, or even that they are Atlantean, but that, like the maritime travellers upon whom he bases much of this 'alternative mythology' of Afro-European culture, they are, like him, explorers on the fringes of 'official' interpretations of self and nation. It is not so much a matter of 'proof' or 'evidence', but of discourse. The purpose of the film is to expand the frontiers of debate on the subject of Irish culture.

There are many layers of analysis within *Atlantean*. It deals with music, sculpture, language, religion, early seafaring and boat designs, each invoking questions of culture, nationality and identity. Quinn's readings of all of them challenge orthodoxy, deconstructing 'traditional' conclusions. He finds alternative explanations for events and characters such as the Brendan Voyage, St Patrick, Irish placenames, Yeats's *Deirdre of the Sorrows* and a plethora of other cultural and historical institutions which Irish people would be familiar with since their school days. He also uses geographical and anthropological research to extrapolate his theory that the culture and people who evolved along the Atlantic coast must have emigrated from North Africa along the coasts of Spain and France, transforming as they did until they settled in Ireland, Wales and Scotland. He argues, quite persuasively, that trading between the seafaring peoples would have continued after initial emigration, and that the culture which evolved separately in each of these places thereafter nonetheless exhibits commonalities which give clues about this shared (and now forgotten) heritage. In a hypothesis central to many of the interpretations of the film as parody, Quinn muses that perhaps the myth of Atlantis is 'a souvenir of the imagination' of this multinational culture.

Amid the irony and self reflection though, there is a current of political anger. This is evident even in the observation which accompanies the Atlantis theory, 'he believes that Atlantic coastal dwellers once shared a common culture. Their contact was shattered by the rise of the nation-states, which turned natural neighbours into unnatural enemies.' Like Kearney, he is clearly concerned with the manner in which the evolution of the nation-state gave rise to the discourse of nationalism throughout Europe, not necessarily merely because it destroyed a semi-mythic cultural federation of trading people, but because of the inevitable nationalistic divisions which came with nation-state identities. More specifically, he is concerned with its effects in Ireland, particularly postcolonial Ireland where the recourse to a mythic pre-colonial past (Celticism) was a form of Aryanism.

It is worth noting in the context of the current discussion, that in attempting to link Ireland to North Africa, Quinn is well aware of the racial prejudice in Irish society. Though racism remains largely unexamined as a subject in its own right, Quinn touches upon it here. He is fully cognisant of the fact that his suggestion of a connection between North Africa and Ireland links white Irish culture with black ones, and he even suggests at one point that this is one reason for resistance to the idea. Again though, it is not that he is eager to prove or disprove the contention. By even suggesting it he forces the viewer to question the racial and cultural heritage of Ireland. He argues that Celticism is an expression of Catholic and nationalist ideology which has been artificially accorded the status of racial authenticity to legitimise orthodoxy. Whether 'fact' or speculation, it is a thought-provoking idea, and this is precisely the point.

Authenticity is one of the key areas of debate in postcolonial studies, and is, in a sense, at the centre of this book. If documentary is a philosophical form concerned with ontological arguments which define a person's relationship with the historical world and upon which suppositions regarding culture, history and identity are based, then it may be seen to be intrinsically related to the discourse of authenticity. Gareth Griffiths points out that there are genuine dangers in this arena of debate, which often represents an ideological confrontation between groups within society in which both sides make use of the same argument to claim the cultural high ground at the expense of the other. He notes that while claims to an 'authentic' voice can represent the postcolonial struggle for the emergence of a repressed cultural identity, the same claims can also represent an attempt to homogenise a new orthodoxy which represses elements of difference or otherness. He argues that postmodern instruments such as 'displacement, disruption, ambivalence, or mimicry, discursive features founded not in the closed and limited construction of a pure authentic sign but in endless and excessive transformation of the subject positions possible within the hybridised' (Griffiths, 1995: 241) are the weapons of resistance to this process of homogenisation, which we see in evidence in *Atlantean*.

As Diana Brydon notes, however, such weapons are usually turned on the colonial rather than the native culture. In fact, as she says, 'when directed against the Western canon, post-modernist techniques of intertextuality, parody, and literary borrowing may appear radical and even potentially revolutionary. When directed against native myths and stories, these same techniques would seem to repeat the imperialist history of plunder and theft' (Brydon, 1995: 140). This observation raises particularly interesting questions with regard to *Atlantean*, which *is* directed against 'native' myths. Given that no discourse of the racial subaltern has been acknowledged within Irish society, the postcolonial struggle for authenticity has been between nationalist and anti-nationalist factions. As Brydon asks, 'whose interests are served by this retreat into preserving an untainted authenticity? . . . Ironically, such tactics encourage native peoples to isolate themselves from contemporary life and full citizenhood' (141). By disputing the Celtic myths which have influenced the course of Irish history in the twentieth century (sometimes directly, sometimes by inference), Quinn turns Griffiths's weapons of resistance onto the culture which itself had been the one seeking independence from the colonial. Thus, in Brydon's terms, it isolates the Irish people from themselves, a reading which is reinforced by our survey of the evolution of Ireland in documentary to date. Ireland had not yet developed the ability to truly explore the limits of self-definition. Tentative examination of the questions of landscape, economy and history throughout the decades had merely begun the process. It is only by exposing the mythology of the state through a demonstration of the principles by which knowledge of its pre-colonial past has been collated and may be problematised that Quinn is able to finally make the breakthrough.

This is a difficult position in which to find oneself, and one which Quinn has responded to with all the force of the reflexive mode of representation. *Atlantean* does not claim to represent the 'authentic voice' of the Atlantean people. On the contrary, it argues that the vagaries of cultural evolution and historical development have wrought differences which have now defined a series of still distinctive European and African cultures. The series thus cannot be understood within conventional postcolonial parameters. Rather it must rank among the first postnationalist documents, a speculative meditation upon a post-postcolonial sensibility which simply did not exist at the time (and still does not, even according to Kearney). It is also the first truly postmodern Irish documentary. Its ability to employ and subvert convention to explore the notion of evidentiality is far beyond the polemical modernism of *Rocky Road to Dublin* or the rhetoric of *Our Country*. It is both formally and politically reflexive and successfully problematises form and content in a way which ultimately makes it a far more affecting and thought-provoking work than any of the more conventional cultural historical investigations which preceded it. Sadly, like *Our Country* and *Rocky Road to Dublin*, *Atlantean* would remain largely alone at the vanguard of Irish documentary for some time. Though subsequent films such as *The Road to God Knows Where* (1988) and *Mother Ireland* (1988) would continue to pressure the boundaries of authorisation and other films would begin to examine areas of the Irish experience as yet untouched, few would evince the genuine formal radicalism of Quinn's film until *The Uncle Jack*, where it was turned to quite different ends. Notably, *The Irish Empire* (1999) later made many of the same arguments about Ireland's early history as a maritime culture without a trace of humour or a suggestion of provocation, as if it were now accepted fact.

After *Atlantean* Quinn seemed spent as a force for change in documentary form. He continued to work as a producer and sponsor of non-fiction and eventually served on the RTÉ Authority (only to resign in protest at the station's policy on children's advertising), but by and large his profile was again of a fiction filmmaker. *Budawanny* (1987) and later *The Bishop's Story* (1994) would contribute significantly to the open debate about the clergy and religious orders in contemporary Ireland and he would continue to write and comment upon developments in the Irish film industry and in film as an art form. He continued to cast himself as the eccentric outsider and remained a figurehead of energy, innovation and lateral thinking. Yet by the time he came to make *Navigatio: Atlantean II* (1998) for Telefís na Gaelige, it seemed too much like an old master revisiting his masterpiece. A one-hour, single-episode documentary, *Navigatio* simply picked up where

15 Iconoclastic, mercurial and brilliant, filmmaker Bob Quinn was involved with the history of Irish documentary from the 1960s. Working initially with RTÉ, he became among the first independent producers to hire himself back to the organisation he left in protest in 1969. Though an important figure in fiction film, his greatest work is the documentary series *Atlantean* (1984), one of the most complex, self-reflexive visions of Irish culture ever produced

Atlantean left off, this time exploring the links between Conamara singing and the people of Tartarstan in the Russian Federation.

Though it was much the same in approach and content, *Navigatio* lacked the impact of its predecessor. Though Quinn managed to include a satirical jab at the obsession with the American-Irish hybrid culture which has sprung up around *Riverdance*, the film had little new to say. His 1997 film *Graceville* had been moderately more successful in recording an unusual angle on emigrant sagas, documenting the history of a group of individuals from Conamara who travelled to the US to work on a Native American reservation. The film was stylistically straightforward, though its exploration of the links between Native American and Irish culture echoed the concerns of his masterwork. His affectionate documentary tribute to then recently deceased actor Donal McCann (who had featured in several of Quinn's fiction films) *'It must be done right!'* (2000) was subtitled 'a film collage', which essentially excused its relative lack of structure and its reliance on a lengthy public interview given at the Galway Film Fleadh shortly before the actor's death. In concluding his 2001 book *Maverick* Quinn summed up:

The Lone Ranger is now a creaking man of sixty-five and has finally admitted that decrepitude of mind and body are creeping up on the ego and libido that he once fancied were indestructible. He has realised that his tastes and opinions are passé, that he should channel his remaining energies into wrestling with trees. As he stomps and splashes over his six acres of bog in Conamara, the process of whose reafforestation coincided with his naive efforts to reform RTÉ, he is capable of nothing more energetic than contemplating Shakespeare:

> 'And this our life except from public haunt,
> Finds tongues in trees, books in the running brooks,
> Sermons in stones, and good in everything.'

And about time, too, he agrees. (Quinn, 2001: 269–70)

Mother Ireland

The site of disjuncture at the intersection between postmodernism, post-colonialism and postnationalism would seem an ideal point of intervention for feminist documentary. Hélène Keyssar writes of the capacity of non-fiction film to dwell in those uncertain spaces between the profilmic and personal lived experience into which a woman can insert herself: 'the constant presence throughout these films of unfixed ideas of women defies essentialist feminisms while invoking women's distinctive ways of seeing and being. These are films, as Cavell might say, the viewing of which is an education in itself' (Keyssar, 1996: 104). She notes that documentary thrives on instability and ambiguity, which is exactly the kind of arena in which it is possible to establish a distinctively female voice, or preferably several different ones which open up different areas of female experience. It is therefore surprising that the majority of films made in Ireland, even dealing with issues of importance to Irish women, tend to be bracketed within conventional frames of reference. They are frequently constrained by debates which shift the focus from the fissures in contemporary Irish society to simply marking the passage of time.

The evolution of feminist documentary began with a series of what Patricia Erens terms 'consciousness-raising' films, often made in either *cinéma vérité* or personal monologue forms in the early 1970s (what Nichols might term observational and interactive modes). She writes, 'these films all had in common a concern for women and women's issues. Women and their environments were made visible in a new way. By eliminating the omniscient male narrator, women could speak in their own voices and validate their experiences' (Erens, 1988: 556). According to Julia Lesage even though these films did not exhibit stylistic radicalism they represented an important parallelism to patriarchal norms. By addressing women's issues with female voices, even if constrained by the representational parameters of tradition-ally patriarchal (or at least male-dominated) documentary formats, these films contributed to 'women's self-conscious, heightened, intellectual dis-cussion of role and sexual politics' (Lesage, cited in Nichols 1991: 64).

This particular strain of documentary is exemplified in Ireland by Trish McAdam's *Hoodwinked* (1997), made nearly thirty years after the US equiv-alents. As observed in Chapter 3 on historical documentary, this was essen-tially an attempt to (re)construct a 'herstory' of Ireland through the use of both archival material and interviews with prominent Irish women. In this regard and in this context, it was successful. It provided an array of female voices which documented women's contributions to Irish history since the foundation of the state and even allowed women of different generations to offer conflicting points of view. As McLoone (2000) notes, many of the debates around which the modernity of Irish culture were centred were issues central to women's experience, including property and succession rights, divorce, abortion, and social and economic equality. Protests by the Irish Housewives Association in the early 1960s led to legislative reform of legal marriage age in 1972, raising it from 16 to 18. The high-profile 'condom train' advocating the legalisation of contraception in the 1970s raised public awareness and contributed to eventual change in the law. The Employment Equality Act was introduced in 1977, legislation which con-tinues to impact heavily on Irish society as the terms of 'equality' spread ever wider. Continuing pressure in the arena of abortion has resulted in much activity, especially during high-profile cases such as the 'Kerry babies' affair in 1984, where a young lone parent was accused of murdering her infant, and the 'X case' in 1992 where a teenage rape victim was prevented from leaving the country because she admitted she wished to have an abor-tion in England. Women also occupy a particular place in Ireland, not least because of the enshrining of the family in the 1937 constitution, which emphasised the primacy of the home and its importance as the foundation of Irish society, and also because of the level of Marian worship associated with Irish Catholicism.

Women have traditionally been central to the representation of Ireland in fiction film, sometimes literally embodying the spirit of the country in the binary opposites of the loving mother and the fiery lover demanding blood sacrifice in her name. This trend has been extensively discussed in the stan-dard books on Irish fiction film, and, as Ruth Barton observes, 'if we look at these images more closely, we can see how much more they tell us about the culture their creators came from than the Irish situation to which they were allegedly indebted' (Barton, 1999: 40). In all of these it is fair to say that the representation of Irish women has not been illustrative of their experience. Each film is inevitably suited to the preconceptions of the producers – either commercial minds seeking to exploit clichés or traditionalists whose goal is the repression of the other or its integration with the status quo.

By the mid to late 1970s feminist filmmakers in general had begun to seek new forms and new modes of representation with which to problematise the ideas of femininity still held by the majority of viewers. This more avant-garde, experimental type of filmmaking was more concerned with defining the issues around which the basic questions of femaleness revolved rather than documenting thoughts and ideas on the subject. As Erens puts it, 'the best films are those that seek to expand their subjects, by providing an analytic context within which the viewer can place the material offered or by challenging our normal perceptions of the world (including film)' (Erens, 1988: 565). This clearly describes the kind of reflexive film which results from a postmodern sensibility, and indeed these are the type of films discussed by Erens, Nichols and partly by Keyssar. *Hoodwinked* certainly falls well short of this level of formal radicalism. To be fair to McAdam, her attempt to incorporate a general analysis of the course of Irish history and include male historian J. J. Lee may be seen as an attempt to delve a little more deeply than the 'talking heads' format allows, but as noted, the series ultimately falls victim to the inherent pitfalls of historical representation in Irish documentary.

The best-known feminist documentary to come out of the island of Ireland is *Mother Ireland* (1988). Located more firmly within a tradition of cultural nationalism than *Hoodwinked*, director Anne Crilly's film charts the relationship between feminism and nationalism in Ireland. The film (shot on video) was produced by the Derry Film and Video Workshop with partial funding from Channel Four (UK), and as such was something of a pioneer in the field of community video. Certainly since its production many more videos have been made by groups seeking to represent themselves, including victims of political violence attempting to deal with their trauma. Writing in 1992, documentarist Marilyn Hyndman drew attention to the project of 'resisting cultural arrest' in Northern Ireland. She pointed out that the majority of non-fiction produced there was made 'by British film makers who have parachuted in for a couple of weeks' (Hyndman, 1992: 16) and gave little insight to life in the country. She argued in favour of a documentary not constrained by the demands of television schedules or subject to the preconceptions of the intended audience. Instead, she claimed, documentaries should allow the communities within Northern Ireland to document themselves as a means of better understanding who they were and how they responded to the challenges of their lives. *Mother Ireland* was very community specific, and unashamedly sectarian. Excluding both males and protestant females, its political specificity and evident rhetoric made it a double threat to the establishment. The film was not broadcast by Channel Four when delivered to them, because they found elements of it problematic. Not only did it feature an interview with Mairéad Farrell, a member of the IRA who had been shot by the SAS in Gibraltar while on active duty, but its over-all message that these women had linked the personal and the political in an inevitable response to the twin pressures of colonialism and patriarchy was obviously troubling. It demonstrated a level of political consciousness out-side the domain of 'women's issues', and thus confronted Channel Four with its own policy of liberalism and giving time to minorities and/or special inter-est groups. When Crilly refused to make changes, Channel Four refused to show the film.

The issue of nationalism is nonetheless an example of the kind of con-text described by Erens which expands the frontiers of debate on the issue of women in society and challenges the 'normal' perceptions of both the world and film itself. Though not formally radical, *Mother Ireland* is at least cognisant of issues of representation and addresses them. Even its title is ambiguous, on one hand perpetuating the myth of 'Mother Ireland' by indi-cating that the programme will deal with material which illustrates contem-porary and historical events in the 'mother country', while on the other hand allowingg Crilly and the interviewees to critique the idea of 'Mother Ireland'. Is it about 'Mother Ireland' as a representational construct, or how Ireland continues to be violated, exploited and repressed as women have always been? This is the paradox the film invites us to consider, but it does not pro-vide resolution. Like the interweaving threads of feminist and nationalist analysis used, the stylistic blend of cutaways, film clips and interviews employs and critiques the means of representation. It is ultimately irresolv-able into discrete contexts of women and/or 'women' as a representational construct within nationalism and ideas of nationality, which is where its polemical force comes from.

Mother Ireland remained contentious and unique in Irish and Northern Irish feminist documentary. Though *Daughters of the Troubles* (1996) followed many years later, this film, exploring the community bonds between women throughout 'the troubles', was produced and directed by American Marcia Rock, and though quite thorough, still evinced an 'outside' perspective. *Mother Ireland* was eventually screened by Channel Four in 1993 as part of a series of films previously banned in the UK, including *Freaks* (1932) and *Monty Python's Life of Brian* (1979), curious company to say the least. Though a number of films followed in the Republic which articulated the viewpoints of female subjects, few films other than *Hoodwinked* could be termed 'feminist', and none has attempted to problematise representational codes.

My Great Grandmother was a Boxer (1997) was a slightly more self-reflex-ive (certainly more personal) attempt to (re)construct the history of a single female life as a sort of exemplar for female self-realisation in contemporary

Ireland. This was an account of the investigation by Dubliner Catherine Moylan into her family's history inspired by an old photograph of her eccentric great grandmother posing as a boxer around the turn of the twentieth century. Using some semi-comic reconstructions and some serious ones, the film attempted to give a sense of the difference between the world of the 1990s and that of the late nineteenth century when Polly Fairclough is supposed to have participated in a variety of pugilistic contests to claim the title of Lady Boxing Champion of the World. The scepticism of the modern-day boxing establishment about Fairclough's career is seen as the inevitable result of patriarchal oppression. Her pioneering efforts are therefore presented in terms of how a woman may establish her own parameters despite social and sexual prejudice. Like *Atlantean, My Great Grandmother was a Boxer* is not so much about the proof as the journey. The film is less concerned with the specifics of whether or not Polly Fairclough was a 'legitimate' boxer or merely an eccentric free spirit than with a project of self-discovery. Moylan demonstrates the same determination not to accept what she is told by the male establishment that she presumes Polly possessed. Her investigation recounts a female experience and *is* a female experience. The film is thus a feminist exploration of the nature of femininity and the legitimacy of female experience within patriarchy far more than it is an investigative documentary.

Barton also draws attention to *50,000 Secret Journeys* (1994), recounting developments in the legal battle over abortion which intercut interviews with three Irish women with news footage. As one of the outstanding key areas in which female political activism remains both high profile and distinctively concerned with the implications of the relationship between Irish women and the Irish state, abortion should presumably prove a suitable subject for radical treatment. The battle over the referendum of 1983 was lost when the Catholic church voiced its opposition to the introduction of abortion both from the pulpit and on television. In 1986 a High Court ruling decreed that even the provision of abortion information was illegal (though the decision was later overturned by the European Court). In 1992, the 'X case' resulted in the Irish courts granting injunctions to prevent women leaving the country to have abortions abroad, and though again after protests and appeals a limited amount of discretion was granted in cases where the life of the mother was in danger, the situation remains unsatisfactory to the majority of pro-abortion campaigners.

The film *50,000 Secret Journeys* is one of the very few to approach the subject. Though Barton praises its avoidance of voyeurism or exploitation, and it allows its three interviewees to tell their stories in the manner of the early American feminist films, she notes that the film was originally shown as part of a longer current-affairs broadcast presented by respected RTÉ broadcaster Marion Finucane. This is the context in which many documentaries are shown on Irish television, a pattern we have already seen emerging from the 1960s onwards, and the bulk of the focus tends to be on the comments of the spokespersons or politicians who participate in the panel discussion rather than the film itself. While this is indicative of the use to which documentaries are put in public affairs, it also robs them of their potential to engage the audience on their own terms. In this case the context does not so much expand the subject as narrow it to a debate between public figures. Viewers do not have the chance to respond personally and emotionally to a film so bracketed. In the case of *50,000 Secret Journeys* abortion is defined not so much as a feminist issue or even a women's issue, but as a current-affairs topic.

Again the difficulty is that with essentially only one potential means of reaching a mass audience, filmmakers must subscribe to the programming demands of the national broadcaster. Therefore, radical, oppositional or experimental documentaries are unlikely to be seen. Within the terms of the current discussion, one might be tempted to presume this represents a concerted attempt to repress women's voices on Irish television. But it is equally true of non-fiction films on any subject and by any director. The majority of non-fiction filmmakers are satisfied merely to have employment. This is understandable, but it is not necessarily healthy. As Alan Gilsenan remarked in an interview in 1996, 'people are doing programmes just because they will get the commission. Obviously RTÉ have certain things they need to fulfil but I think you have to be very careful to retain the passion and the interest in what you are doing . . . There is a careerism at the expense of the work' (cited in Collins, 1996: 22). This results in the majority of Irish documentaries remaining within journalistic parameters, serving as news documentaries rather than theme documentaries such as *Atlantean* and *Mother Ireland*. This leads to a level of frustration, and has encouraged several young directors to work abroad or to work on contract for the BBC, ITV or Channel Four. Yet this has not necessarily always been unhealthy for Irish documentary, especially because this period of self-imposed exile often results in a maturing of style and the establishment of a reputation which gives filmmakers sufficient weight to develop more personal projects when they return to Ireland.

Inside and out: Alan Gilsenan and John T. Davis

By the late 1980s, Ireland seemed to be on a downward spiral of resurging conservatism, unemployment and emigration which many young people found depressing and intolerable. The decade had begun with pronouncements by Charles J. Haughey (the son-in-law of Seán Lemass) that it would be 'a decade of endeavour' which would make Ireland one of the great nations of the world. Time proved his exhortations to be empty rhetoric. The defeat of the referenda to introduce abortion and divorce, the closure of factories and businesses, the decay of inner-city Dublin and the continuing allure of employment in Britain and the US inspired few school leavers to remain at home. The 'slow bleeding to death' of the country decried in *Our Country* had reached ruinous proportions and there seemed little hope despite the attempts by government agencies and promotional bodies to encourage indigenous industry and keep young people on Irish soil.

Though the situation would have turned around dramatically in less than ten years, when Alan Gilsenan, then twenty-four years old, made *The Road to God Knows Where* in 1988 it captured the moment. A much-needed injection of energy in Irish documentary, dealing more frankly and directly with the subject than anything produced to date, It was an angry assault on the institutions which its maker saw as being responsible for the conditions of the time in the mould of *Rocky Road to Dublin*. It was more than a direct-address polemic though, and demonstrated a sense of juxtaposition and irony which went beyond the *nouvelle vague* trappings of its predecessor. It was also an evocative study of the contrast between the state and the citizen which established a dialectic between the desolation of the dispossessed and the rhetoric of progress.

The film begins with an extract from a poem by Padraig Pearse, immediately establishing a link with the ideals of 1916 and taking on the legacy of Ireland's past, not to mention the dark tone:

I have turned my face
To this road before me,
To the deed that I see
And the death I shall die. (Pearse)

This gives way to an eerie image of a young blonde child with a dirty face standing on a windswept hill as the camera swoops around him/her. A series of images follow of graveyard headstones, signposts on empty roads in semi-darkness and barren hills and open bogland. An interviewee speaks about traditional Irish culture, where everyone was neighbourly and where proud and noble people lived happy lives. The shots of headstones which continue throughout the speech undercut his optimism with a clear message that such an Ireland is long dead. The titles then come (in green, white and gold) and a mournful female voice performs 'The Soldier's Song'. This is traditionally a cheerful tune celebrating unity and a devil-may-care approach to trouble. Here it becomes an unsettling dirge forecasting a future of despair and uncertainty. The image dissolves to a lonely country road in the evening darkness along which a single car is driving and where the wind is heard howling.

This opening sequence sums up the attitude and approach taken by Gilsenan towards both the formal and thematic content of his film. It is reminiscent of the first scenes in *Rocky Road to Dublin*, not only in its symbolic concern with a road and the use of a traditional song, but in using its precredit sequence to establish the frames of reference for the subsequent argument. The film which follows continues to counterpose images of Ireland and the Irish, and establishes an opposition between ideals and reality. The opening sequence is followed by a further montage of suburban housing developments ringed by barbed-wire fences where strips of dirty plastic flutter in the breeze and where pollution and litter surrounds scattered children who play there. One child hesitantly reads the 1916 proclamation, which speaks of the happiness and prosperity of the Irish people in the name of God and the dead generations. The images of the urban landscape and the dirty faces of young children make a poignant rejoinder to its aspirations. The blame here is being laid both on the state (in the guise of the proclamation) and on the romantic ideals of the past which have, in Gilsenan's view, stifled progress because of people's obsession with them. Like an increasing number of directors at this time, he was both aware of the constructed nature of Ireland's image of itself and eager to question it. Unlike most, he actually succeeded.

Throughout the film, Gilsenan demonstrates a scepticism about 'official' representations of Ireland and the Irish. Like Lennon before him, Gilsenan does not expect us to take all that is said by his interviewees at face value. The smugly upbeat comments of a neatly dressed interviewee speaking about how young people can accomplish anything if they put their minds to it are juxtaposed with shots of dirty children playing on littered streets. A spokesperson from the IDA speaks of progress and investment over images of abandoned factories. Gilsenan's anger is manifest not in a spoken commentary as in Lennon's film, but in this type of constant sense of irony and the visual undercutting of the verbal referent. Title cards are flashed up bearing familiar, upbeat slogans and common phrases like 'it's a long road that has no turns', 'the youth are our greatest national asset' and 'may the road rise up to meet you'. These are not chapter headings, but appear as random thoughts which relate to the general thematic content of the film. They also provoke viewers into disengaging from the expositional material, and force them to treat their positive exhortations with incredulity. Devices such as this demand that the audience remains active. The techniques of fragmentation, parody and confrontational editing constantly draw attention to the film as discourse, not data.

The stand-up comedy sequences featuring Karl McDermott work the same way. The comedian first appears standing in the foreground of an image of a housing estate in which a group of small children are visible in the background tipping the remains of a car end over end. Each time it hits the ground, a loud crash is heard (obviously non-synchronous). McDermott mimics the upbeat attitude of the earlier interviewees, speaking about how great a race of people the Irish are and how they can accomplish anything, before giving a brief rendition of 'Danny Boy'. All the time the children progress across the littered green area of their estate, from the left-hand side of the screen to the right. When they reach the far side, the sequence ends. On one level there is the obvious parody of the spoken word and the sentiments it expresses. McDermott's delivery is stylised and ironic, and eventually descends into a series of meaningless and unrelated aphorisms. Lest anyone still take his words seriously, the constant presence in the image of the children, the litter and the wrecked car is a reminder of the physical condition of the landscape – a profilmic referent even in traditional documentary terms. The strangeness of what the children are doing is emphasised by the artificiality of the noises dubbed on the soundtrack, and McDermott's apparent unawareness of what is going on behind him obviously suggests the refusal of people who speak in all seriousness as he does in jest to acknowledge 'reality'. His final reference to 'two great Irish tenors no longer in the land of the living . . . John McCormack and Frank Patterson' (the latter of whom was still alive) is both an obvious joke and a pointed bit of satire, especially when taken in the context of the film's overall deconstruction of Irish culture.

The film incorporates a broad range of interviewees living abroad and collates their comments. But even here irony and paradox are more interesting to Gilsenan than basic information. One Irish woman living in New York speaks about her pride in being Irish and her refusal to renounce her Irish citizenship, yet she tells us that she would never go back to Ireland unless she was terminally ill. Another interviewee, living in London, expresses similar pride in his Irishness but an equal reluctance to live in Ireland. As he begins to elaborate on the national pride felt when Stephen Roche won the Tour de France, the soundtrack fades up U2 singing 'Pride', effectively drowning him out. No one, it seems, is spared Gilsenan's ire. The film works in material regarding morality and religious issues, contrasting pious people with those who feel bitter about the church's legacy in the abortion referendum and in homophobia in Irish society. The Pope's famous goodwill message to the 'young people of Ireland' is juxtaposed with the title card, 'It's a rat trap, and you've been caught'.[1] Similarly some observations regarding the situation in Northern Ireland appear as part of the tapestry of oppression which Gilsenan weaves, but he is less concerned with Northern Ireland *per se* than with the schisms within Irish society: industrialisation/unemployment, national pride/emigration, religion/despair, peace/war, etc. This makes it very much an expression of the postmodern condition in contemporary Ireland, an explicit illustration of the decay of traditional boundaries and forms of understanding.

The film's conclusion returns us to the child featured at the beginning, standing again on the windswept hills of a littered suburban 'green area', where he/she comes across the Dublin band Aslan playing songs about contemporary Ireland. The film constantly returns to images of children, especially pre-teens and toddlers. There are many inserts of children playing on the streets or in playgrounds and there is a recurring image of a group of children in school uniforms jumping up and down in slow motion which is employed in different contexts to suggest energy, conformity and (perhaps) rebellion. While it is clear that the film is aimed at a young audience, the use of children also exerts a powerful emotional hold over adults. The film is not necessarily a work of social advocacy, or even strictly what we might term a social documentary despite the fact that it demonstrates a concern with the state of Irish society. It does outline the problems facing certain segments of the population and attempts to give a sense of the environment and the people, but it does this through confrontation and subversion.

The film is a response not only to decades of social and political conformity, but to both the image of Ireland proffered by uncritical documentaries and to the form with which it has been represented. It is a document of the times and a summation of the frustrations of the younger generation, only understandable within the context of the indefinable moment of 'post' modernism. It comes after years of industrialisation and economic expansion which had been presumed to have been progressive but which the film reveals to have been merely a slow journey down the 'road to God knows where'. It treats the 1980s the same way that *Rocky Road to Dublin* treated the 1960s. It asks, have the cultural myths of Celtic warriors and smiling villagers really been dispelled? Is the country really any better off? Who are the 'real' Irish and what is the real Ireland? Its concern with cultural myth and economic conditions gives it the means to deconstruct both the filmic and the *realpolitik* Ireland and problematise our assumptions about both.

It is noteworthy that the film was commissioned by Channel Four and originally screened on British TV as part of a series of Irish documentaries entitled *The Irish Reel*. RTÉ picked it up for broadcast in October 1988, when its screening sparked predictable controversy. The IDA publicly criticised the film for its portrayal of Ireland, and it provoked discussion on television and radio talk shows not only of unemployment and emigration, but of the type of Ireland that was emerging at the end of the twentieth century. It was the conditions it captured which caused shock and outrage, not the film, and though there were some who claimed it was a distortion of 'reality', on the whole the film was popular. It won an Irish National Television Award and later a European Film Special Jury Award. Famously, at the ceremonial presentation of the former, Gilsenan criticised the then Fianna Fáil government for the closure of the Irish Film Board, firmly establishing his reputation as an angry young man.

Gilsenan went on to become one of the most successful and high-profile Irish documentarists of his generation. First followed an equally provocative account of the treatment of AIDS patients in Ireland, *Stories from the Silence* (1990), which offered a dark counterpoint to the ultimately upbeat and pro-state account of the treatment of TB in *Voyage to Recovery*. Like *The Road to God Knows Where*, the film exhibited anger and dealt with a subject not examined before. This was followed by *Prophet Songs* (1991), a study of Irish Catholic priests who have left the church. Again confronting taboos by expressing dissatisfaction with organised religion (albeit mediated by inter-viewees), the film did attempt to retain some respect for spirituality while condemning the repressive institution that had driven these men away from something they loved (rather like the emigrants in *The Road to God Knows Where*). Gilsenan noted that 'we've rid ourselves of the yoke of Catholic oppression in institutional terms but there was a spiritual legacy that came with Catholicism that is still very much in the psyche and to neglect that or pretend it doesn't exist is dangerous and counterproductive. The imaginative and transcendental part is valuable and we shouldn't be so quick to throw out the baby with the bathwater' (cited in McKeone, 1998: 41). This kind of opinion is at the heart of Gilsenan's sensibility (and uncannily echoes both Louis Marcus and Fr Joe Dunn). *The Road to God Knows Where* was bleak, but its anger encouraged action, not despair. Its constant referral to children, like in *Rocky Road to Dublin* and *Our Country*, evoked thoughts of the future. Gilsenan used the camera to reveal a dark underside to empty rhetoric, but also to find a glimmer of hope in the eyes of those with most to lose.

In 1995 Gilsenan was hired by ITV to make the six-part series *God Bless America* (1996) profiling major American literary figures. In this series he employed his sense of visual counterpoint to American culture, exploring myths and juxtaposing the icons of progress and development with profilmic images of decay and deprivation. The level of invective and penetration varied from programme to programme and Gilsenan demonstrated an ability to match himself to the subject's voice rather than foreground his own. While Gore Vidal was obviously an inspiration for some pointed vitriol on Washing-ton DC (tinged with a melancholy affection with which Gilsenan identified), Scott Turow more tamely spoke of the work ethic in Chicago. Throughout, Gilsenan endeavoured to match form to content, and in a sense went from being an angry young Irish director to a very competent observer of life, wher-ever it took him. He allowed himself to see with other people's eyes, and this became a vital skill which he applied to his next project.

Home Movie Nights (1996) is an example of what Corner in his section on the future of documentary categorises as 'do-it-yourself documentary'

(Corner, 1996: 185), a series structured around home movies made by amateurs. As Corner points out, this new genre has divided commentators into two schools, one which argues that it represents a democratisation of the form and another which expresses caution about voyeurism and exploitation. First broadcast in 1996, but rerun several times, *Home Movie Nights* was a pleasing variant on the established format pioneered in Britain by *Video Diaries* (1991). Rather than farm out equipment to contemporary Irish citizens and compile the results, Gilsenan delved into the extensive archives of amateur filmmakers working with 8 mm and 16 mm stock from the 1930s on. The raw footage was then combined with contemporary interviews with either the filmmaker or persons otherwise involved with the films or the events which are captured on them. This cleverly combines three frames of documentary reference. Firstly, it invokes the democratising effects of the video diary. Secondly, it has the historical interest of being archival footage. Thirdly, it has the contemporaneity of allowing people of the 1990s to reflect on how the events of the past have shaped their subsequent lives.

Home Movie Nights restored to documentary some of the fascination and spontaneity that the early films of Alexandre Promio offered to the Dubliners of the 1890s. The subjects of the individual films are frequently off-beat, rarely concerned with major political events or significant moments in Ireland's past, and always seem to capture a sense of the everyday often lacking in contemporary *video vérité*. In a single episode, as many as eight or ten segments might be featured (though it was often less), mostly unrelated to one another except by the locality in which they were shot or by the filmmaker. The addition of the commentary introduces an element of reflexivity. Participants will frequently discuss the conditions under which the film was shot and the type of equipment used, and supplement what is seen with memories of the process of recording it. Frequently this does not so much envelop the viewer in a happy fog of nostalgia as evoke powerful identification. It also gives a strong sense of time and place which surprisingly does not prevent it from dealing with contemporary Ireland. In one episode, a man who had shot amateur footage of Bishop Eamon Casey reflects on more recent events in the bishop's life (the paternity scandal) and the implications this has for the future of Catholicism as the filmmaker sees it. The fact that his footage of Casey is utterly inoffensive makes it all the more affecting. The viewer is engaged on two levels, reflecting on past and present in a unique manner.

The success of *Home Movie Nights* inspired the more conventional do-it-yourself documentary series *Citizens* (1999) which, while admittedly contributing to the multiplicity of Irish voices beginning to be heard in the late twentieth century, lacked the reflexivity and contextuality of Gilsenan's series. *Home Movie Nights* is testament to Gilsenan's evolution as a documentarist, and though his next project was the experimental drama *All Soul's*

Day (1997), which McLoone says 'quietly irritates rather than shocks' (McLoone, 2000: 167), he then wisely returned to non-fiction. His subsequent films were less remarkable though, and he seemed to become a victim of the careerism he once identified as a problem. Though flawed in some respects discussed previously, *The Green Fields of France* (1999) was at least a demonstration of how far both Ireland and documentary have developed, in that, on one hand, Ireland's contribution to the First World War has been acknowledged, and on the other, a film as stylistically abstract and poetic as this should be deemed a suitable treatment of the subject.

The internationally co-produced *The Irish Empire*, of which Gilsenan directed two episodes, took him again away from Ireland to explore the legacy of emigration in Irish diaspora around the world. The series was something of a rejoinder to the Disney-produced *The Long Journey Home* (1997) in its insistence not only on a more international selection of Irish emigrants than those who had gone to America, but also on the importance of the outward flow rather than the journey back. It featured interviews with emigrants and their descendants in an attempt to argue that the borders of Ireland stretch well beyond its coastlines in 'an empire of memory and imagination'. Historians from various Irish, Australian and American universities speculated on the meaning of Irish identity in the context of late twentieth-century ideas of nation, self and culture. Series consultant Fintan O'Toole made the observation that 'Irishness is going to be this kind of infinitely expandable ethnic identity that will make people feel they have a place in the world – even if they don't', which was a summary of the argument presented by the series on the whole. In this it was vaguely reminiscent of *Saints Went Marching Out* (1967), and with its all too soft-voiced narration by Fiona Shaw and overbearing musical score by Deborah Mollison, it frequently threatened to overwhelm the wealth of academic investigation and the volume of human experience presented in the course of five hours of television with the romantic ideal that the Irish had 'saved civilisation'. In a sense *The Irish Empire* represents an expansion of elements of *The Road to God Knows Where*, though it is far less anxious about the consequences of this emigration for contemporary Ireland, because it no longer threatens the health of the nation. On the contrary, given the increased concentration on the diaspora in the 1990s, it is an assertion of strength, hinted at even in the title's reference to 'empire' (a term used with all due irony, of course). The diaspora was also the subject of the four-part series from Graph Films, *The Morrison Tapes* (1995), following the experiences of four different Irish emigrants abroad, which will be discussed in the next chapter.

The true sequel to *The Road to God Knows Where* followed in 2001. In between Gilsenan helmed *Julie's Story* (2000) and *Private Dancer* (2000), the former a film on the life of novelist Julie Parsons which was a kind of variant on *God Bless America*, the latter a disappointingly shallow profile of the lap-dancing scene in contemporary Dublin. Expectations were high for *Road II* (2001), into which observers presumed Gilsenan had been putting all of his energies. In the event, *Road II* was a major disappointment. Shot mostly on digital video, the film incorporated clips from its predecessor, which it jux-taposed with new footage and new interviews with some of the participants in the original film. Like a doubly self-reflexive variant on *Home Movie Nights*, it attempted to put its image of the new Ireland in counterpoint with that documented thirteen years earlier by Gilsenan himself and tried to signal the distance between them by putting pronounced black borders around scenes from the first film (as he had with the archival material in *Home Movie Nights*). The contemporary footage was blurred and impres-sionistic, replicating the visual style of *All Soul's Day* in what seemed an attempt to comment upon the nature of the postmodern landscape. Rapid-fire, almost meaningless images of car dealerships, video shops, phone booths, supermarkets, signposts and traffic lights seemed to represent the empty whirl of modern life, and yet this amounted to less than any of the same montage sequences in any of the city films of the 1920s and 1930s.

The issue was one of context. These scenes of the city were juxtaposed with interviews which had nothing to say. Though the film purported to attack the excesses of the Celtic Tiger (partly by correlating the imagery from contemporary Dublin with scenes shot in the US), most of its interviewees seemed visibly better off than they were in 1988. Their complaints about the Ireland they now lived in seemed petty in the face of obvious counter-evi-dence of their comfort. This dissipated whatever polemical force their views may have contributed to Gilsenan's overall argument, and effectively self-destructed the film. There was some evidence of social frustration in the impressionistic account of the economic scandals and tribunals of the late 1990s featured deep in the *mélange* of images and free-association musings of the film, but Gilsenan refused to provide a clear articulation of the issues or illustration of the facts. This was precisely the point from a formal point of view, of course: to immerse the viewer in the maelstrom of greed and con-sumerism which rendered the physical and socio-economic 'landscape' of Ireland as an abstraction. It also had the effect of leaving the viewer without any frame of reference to understand what it was about. *Road II* literally became a 'road' 'to' nowhere (which is the paradox suggested by its title), but the journey wasn't especially interesting. It quickly became meaningless and tedious, and ran out of even curiosity value long before its fifty-four minutes were up. The film was largely negatively reviewed and quietly ignored by the public.

The increasing importance of the subject of emigration and immigra-tion, which remained at the centre of *Road II*, is of course indicative of the expanding borders of the idea of Ireland in the late twentieth century which has necessitated the growth of a postnationalist, multicultural identity. Including 'foreign' histories within the canon of Irish cultural nationalism is a sign of the beginnings of the kind of redefinition with which Kearney is concerned. Gilsenan himself remains ideally placed to continue to challenge expectations of documentary form and content in Ireland. For all of its failures, *Road II* was at least unconventional and tried to use form to explore content. Gilsenan's experience is indicative of the restlessness and sense of blurred boundaries which has defined postnationalist Ireland with which we are currently concerned, and though he often reflects its confusion, Gilsenan has also proved that documentary can help to make sense of it.

The same is true of John T. Davis, a Belfast-born filmmaker whose work as a director and cinematographer spans not only north and south of the border, but, like Gilsenan's, the United States.[2] In Davis's case the US has significance in terms of understanding Ireland. America often fulfils a thematic function, providing an illustration of certain principles which help Davis to understand both his country and himself. *Route 66* (1985) configured the

16 Belfast-born John T. Davis has made some of the most personal, introspective films ever to come out of Ireland, yet he has consistently matched his authorial concerns to external subject matter. He is pictured here enjoying ice cream with 'Beargrease', one of the subjects of *Hobo* (1991). It is not easy to tell the subject and the director apart (Davis is on the left), which is typical of Davis's immersive filmmaking practices. In making *Hobo*, he lived on the road with these men for several months landscape of the famous highway and the people who live along it in a way which has resonance for Ireland (especially in the light of the significance of the 'road' in two of the films discussed so far). *Dust on the Bible* (1989) examined the evangelical tradition within Northern Ireland's Protestant community. *Power in the Blood* (1989) followed religiously inspired Nashville singer Vernon Oxford on tour in Northern Ireland, where a seemingly alien musical tradition found popular success. *Heart on the Line* (1990) was a study of creativity and the creative personality focused on veteran and struggling writers in Nashville. *Hobo* (1991) studied the lives of American transients whose sense of identity was defined by a restless nature. *Atlantic: The Independent Years* (1993) profiled the development of Atlantic records from a small operation to a thriving conglomerate.

It was only after all these that he returned home literally and spiritually to make *The Uncle Jack* (1996), a reflection on his own creative personality and the inspiration for his filmmaking which attempted to explore his sense of self and the meaning of his life and art. A disastrous fire at his home but a short hold on Davis's directing career, but he returned some time later with *Travellers* (2000), co-directed with photographer Alen MacWeeney, whose 1960s photographs of Ireland's travelling community provided the inspiration for a return journey to the people and places recorded thirty years before. After much freelance cinematography work and service as an instructor on film production training courses, he finally directed *A House Divided* (2003), a film portrait of a painted portrait of the members of the Northern Ireland Assembly intended for display at Government Buildings.

Davis was inspired to become a filmmaker by the peculiar combination of his uncle, John McBride Neill, an architect who designed cinemas and encouraged his nephew to be creative, and D. A. Pennebaker, whom he saw on the streets of Belfast in 1966 filming Bob Dylan for the documentary *Don't Look Back* (1966). After attending art college he began making experimental films with an 8 mm, then a 16 mm, camera. His first film 'that anybody took notice of' (cited in O'Regan (ed.), 1993: 9) was *Shellshock Rock* (1978), a low-budget profile of the punk music scene in Belfast. During the production he formed a company called Holywood Films[3] to make commercial documentaries. *Shell Shock Rock* gained instant notoriety when it was refused entry to the Cork Film Festival on grounds of insufficient technical quality. Infuriated by what he saw as censorship, Davis arranged for a public screening of the film at which some of the featured bands played live and to which members of the press were invited. It was a success and the festival committee was forced to retract its statement. Davis did not rest though. He took the film to America, where it was screened at the New York Film and TV Festival and won a Silver Award. Afterwards it was picked up for art-house distribution and sold for cable screenings.

After living in the United States for three years, Davis returned to Ireland to make another music documentary, *Self-Conscious Over You* (1981), again featuring punk bands, but now at the end of their popularity. The film reflected 'the end of an era in Belfast' (cited in O'Regan (ed.), 1993: 13) in more ways than one. Music remained a fascination of Davis's throughout his career, and a frequent subject of his films. His attention now turned back to America, specifically Route 66, which he saw as a symbol for the whole of the United States. Inspired by 'beat' writers such as Jack Kerouac, the songs of Bob Dylan and Peter Bogdanovich's *The Last Picture Show* (1971), Davis sought an America which was empty, ravaged and torn, but in which people lived with a pride and dignity. Though it takes an imaginative leap to appreciate it, this was, for Davis, also a study of Ireland and the Irish, or at least of a certain way of seeing the world with which Davis empathised having been raised in Ireland. To him Ireland represents a wilder and more barren place than the rest of Europe, a kind of peripheral state of the United States where the attitudes of the people differ greatly from those of the British or other European countries. This places Ireland on the periphery of an 'official' (perhaps 'civilised') culture where it negotiates its own space by drawing on different traditions. It is a classic postcolonial situation and a postmodern response.

This may be a problematic contention, but Davis does not attempt to rationalise his instincts. He expresses his feelings on film. Filmmaking is, for him, a creative and therapeutic act, something he is driven to do by his artistic temperament. He despises 'journalistic documentaries' which he dismisses as 'wallpaper' (cited in Lavery, 1992: 20) in which visuals are secondary to data. To him the medium offers an opportunity to express himself with images: 'When they [the audience] watch my films, I feel that, you know, I'm exposing myself. I feel naked. And that's the way it should be really, if it means anything to you, because that's what it's about, it's about self-expression, it has to be' (21). Kathleen McCracken explores Davis's visual style in terms of poetic expression. She notes that his juxtaposition of word and image offers a counterpoint to traditional documentary forms which emphasises the presence of the personal without sacrificing the subject matter to self-indulgence (though she confines herself to an analysis of *Route 66* and *Dust on the Bible*). She observes, 'there is a fine balance between the lyrical "I-centered" elements and social realities, which in turn directs the audience's emotional and intellectual response. Again, the analogy with the lyric poem, which is an integration of private and objective experience, presents itself' (McCracken, 1999: 14). Though it becomes more evident in the light of his later work, especially when it was the specific subject of *The Uncle Jack*, all of Davis's films are bound up with his sense of self, a sense in turn defined by, on one hand, his artistic temperament in an industry which emphasises pragmatism and, on the other, an exploration of what it means to be part of an 'Irish' culture.

Route 66 and *Hobo* are an example of this expression at its most metaphorical. Both films are concerned with America and American culture, and have the appearance of conventional documentaries which would not look out of place in the filmography of any American director. But both films examine a fringe culture, a reflective sensibility which is capable of taking the stance of outsider from within. The peoples of the Mid-West living in dust-ripped settlements along Route 66, the transients who comment on trends in popular culture but have opted out from it, and Davis himself, the art student from Belfast making films about punks, drifters, hobos and musicians, are fundamentally interrelated. All of Davis's films are intensely personal. As Ted Sheehy observes, '*Hobo, Power in the Blood* and his other films all have subjects which are like manifestations of Davis himself in a celluloid parallel universe' (Sheehy, 1996: 17). *Heart on the Line* and *Power in the Blood* both concern themselves with country music, again one would presume a particularly American phenomenon. However there is a strong tradition of so-called 'Country and Irish' music which thrives in contemporary Ireland, especially Northern Ireland and northern counties of the Republic, as revealed in *Power in the Blood*. *Heart on the Line*'s concern with artistic integrity would later find direct expression in *The Uncle Jack*, but again, Davis was interested in seeing where creative inspiration comes from and how it flowers or dies in the face of an often uncaring music industry, echoing his own experiences as an Irish filmmaker.

Power in the Blood and *Dust on the Bible* were also both concerned with religion, and Davis indeed has said he considers them both part of one work on Northern Ireland. *Dust on the Bible* dealt with street preachers in Belfast, to Davis a symbol of the city and an exemplar of the fundamentalist point of view which informs so much of Northern Irish culture, especially the culture of resistance which underlies the Unionist struggle to maintain its identity. He says:

You can listen to a preacher in Cornmarket on a Saturday afternoon here, or see Paisley standing in front of City Hall on a Friday at lunch-time. I've been up in Stormont, shooting news, when Paisley has started talking about the Bible – in the middle of a press conference! The problem is that one-track narrowness that's best described in the slogan 'Ulster Says No'. It just shows the attitude of some people – from fundamentalist religion right through to politics. That nihilistic attitude, 'we will not change' has torn Northern Ireland apart. (cited in O'Regan (ed.), 1993: 17)

He also admits to being fascinated by 'the madness in their eyes', which he saw as 'a projection of the madness in this country' (cited in O'Regan (ed.),

1993: 17). He identifies this with the character of Preacher Casey in *The Grapes of Wrath*, again linking his sense of events and people in Ireland with those of the US. However, its juxtaposition of the wild eyes and screaming lips of the preachers with scenes of army and police activity on the darkened streets of Belfast also locate the film very specifically within the political geography of Northern Ireland. *Power in the Blood* focused on Vernon Oxford, a man with a reckless youth who had turned to God and to music to spread his word. Davis admits to identifying with Oxford's life story and his quest for spiritual meaning. He was also canny enough to relate the singer's tour to political concerns, such as when he visits the Maze prison to meet a fan. Davis does not separate religion from politics. Whatever the difference between a spiritual world and the material one, he is aware that in contemporary Ireland (and Northern Ireland) religion is intrinsically related to a sense of social and political identity.

The Uncle Jack was undoubtedly the pinnacle of Davis's achievement, and a milestone in Irish documentary. Like all such milestones, however, it remains unique for the time being and has yet to inspire a fully self-conscious documentary practice which might truly lead the form through the labyrinths of postmodernism and postnationalism to the kernel of human truth which non-fiction film has the capacity to touch upon. Ian Thullier's *Darkroom* (2002) had some trace of its sense of personal insight, a moving homage to photographer Harry Thullier Jr. directed by his younger brother which attempted to understand his life, his death and his art relative to parts of their world the brothers shared and those they did not. But like Michael Moore's *Roger and Me* (1989) and Ross McElwee's *Sherman's March* (1986), *The Uncle Jack* is a specifically autobiographical film which also addresses topics arising out of the life experience of the director, who is also the subject. For McElwee it was the historical significance of General Sherman's march across the United States which paralleled his own quest for romantic resolution; for Moore it was the death of the industrial town in North America where he was raised. Both films were an explicit reversal of the conventions of classical documentaries. They inscribe the author within the text to the extent that their ordering presence is not only felt, but acknowledged and discussed.

As Jim Lane points out, the autobiographical genre is inherently reflexive and subjective. Emerging from the 'personal is political' debate of the late 1960s, autobiographical documentary is socially and politically engaged, and has been an important genre in postmodern non-fiction film. It shifts the boundaries between proscription and discourse, problematising referentiality to the point where traditional notions of 'truth' and 'subjectivity' break down. As Lane observes:

Autobiographical documentaries constitute a site of struggle between the collective political groups of the late sixties, exemplified by the New Left and the Civil Rights Movement, and the more personal, self-directed political or apolitical movements of the seventies and eighties, movements that were initiated by the breakdown of the political collective, developed by the Women's Movement, and elaborated by the new multiculturalism. These films represent a range of attitudes toward the self in history by inscribing a variety of positions for the subject in the film text. Starting from the point that the enunciative subject is the filmmaker in the film, these films open out, presenting multiple possibilities for cinematic self-inscription. (Lane, 1993: 22–3)

Autobiographical films therefore allow viewers to experience documentary subjectivity in a more intimate and immediate way. In viewing aspects of the filmmaker's life experience relative to the subject under discussion, we are forced to consider our own reactions and our own subject positions. Whether or not we then 'get to know' the filmmaker is not the point. The important thing is that we acknowledge their presence, place their argument in context because of this, and therefore understand that non-fiction filmmaking is a discursive practice. This gives us the necessary sense of negotiated space within the discourse on contemporary Irish identity found in Davis's work, especially *The Uncle Jack*.

The film is introduced by Davis seated in a studio. He explains that it was intended as 'a sentimental journey' through his own past and a homage to his deceased uncle, John McBride Neill. He acknowledges however that the past is a 'treacherous' and 'haunted' landscape where reality and nostalgia become entwined and it becomes difficult to separate memory from lived experience. The film which follows is a melancholy and emotionally charged exploration of Davis's own journey from being the infant nephew of McBride Neill to the maker of the film we are watching. Scenes of him working in his studio, running projectors – assembling the building blocks upon which the filmic text is to be constructed – are juxtaposed with his rediscovery of model aeroplanes, a hobby encouraged by his uncle and which is seen as a metaphor for their shared fascination with shaping raw material into concrete objects. Dramatically lit inserts show the camera panning across the eerie landscape of a model town and of buildings designed by his uncle, and these are juxtaposed with scenes of Davis building a model plane which he will fly before the film's conclusion. McBride Neill the architect is reflected in Davis the filmmaker and vice versa. The transposition of past and present is seen in terms of the personal, and while Davis documents his uncle's sometimes troubled and unhappy life, he also celebrates his achievements, just as Davis himself recounts his early experiences as an avant-garde psychedelic artist and later filmmaker.

Not unlike *Home Movie Nights*, Davis uses amateur footage of his uncle and family to help us understand his relationship with his own past. He uses these scenes both as an archival record and as a documentary tool, showing us Jack as he was, but also revealing to us how he sets the projector in operation and studies the footage for potential inclusion in the film itself. As Bob Quinn did in *Atlantean* and *Caoineadh Airt Uí Laoire*, he juxtaposes scenes of himself watching the films with scenes from the films themselves shown for our benefit. All the while he describes his feelings and relates stories from Jack's life which are not evident in the footage. He constantly shifts the boundaries between the profilmic and the referential and ultimately brings us on a journey to the past which can only be understood in terms of discourse. The film is a meditation upon how Jack and his life have influenced Davis. It is also about his realisation that in many ways their lives are mirrored, and that Jack's obsession with building cinemas and model planes is echoed in Davis's ability to shape and mould film stock into documentary. The recurring images of the model buildings and the model planes are matched to images of VCRs, film reels, projectors, lamps – the physical objects with which a film is made. He seems to be reaching towards a Vertovian idea of film as a physical process and therefore a legitimate part of human endeavour.

Early in the film Davis shows us the demolition of the Tonic in Bangor, one of his uncle's cinemas. He crosscuts between images of the building in its prime and its ruins, acknowledging that like human life itself, or the artistic consciousness, even the most magnificent edifice can be demolished. It is not difficult to see this as a comment upon the nature of his own art, and on how film can also be 'destroyed' through the kind of self-reflexive deconstruction which he employs. Film becomes not so much a solid object then as a shadowy reflection of solid objects – in short, a representation. As a representation, the film then becomes less a 'documentary' as it is normally understood (at least in Ireland) than a shadowy and ephemeral journey through the 'haunted landscape' of memory and perception. He notes, 'I don't know what my films are. I don't think of them as documentaries and they're not fiction, but there's drama in them of some description even though they're not acted. This journalistic approach to documentaries which you see on television every night is so boring, and unfortunately, that's what most people regard as documentary. I use the film itself to tell the story' (cited in O'Regan (ed.), 1993: 25). The question is, what story is he telling? What precisely is he trying to get to the heart of and what meaning does this have for the ordinary viewer?

While it is obvious that on one level he is concerned with himself, there must be another communicative dimension to the film, otherwise it would seem narcissistic. If we look at Davis's work within the context of a culture of repression against which he personally rebelled (as an archetypal 1960s counter-culture art student) and within that of a film industry crippled by internal and external pressures, his quest for self-realisation takes on greater significance. Like *The Road to God Knows Where*, the film is best understood relative to that which has gone before it. *The Uncle Jack* recounts facts and charts the histories of both successful architect John McBride Neill and struggling artist/filmmaker John T. Davis. Both lived and worked within a community not discussed in political terms, but within which definite ideas of self, of work and even of art were evinced. Davis nonetheless sees his uncle's work on a creative, imaginative plane (captured visually by the lighting and photography employed in representing his models) which somehow 'escaped', however temporarily, from the stranglehold of 'official' culture. Similarly Davis's art (filmmaking) becomes a channel for the creative and rebellious spirit, even though he acknowledges that much of his work as a cinematographer is in the commercial vein and he is himself a culturally determined subject. In making a film of this kind – reflexive, autobiographical, aesthetic – he allows himself a moment of freedom. Like the model aeroplane he sets to flight in an emotionally charged climax, he knows it may crash (one scene recalls the death of an airman who lived next door to him as a child), but this does not mean it should not fly at all.

The Uncle Jack then is an exploration of his own sense of self, but also of the self's relationship with the external world, which can be read in general as well as in specific terms. The film acknowledges that people are both influenced by others and defined by the forces of social and political determination which surround them. Perhaps as much as *Our Country*, *Rocky Road to Dublin* and *The Road to God Knows Where*, certainly more than *Atlantean* and *Mother Ireland*, *The Uncle Jack* calls for action, if on quite a different level. It argues that non-fiction film is a medium of philosophical enquiry through which questions about society on the whole can be addressed, and though resolution is impossible, the debate goes on. While John McBride Neill is dead, his memory lives in his nephew, and now in this film. Though he is not our uncle, our sense of ourselves is brought into question through joining Davis on this journey into their shared past. We are therefore invited to weigh our own relationship with others and with the world itself against those things that we feel about them in an attempt to sort out what is real from what is represented. Situated at a juncture between the reference and referentiality, its solution is a simple, humanistic appeal to human emotions, which transcend and inform events in the historical world. Davis does not ask us to share his emotions, yet the film evokes a powerful emotional response. It touches us in a way which is unique to Irish documentary.

Speaking in 1993, Davis noted, 'you really only make one film in your life, or write one song or do one painting, but you keep doing it over and over again until you get to the heart of it' (cited in O'Regan (ed.), 1993: 25). It is easy to see *The Uncle Jack* as something of an arrival at that heart, especially because of the way it crystallises all of the issues which are raised in viewing Davis's work as a body of films. The last lines of the script suggest something similar: 'And you hope you will eventually reach that flat calm day, that day when the wind is only a whisper. That holy day when you are finally at peace with the whole spirituality of time blowing gently around the planet.' Its concrete, identifiable concerns with the life of John McBride Neill give it a rootedness which keeps it in the realms of conventional documentary. It provides an anchor with which to ground Davis's musings on the self, and provides a resolution in that the film clearly has allowed him to come to terms with the role McBride Neill has played in his life. Yet it suggests that life continues, and that discourse upon these questions likewise goes on for those who see the film. It expresses a concern with a spiritual search, and though for Davis it has reached an important juncture, the audience must now act upon what they have seen and question themselves and their own worlds in similar terms.

This is what all autobiographical documentaries ultimately do, mediated through the notion of self which the autobiographical process inevitably involves. As Lane notes, the paradox they represent is that the life of the documentarist inevitably continues even after the cinematic narrative has ended. For Davis, this represents the continuation of the discourse which he has begun about the meaning of the past for the present about how one's sense of self may be defined relative to both the environment and people who are close to you. In this it is an important and challenging Irish documentary film which advances the medium both in terms of content and form. It problematises our expectations of what documentaries can do, and questions the very basis of reality itself, or at least the perception of reality which has traditionally defined documentary practice and upheld the status quo. Though it does not tackle the mechanisms of church and state or concern itself with social problems which require critical reappraisal in postmodern, postcolonial, postnationalist Ireland (if such a thing even exists), it delves into Yeats's 'foul rag and bone shop of the heart' and asks that we look within for the solutions. While it could be argued that this represents an idealistic contribution to practical debate on social and political affairs in contemporary Ireland, it might also be fair to note that Davis is simply reminding audiences of their own subjectivity. He therefore intervenes at a deeper level than the 'journalistic documentaries' he so dislikes. As Kiberd reminds us, the utopian impulse can never be wholly suppressed. It fulfils an important function as a dormant force poised to re-emerge at a time of crisis. As he puts it, 'at times when an old order of life has lost its meaning, and a new world has not yet been born, Caliban may indeed be tempted to plot the murder of Prospero' (Kiberd, 1995: 561). *The Uncle Jack* may be, in this sense, a utopian documentary, at least in that it implies that utopia (or spiritual peace with oneself and one's past) is within reach of the self-conscious, questioning and exploring mind.

Travellers is quite a different film, and though co-credited to Davis is as much the work of photographer Alen MacWeeney. Originally entitled *May the Road Rise Up*, it is more a record of MacWeeney's inner journey than Davis's, which may be something of a missed opportunity given the possibilities offered by a study of Ireland's own resident disenfranchised outsiders by this particular filmmaker. The travelling community are a group of people who prefer life on the road in caravans to 'settled' norms and who have been the constant victims of prejudice. The traveller issue was, until the influx of immigrants in the 1990s, the nearest equivalent to a racial question in Irish culture, and it was frequently cast in these terms in news and current-affairs programmes. In the 1960s MacWeeney took a series of images of travelling families in Dublin and Galway. He also made audio recordings of their singing and storytelling. In 1999 he returned to some of those families to see how their lives had changed. Accompanied by Davis and armed with his recordings and images, MacWeeney's journey was partly personal and partly socio-cultural. The film is the result and the site of a unique series of collisions – between still and moving images, between photographer and cinematographer, and between travellers and observers delving into what the voice over terms a 'hidden' part of Irish culture.

It begins like a standard nostalgic television documentary and threatens to remain superficial and overreliant on the stills themselves for impact. MacWeeney's photographs are remarkable, shot in rich black and white and capturing an enigmatic yet realistic world, visible yet partly shielded. His signature image for the series, reproduced on the cover of this book and also MacWeeney's own compilation of the photographs, is of a little girl holding a plastic bag over her face. The landscape behind her is blurred, yet plainly visible, a caravan cast against a bright white sky. The girl is hidden, yet her features are discernible underneath the plastic, a ghostly and yet not sinister image of a real person in a real environment which invites scrutiny and yet provides no definite resolution as to the status of place or person.

Early scenes in the film depict MacWeeney and Davis discussing which images to use and show them setting up stills for filming. It is a small concession to self-reflexivity, certainly an illustration of the fact that this film is a collaboration between two artists with differing points of view, but the film doesn't immediately suggest an intention to penetrate very deeply into this element. As it progresses the film finds its way deeper into the lives of the travellers themselves, attempting to move beyond the image and into the referent. It gradually exposes a rich and tantalisingly ambiguous tapestry of personality and culture without ever successfully penetrating it. MacWeeney shows his photographs to some of the people they feature and Davis's camera observes their reactions. Though the results are initially a mixture of anecdote and performance, a series of themes begin to emerge which find fuller exploration later. Individuals comment vaguely about changes in traveller culture and MacWeeney remarks on the difference between the Dublin suburb of Cherry Orchard in the 1960s and the 1990s. But it takes some time before the true face of these changes both in the lives of individuals and traveller society on the whole becomes evident.

The film begins to take hold with the introduction of 'colourful' Pat Stokes, who first comes across as one of those 'characters' who populate so many representations of Ireland and the Irish. He appears on *Winning Streak* wearing a hat which Mike Murphy tells the audience he was born with. The dry drollery of the moment seems to be matched by Pat's interaction with MacWeeney in a more personal interview. Then at one point when they are discussing the photos taken of him in his prime, Pat begins to accuse MacWeeney of exploitation. The moment seems fraught with tension despite the jovial tone, and here the film first provides a flash of the ambiguities which make this world truly 'hidden'. The confrontation ends as soon as it began with Pat singing the first lines of 'Danny Boy' and we are then treated to a scene of the two men dancing and laughing to show that there have been no really hard feelings. But one comes away with an impression of the inscrutability of the old man and a sense that there is far more to him than meets the eye.

From this point on the film becomes increasingly comfortable with ambiguity and begins to chart a path around the edges of this fringe culture. As they begin to follow the story of an ongoing feud between families, Davis and MacWeeney find themselves getting a peep through the curtains without ever seeing the full picture. Gradually, our sense of the people themselves becomes more layered with the mixture of nostalgic anecdote, stories of tragedy, and comment on current conditions for travellers the film begins to explore its subject more meaningfully. While MacWeeney desperately tries to understand the nature of the conflict which leads to the destruction of a family's grave, Davis films an encounter between documentarist and subject which is just as revealing as any of the scenes of men and women telling stories of what they see in the photographs.

Travellers is finally a powerful document of distance, difference and the rejection of representation. The distances between the 1960s and the 1990s become merely a springboard from which deeper questions are raised about the nature of travellers and our perceptions of them. It is never as obvious as it seems at the outset and avoids the trap of becoming a magazine report with spokespersons and dogma. It makes full use of its eighty-four minutes to build up visual and aural information which both informs and is informed by MacWeeney's work. As he notes himself, the film gives those images and sounds a new life. With the collaboration of Davis and editor Sé Merry Doyle, the film fits part of a cinematic project of exploring the periphery of the Irish experience which Davis began not long after MacWeeney. Their subjects may have been different, but their search has been along similar lines. The film is therefore a blending of personalities which makes the co-directing credit appropriate.

Davis's most recent film at the time of writing is *A House Divided*, a return to the subject of life in the place of his birth. It is a peculiar film in that its premise is literally to allow the audience to watch paint dry, or at least to watch the evolution of a painting, specifically a painting of the members of the historic Northern Ireland Assembly elected following the Belfast/Good Friday agreement. The film intercuts the comments and observations of its participants with scenes of their posing session with the artist, and, like the painting itself, gradually builds into a collage of representations encompassing the face of Northern Irish politics. Again Davis's distinctive camerawork enlivens what could have been a disastrously dull subject, continually drawing attention to the interrelatedness of representation, aesthetics, politics and the expression of self.

The fall of the church

Tom Inglis notes that the decline in influence of the Catholic church in Ireland in the late twentieth century did not necessarily represent merely a reaction to the revelations of child abuse, sexual relationships of clergy, and institutional mismanagement which came to light in the 1990s. Change came as part of an overall process of secularisation as Irish people increasingly dealt directly with state institutions or organised action with community groups to deal with social and personal affairs. Inglis observes, 'in effect, the main change in Irish society is the decline in the symbolic domination of the Catholic Church and the rise of the symbolic domination of the media' (Inglis, 1998: 208). It is significant that he speaks in terms of 'symbolic' domination rather than logistical control. Though he charts the lessening of influence of the church in the spheres of Catholic practice, moral authority and the institution itself, and in the fields of education, health and social welfare, he notes that it remains a presence in many of the areas of Irish life which it previously dominated, if a less formidable one. In a sense, this 'symbolic' domination of Irish life has been evinced throughout this book. As we have seen, church and state exerted a powerful influence over the projection of 'official' images of Ireland throughout the twentieth century (certainly after Independence). They remained the dominant ideological forces in Irish society even when their intervention in the production of documentary films was only tangential.

The kind of fragmentation of consensus and emergence of multiple points of view seen throughout this chapter is one of the signs of encroaching postmodernism (and arguably postnationalism). It is unsurprising, then, that such dominant ideologies should begin to crumble. The fall of the church is not a complete end to the institution, or to the belief in God, or even moral teaching, nor it is likely to be the end of the story. It is a fall from a position of dominance to one of relative equality with the alternative voices. Inglis concludes that 'the Catholic church's monopoly on Irish morality has been broken. It no longer commands the same awe and respect it did thirty years ago. In civil society it has moved from having a close relationship with the state, especially in relation to social and moral issues, to being one interest group among many others. It is no longer the conscience of the Irish people' (241). Religious programming is still a feature of RTÉ's programming policy. Though *Radharc* has departed, RTÉ's in-house series *Would You Believe?* has taken its place, at least in scheduling terms (the series rarely exhibits the penetration of the best of *Radharc*). Religious authorities still speak out on public issues and despite the scandals and revelations of recent years, they still carry some weight. Yet the secularisation of Irish society, the influx of emigrants and asylum seekers of other religious denominations, the decline in direct control of educational institutions, and the scepticism of younger generations of Irish people about the church have made the previously unquestionable and monolithic presence as much a subject for interrogation and analysis as any other social institution.

It nonetheless took some time for this interrogation to become visible. Cathal Black's *Our Boys* was made in 1981, but was only finally screened on Irish television ten years later. This melancholy drama was concerned with the final days of a Christian Brothers' school, focusing in particular on a brother, played by Mick Lally, whose quick temper results in a beating which brings a concerned father to the school in protest. The brother's anger is placed in the context of his claustrophobic life within the community and amid the decaying building itself. He is shown as lonely and isolated, and the closure of the school represents the encroachment of secular authorities (the land is to be sold to a developer and the school is to be merged with a secular community school), threatening to destroy his sanctuary from criticism and 'reality'. This drama is intercut with documentary interviews with former students who attest to the brutal conditions under which their education took place. They speak of beatings, hypocritical codes of discipline (bodily contact was forbidden, but if the students wrestled with one another, they were physically beaten by the brothers), and the effects of this upon their attitude to the world and to other people.

Our Boys was the first significant shot across the bows of the church, though its focus was upon the Christian Brothers, who are not priests. It was nonetheless clear that institutional education and the psychological repression by religious orders was being questioned. Though its delay until 1991 meant that Bob Quinn's *Budawanny* preceded it to television, it is interesting that it was only in the 1990s that the questioning of the church became more widespread. Even throughout the 1980s, the church had demonstrated the ability to influence social and political events, including the referenda on abortion and divorce. While the screening of *Our Boys* did generate debate, it was the revelation in 1992 that Bishop Eamon Casey had a teenage son which impacted most heavily upon the image of the church. The events and their consequences are discussed in detail by Inglis. It suffices to note that this was the first in a chain of public revelations about religious figures which became media events throughout the 1990s, including paedophilia, adultery, physical abuse and institutional cover-ups. Quinn's *The Bishop's Story* followed in 1994, and though essentially a remake of *Budawanny* (based on the same 1983 source novel), it was widely discussed as a reflection of Casey's indiscretion and the decline of the sacred image of priests and bishops.

While all of this is important in terms of the climate of change in 1990s Ireland, *Our Boys* and *The Bishop's Story* were both primarily fictional. It was not until 1996 that a documentary on the subject was made. RTÉ had broadcast numerous talk shows and current-affairs programmes to discuss the scandals as they arose, especially on radio. In contrast to the respectful distance maintained in the past by Irish television and even the print media (occasional editorial vitriol is no substitute for investigative reporting or a sustained campaign of protest), these events had finally led to open criticism of the hypocrisy of the Catholic church. Inglis maintains that there had been a steady erosion of respect for the church's interpretation of the role of the media since the 'Bishop and the Nightie' affair in 1966, but concedes that by 1996, 'it would appear that the backlog of stories had built up so much that once the climate changed, the lid was suddenly lifted, and what had remained private and individual quickly became public' (Inglis, 1998: 229–30).

In 1995 Donald Taylor Black's *Hearts and Souls* became the first significant non-fiction film to tackle the issue of divorce in Ireland, treading on ground previously dominated by the church. But this *cinéma vérité* account of the 'no' campaign in the referendum did not directly tackle religious authority. It confined itself to observational ridicule of the (secular) conservative campaigners, whose vehemence frequently made them appear foolish and irrational. We will return to this film in the next chapter. Louis Lentin's *Dear Daughter* (1996) was the first and most important documentary to actively identify and accuse religious orders of impropriety. Despite its now considerable reputation, it is interesting to note that the revelations of physical abuse and economic exploitation of children in the Goldenbridge orphanage run by the Sisters of Mercy upon which the controversy centred, and for which the film is most praised, constitute a relatively small part of the whole film.

It begins with the bitter words of Christine Buckley, formerly of Goldenbridge. She says, 'I wanted to find my parents and kill them for every ounce of pain I suffered.' This introduces us to her quest to find the people who left her to the Sisters of Mercy in the late 1940s. Though the film follows on from *Our Boys* in its expressionistic evocation of the haunted hallways and menacing robes of the religious during the many reconstruction sequences, it is as much concerned with evoking Christine's sense of loneliness and abandonment as demonising the Sisters themselves. The story of her life is told to us not as an example of a child abused by the childcare system, but of a woman seeking her identity in a troubled past.

The film is mostly concerned with Buckley's attempt to trace her birth mother and confront her with the woman she is now. This she finally does, and though her anger has now dissipated, she is seeking to understand why the woman did what she did in the face of the social pressures of 1940s Irish society. Among the difficulties her mother had to face was the fact that Christine's father was an African student, and the film thereby touches briefly and tangentially upon racial issues and the ambiguity of traditional Ireland's relationship with 'black babies' (a feature of so many charitable campaigns directed abroad yet one which was far from welcome in Ireland itself). In many ways, *Dear Daughter* is as much a product of the evolution of female consciousness evinced by *Mother Ireland, Hoodwinked* and *My Great Grandmother was a Boxer*. It is a story of self-discovery framed by a strong female voice, and resolves itself when she meets and talks with her mother and finds some sense of peace about what has happened.

This can be seen however as a filter through which the more sensitive and controversial material was explored. Though *States of Fear* would later eschew such bracketing, *Dear Daughter* did not have the luxury of precedent (though Buckley's story had first come to light in the early 1990s on radio). It also chose a circumspect method of representing the horrors of abuse and exploitation endured by Buckley and her fellow orphans which is perhaps not surprising from the director of *Insurrection*. The reconstructions used here went beyond the 'dramatic' material featured extensively on many docudramas. They were rather interactive flashbacks, where the adult Buckley stood in shot observing scenes from her own early life being played out by actors, and where she and others played themselves as children, acting out the rituals they had to undergo while commenting upon them. It was an intriguing approach which avoided the trap of fictive engagement to which docudrama is prone. It was also unprecedented on Irish television, and further contributed to the impact of the programme. It also ensured that the material remained in the realm of the discursive rather than the informational. The revelations were presented in terms of their effects upon Christine, which in turn informed her quest for self-realisation and her initial desire for revenge upon her parents, which eventually became more reflective. So rather than an investigative documentary about child abuse in Goldenbridge, which is how the film is often construed, it became a reflection upon the emotional and psychological consequences of that abuse on one woman in particular.

It nonetheless provoked massive public response, most immediately from the Sisters of Mercy, who were aware of the production and had cooperated. The film concluded with an advertisement for a special hotline for victims of abuse and an apology. Shortly after its broadcast, members of the Provincial of the Congregation appeared on *Kenny Live* (a light entertainment/human interest talk show used to fill in for *The Late Late Show* in the off season) to explain the history of their Order and apologise publicly to anyone who suffered abuse. Two weeks later they released a list of names of people who were willing to testify to positive treatment by the nuns during their time in care, and though they did not attempt to refute the allegations made by the programme, they essentially argued that it had been one sided in its presentation. The media frenzy continued, and arguably has still not abated. The film was followed by other programmes and series, many of them originating abroad, such as *Sex in a Cold Climate* (1997), *Suing the Pope* (2000) and a plethora of films about the Magdalene Laundries culminating in the TV serial *Sinners* (2000) and the fiction film *The Magdalene Sisters* (2002). As Inglis points out, the importance of *Dear Daughter* was not even the specific details but the implications its production had for the role of the media in contemporary Ireland:

The documentary also indicated how the perception and understanding of nuns and the Church had changed in RTÉ. It it unlikely that such a programme would have been broadcast ten years previously, particularly since it took such a negative, one-sided view. It indicated that there was a change within RTÉ regarding stories about the Church. In the changed climate of opinion, it was not only permissible to produce programmes critical of the Church, it became a mechanism of increasing one's symbolic capital. It was as if it was open-season on the nuns and the Church. (Inglis, 1998: 228–9)

The media now occupied the moral high ground, capable of revealing the hidden truths about Irish society and of criticising the institutions upon which the very idea of Ireland had rested for so long.

The irony of the situation, as Inglis points out, is that the role of the state was never questioned in this film, or in much of the debate which followed. RTÉ's willing collusion in the assault upon the church was on one hand a liberation, but on the other it represented the ongoing cooperation between the state and the media. As Inglis concludes, the symbolic domination of the media was in question here, and in a sense the media frenzy was merely a refiguration of the locus of power in Irish society. The secularisation of Ireland is of benefit both to the state and the media. Given the continuing influence of the state over the 'official' media in the form of the RTÉ Authority, it is arguable that the explosion of anti-clerical sentiment was thereby acknowledged by the state as a legitimate expression of the public's concerns.

States of Fear (1999) then seemed to shift the frames of reference by evoking, even in its title, a sense that authorities other than the church were responsible for the systematic abuse and exploitation of children by the industrial schools and child-care institutions. It drew attention to the historical unwillingness on the part of local and government authorities to interfere with the operation of the schools. One of the most compelling and important arguments presented by the series was that the conspiracy of silence which prevented these stories from becoming public earlier was a social consensus that religious orders were above reproach and that they knew best how to care for God's children. Stories were told by interviewees about how their parents were aware of certain levels of violence, but dismissed this as ordinary discipline (this was also a theme in *Our Boys*). Stories of sexual abuse were often simply not believed, even when children had the courage to tell them. In this way, *States of Fear* retrod the territory covered in *Rocky Road to Dublin*, exploring the authoritarian, patrimonial and institutional nature of Irish society. It posited a culture of obedience, the result of religious education and the constant reminders of the authority of the state we have seen throughout this book, a system of manufacturing consent in which the dominant orthodoxy exerted so powerful an influence that even those who questioned or disapproved in private said nothing in public. It was perhaps the first documentary to address this so directly since Lennon's, but even so, much of this argument is buried beneath a wealth of evidential material concerning the abuse itself. As with *Dear Daughter*, which used Christine Buckley's personal story to address something entirely different, the most telling material in *States of Fear* is not on its surface.

Its reception was predictable. The series had unflinchingly presented a distressing amount of detail on the physical, sexual and economic abuse of children in institutions under religious administration throughout the twentieth century. The first industrial school had opened in 1868, but understandably, records reflect little of the horrors which more contemporary interviewees recount as eyewitnesses and victims. Several religious orders and even individuals were named, including the beloved media celebrity Brother Joseph O'Connor, leader of the Artane Boys Band. The series was thick with blame and eager to present statistics, reports and interview material never seen before. By and large the public responded with numb acknowledgement. *States of Fear* was broadcast three years after *Dear Daughter* (which it credits as a catalyst). The intervening period had seen much more of the same material coming to light on radio talk shows and print-media investigations. It was no longer surprising, though its scale was shocking. The communications director of the Dublin archdiocese of the Catholic church responded by claiming an opportunity had been missed to put things in proper perspective by showing how attitudes to child care in general had changed over the last fifty years and to tell both sides of the story. Dublin's Archbishop Desmond Connell emphasised the need for healing, not blame, and called for attention to be paid to the contemporary treatment of the homeless and prisoners as well as the past abuses featured in the series.

The most interesting omission in *States of Fear* however was an acknowledgement of the role the media itself had played in the history of silence. Though some responses in the press maintained that it was laudable that RTÉ had finally made this contribution to openness and self-assessment in Irish society, it might be argued that more weight should have been given to the journalistic negligence and irresponsibility of current-affairs documentaries in the past. The series featured clips from a variety of news and documentary programmes such as *7 Days* which had filmed inside these institutions in the 1960s. Most of these films had been promotional, respectfully congratulating the church for its work (some of them had been made by the *Radharc* team). Though this is understandable and the filmmakers would not have been searching any deeper given the constraints of the time, *States of Fear* did not address this as an issue in itself. It acknowledged that RTÉ was not aware of and did not seek to investigate any abuses until the 1990s when these stories began to break. Interviewees who had been in the films as children, absolving the reporters of blame, explained how everything was cleaned up and made presentable for the arrival of the television crews, and then returned to 'normal' afterwards.

There are also questions which have not been asked regarding the media's long-term collective responsibility and the role played by non-fiction in particular in the redefinition of Irish society. *States of Fear* was quite triumphalist in its approach to presenting evidence. While undoubtedly an important moment in late twentieth-century Ireland, its failure to question its own production is indicative of the absence a self-reflexive mode of documentary representation. It does not problematise representation itself, or the one-sidedness of the process of evidence gathering. It does not contextualise the utterances of individuals clearly suffering psychological stress, or drawn attention to the ways in which our very concept of investigative reportage needs to be questioned before we can understand why the series was made in the first place. This is not a subversive underground documentary, but a high-profile three-part television series which was greeted, as noted, with carefully prepared responses by the various parties concerned. It is every bit as much an 'official' film as any of the nationalistic or romantic films from the past which we have discussed here. Perhaps even more frightening than the suggestion that *Dear Daughter* represents a state-sponsored challenge to the church, *States of Fear* is an apotheosis of the media to the point where it may be trusted to an even greater extent than before because it has spoken so freely on the wrongs of both church and state. This is a worrying concept, and one which Inglis sounds as a note of caution in his assessment of the events of the 1990s in Ireland.

It may also represent a redefinition of the public sphere in which the emergence of multiple viewpoints and diverging voices is representative of a long-overdue fragmentation of the dominant ideology and the 'commonsense' understanding of the reality of life in Ireland. This more optimistic reading is in accordance with the ideas of postmodernism and postnationalism with which this chapter began. We have seen evidence of a postmodern sensibility in which fixed and stable ideas of public discourse have begun to dissolve, along with equally absolute concepts of documentary form and function. Filmmakers like Bob Quinn, John T. Davis and Alan Gilsenan remain the exception rather than the rule, however, as do programmes like *States of Fear* and *Dear Daughter*. Ireland is not a martriarchal state, despite the feminist or female-centred films discussed. It has not yet reached a state of social consensus where tolerance and multiculturalism are the norm. The majority of non-fiction films still tend towards the journalistic and the expository and do not attempt to challenge either representational or thematic convention. There remain vast numbers of tourist films and romantic evocations of the glorious Celtic past which do not even warrant fuller analysis. It is nonetheless worth concluding this book with a survey of the output of Irish documentarists working within a less formally or politically radical vein but who still address important subjects. Their films also represent explorations of contemporary Ireland, albeit not necessarily at its boundaries. They are an equally important part of the overall project of Irish documentary, and indeed arguably its mainstay. For this we must turn to a final chapter.

Notes

1 This is a lyric from a hit song by the Irish band the Boomtown Rats, but Gilsenan here specifically relates it to Irish Catholicism rather than urban gang culture, to which the original song referred.
2 Portions of this material have been previously published. See O'Brien, 2001.
3 This is not a typo. Holywood was the place in Co. Down where Davis's uncle lived and where Ben Eadar, the house he willed to his nephew, stood until it burned down on 1 December 1999, destroying Davis's base of operations, his camera, editing

equipment and personal archive of films, some of which had never been seen by the public. Producer Sé Merry Doyle launched an appeal to assist the Davis family, part of which was a screening of Hobo, held at the Irish Film Centre on 12 December 1999. In introducing the film, Davis commented that it was an appropriate choice given that it focused on those whose lives were without a centre of the type provided by a family home. He noted that he himself was now at ninety degrees to where he had been, and his own sense of dislocation and personal loss was very great.

6

Unto the breach: redefining the public sphere

This book has been centrally preoccupied not with the manner in which documentaries have directly affected or prophesied changes in Irish society throughout the twentieth century, but with how the evolution of Ireland has been both visible within and represented by non-fiction films. As Gibbons argues, it may be that an undue emphasis on the modernising role of the media can reduce the complexities of cultural transformation to a model of cause and effect in which, 'in combating "tradition", the mass media and related versions of modernity are often tilting at windmills of their own making' (Gibbons, 1996: 4). Yet as Nichols has observed, documentaries represent an argument on the levels of both form and content which positions the viewer within the historical world relative to 'things as they are'. As he puts it, 'we become better qualified through the knowledge provided us by the text's argument and through the subjectivity conveyed by its rhetoric to take a specific position within the arena of ideology' (Nichols, 1991: 140). The films which follow exemplify the concerns of Irish documentarists relative to the perceived interests of the viewing public at the turn of the millennium. Some of them attempt to explore areas and tackle issues previously not confronted or otherwise muted by dominant discourse, although few use radical formal styles in doing so. Many merely offer new perspectives or contexts, and some are no different from their earlier counterparts.

Though many postmodern interpretations of the mass media discuss the surfeit of information and the fetishisation of knowledge in the consumer society as products of, as Baudrillard puts it, 'fragmentation and spectacularisation, of misrecognition of the world and the valorisation of information as commodity, the exaltation of content as sign' (Baudrillard, 1999: 89), and though it has become commodified in the era of the *video vérité*, documentary still occupies a unique position relative to what we might call the public sphere. For Jürgen Habermas, the public sphere represents a space where the free exchange of ideas on matters of public concern takes place outside the domain of government institutions or other vested interests.[1] Mark Warren summarises the argument as follows: 'a public sphere is an arena in which individuals participate in discussions about matters of common concern, in an atmosphere free of coercion or dependencies (inequalities) that would incline individuals toward acquiescence or silence' (Warren, 1995: 171). Peter Dahlgren (1996) makes the point that this is also a historically conditioned social space, explained by Habermas in terms of a historical narrative whereby the encroachment of industrial capitalism and mass media fragmented the public itself into spectators at the fringes of true social discourse.

Habermas originally conceived of the public sphere in terms of the participation of the free press in a democratic society, where citizens could read about matters of common concern and thus be informed and aware of the important issues. As we have seen throughout this book, documentary can be seen as hermeneutic structure which, ideally, contributes to the kind of enlightened public discourse which Habermas believes to be at the root of a truly democratic society, if not in itself (Habermas is sceptical of the technological mass media because they are too easily subject to vested interests), at least insofar as it provides viewers with sensory and cognitive information which allows them to participate in public culture. Though it might be argued (and indeed it has been throughout this book) that documentaries are all too often subject to ideological constraints, as Nichols points out, documentaries cannot in themselves prescribe the limits of knowledge or information which may be derived from them. Because of their relationship with history and the historical world, even films which are formally unchallenging can contain an excess of knowledge outside the frames of reference of rhetoric which viewers have access to by virtue of cognitive perception. He explains: 'always referred to but never captured, history, as excess, rebukes those laws set to contain it; it contests, qualifies, resists and refuses them' (Nichols, 1991: 142). It is not so much the literal 'reality' of modern Ireland which is in question here, but the limits of discourse. In surveying films which have sought to examine Irish society and culture in the millennial years, we can perhaps reach an understanding of how history continues to be actively transformed by social, political and cultural forces including the media, but also how society defines the parameters within which examination occurs.

In the late 1990s, two new television stations began broadcasting in Ireland. Telefís na Gaelige commenced in 1996, partially funded by RTÉ's operating surplus, but also generating commercial revenue from advertising. It offered a schedule of Irish-language programming, including news and documentaries, but also game shows, drama and sports coverage. It also provided a showcase for the history of Irish documentary, featuring many reruns of classic films and archival compilations based upon the long history of Irish-language non-fiction from *Amharc Éireann* on.[2] The second new station, TV3, began broadcasting in 1998. This was a wholly commercial operation primarily featuring American- and British-produced programmes, though with its own news and sports divisions. To date it has not significantly contributed to Irish documentary. Together these two bodies represented the first intrusion into the arena of television broadcasting dominated for almost forty years by RTÉ alone.

In 1999, TnaG was renamed TG4 in anticipation of the switch to digital broadcasting. Fearful of finding itself ranked low in the menu of available channels, the station was eager to ensure it would remain alongside RTÉ One, RTÉ Network 2 and TV3. How successful this gambit will prove remains to be seen. Iarfhlaith Watson notes that the position TG4 has found itself in, negotiating a space for Irish-language broadcasting amid the arguably contradictory demands of public service and entertainment and between Irish and non-Irish speakers, has left the station torn between ideological and market forces: 'TG4 today provides popularised programmes, emphasises drama and provides English-language subtitles in an attempt to attract as large an audience as possible to entice advertisers. While RTÉ was accused of neglecting Irish-language programming because of the market, TG4 is forced to structure the schedule around market forces in providing Irish-language programmes' (Watson, 2003: 127). Watson observes that wholesale changes in the legislation governing broadcasting in Ireland could leave the station wholly in the grip of the market, which may overwhelm the public service dimension of its attempts to keep the Irish language in the public eye.

Indigenous narrowcast digital television had not yet arrived in Ireland at the time of writing, but the legislative infrastructure was being debated. A green paper on the future of broadcasting was published in 1995, followed by moves towards a new infrastructure in the age of multichannel digital communications. The green paper stressed, 'it is Government policy to ensure that Irish television and radio programming is of the highest quality and that it remains the preferred choice of a majority of Irish viewers and listeners' (p. 136), expressing the common and obviously continued desire to ensure that the organs of public opinion remain under legislative direction. In a statement on digital terrestrial television in 1998, RTÉ added, 'Irish national interest and the requirements of the Irish public dictates that digital is too important in its impact on cultural and economic activity to be left to international market forces' (cited in McNally, 1998: 3).

As we have seen, the increase in the influence of the media in Ireland has accelerated with the gradual disintegration and refiguration of the dominant ideologies of nationalism and Catholicism and their respective institutional purveyors. Tom Inglis has sounded a note of caution in this regard, and he is not alone in speculating that the triumph of secular liberalism may have unforeseen disadvantageous effects upon Irish society. David Begg notes the irony that the move towards a free market has resulted in the domination by multinational conglomerates and a resultant *reduction* of democratic access to the most prominent means of cultural self-expression in the modern world.

Market forces have, it is quite widely believed, leaped free from government control and now control governments instead. Economic liberals hail such glob- alisation as the chariot of progress; democratic socialists fear that its scythed wheels are cutting down the hopes of socially beneficent intervention. . . . I have no doubt that there are huge benefits to be gained economically by the capabil- ity of information technology to reduce the effect of distance and peripherality. In the right circumstances, Ireland could be a real beneficiary of these advances. I am equally certain, however, that if governments don't find a way to effectively re-regulate it, society will suffer the consequences. (Begg, 1997: 67)

Groups such as the Community Media Network (who publish the magazine *Tracking*) and lobbyists for socially disadvantaged communities in Ireland continue to follow the debate on digital television with interest, hoping that some of the new channels will be allocated to special interest groups. A struggle between local and national media may well be developing in which the forces of cultural production will be arrayed along lines of opposition between established and emerging broadcasters. The terms of public service broadcasting must shift to accommodate public access. Before long Irish documentary will find itself facing a democratisation which the medium achieved long ago in the US, but which brought as many challenges as opportunities. The question will then not be whether non-fiction films will be able to tackle previously neglected subject matter, but whether anyone will watch such programmes as the viewing options increase.

In a situation roughly analogous with the larger political question of what Kearney terms 'double minorities' (Kearney, 1997: 77), the specialisa- tion of the media might result in a situation where rather than deconstruct- ing the totalising influence of dominant orthodoxy, the 'democratised' media may represent a profusion of subject positions clamouring for authentication and supremacy over one another. This may also be seen as a technocentric version of the postcolonial condition of counter-hegemony, where, as Benita Parry puts it, 'the hegemonic discourse is ultimately abandoned as scorched earth when a different discourse, forged in the process of disobedience and combat, occupying new, never-colonized and "utopian" territory . . . is enun- ciated' (Parry, 1995: 43). Writing in a review of *Suing the Pope* (2000), Liam Fay remarked, 'Trial by television is reviled by the powerful precisely because of its potential for achieving a brand of justice that is poetic and practical' (Fay, 2000: 26). The implications of this statement are best understood rel- ative to a more detailed study of some of the documentary material serving this 'brand of justice'.

Taboos

Before *Dear Daughter* (1996) Donald Taylor Black's *Hearts and Souls* (1995) was the highest-profile non-fiction film of its time. Its appeal was in Black's insistence upon *cinéma vérité* methods in documenting the second divorce referendum. Focusing solely on the activities of 'no' campaigners, it is an example of what Michael Rabiger terms the 'walled city' film which, in his terms, 'uses a microcosm to imply criticism upon a much wider scale' (Rabiger, 1992: 291). Though Black vehemently claims the film is strictly *cinéma vérité* (a form, remember, some thirty years out of date by now), it blurs the boundaries between observational and interactive modes of representation. It features a great deal of interview material – interviews conducted by members of the press, not by Black himself, granted – and his insistence on covering press conferences and filming situations where 'no' campaigners explain themselves makes their behaviour much more rehearsed than is usual in *cinéma vérité*. The result is not strictly observational insofar as we are given a great deal of verbal information to which the visuals add little.

Yet there are times when Black succeeds in revealing the hidden tensions between different factions of the overall 'no' vote though observation alone. The squabble between the 'No Divorce Campaign' and the 'Anti Divorce Campaign' about their respective identities and legitimacy resembles the scenes in *Monty Python's Life of Brian* (1979) where the 'People's Front of Judea' fight the 'Campaign for Free Galilee' over whose plan to kidnap Pilate's wife came first. Black's ability to stand back and adopt a nominally 'neutral' stance allows him superb access. His inclusion of sequences in which members of the campaign appear disorganised, smug or slightly crazed (Úna Bea Mhic Mhathúna's condemnation of the assembled members of the press as 'wife-swapping sodomites', which results in peals of laughter, is an obvious example) signals his distance from them. The most obvious shortcoming of this method is that there is no counter-balance between the personal and the public lives of its participants, who are presented merely as political subjects within the limited boundaries of their campaign life. The film lacks a true sense of social observation because of its specificity. It is not a microcosm of Irish society as a whole because the 'walls' of this particular 'walled city' are too close to allow the light of the everyday to fall upon it.

Black's subsequent four-part series *The Joy* was more successful in this respect. This was a profile of life inside Dublin's Mountjoy Prison, a Victorian institution still in use despite constant pressure to reform the prison system and upgrade its facilities. It was the first major documentary series made inside an Irish prison, and one of the first on the subject since *The Young*

Offender (1964). Though made with the full cooperation of the prison authorities, it painted an unflattering portrait of the institution. Guards acknowledged the drugs problem and the impossibility of preventing it. Prisoners
explained the shortfalls of the substandard facilities. Confrontations between
prisoners and the prison authorities were presented without apology, though
prison governor John Lonergan frequently sought to explain his point of view
directly to the camera afterwards.

Black successfully maintained a sense of balance on this occasion and
lent undue weight or sympathy to neither the population nor the authorities.
Each issue was presented as it arose by the people involved, and though
intertitles explained developments and provided factual clarification, by and
large it followed an interactive formula in having the subjects both explain
and demonstrate situations by word and witnessed deed. As in *Hearts and
Souls*, Black had excellent access and succeeded in capturing the natural
tensions despite the presence of the camera. Though behaviour was
undoubtedly modified to some degree, on the whole there was an authenticity here which was lacking in its predecessor. Ironically, it was as if being
aware of and acknowledging the organising presence of the filmmaker freed
the participants from the kind of publicity-conscious pandering exhibited by
the 'no' divorce campaigners.

If, as Dostoevsky once claimed, a society can be judged by how it treats
its criminals, then *The Joy* was a vision of Irish society which was neither
romantic nor dystopic. Its ability to penetrate the rhythms and concerns of
prison life and indirectly raise questions regarding crime and punishment
provides a fascinating insight into late twentieth-century Ireland. It neither
praises nor condemns the prison system, but it does highlight its problems. It
does not exonerate or glamorise prisoners and their attitudes, but it does
attempt to give a sense of their difficulties as human beings. Defined by a very
specific space, well photographed by Seamus Deasy, the film even succeeded
in creating a visual counterpoint between images of freedom and of enclosure, suggesting – as many fiction films on the subject of prison do – that the
guards are equally as confined as their charges. It represented a previously
hidden world in a way which gave sight of one part of Ireland to a different
part, thus fulfilling one of the medium's most important functions.

Its objectivity is in contrast to the redemptive vision of rehabilitation
evinced in *The Hard Man* (1995). This RTÉ-commissioned project profiled
former notorious criminal Michael Kelly, now reformed and contributing to
his local community in Limerick by training the local football youth team.
Like a generic narrative, the film employed procedures of fictive engagement,
establishing empathy for the subject and an expectation of his fate. Life, it
seems, duly obliged, as his stint in prison brought about an encounter with a
priest which gave him a transforming new sense of morality and community

spirit. It was a compelling true story which gave insight into the mind of a brutal thug (Kelly was most candid about his desire to hurt people and control their destinies), but its almost too perfect narrative resolution of social service and religious inspiration closed off the story too completely. *The Joy* left many questions unanswered, and indeed the broadcast was followed by public debate on the prison system. An official report on conditions in Mountjoy was published shortly afterwards, and though the film did not necessarily directly influence its production, it contributed to the high profile it received when released.

Black's *Dear Boy: The Story of Micheál MacLiammóir* (1999) was among the first high-profile documentary productions to address homosexuality in Ireland, albeit through the filter of the biographical details of the famous actor. Louis Marcus had directed a short piece in Irish, *An Saol Gay* (1992), which profiled writer and activist Ger Philpott, and later Bill Hughes directed the interview-based *The Love that Dare Not Speak its Name* (2000), but Black's film was more subtle and far-reaching. The film counterposed an exploration of how MacLiammóir invented a persona for himself which encapsulated his obsessions with theatre and Irish culture, but which also allowed him to flaunt his sexuality in a country where it was doubly disapproved of (and illegal). Born Alfred Willmore in London, MacLiammóir moved to Ireland and embraced Irish culture to the extent that he often denied his actual roots. For Black this was a metaphor for his sexuality, which the programme explored relative to how MacLiammóir subsequently became such an icon of the Irish stage, and, latterly, of gay culture in late twentieth-century Ireland. Typical of Black's approach, the film succeeded in raising issues without taking an obvious stance, and for the most part it seemed to concern itself with chronicling the details of MacLiammóir's life. It was nonetheless clear that because that life had been so defined by his sexuality, the film was in fact addressing a largely hidden aspect of Irish culture which was only beginning to find a voice at the time the film was made following the decriminalisation of homosexuality in 1993.[3] By approaching the subject in this way, Black was able to avoid marginalising it into 'an issue'.

In 1993, Liam McGrath's short documentary *Boys for Rent* also delved into a secret world – male prostitution. In many ways the opposite of *The Joy*'s authenticity, the film fulfilled the same social function by bringing the issue to light. While its subject matter is daring and contemporary, the film chose an abstract style through which to represent it, which was more distracting than revealing. Its footage of boys and cars in public parks and silhouetted figures speaking about their experiences were all reconstruction. Only the testimony itself was real, though spoken by actors. On one hand this is testament to how hidden this world really is, but on the other the film amounts to little more than a radio documentary with moving pictures. It presents nothing evidentiary on a visual level. The profilmic is a fictive rather than a documentary space, one that is as easily ignored as considered. McGrath made the film while still a student at the Dun Laoghaire College of Art and Design, and it reveals a film-school student's concern with expressionist imagery. It is atmospheric and suggestive, and in one sense this complements the spoken evidence of the hardships and terrors of a life of sex, drugs and disease, but this visual material is fictive.

Boys for Rent won an award for best Irish short at the Cork Film Festival, and its success brought McGrath further work as a camera assistant and director. He also directed *Male Rape* (1996), a study of the psychological trauma endured by males who had been the victim of rape or other sexual abuse. Predating *States of Fear* and contemporaneous with *Dear Daughter* (screened one week after it in the same time slot), the film was notable again as an exploration of hithertofore unseen aspects of Irish life. Unlike these others, it was not concerned with abuse by institutions or religious orders, or even particularly with the details of the acts of violation which the six interviewees suffered. It was rather about exploring their emotional states in the wake of their experiences, and assessing the impact on their lives. In this it closely resembles many of the American feminist films of the 1970s which dealt with female rape in the same terms.

Male Rape also featured reconstructions filmed in the same grainy, handheld, black and white, slow-motion style as its predecessor. As in the earlier film, this was a constant distraction from the spoken testimony and squandered the opportunity to use the space to expand the range of analysis and include some discussion of masculinity in Irish society, or indeed the response to rape and the work of rape crisis centres. Only one of the interviewees actually showed his face, and he explained his reasons for doing so: 'If you want to see results, look at my personal life. No one wants to show their personal life. Nobody wants to be stripped bare and to be exposed for the world around to see, and I do not want that. But I know that if I'm going to have any effect, that I have to go that extra mile.' It is interesting that this man speaks of wanting to have an effect, and therefore acknowledges that the documentary has an important role to fulfil regardless of its stylistic excesses.

The same is true of Alan Gilsenan's AIDS documentary *Stories from the Silence* (1991), which evinced the director's characteristic frustration and spoke more openly of the prejudice and ignorance of some Irish people. It broke the 'silence' of its title and therefore brought the issue into the public spotlight. Writing on AIDS documentaries in the United States, Bill Horrigan (1993) notes that regardless of the actual content or even the argument of an AIDS-related non-fiction film or television programme, the very acknowledgement of the issue represents a progressive awareness of the needs of muted groups within a society. In these terms *Stories from the Silence* fulfilled the twin functions of drawing attention to AIDS sufferers in Ireland (thereby acknowledging the problem) and of representing a minority voice in a mainstream documentary production. It is an indication of the increasing sense of multiple points of view and diverging identities. This film was followed by *The Moon on My Back* (1996), a profile of poet and campaigner Pat Tierney (based on his autobiography). The film featured Tierney himself, dying of AIDS, speaking about his life as an outsider and commentator upon Irish society. As with *Hearts and Souls*, *The Joy* and *Boys for Rent*, the very fact that these taboo issues are presented in documentary form is important. It represents the gradual acknowledgement not only that these matters are real problems in contemporary Ireland, but that Irish people have begun to address them publicly in a manner which can only benefit society at large.

Northern Ireland: the last taboo

Documentary representation of Northern Ireland continued to be largely confined to news items and panel discussion programmes throughout the peace process. As noted previously, it frequently fell to the BBC to cover current events in a more considered documentary form. From the 1970s on, documentaries like *'last night, another soldier'* (1973), *Ireland: Behind the Wire* (1974), *The Unfinished War* (1976) and *The Troubles* (1981), leading right up to later programmes and series including *Bloody Sunday* (1994), *The Dead: 25 Bloody Years* (1994), *Provos* (1997), *Loyalists* (1998) and *Endgame in Ireland* (2001) originated in the UK. Though most of these productions credited RTÉ with some measure of assistance or cooperation and most of them were screened on Irish television subsequent to their original broadcast, the social imperative for their production did not seem to come from the island of Ireland. In Northern Ireland, though BBC Northern Ireland was part of these activities, local filmmakers were mainly confined to seeking one-off funding from UK bodies such as Channel Four (which sponsored *Mother Ireland*).

Among the more courageous attempts to examine recent history within Northern Ireland itself was director Margo Harkin's *Twelve Days in July* (1997), also sponsored by Channel Four. This film followed the build-up to the Orange Order Parade at Portadown and the increasingly hostile showdown over the right to march along the nationalist Garvahy Road which became the flashpoint for sectarian riots throughout the late 1990s. Harkin is best known in Irish film for *Hush-a-bye-baby* (1989), a taboo-breaking drama about teenage pregnancy. Often seen as a companion piece to *Mother Ireland*, it was also produced via the Derry Film and Video Workshop and with the support of Channel Four. *Twelve Days in July* begins with faint echoes of *Hush-a-bye-baby* through scenes showing a pregnant woman watching TV footage of herself screaming at the barricades in 1996. She cries as she watches, as does her teenage daughter seated nearby. The foregrounding of the female experience is resonant, yet it is not necessarily a focal theme. It is more an underlying image. Like Ophüls's *A Sense of Loss* (1972), Harkin's film attempts to put a human face on political events, though she is more successful in recounting the specific political and historical details which form the background.

The film is not entirely formally comfortable, shifting between observational coverage of the build-up to the parade and the riot which followed and interviews which outline stridently conflicting points of view. It demonstrates the influence of *Harlan County USA* (1976) in its intimate evocation of a community's struggle with seemingly implacable external forces, and there are many suspenseful and visually resonant scenes depicting social conflict. The problem is that Harkin is well aware that the situation here is no more analogous to that filmed by Kopple than was the Holocaust for Marcel Ophüls. Her access to both sides of the conflict shows participants with firmly held points of view and equal measures of hostility not only towards each other, but towards the media itself, which both sides seem to want in attendance under their own direction. The crew are 'directed' by participants on several occasions, by Orangemen, RUC, and during the riots when Garvaghy Road Residents' Coalition spokesman Brendan McKenna orders the camera operator to film scenes of RUC officers beating protesters with batons. The operator angrily tells McKenna that he needs no direction from him. The film is at its best when seemingly least concerned with context (during the riot), but it is paradoxically most worthwhile because of the strength of its contextual bracketing, aware as Harkin clearly is of both the personal and community perspectives which inform the events being filmed.

After *Mother Ireland*, community film and video groups continued to produce work, mostly testimony-based personal histories which received very limited distribution. A more polemical strain of representation may be seen in the work of academic filmmaker Desmond Bell, whose video productions *We'll Fight and No Surrender* (1990), *Redeeming History* (1990) and *Facing the Future* (1991) made important contributions to the representation of Protestant and loyalist points of view on a history and culture usually referred to only in terms of its relationship with republican nationalism. As McIlroy points out, Bell's work is motivated by the belief that 'young working-class Protestant males have had little opportunity to question their culture' (McIlroy, 1998: 151). These films used interviews with outspoken youths to articulate the sense of siege under which these individuals felt their culture to be, and to explore the nature of the Protestant sense of 'national' history on the island of Ireland.

Bell later went on to explore Protestant culture from another angle in the personal history in *Rotha Mór an tSaoil* (1999), an account of the travels of Donegal-born Mici MacGabhain, who emigrated to the United States in the nineteenth century and worked as a prospector in the Yukon. Like Black's *Dear Boy*, the film explored deeper questions of a particular personality and culture amid an easily digestible narrative (familiar from the book's appearance on school curricula). Ironically enough, virtually the same process was underway in *Voice of Generations* (1998), a film on the life of Blasket islander Peig Sayers, whose story of peasantry and hardship in rural Ireland was accorded the same 'official' status in Irish education and also fulfilled the same ideological role on a deeper level, routing 'history' through 'personality' via the process of biography. This was also the project of *An Irish-American Story* (1996), an independent US-produced study of the life of Mary Crehan Dillon, who emigrated from County Clare in 1911 and forged a new destiny in an increasingly multinational America. In this case the film was made more personal by the fact that the director was the grandson of the subject.

The belated establishment of the Arts Council of Northern Ireland and the Northern Ireland Film Council began to contribute to the production of higher-profile television documentaries in both Northern Ireland and the Republic, though a fairly circumspect or at least tangential approach was still notable. 'Dragon's Teeth' (1990), for example, followed on the heels of *Mother Ireland* in concerning itself with the conflict via the medium of a convenient metaphor. "Dragon's Teeth" were security barriers which prevented cross-border access along old, secondary or local routes not patrolled by the British Army. The film explored the significance of the barriers as both physical and metaphorical impediments to cross-border communication, focusing primarily on families who lived in the area with relatives on either side of the divide. It did not attempt a comprehensive overview of the political situation, but rather deferred to this apt symbolism to comment upon the concept of Ireland it implies. Similarly *The Kickhams* (1992) deferred its analysis of the troubles to the story of a Belfast Gaelic football team. In the guise of a conventional sports documentary, the film dealt with the cultural and emotional significance of the sport to the nationalist community. Evidence of political meaning was plentiful, including the scene where a member of the club indicates all the members of a famous Kickhams team who have since been killed in the violence.

This circumspect approach continued in the TnaG film *I gCillín na mBháis 1980-81* (1998) even though it dealt directly with one of the key events in the history of northern nationalism, the hunger strikes of 1980–81. The film refused to provide a contemporary context for the first-person accounts presented by survivors of which it was almost entirely composed. It deferred to its evidence in the manner of the interactive mode, allowing audiences to respond to the information as presented by eyewitnesses without intervention or guidance. The earlier *How Far Home* (1997) employed similar methods to much greater and more profound effect. This was a profile of Gerry Conlon, the man accused of the Guilford pub bombings of 1974 and imprisoned but later exonerated and freed, and the subject of the feature film *In the Name of the Father* (1993) based upon his autobiography. Rather than recount events in the past, Byrne's film was a portrait of the man as he is now, a shattered and damaged soul whose sense of himself has been destroyed not only by prison, but by his life after prison: first a media celebrity, then hailed as a champion of a political cause he felt he had nothing to do with, finally a lonely and desperate man attending psychological counselling and failing to adjust to a world with which he cannot engage. Allowing Conlon to speak of his experiences and combining interview material with observational techniques following him to his therapy sessions and on his travels, the film constructed an affecting portrait of the consequences of Northern Ireland's political history. Evocative cinematography by John T. Davis enhanced its visual power, capturing Conlon's sense of loneliness and desperation both through the use of the natural environment and through images of his expressive face.

Again the question becomes one of both form and forum. While public debate, radio and television talk shows and panel discussions, books, articles and fiction films seemed happy enough to explore direct questions about Northern Ireland, the subject seemed to remain taboo in Irish documentary film. The historical, social, political and cultural status of this country admittedly raises a series of complex and emotive questions, and, as *Housing Discrimination* and *Radharc in Derry* proved, those who asked them were not always free to suggest their own answers. It remains a curious and telling sign of both a basic satisfaction with the talking cure provided by radio and television programmes and an unwillingness to expend logistical and financial resources of making films which it seems others are happy to make anyway. Is this an Irish solution to an Irish problem or does this lack represent a more fundamental reluctance to engage with the question of whether or not it is an 'Irish' problem, and what nature of 'problem' the history and culture of a neighbouring country should be?

Sport, music and the performance of culture

Sports documentaries have a long legacy in Irish non-fiction film, including Louis Marcus's films for Gael-Linn and others including *Ireland: Isle of Sport* (1959/60) and *Cork Draws the Sportsmen* (1965) in which sporting events are merely a platform from which to extol the virtues of tourism or the product of a sponsor. Even within Ireland, however, documentaries on sporting subject fulfil an important national and indeed local function in asserting and reaffirming community identities. *The Road to America* (1993), an account of Ireland's struggle for qualification for the 1994 World Cup, became the best-selling Irish-produced videocassette of all time, and was a broad affirmation of the 'never say die' attitude of the Irish as competitors on an international stage. *They Called Him God* (1998) was an RTÉ-produced profile of soccer star Paul McGrath similar to *How Far Home* in its attempts to integrate psychological profile with more conventional biography. *A Year 'Til Sunday* (1998), which dealt with Galway's football championship of 1998, was remarkable because it was made by a member of the team and thus shot from the inside out. This gave it a much greater intimacy than its many predecessors and contemporaries, and the film successfully demonstrated the importance both of the sport and the win itself to the people of Galway and the families of the players. It typified the kind of local concerns evident with Gaelic Athletic Association competition. RTÉ continue to broadcast a programme called *Up for the Final* in the days before the hurling and football finals in which performers, personalities and ordinary people from the counties involved in the competition visit the RTÉ studio to participate in a night of music, chat and the proverbial 'craic'.

A different level of potential social analysis arose with the release of *Southpaw* (1998). Directed by Liam McGrath, the film told the story of Francis Barrett, an amateur boxer who represented Ireland in the Atlanta Olympics and afterwards went on to win several amateur boxing titles in Ireland and Britain. The additional cultural resonance of this story lies in the fact that Barret is a member of the travelling community, and the film establishes this as an important consideration early on. Interviewees including journalists and Barrett's trainer explain how his being a traveller politicises his boxing for Ireland.

Southpaw seems initially to present itself as the first non-fiction film to address the role of travellers in Irish society. It attempts neither to naturalise Barrett within mainstream Irish culture nor to deny his social origins. It foregrounds the traveller question from the opening, and clearly Barrett's life path is influenced by his family and environment. Yet in terms of documentary analysis, the film then seems to sideline this issue and ultimately fails to articulate a clear point of view. It shies away from a thorough sociological, interpersonal or even ethnographic profile of the community, and even fails to elicit Barrett's reflections upon his reasons for remaining at home. It is somewhat disingenuous for McGrath to assume he has adequately served his subject simply by including it at all despite the fact that, as we have seen, the very mention of a sensitive topic is often the most important first step. The film presents an issue, then abandons it, as if suddenly troubled by it or simply unable to find a means of adequately representing it within the chosen generic format.

Notably, *Southpaw* was the first Irish documentary to be released into commercial cinemas for decades. It was subsequently selected for the 1999 Sundance Film Festival, and though it failed to win any awards there, this was a major achievement for an Irish-produced film and a boost for the industry. It is remarkable that such attention was lavished on an ultimately disappointing film, but it seems that even the whispered presence of potent subject matter was enough to draw audiences to it. Inspired in part by Barrett's story, the question of travellers was raised in the public discussion of the film. Again though, it was the other media in the public sphere – print, radio and television – which took up the slack left by the film itself.

Like sport, music has remained a constant presence throughout the history of Irish documentary, both as a feature of films from *Mise Éire* on and as a subject in films about Ireland, which inevitably refer to song and dance as integral elements of the personality of the country. Harry White has argued that the study of Irish music should be as central to discourse on Irish culture as literature, and has explored the links between them in great detail. Music, he argues, is 'an essential conduit of intellectual and cultural formation' (White, 1998: 2). With the astonishing international success of *Riverdance*, music (literally) assumed centre stage as the conduit via which people could be introduced to 'Irish' culture. There have been many one-off documentaries on bands and musicians, most of them assuming an unproblematic link between the artist and the culture following the pattern of *W. B. Yeats – A Tribute* (1950) and its many successors. There have been notable exceptions, among them *Christy* (1994), *Luke* (1999) and *If I Should Fall from Grace* (2001), all of which successfully drew the threads of socio-cultural commentary through the unique personalities of their subjects.

Philip King's *Christy* examined the life of songwriter and performer Christy Moore, 'with a metaphorical placard in one hand and a bodhrán in the other' (Corr, 2001: 4). Touching on his past relationship with political music, his links with and revisions of traditional Irish forms, and his emotional difficulties, *Christy* created a portrait of the artist which exemplified the struggles of the creative personality without necessarily turning him into a metaphor for Ireland itself. Sineád O'Brien's *Luke* (1999) did subtly shift the story of singer Luke Kelly (formerly of the Dubliners) in that direction in the manner of Black's *Dear Boy*. Kelly's commitment to a broadening of perspective throughout his art and his life allowed the film likewise to broaden and deepen into a significant study of the role of art in Irish political consciousness. Interviews with commentators as diverse as John Hume and Bono noted the deep resonance of Kelly's rendition of songs like the Derry homage 'The Town I Loved So Well', the Union ballad

'Joe Hill' and the CND anthem 'The Sun is Burning', and this allowed O'Brien to quietly document the political shifts throughout the period of Kelly's life to which he made a significant if tangential contribution. *If I Should Fall from Grace*, meanwhile, sank into the depths of the alcoholic and self-destructive personality of Shane MacGowan, who became another in a line of two-fisted hard-drinking 'Irish' artists. Harrowing as the images of the ravaged face of this iconic performer certainly were (which seemed inspired by the use of such images in *How Far Home*), the overall idea that his Irish roots served to explain both his genius and his weaknesses lacked analytical nuance.

A similar mixture of themes of music, creativity and personality under-pinned *Aidan Walsh: Master of the Universe* (2000), which followed *Southpaw* into commercial cinemas and *The Road to America* onto videocassette. Directed by Shimmy Marcus (son of Louis) over the course of four years' filming, it profiled eccentric recording artist and performer Aidan Walsh, whose peculiar brand of performance art won him an unexpected record deal (allegedly agreed while the producer was intoxicated) and instant celebrity in 1987. His shortlived fame carried him to radio and television and even into the fringes of the recording industry in the late 1980s before he faded from public view. Walsh's behavioural and psychological divergences are not portrayed by Marcus in terms of insanity or disablement, but are positioned thematically as a celebration of his individuality.

The film's real appeal is in the outrageous nature of the world Walsh has made for himself, which Marcus accepts at face value. What might be insane rambling and evidence of mental illness in another film is here celebrated as a unique viewpoint which has given birth to singular art – in this case Walsh's now rare collection of bizarre 'songs' on the album 'A Life Story of My Life'. The result is almost akin to a documentary from another reality altogether, which Marcus places in relation to our own. Though the film explores questions of exploitation and foregrounds music and media indus-try personnel whose 'admiration' for Walsh seems tinged by irony, it is itself open to criticism on the same level. This did not prevent it from earning pos-itive reviews, and even comparisons to Terry Zwigoff's *Crumb* (1994), which also explored a divergent personality in terms of his performance within an 'alternative' culture. What precisely Aidan Walsh represents in terms of Irish culture is another question. Certainly this character fits a pre-existing arche-type of the 'holy fool', seen in the much-maligned *Ryan's Daughter* (1970) in the character played by Oscar-winning Sir John Mills. In that case the char-acter was a kind of all-seeing 'outsider' whose clarity of perception was shown to be greater than that of nominally 'sane' individuals. It is doubtful the same can be said of Aidan Walsh, although the general point about divergence, difference and creativity is well taken.

Philip King returned with a more general overview of the mixing frames of reference in the study of Irish music in *Freedom Highway* (2000). This was an even more explicit exploration of political discourse through music, though it was not focused exclusively on Ireland. By contrast, the RTÉ series *From a Whisper to a Scream* (1999) attempted to construct a history of Irish music in terms of the paradigm suggested by its title, a progression from the safe domesticity of Dana to the postmodern political agitation of U2. Though King was able to give substance and texture to his film, the latter series was unsurprisingly superficial. *Freedom Highway* employed archive footage and details from political and social history to trace a continuum of musical agitation across several cultures. *From a Whisper to a Scream* was confined to the repetitive 'talking heads' format, and though it did incorporate developments in Irish history in general, the emphasis seemed to be placed on anecdote and opinion from the performers themselves rather than an overarching sense of the context of music in Irish culture as a whole. Perhaps the issue with such films is that addressed by White himself, whereby it is the lack of an analytical paradigm which limits the level of discourse. Without fully exploring the complex dynamics of music as an art and an industry, it is difficult to arrive at nuanced conclusions. As such most of these films, and many others like them originating in other countries, simply lionise the activities of Irish musicians as an unproblematic exemplar of the creativity of the nation.

Dublin and the millennium

The construction of the Spire of Dublin in the late 1990s was to be an important statement of the face of the new Ireland, the centrepiece of a revived O'Connell Street (which had become a glum and ugly thoroughfare fronted by fast-food outlets and bargain stores and frequented by junkies, muggers and violent drunks). Originally called 'the millennium spire' (but renamed because it failed to meet its original construction deadline in the year 2000), this 120 m metal spike was erected on the site of the Nelson pillar. It was finally completed in 2003. The public response was largely one of bemused bewilderment. The consensus was that regardless of what notional significance it may have had in the minds of the city planners or the architect who designed it, the spire definitely was a symbol of the Celtic Tiger: it was conspicuous, self-serving, and ultimately meaningless to the ordinary citizen.

The decline of the city through the twentieth century had been seen perhaps most forcefully in Jim Mulkerns's *Capital City: Dublin 1974–1975* (1974), a film shown privately while international audiences were treated to Micheál MacLiammoir in *The Importance of Being Dublin* (1973) and Blue

Peter's *Touring Great Cities: Dublin* (1974) with Valerie Singleton. Mulkerns's film received something of a follow-up with *Bargaintown* (1989) a bleak, black and white, expressionistic study of urban decay in the inner city before the property boom which transformed the area. Made by two German visitors working independently of any television station or sponsor, it had a poetic, reflective style that was very atypical of Irish-made non-fiction films at the time. Not dissimilar to Mulkerns's film in its depiction of the urban landscape, the film incorporated interviews with Quayside antique dealers, publicans and other individuals who populated an area otherwise dominated by empty lots and 'for sale' signs. The film seemed able to find darkness in every corner of this hidden world, with interviewees often barely visible in a field of vision defined by light and shadow.

This is Dublin (1990) was a less poetic but entirely indigenous effort which evinced some of Alan Gilsenan's anger in its portrait of the city. The film focused on the destruction of Dublin's architectural heritage by urban renewal. Consisting mostly of rapidly edited, high-speed montages of parts of the city featuring time-lapse photography and a variety of film and video formats, it was a stylistically unusual film with great energy. Scrolling intertitles recounted the history of the city from Viking times to the 1980s, commenting on how contemporary buildings reflected the emptiness of contemporary Irish culture. Like *The Road to God Knows Where*, it prominently featured music by Irish bands and seemed designed to attract the attention of a youth audience. It occasionally resembled some of the modernist city films in its application of montage to create a sense of busy urban chaos, but was notably absent of a human presence, and seemed more concerned with architecture and public monuments than the inhabitants and their histories. By contrast the community video *Whitefriar Street Serenade* (1990) focused on the social aspects of inner-city life with a profile of the place and the people who lived there. Intended for local distribution, it is evidence of the continuing project of amateur filmmaking through the greater logistical resources provided by the activities of community groups.

Donald Taylor Black took a sidelong look at the city in *In Flags or Flitters: Pictures of Dublin* (1991). A conscious attempt to redress the mythology of the city through the critical reflections of artists and poets who treated official culture with scepticism, this was another of the director's ironic reflections on Irish life. Taking its cue from *The Road to God Knows Where*, the film included comic interjections, though this time the humour was that of authors and commentators like Joyce and Yeats. Featuring a vast amount of interview material from a large number of public figures and copious archival footage of events in the city's past, its production was partly motivated by the 1988 city millennium celebrations, which Black treated with characteristic scorn. Though in its own way celebratory of the city's character, the film was highly critical of romantic interpretations, and included images of the destruction and decay of buildings and monuments alongside scenes of protests, marches and other preservation-related activities (including footage of a young Mary Robinson). All of this was set against a 'traditional' opening which featured travelogue footage of the city and a cheerfully vapid voice over of the kind familiar to viewers of previous films. Black then cut from footage of Patrick Kavanagh singing traditional Dublin songs on black and white television, to U2's 'Where the Streets Have No Name', and images of contemporary Grafton Street thronged with young people and tourists.

As the city benefited financially from the advance of the economic boom, subsequent films tended to be less hostile. As if heeding the call of *Tourism is Everyone's Business* (1978), few overviews of the city produced during the prime years of the Celtic Tiger were sceptical of its effects. Sé Merry Doyle's *Alive Alive O: Portraits of Dublin* (2001) was an exception, a conscious attempt to examine the underbelly of the city's 'rejuvenation' by focusing on the demise of its traditional street traders and open markets. Using the same combination of imagery and interview seen in *Bargaintown*, Doyle's film was at once nostalgic and belligerent. Doyle, who is better known as John T. Davis's regular collaborator and editor, had also directed *James Gandon: A Life* (1996), a film about the life and work of the English neo-classical architect who had designed many of Dublin's most important civic buildings. *Alive Alive O* also touched on the colonial past, with one interviewee even suggesting that the paternalism of Victorian aristocrats was at least in some cases philanthropic enough to provide for leisure space and accommodation for their workers, which the contemporary authorities were not.

The film attempted to draw connections between the working-class experience of 'old' Dublin and that of the 'new', essentially a more economically polemicised version of the pattern seen in Louis Marcus's *Dubliners Sean agus Nua* (1971). The film featured comments from independent politician Tony Gregory as well as the views of various street traders and observers of urban culture in an attempt to give a voice to those for whom the rejuvenation of the city represented the end of a way of life. Not entirely free of sentiment, and using the device employed in *Travellers* where participants are shown pictures of themselves and others like them in years now gone by, it was nonetheless a welcome antidote to the numerous promotional films distributed on video to visitors and tourists. Its awareness of the fact of habitation and the human dimensions thereof compensated for its over-the-top soundtrack and some less pointed teary-eyed reminiscences by some of the participants.

Docusoaps, *video vérités* and 'reality shows'

The proliferation of new 'reality' formats in the 1980s and 1990s has been a cause of both celebration and alarm in the analysis of non-fiction forms. As Izod et al. remark, 'much as these new modes have succeeded in getting factual programming noticed, they may – ironically enough – have made it easier for broadcasters to turn their face against the commissioning and production of more challenging work, most of which requires much higher levels of investment in terms of time, planning and resources' (Izod et al. (eds), 2000: 4). It is not surprising that RTÉ should have leapt on the low-cost bandwagon with do-it-yourself reality shows, and *video vérités*, which, as John Corner is careful to point out, draw their inspiration not from *cinéma vérité* but from other forms of popular television programming such as game shows and soap operas.

The 'reality show' achieved its highest public profile in Ireland in 2003 with *Cabin Fever* and *Celebrity Farm*. The former was a game show inspired by the *Survivor* format, the latter a variant on *Big Brother*. *Cabin Fever* became a talking point quite literally by accident. The premise was to follow a group of individuals on a journey around Ireland on a sailing boat which they would crew while also completing the usual weekly tasks. The show went on the air in late May, and received average viewing figures. It made headlines however when on Friday 13 June the boat sank off the coast of Donegal. A special episode was broadcast the following Sunday night (running into the time slot usually allocated for the main evening news), amid speculation about the future of the series and potential litigation by traumatised participants.

The public interest (and amusement) was enough to hold *Cabin Fever*'s ratings at higher levels than expected throughout its remaining weeks (a new boat was obtained and two new competitors were brought in to replace those who refused to return), but in documentary terms, even the special episode offered little to no insight into contemporary Irish culture over and above any other type of game show. Its study of disparate individuals in confined conditions produced the usual personality clashes and role-playing exercises, but the only surprising moment was not even captured by the makers' own cameras. The crucial footage of the ship floundering on the rocks off Tory Island was captured on home video by a passer-by.

The appeal of *Celebrity Farm* rested on the collision between (post)modernity and rurality inherent in the idea of putting a group of prominent personalities to work on a farm, where they were the subject of twenty-four-hour scrutiny and a daily television broadcast. Though many observers noted the relative lack of actual farm work carried out by the contestants, audiences enjoyed the gradual fraying of nerves which came with the public vote each evening. One after another, the rejected 'celebrities' began to appear on radio and television talk shows complaining of how they had been treated and accusing the makers of the show of manipulating the footage to make them appear more 'villainous'. Arguments like these had been heard on American television as far back as 1973, with the famous Loud family protesting their innocence upon the broadcast of the fly-on-the-wall series *An American Family*.[4] Nevertheless Irish audiences enjoyed the ever-widening arena of gladiatorial spectacle as the ripples from the show spread across the visual, sound and print media with a stream of ill-tempered observations from the participants.

Not all of these shows have been a complete waste of time. Corner speaks of 'hybridising' as a feature of generic evolution, and notes that 'as a public form, documentary has the capacity to survive both postmodern skepticism and the constraints of the audio-visual market' (Corner, 1996: 190). Graph Films have been among the most interesting companies making docusoaps in Ireland in their attempts to reach the limits of the Irish experience both at home and abroad. Graph were the producers of *The Morrison Tapes*, dealing with the Irish abroad, *Hallelujah Love and Stuff* (1996), on marriage in modern Ireland, *D-Watch* (1999), an 'emergency services' film about the Dublin Fire Brigade, and *The Leaving* (1999), charting the final school year for students from different Irish secondary schools. Three of these four series were directed by Darragh Byrne.

Among the more important results of this genre has been the capacity to present multiple perspectives on a single topic, as the views of participants often differ widely. *The Morrison Tapes* was an ambitious project which obviously took some inspiration from *The Road to God Knows Where* in its focus on the diasporic experience. Its premise was to follow four separate emigrants from different strata of Irish life who had been granted Morrison Visas[5] to work in the United States and see how they adjusted to life abroad. Its structural conceit of interviewing its subjects first in Ireland, then several months later in the US, also allowed contrasts in their attitudes to emigration to emerge. Yet it was clear that Byrne had yet to develop a sense of balance which would allow the subjects' character and environment to emerge from the profilmic via observational techniques. The series relied too heavily upon intimate conversation without acknowledging the inevitable subjectivity of this method, resulting in a frustrating combination of elements.

Hallelujah Love and Stuff was more effective. The series explored attitudes towards marriage, focusing on four couples in the months and weeks prior to their weddings. Each couple represented a different social stratum, beginning with a working-class couple, then an archly conservative upper-middle-class pairing, then a middle-aged widower with children and a slightly younger woman, finally a couple from opposite sides of the Irish border. Though the series retained the emphasis on interviews, it had a much stronger sense of the social milieu, captured by more carefully selected shooting situations and well chosen cutaway material to establish the environment. The interview material evolved more naturally from the wedding preparations, following specific moments and events in each case. Each episode also contrasted with the previous one, which added to its broader social critique. The contrast was especially strong between the first and second episodes. The young working-class couple (who already had a child) were seen to be casual about propriety but serious about one another. Meanwhile the sense of tradition, discipline and upright morality which pervaded the many pronouncements by the upper-middle-class male (who was also a navy officer) was juxtaposed with the passive acceptance of his fitness-instructor bride-to-be.

This series successfully addressed attitudes towards morality, tradition and personal choice in contemporary Ireland through the medium of its participants. Without losing sight of the pleasures of process-centred documentary form (each episode followed the same structure in charting the events leading up to the wedding and the ceremony itself), it clearly concerned itself with these wider questions, and offered its eight subjects as a cross-section of Irish society. On the whole it strongly demonstrated the changes which had taken place in the past few decades. All but one of the couples had cohabited for long periods prior to the wedding, and while all of them discussed religion and the church, none (including the 'traditionalist') seemed concerned with their approval or disapproval (the traditionalist seemed more concerned with propriety and etiquette than with any particular moral authority). The series also used a wider range of interviewees from the immediate families to tell parts of the relevant story. This provided more than a single perspective on the events and people in question. It demonstrated the importance of the ritual to large groups of people beyond the couple themselves (and, by implication, in society in general).

Hallelujah Love and Stuff was followed by a comparable series on the subject of divorce, but it came seven years later, at a time when, according to the programme, up to 134,000 people in Ireland were either separated or divorced. *For Better or Worse?* (2003) followed the stories of several couples at different stages in their divorces. Combining interviews and voice over, the film was also distinguished by a visual style which sought to inject a note of 'sensitivity'. This was embodied by the reflective music (including the 1980s power ballad 'Total Eclipse of the Heart') and the use of superfluous footage of trees, sky, water and an emblematic image of a doll's house in an open field to provide 'space' for viewers to contemplate the stories being told. Though illustrative of an emerging phenomenon in Irish culture, and the first sustained examination of the subject since *Hearts and Souls*, the series was perhaps limited by its insistence on the serial format and the primacy of the interview. Each episode dealt with aspects of divorce, from emotional to financial, almost taking the form of a video textbook at times. Too bound by the conventions of the serial documentary genre, it conspicuously lacked a wider view of the experience of divorce for Irish society as a whole. Still, it was a useful beginning, and, as with so many of these shows, the discussions it provoked in the public sphere (radio, press, pubs) were at least illustrative of the fact that the issue was finally under open discussion.

Less successful by far was the elaborate 'emergency services' series *D-Watch* (1999) which more strictly followed the docusoap format of developing a serial narrative. It was a more ambitious project than its predecessors. Shot over six months *in situ* with the Phibsborough branch of the fire brigade (which also operates the emergency ambulance services), it attempted to demonstrate the role played by the service in public health. Not only did these men fight fires, they were also shown calling to aid elderly people in distress, picking up drunks from the streets, assisting in a case of suspected suicide and generally working at the heart of the troubles of Dublin city. Director Niamh Walsh tried to use the characters of the men on duty to give the film a personal dimension, introducing them during the credits by name and age and frequently featuring interludes of conversation and merriment in the station house. This was intercut with the action scenes, most of which were filmed handheld and improvised, depending on the situation. The result however was cluttered and superficial. Firemen would make barely audible passing comment as the ambulance or fire truck hurtled noisily along Dublin streets while the camera unsteadily took in the rushing scenery. This quickly became tedious, and though Walsh attempted to expand upon such scenes with location shots and reflective comments afterwards, the entire series felt empty and resembled the type of 'reality programming' represented on Sky TV by *Cops* and its many offshoots. The 'psychodynamics of anxiety and insecurity' identified by Corner (1996: 184) as the principal feature of the 'emergency services' genre were singularly absent.

If *D-Watch* did accomplish anything, it was by inference and as a pale echo of the fire brigade films of the late nineteenth and early twentieth centuries. It was a reassurance to viewers that the state was looking after their interests in the form of this dedicated group of individuals who were on call and prepared to help with an emergency. It is arguable though that the subject would have been better served by a single documentary feature with a more measured approach and a more judicious selection of incidents. The fact that it was not is indicative of the programming policies which are largely responsible for the growth of these genres. RTÉ, like any other television station, is happier with six half-hour episodes of a show than with a single programme. It is easier to market, guarantees an audience and establishes advertising time slots for six weeks (if it is successful). In this regard also, *D-Watch* may be seen to exist in the service of extrinsic forces. The subject did lend itself naturally to a deeper examination of Irish society and its problems, but the directorial approach taken reflects an uncritical, careerist sensibility.

The same might be said of Treasure Films' multipart series *Home* (1998), a generally lightweight profile of the attitude to home and habitat in modern Ireland. Each episode profiled a different type of home and the people who lived there or were trying to live there. Produced in the midst of a developing housing crisis in which price increases were preventing people from owning property, the series steadfastly refused to delve any deeper into the economics of the situation or question the values of Irish society in the light of such mercenary and material attitudes. *Home* was remarkable for its last episode: a sudden, uncharacteristic and very powerful piece of social documentary which dealt with the homeless in Dublin city. In contrast to the cheerful tone of its predecessors, the final episode chillingly detailed the difficulties of those without homes in modern Ireland, following them to various squats, doorways and miscellaneous shelters in which they were forced to live and interviewing them about their experience of life.

While not sentimental in approach or quick to make broad generalisations, this episode pointedly achieved a sense of social engagement which its predecessors had not. Director Liam McGrath (*Boys for Rent*, *Southpaw*) mixed interviews with observational footage in the manner of the Graph programmes and without recourse to reconstruction or any of his usual stylistic extravagances. This produced an effective representation of a genuine social problem. Different people had different experiences, from long-term homeless to those struggling to remain part of the system while in severe financial difficulty. All of them attested to the existence of serious gaps in the 'Tiger' economy – gaps through which people had fallen. Viewers could sense the frustration of one interviewee who repeatedly phoned various shelters for bed space, knowing that he could not call until late at night, and that the window of opportunity was extremely small. Others discussed the best spots for panhandling in Temple Bar, the centre of entertainment for the affluent young in Dublin city, before demonstrating how to keep warm outdoors in cold weather.

There was no voice over and no interviews with helper organisations that might turn the material presented in this episode into a promotion for a particular group or even into a Griersonian problem–solution piece. It observed and chronicled, and allowed the sense of despair and anger to arise naturally out of the material – a most effective documentary in every sense of the word. It was followed by one-off short documentary made by RTÉ as part of their *Townlands* series, also called *Home* (2000), a strikingly photographed meditation on the same themes following a small number of homeless men in different types of temporary accommodation. It is interesting that in both cases the issue needed to be bracketed: in the case of

McGrath's film by an otherwise unremarkable lifestyle show, and in the other by a potpourri series with no over-arching polemical ethos. It again demonstrates the potential value of popular television formats, however, as in both cases, valuable documentary was carried out under the auspices of entertainment programming.

After the disappointment of *D-Watch*, Graph Films' *The Leaving* was a considerable relief. This charted the final school year of four individuals taking their leaving certificate examination in 1998. In keeping with the methodology of previous Graph Films series, each student had a different life experience and a different set of expectations. *The Leaving* also employed a variety of filming methods, beginning with traditional interviews and location work, but including video diary footage which allowed the students to elaborate upon their feelings at crucial and private moments as the exams came closer, when the presence of the film crew would have been intrusive. Because the video diaries were part of an overall palette of documentary techniques, they did not appear narcissistic and trivial. Director Darragh Byrne provided a series of backgrounds to contextualise the confessional material, and when the films did switch to the personal ruminations of the four individuals, the audience had already been presented with enough evidence of their economic situations, educational expectations and social environments for their thoughts to become meaningful.

The series was also unafraid to comment upon questions of class and social prejudice, contrasting the environments of a young Dubliner living in poor circumstances whose attitude was wholly positive with the constant self-serving self-doubt of a Cork girl bound to study medicine. As in *Hallelujah Love and Stuff*, Byrne allowed his camera to roam around his subjects' habitats and used judicious cutaways to give a sense of the milieu from which they came. When juxtaposed with those of the other individuals, these observations effectively contributed to an overall sense of the differences which define the experience of modern Ireland as a whole. Though its structure leaves the series open to questions of narrative manipulation, there is a tangible feeling of relief when the exam results arrive, and though not all of the four get what they wanted, there is a sense of narrative resolution which none of the other series has. Yet it does conclude with some moments of reflection about the future, with one student remarking that it represents 'the end of one phase of my life and the beginning of another'. A project for a later date might be for Byrne to return to these people's lives and assess their progress in the manner of Michael Apted's *7-Up* (1963) upon which Barnouw commented, 'the continuing glimpses of the others, with their ups and downs, twists and turns, surprises and ironies, always against the background of current history, provide a deeply absorbing panorama of a society in motion' (Barnouw, 1993: 324–5).

In a sense this is precisely what the documentaries in this section have the potential to provide. As a 'panorama of a society in motion' they show a country in which the ideas of Ireland and Irishness have broadened to accommodate a range of personalities with different ideas on questions which concern society as a whole. In contrast to the monolithic rhetorical documentaries of the past, contemporary Irish documentaries have begun to represent conflicting, oppositional and simply alternative points of view. That noted, the subject of race in Ireland has yet to receive a thorough documentary examination. In spite of the diversifying racial profile of the Irish population, relatively little has been heard of the voices of the new Irish minorities. The magazine series *Mono*, which began broadcasting at the turn of the millennium, was an attempt to incorporate different perspectives on Irish events, or at least events on the micro level as they affected the new communities. Hosted by Asian and African presenters, *Mono* was a well-meaning attempt to acknowledge the increasing ethnic diversity of twenty-first-century Ireland, but inevitably its very nature (as a magazine show) left it open to accusations of tokenism and marginalisation as it separated out the needs of the immigrant communities from the 'homogeneous' whole.

Though the infrastructure of documentary production still limits the range of free expression, it is evident that Irish documentarists have evolved strategies of response. From Gilsenan's dialectical counterpoint and Davis's self-reflection to Black's irony and Byrne's humanism, it is clear that the millennial years have seen a considerable development in formal style and philosophical approach. It is also evident that the frames of reference of public service have changed, and that the public sphere is itself subject to fluctuating gravitational forces of economic necessity and social advocacy. The matter will become more urgent in the next few years, especially with the introduction of new technologies and the new multiculturalism of postnationalist Ireland, which also promises to transform the landscape of broadcasting. We might hope that based upon what it has accomplished in the preceding twenty years, Irish documentary may continue to reflect and contribute to the evolution of Irish society as a questioning and discursive voice.

If this study of the evolution of non-fiction film in Ireland has accomplished its aims, it has demonstrated that though the pace of change has been slower than elsewhere and the results have been less dramatic, Irish documentary has both itself evolved and reflected the evolution of Ireland. From the earliest factual representations to the most contemporary, Irish documentary has played a part in the way in which Irish people have concieved of their physical, social and political environment. It is not the sole determinant (though it has often assumed it is), nor is it developed to the point where it has established a discursive relationship with the representation of reality itself. Yet as elsewhere in the world, documentary has been a continuing presence in the projection and investigation of the image of Ireland which is prevalent during any one historical period. As it has developed, the medium has taken different attitudes to the world, to itself and to its audience. These attitudes have reflected changes in Irish society. Documentary film has never been at the vanguard of change in Ireland, nor has it ever achieved the impact of more traditional forms of oral communication in their modern guise (the talk show/current-affairs discussion programme), but it has sometimes provided the most sober and reflective comment upon broad trends and shifts in perception.

It is difficult to arrive at a single conclusion regarding over a century of history still within living memory and still impacting on current events. I think it is fair to argue, however, that documentary film is as relevant to an examination of Irish culture or society as studies of literature, philosophy and fiction film are. Documentary is a discursive practice, the study of which reflects as much as the films themselves represent directly. If we accommodate questions of how non-fiction film has facilitated the understanding of Ireland for those who make and view documentary films, then we may study documentary in terms not just of its texts, but of its contexts (of production, of reception, of role and function relative to ideas of society, state and nation). This approach facilitates the evolution not just of ideas of Ireland, or of projections of ideology, but of Ireland itself, insofar as we take the word to refer not to some abstract notion of national identity, but of a people and a place whose relationship with one another continues to grow and change.

Notes

1 For further detail on Habermas and his theories see McCarthy, 1978; Dahlgren, 1995; Edgell et al. (eds), 1995, and White, 1995.
2 See Watson, 2003.
3 For a discussion of images of homosexuality in Irish films see Pettitt, 1999.
4 See Gilbert, 1988.
5 Morrison Visas are special lottery-based visas issued by the US Embassy to allow Irish citizens to emigrate legally to the United States and work freely. They are advertised every few years and applications are invited.

Filmography

This filmography is not intended to list every documentary ever produced on the island of Ireland. It is a record of the films viewed and/or referenced in the course of the research for this book. A purely filmographical reference book is in preparation under the supervision of Kevin Rockett (ed.), *The Irish Filmography: Non-Fiction 1896–2006* (forthcoming, 2006).

Titles The titles listed are the titles as they appear on screen on the print viewed.

Titles in Irish Titles in Irish are usually followed by an English translation.

Date Dates for theatrical productions indicate year of release. Dates for television material denote year of first broadcast (where known). Films which have been neither distributed nor broadcast are listed by copyright or stock date (where appropriate). Where dates have not been ascertained, they are either approximate or have been omitted.

Duration Titles were viewed in a variety of formats in the course of this research, including 16 mm, 35 mm, recorded videotape, DVD and television broadcast. All times shown are approximate and based on the print and format viewed. In some cases the footage length is given. In some cases the category is omitted.

Director Where no director has been credited and no research could uncover the appropriate name, the name of the producer or production company is usually substituted.

Summaries The brief summaries give a general indication of the contents of the film and note whether dramatic reconstruction has been used. Fuller comments on individual titles can be found in the body of the book.

Credits Credits are reproduced as they appear on the print viewed, or, where appropriate, are based on the records of the Irish Film Archive or other sources. In the case of television series, credits are drawn from a sample programme. Certain credits have been omitted, as stated in the entries concerned, on grounds of length.

Credits in Irish Where credits appeared on the original print in the Irish language, they have been reproduced in that form here without translation. An appendix of translation is included below.

Names in Irish Care has been taken to note the proper accents for names credited in Irish. If accents were not indicated on the credits, they have not been added.

Translation guide

The following translation of credits in Irish is intended for reference only. It is not intended to be a comprehensive listing of job titles. Only credits which appear in the filmography are reproduced here.

Irish – English

Áiseanna: Locations
Amhrán/Amhránaí: Song/Singers
Búiochas le: Thanks to
Ceamara: Camera
Ceámaradóir: Camera Operator
Ceol: Music
Ceol Nuachumtha: Original Music
Coin-Léiriú: Co-Production
Comhairleoir Léiriúcháin: Production Consultant
Comhairleoir Staire: History Constultant
Comh-Léirtheoir: Co-Producers
Cúntóir Ceamara: Camera Assistant
Cúntóir Léirúcháin/Léirithe: Production Assistant
Dubáil: Dubbing
Eagarthóir/Eagarthóirí: Editor/Editors
Eagarthóir Coimisiúnaithe: Commissioning Editor
Eagarthóir Líne: Line Editor
Eagarthóir Réamhline: Off-Line Editor
Eagarthóir Script: Script Editor
Fuaim: Sound
Fuaim ar an Láthair: Location Sound
Fuaimrian: Soundtrack
Grafác/Graificí: Graphics
Griangraf: Photographs
Léiritheoir/Léiritheorí: Producer/Producers
Léiriú de chuid: Produced by
Meascóir Fuaime: Sound Recordist
Taighde: Research
Taighde Breise: Additional Research
Taighde Fístéipe: Videotape Research
Taighdeoirí: Researchers
Trachtaire: Narrator
Rostrum/Rostram: Rostrum
Scannán de cuid: A film by
Scéalaí: Narrator
Scriopt: Script
Stiúrthóir: Director
Stuideo: Studio
Teidil: Titles

English – Irish

Additional Research: Taighde Breise
A film by: Scannán de cuid
Camera: Ceamara
Camera Assistant: Cúntóir Ceamara
Camera Operator: Ceámaradóir
Commissioning Editor: Eagarthóir Coimisiúnaithe
Co-Producer: Comh-Léirtheoir
Co-Production: Coin-Léiriú
Director: Stiúrthóir
Dubbing: Dubáil

Editor/Editors: Eagarthóir/Eagarthóirí
Graphics: Grafác/Graificí
History Consultant: Comhairleoir Staire
Line Editor: Eagarthóir Líne
Locations: Áiseanna
Location Sound: Fuaim ar an Láthair
Music: Ceol
Narrator: Trachtaire/Scéalaí
Off-Line Editor: Eagarthóir Réamhline
Original Music: Ceol Nuachumtha
Photographs: Griangraf
Produced by: Léiriú de chuid
Producer/Producers: Léiritheoir/Léiritheorí
Production Assistant: Cúntóir Léirúcháin/Léirithe
Production Consultant: Comhairleoir Léiriúcháin
Research: Taighde
Researchers: Taighdeoirí
Rostrum: Rostrum/Rostram
Script: Scriopt/Script
Script Editor: Eagarthóir Script
Song/Singers: Amhrán/Amhránaí
Sound: Fuaim
Sound Recordist: Meascóir Fuaime
Soundtrack: Fuaimrian
Studio: Stuideo
Thanks to: Búiochas le
Titles: Teidil
Videotape Research: Taighde Fístéipe

50,000 Secret Journeys (1994) 25 min.
Director: Fintan Connolly, Hilary Dully
Women who have had abortions tell their stories intercut with news clips recounting recent events in the ongoing legal struggle between pro and anti abortion campaigners.

Credits The Picture Company wishes to thank all the women who shared their stories with us. Interviewer: Hilary Dully, Researchers: Fiona Bergin, Nicola Byrne, Marie Louise Kenny, Camera: Declan Emerson, Peter Robertson, Ciaran Tanham, Sound: Paul Emerson, Dubbing Mixer: Noel Storey, Video 8: John O'Donnell, On-Line Editor: Mark Nolan, Post-Production: Screen Scene, Co-Producer: Fiona Bergin, Produced and Directed by: Fintan Connolly and Hilary Dully. A Picture House Production for RTÉ.

Achill Island (1972) 25 min.
Director: Kevin Marsland
Portrait of life on Achill Island which attempts to locate the islanders in terms of economy and agriculture though it also bows to touristic expectations as a homage to the rugged and romantic aspects of the landscape.

Credits Director: Kevin Marsland, Script: Kevin Marsland, Assistant Producers: Peter Brown, Susan Morrall, Narrator: Cyril Cusack, Director of Photography: Stephen Haskett, Music: Richard Hartley.

Aidan Walsh: Master of the Universe (2000) 70 min.

Director: Shimmy Marcus

Profile of eccentric media celebrity Aidan Walsh, whose peculiar personal style and unique musical career are presented as daring to be different, although undercurrents of emotional pain and mental disarray are in evidence.

Credits Sound: Kieron Horgan, Dan Birch, Alan Poole, Ken Fogerty, Camera: Seamus Deasy, Ronan Fox, Michael O'Donovan, Mick O'Rourke, Erol Reeves, Liam McGrath, Editor: Shimmy Marcus, Grainne Gavigan, Producer/Director: Shimmy Marcus, Executive Producers: Adrian Lynch, Darragh Byrne, Rod Stoneman, Edwina Forkin. A Let's Not Lose It Production.

Aiséirghe (1941) 20 min.

Director: Liam O'Leary

A film which argues that the spirit of 1916 has yet to be fully realised in 1940s Ireland.

Alive Alive O: Portraits of Dublin (2001) 52 min.

Director: Sé Merry Doyle

A study of the slow death of traditional urban enterprise as Dublin's inner city is developed for commercial use and street traders and markets are phased out.

Credits Poetry: Paula Meehan, Narrator: Jasmine Russell, Original Music: Ger Kiely, Musicians: Trevor Knight, Frankie Lane, Ger Kiely, Songs performed by: Frank Harte, 'Molly Malone' arranged by Frank Harte, 'Biddy Mulligan and the Charladies' Ball' arranged by Harte and Lunny, Principal Photography: Donal Gilligan, Additional Camera Work: John T. Davis, Liam McGrath, Robbie Ryan, Michael O'Donovan, Location Sound: Owen 'Dicey' O'Reilly, Brendan Campbell, Enda Cahill, Philippe Faujas, Simon J. Willis, Editor: Sé Merry Doyle, Assistant Editors: Linda Nartey, Marino Marolini, Additional Editing: Gaye Lynch, Sound Editor: Linda Nartey, Sound Mix: Peter Blayney, Lime Street Studios, Art Director: Marie Tierney, Opening Title: Timothy Booth, Research: Oda O'Carroll, Production Coordinator: Helen Curtin, Telecine Colourist: Glenn Kyte, Mastering: Shayne Murphy, Photos and Illustrations courtesy of: Derek Speirs, the National Gallery of Ireland, the Royal Society of Antiquarians, Film Archive Courtesy of: RTÉ Archive, the Irish Film Archive, Dept. of Foreign Affairs, Sé Merry Doyle. Many thanks to the street traders of Dublin. Special thanks to: Mick Rafferty, Catriona Crowe, Dave Reddin, Jimmy Walsh, Cúán MacConghail, Jim McGuirk, Barbara Durac, Sunniva O'Flynn, Glen Gorman, Glaire Duignan, Rod Stoneman, Ronnie Drew. Our film is dedicated to Owen 'Dicey' O'Reilly and Pat Stokes. Producer: Bernadine Carraher, Director: Sé Merry Doyle.

Amuig Faoin Spéir / Out Under the Sky (1960) 25 min. each episode

Director: Éamon de Buitléar

Ireland's first indigenous nature programme, presented by conservationist and cameraman Éamon de Buitléar. Filmed and broadcast in black and white, but enlivened visually by drawings and paintings by Dutch artist Gerrit Van Gelderen.

Credits Production Team: Éamon de Buitléar, Oscar Merne, Gerrit Van Gelderen.

An tAirgead ag Obair / Our Money at Work (1957) 12 min.

Director: Colm O'Laoghaire

Film promoting Lemass-era economic policies of trade and foreign investment rather than self-sufficiency which encourages viewers to contribute in the form of taxes: 'we are all of us shareholders', it explains. The film was released in both Irish and English-language versions.

Credits Photography: Uinsionn Ó Corcorain (Vincent Corcoran), Editor: Ted Richards, Sound: Peter Hunt, Leevers Rich, Sponsors: National Savings Committee (Department of Posts and Telegraphs), Production Company: National Film Institute, Script: Gerard Healy, Narrator (English-language version): Denis Brennan, Musical Advisor: Gerard Victory, Director: Colm Ó Laoghaire.

'Aon Seans Ort?' / 'Any Chance?' (1999) 35 min.
Director: Jennifer Keegan
An account of young Dubliners on the town one Friday evening in summertime.
Credits Ceámaradóir: Ciaran Tanham, Fuaim ar an Láthair: Joe Dolan, Cúntóir Léirúcháin: Sinád NÍ Ghuidhir, Taighde Breise: Natasha Fennell, Meascóir Fuaime: Réamonn de Brún, Eagarthóir Líne: Julian Charlton, Eagarthóir Réamhline: Cóilín Ó Scolaí, Comhairleoir Léiriúcháin: Dearbhla Walsh, Ceol: Sala Brava, Bumble, Forefront, JV, Niall Byrne, Búíochas le: Máire Moriarty, Jane O'Connor, Denise Dunne, Aedín Chonalláin, Tomás Ó Súillebháin, Cearbhall Ó Síocháin, Caitríona Ní Threasaigh, Billy O'Hanlon, Léiritheoir/Stiúrthóir: Jennifer Keegan. Lennon St. Films do TG4. Léiriú le Lennon St. Films. 'Aon Seans Ort?' ©TG4 1999.

Aran of the Saints (1932) 21 min.
Producers: the Catholic Film Society of London
A study of the Aran Islands dealing with the influence of Christianity and Catholicism on the native population.
Credits Producers: the Catholic Film Society.

Art of the State (1993) 52 min.
Director: Séan Ó Mórdha
Study of the relationship between art and nation.
Credits Director: Séan Ó Mórdha. Araby Productions for the Arts Council in conjunction with RTÉ and BBC Northern Ireland.

Atlantean (1984) 3 × 45 min.
Director: Bob Quinn
An exploration of the links between Irish and North African cultures which problematises a great many assumptions about Irish history and heritage. Followed by *Navigatio*.
Credits Heinrich Wagner, Joseph Raftery, Cliodna Cussen, Igor le Floch, Tráctaire: Alan Stanford, Ceol: Seán Ó Domnaill, Nóra Uí Meacair, De Danann, Sorca Uí Congaile, Seán Ó Conaire, Aisteoir: Noel O'Donovan, Ceamara: Sean Corcoran, Seamus Deasy, Abdelhadi Tazi, Joe Comerford, Thaddeus O'Sullivan, Halim Fahim, Nick O'Neill, Kevin Duggan, Cúntóir Ceamara: Des Whelan, Repeah Sapan, Gerald Lewis, Mohammed El Halim, Fuaim: Pat Hayes, Darby Carroll, Salama Sallam, Bob Webber, El Khabaz, Eagarthóir: Daibi Dorab, Cúntóir: Anne O'Leary, Fuaimrian: Tony McHugh, Cúntóir Lírie: Cathal Black, Miriam Allen, Mohammed Hassini, Taigde: Kathryn Hone, Rhiannon Thomas, Griangraf: Bob Hobby, Mark Quinn, Bord Fáilte, Bob Quinn, Grafác: Al O'Donnell, Rostrum: David McGarry, Ceol: Roger Doyle, Scríofa agus Stiúrta ag Bob Quinn, Coin-Léiriú: Radio Telefís Éireann, Sianel Pedwar Cymru, Bord Scannán na hÉireann, Radio Television Marocaine, Egypt TV, Búíocas do: National Museum Dublin, National Museum Cardiff, British Museum, Chester Beatty Library, National Library Dublin, Museums i Fez, Meknes, Rabat, Marakech, Cairo, Filmian TV Gwyn, Scannán de cuid: Cinegael. Bob Quinn © 1983.

Atlantic: The Independent Years (1993) 104 min.

Directors: John T. Davis, Uri Fruchtmann

The history of how Ahmet Ertegun and Herb Abramson built up Atlantic Records from a small recording label to a multinational corporation.

Credits Directors: John T. Davis, Uri Fruchtmann, Producer: Brendan Hughes, Photography: John T. Davis, Sound: Tim Lay, Editor: Sé Merry Doyle, Commissioned: Channel 4.

At the Cinema Palace: Liam O'Leary (1983) 53 min.

Director: Donald Taylor Black

A profile of documentarist and archivist Liam O'Leary featuring interviews with O'Leary and others including film historian Kevin Brownlow. The film is also a thumbnail portrait of the evolution of cinema in Ireland, with particular focus on the activities of the Film Society of Ireland of which O'Leary was co-founder.

Credits Music: Bill Whelan, Editor: J. Patrick Duffner, Photography: Sean Corcoran, Executive Producer: Kieran Hickey, Co-Producer: James Hickey, Produced and Directed by: Donald Taylor Black, Sound Recordists: Kieran Horgan, Liam Saurin, Dubbing Mixer: Bob Bell, Make-Up: Toni Delaney, Marie McLoughlin, Graphic Design: Brendan Foreman, Camera Assistants: Ken Byrne, Aidan McGuinness, Electricians: Tony Byrne, Gerry Donnelly. Thanks: the Liam O'Leary Archive, Irish Film Institute, Radio Telefís Éireann Film Library, Dublin Public Library, National Library of Ireland, G. A. Duncan Collection, National Film Archive London, British Movietone News, CND London, Rank Film Distribution, SOVexport Film, Svensk Filmindustri Stockholm, Kevin Brownlow Collection London, BAC Films, Consolata Boyle, Rupert (U Turn) Christie, Federation of Irish Film Societies, James Morris, Radio Telefís Éireann Film Department, Kevin Rockett, Mary-Jane Walsh, Staff of the National Film Archive (London). Made with the assistance of: Bord Scannán na hÉireann/the Irish Film Board, Channel Four Television, Radio Telefís Éireann, British Film Institute, Susan Langley Trust.

Autumn in Dublin (1962) 9 min.

Production Company: Coronet Productions

Touristic overview of Dublin locales sponsored by a car rental agency.

Credits Narration: Terry Wogan, Script: Frank Foley, Photography: Joe Crassen, Norman Sparksman, Sponsor: Joe Malone Self Drive Ltd, Production Company: Coronet Productions.

Ballyseedy (1997) 91 min.

Director: Frank Hand

Docudrama detailing an atrocity which occurred during the Irish Civil War. The film was the final result of some five years' research by writer Pat Butler.

Credits Acknowledgements: Nuala Jordan, the Defence Forces, Military Archives, Cathal Brugha Barracks, the National Library, UCD Archives Dept., Fitzgerald Papers, Moss Twomey Papers, Ernie O'Malley Papers, the BBC, Kathleen Browne, Kerry County Librarian, Hugh Lane Gallery, Group Theatre, Tralee, Zyber Theatre Company, Tralee, 'The Kerryman', Pádraig Kenneally of 'Kerry's Eye', the *Examiner*, Con Casey, Kathleen Larkin, Eoin Neeson, Robert Casey, Luke Kane, George Rice, John O'Shea, Joe Taylor, Martin Moore, Annie Boyle-Lenihan, Paudie Fuller, Nora Nolan, Bryan MacMahon, Anne O'Brien, Thomas O'Connor, Thomas Thompson, Peig Hickey, Nora Fleming, Eddie Barrett, Richard Boylan, Seán and Michael Buckley, Jim Dukes, Jack Godfrey, Larry Keane, John and William Lenihan, Tom

McEllistrim, Mary McSwiney, Áine Meade, Dermot O'Connor, Michael O'Connell, Rory O'Connor, Ted O'Donoghue, Sheila Stack, Peig Hayes, Gerry Twomey, Donie and Kathleen Walsh, May Stack, Ann Walsh, Marion Fitzmaurice, Bryan McManus. The Players: Barry Cassin (Lt. Col. Niall Harrington), Michael McElhatton (Comdt. Ed. Breslin), Alan O'Neill (Capt. Jim Clarke), John Fraher (Paddy Pats O'Connor), Michael O'Sullivan (Stephen Fuller), Malachy McKenna (Maj. Gen. Paddy O'Daly), Ciaran McMahon (Gen. Richard Mulcahy), Justin Aylmer (Bill Bailley), Fran Brennan (Maj. Gen. Price), with: Tracey Bolger, Charlie Bonner, Robert Devance, Brenan Dineen, Claire Dowling, Katie Dowling, Graham Doyle, Michael Dunphy, George Fields, Brendan Galvin, Tom Herlihy, Finbar Higgins, Paul Hughes, Frank Keane, Mark Kiernan, Eoin Kingston, Gerard Lee, Andrew Lovern, Kevin Lynch, Les Martin, Pat Melia, Richard Moloney, Keith Moynihan, Dermot Murphy, Brendan McDonald, John Niland, Robert O'Connor, Eunan O'Neill, Hugh O'Neill, Brian O'Rourke, Tanja Raab, Michael Rogers, Damien Ryan, Catherine Spangler, Charlie Walker (Catherine Spangler appears by permission of 'Siamsa Tíre', Tralee). Research, Script and Original Teleplay: Pat Butler, Music composed by Peadar Ó Riada, Performed by: the RTÉ Concert Orchestra, Conductor: Proinnsias Ó Duinn, Sound Engineer: Aodán Ó Dubhghaill, Graphic Design: Jill Simpson, Rostrum Camera: Nico Vermuelen, Vista Operator: Martha Powell, Make-Up: Antoinette Forbes-Curham, Eveleen Lunny, Wardrobe: Brigitte Horan, Catherine Manning, Property Master: Liam Cummins, Property Buyers: Joanne MacAvin, Ruth McDonnell, Staging: Conor O'Brien, Studio: Carpenters: Ned O'Byrne, Jim Mooney, Painter: Des Davis, Stage Manager: Maggie Stewart, Vision Mixer: Gerry Ring, Floor Manager: Niamh Farren, Video Tape Recordist: Phil Gavin, Cameras: Pat O'Reilly, Sound: Paul Dowley, Lighting: Bernard Kavanagh, Location Special Effects: Maurice Foley, Armourer: John McKenna, Electrical Supervisors: Eddie Bolger, Joe Kerins, Assistant Cameramen: Simon Culliton, Oisín Kelly, Lighting Cameramen: Breffni Byrne, Cedric Culliton, Location Sound: Eddie Duffy, Alan Seavers, Production Assistant: Úna McHenry, On-Line Editor: Tom Bannon, Post-Production Sound: Peter Fletcher, Gerri McCaffrey, Avid Editor: James Dalton, Design: Jay Clements, Paula Farrell, Executive Producer: Mick McCarthy, Produced and Directed by: Frank Hand. © 1997.

Bargaintown (1989) 70 min.
Directors: Dávid Jászai, Judith Klinger
Poetic meditation on urban decay and the change in property values in Dublin's inner city in the late 1980s, just before its reconstruction. The film features interviews with the owners of antique shops, publicans and other assorted commentators.
Credits With: Seamus Doyle, Michael Rynne, Michael Hoban, Dick Tynan, Frank Quigley and Alias Geraldine and Raymond Duffy, Photography: Dávid Jáaszai, Sound/Camera Assistant: Judith Klinger, Camera Assistant: Thomas Boetsch, Edited by Dávid Jászai and Judith Klinger. Thank you: Heiner Stadler, Áine and Tony Meade, Jocelyn Braddell, Laura Magahy and the Irish Film Institute, Ryanair, Executive Producer: Evi Stangassinger; Bargaintown HFF 1988/89.

Belfast Building (1998) 6 min.
Director: Declan McGrath
A child cycles through the streets of Belfast, a city of walls and boundaries, many of which are still being built as others lie in ruins.
Credits Video Images: Felim Mac Dermott, Camera Assistant: Claire McGrath, Sound Mix: Paddy Gibbons, Photography: Liam McGrath, Editor/Director: Declan

McGrath. Special thanks to: Frankie Quinn, Mike Hewitt, Dermot Lavery and Felim McDermott. Double Band Films, Ardmore Sound, Pancom, Loopline, RTÉ, Dun Laoghaire College of Art and Design, Keith Nolan, Colum Stapleton, Sé Merry Doyle, Gerry McTeague, John McGregor, Anne O'Leary, Anthony Litton, Brian Martin, Michael Doyle, Colm Austin, Colin McKeown, Fiona McGrath, Carolyn McCambridge, Frank and Rosemary McGrath.

'The Best Catholics . . . ' (2002) 24 min.
Director: Moira Sweeney

Exploring the significance of the 1932 Eucharistic Congress to the fledgling Irish state. The programme features footage from Fr Browne's film. An episode of RTÉ's *Leargas* series.

Credits Láithreoir/Tuairisceoir: Facthna Ó Drisceoil, Taighdeoir: Rhenda Sheedy, Comhordaitheoir Craolta: Aedín NÍ Chonalláin, Fotheidh: TMI, Ceamara Rostraim: Lorraine Sherry, Fuaimthaifead: Jim McDonnell, Fuaimrian: Steven Spoor, Soilsú: John Daley, Cuntóir Ceamara: Conall McGarrigle, Ceamara: Breffni Byrne, Eagarthóir Fistéipe: Tom Mongey, Léiritheoir/Stiúrthóir: Moira Sweeney, Léiritheoir Straithe: Tommy McArdle. © RTÉ 2002.

Between Heaven and Woolworths (1993) 52 min.
Director: Alan Gilsenan

Study of artists and their inspiration featuring, among others, John B. Keane, John Banville, Shane McGowan and Neil Jordan.

Credits Director: Alan Gilsenan, Camera: Peter Dorney, Research: Victoria White, Editor: Martin Duffy, Production: Martin Mahon. A Yellow Asylum Production.

Bird's Eye View: Inis Fáil – Isle of Destiny (1973) 62 min.
Producer: Edward Mirzoeff

Elaborate meditation upon the landscape and culture of Ireland filmed with a plethora of panoramic helicopter shots. James Plunkett narrates and presents.

Credits Presenter: James Plunkett, Production Assistant: Pennie Denton, Photography: Ian Stone, Editor: Edward Roberts, Dubbing: Mike Billing, Readers: T. P. McKenna, Richard Pasco, John Betjeman, Music Composer: John Beckett, Singer: Frank Patterson, Orchestra: RTÉ Symphony Orchestra, Pilot: Capt. Peter Peckowski. A BBC/RTÉ co-production.

Book of Kells (1972) 26 min.
Producer: Andrew Crockart

History of the famous Book of Kells also incorporating study of the typography and design presented by the archbishop of Armagh.

Credits Producers: Andrew Crockart, Associate Producer: Paddy Scott, Narrator: John Keyes, Photography: Ramsey Nelson, Joe Lyttlella, Presented by Dr G. O. Simms, archbishop of Armagh.

Boys For Rent (1993) 16 min.
Director: Liam McGrath

Interviews with male prostitutes in Dublin city are repeated on camera by actors shrouded in shadow as if they were the people in question. This footage is interspersed with grainy, handheld, slow-motion images of actors playing out typical rent-boy scenes.

Credits Actors: Bernard Deegan (Boy 1), Ross Hamilton (Boy 2), Patrick Brennan (Boy 3), Eamon Rohan (Man). Crew: Garry Keane, Conor O'Mahony, Liam McGrath,

Additional Assistance: Linda Nartey, Music: Tim Boland, Processing: Ranks Laboratories Ltd, Sound Dubbing: RTÉ, Tutorial Supervison: Anne O'Leary, Philip Davison, Michael McNally, Maurice Healy, Supervising Editor: Sé Merry Doyle. Thanks to: John Leinster, Rev. Peter McVerry, Kieran McGrath, Liam Regan, Edmund Lynch, Dave Kelleher, Mark Lowry, Dan Donnelly. Special Thanks to: Declan Reddy, Anastasia Clafferty, Mick Quinlan, Sr Fiona Pryle. Film Stock sponsored by Kodak Ireland. Producer and Director: Liam McGrath. A Liam McGrath and Dun Laoghaire College of Art and Design Production. 1993.
Best Irish Short – Cork Film Festival 1993.

The Bridge of the Ford: The Story of Drogheda (1948)
Director: Henry Cooper
A history of Drogheda featuring various sites of architectural and anecdotal interest.
Credits Producer, Script: Andrew Buchanan, Narrator: Nigel Fitzgerald, Music: M. De Wolfe, Camera: George Fleischmann, Editor: James Anderson, Sound: Peter Hunt, Leevers Rich, Director: Henry Cooper.

'*Building a Curragh at Dingle Bay*' 13 min.
Silent Kodakchrome film featuring a detailed look at the construction of a traditional fishing boat in the west of Ireland. It concludes with one such boat putting to sea in search of Mackerel.

Cabin Fever (2003) 50 min. each episode
Director: Liam McGrath
'Reality' gameshow, almost scuttled when the ship upon which it was set ran aground on Friday 13 June 2003, forcing the rescue of contestants and crew by emergency services. The third episode detailed the build-up to and aftermath of the wreck. The show resumed with a new ship and several new contestants some weeks later.
Credits Narrator: Enda Oates, Music: Gregory Magee, Script Writer: Niall Murphy, Camera: Ken O'Mahony, Sound: Stephen McDowell, Electrician: Kevin Scott, Consulting Psychologist: Fíona Kelly Meldon, Researchers: Tony Brady, Michelle Connolly, Cabin Fever Skipper: Peter Culleton, Ship Master and Owner: Rodger Barton, Carrie of Camaret, Sea Survival Training: Sea and Shore, Safety Services, Chopper Pilot: Loy McParland, Graphics: John Kennedy, Games Specialist: Jamie Young, Games Assistants: Sean Flynn, Deirdre Fitzgerald, Courier Service: Philip Higgins, Publicists: Karen Fitzpatrick, Gillian Rowntree, Production Accountant: Stephen Kennaugh, Production Assistant: Suzanne Bailey, Production Secretary: Jacqueline Drohan, Production Trainee: Colm Nicell, Dubbing Mixers: Peter Blayney, Keith Alexander, On-line Editor: Alan Sullivan, Edit Assistant: Stephen Doran, Assembly Editor: David Dillon, Editor: Stephen Vickers, Production Coordinator: Sonia Patterson, Production Manager: Hilary O'Donovan, Post-Production Director: Cúán Mac Conghail, Director: Liam McGrath, Executive Producer for RTÉ: Julian Vignoles, Executive Producer: Stuart Switzer, Producer: Linda Cullen. A Coco Television production for RTÉ © 2003.

Campa (1942) 13 min.
Director: Liam O'Leary
Film of the activities of the Irish Boy Scouts. Long believed lost, this film has recently been reconstructed by the Irish Film Archive.

Credits Production Company: Scannán o Cumman na Scannán, Grafadoiri: Liam Ó Laogaire, Caoimgin Ó Ceallaig.

Capallology (1968) 19 min.
Director: Louis Marcus
Study of the role played by the horse in Irish sporting culture. The film compares the decorum of showjumping at the RDS to more frantic hunting and racing events and includes some interviews with jockeys. The commentary is in Irish, with snatches of English and German included for comic effect.
Credits Director: Louis Marcus, Script: Brendan Ó Heithir, Narrator: Niall Toibín, Photography: Robert Monks, Assistant Cameramen: Nick O'Neill, Val Ennis, Sound: Peter Hunt Studios, Production Company: Gael-Linn.

Capital City: Dublin 1974–1975 (1974) 17 min.
Director: Jim Mulkerns
Silent montage of urban decay in inner-city Dublin. Commissioned by the Labour Party as part of their 1974 election campaign.
Credits Director, Photography, Editor: Jim Mulkerns.

Celebrity Farm (2003) 7 × 50 min.
'Reality show' featuring a range of stage, art and television personalities trying to survive a week on a farm as the public vote one off each night.

Celtic Gas (1979) 34 min.
Producer: George Fleischmann
Promotional film detailing the mining of natural gas in Ireland.
Credits Photography: George Fleischmann, Script: John Kelleher, Narrator: Eamonn Andrews, Music: Jol Jackson, Editor: Merritt Butler, Sound: Liam Saurin, Animation: Theo Hodges, Graphics: Pat Cody, Acknowledgements: Bord Gais Eireann, Electricity Supply Board, Marathon Petroleum Ireland Ltd, Nitrigin Eireann Teo.

Celtic Gold (1966) 14 min.
Director: John Fitzmaurice Mills
History of the National Museum of Ireland's collection of Celtic gold. The film features scenes of dramatic reconstruction.
Credits Music: Sean Ó Riada, Script, Direction, Narration: John Fitzmaurice Mills, with (cast): John Murphy, Billy O'Connor, Michael O'Neill, Tom Hayes, Liam Og Miller, Eddie Clarke, Denis Merrill, Austin O'Malley, Paul Clarke, Paddy O'Broin, Photography Production: Rex Roberts, Sponsors: Bord Fáilte, Dept. of Foreign Affairs.

Citizens (1999) 6 × 25 min.
Series Producer: Peter Mulryan
Potpourri of *video vérités* filmed by ordinary Irish people, assembled in multipart episodes.
Credits Production Team: Helen Barry, Michael Frawley, Eoin O'Shea, Production Coordinator: Clare Carr, Associate Producer: Eamon Keane, Will Harris, Series Producer: Peter Mulryan; citizens@rte.ie; RTÉ Cork.

City Folk (2003) 28 min.
Director: Sarah Ryder
Profiles of Dublin residents. Part of an internationally co-produced series.

Credits Thanks to: Dublin Corporation, Dublin Fish Market, the Front Lounge, Gaiety School of Acting, An Garda Síochana, Open Heart House, the Shakespeare Bar, Shelbourne Park Greyhound Stadium, Travel Hewitts, Yamamori Restaurant, and all the people who helped to make this programme. Sound: Stephen Spoor, Enda Cahill, Pat Murray, Camera: Aidan McGuinness, Cormac Downes, Dubbing: Seán Higgins, Titles: Réné Gast, Editor: Nathan Nugent, Producer/Director: Sarah Ryder, Executive Producer for RTÉ: Mairéad Ní Nuadháin, Executive Producer: Erik Hogenboom. City Folk is a co-production of the EBU sub-group for multicultural programmes: BR, DK4, MTV, NPS, NRK, ORF, RTÉ, RTP, SVT, TV de Catalunya, TV Slovenija, YLE. © RTÉ 2003.

City of James Joyce (1963) 9 min.
Director: Bill St. Leger
Introduction to Dublin landmarks portrayed by James Joyce in his writings.
Credits Producer, Director, Photography: Bill St Leger, Script: Irene French Eagar, Commentator: Andy O'Mahony.

Charm of Ulster (1950s) 14 min.
Producers: British Travel Association Films
Bizarre travelogue which makes vague reference to 'St Patrick's Ulster' while also giving hard factual details about Northern Ireland's industries and political independence from the Republic.
Credits Presented by: Associated British Pathé, Producers: British Travel Association Films.

Christy (1994) 55 min.
Director: Philip King
Profile of singer/songwriter Christy Moore examining his ability to combine traditional song styles with contemporary political and social issues.
Credits [Song list omitted.] For Christy Moore; Management: Mattie Fox, Assistant: Bernie Mulfaul, Tour Manager: Jim Donoghue, Stage: Dickon Whitehead, Assistant: Sean Duggan, Family Stills courtesy of the Moore Family. Thanks to: the Irish Traditional Music Archives, Irish Film Archive of the Irish Film Institute, the National Library of Ireland, the FÁS Leinster Leader Indexation Project, ESB, Travellers Stills courtesy of Derek Spiers, Ian Lee for the RTÉ Radio Sound Archive, Stephen Darcy for the RTÉ Library, Oliver McCrossan, Eilis Moore, Anne Byrne, Tom Munnelly, Kevin Saunders, Niall O'Callanain, Conor Byrne, Con Collins, Sheena Collins, Eugene and Mary Lambert, the Hangedman's Arch, Milltown, Newbridge, Co. Kildare, Roadstone Ireland Ltd, Mother Redcap's Tavern, Slattery's Pub, J. McNeill's Music Shop of Capel Street, the Point, the Baggot Inn, the Factory. Cameras: Panavision Ireland Ltd, Film Stock: Kodak Ireland Ltd, Lighting: Film and Lighting Facilities, Insurance: Network Insurances, Couriers: Aerlybird Couriers, Staging: Rock Solid Staging; Additional Crew; Camera: Cian De Buitlear, Focus Pullers: Brendan Galvin, Ken Byrne, Clapper Loader: John Moore, Camera Trainee: Harry Purdue, Electricians: David Durney, Tony Swan, Grips: Philip Murphy, Joe Quigley, Stage and Set Design: Jimmy Hickey, Transport: Peadar Gaffney, Production Accountant: Niall McHugh, Legal: Anne Corrigan, Production Assistant: Aoife Dorney, Research: Nuala O'Connor, Terry Moore, Rostrum: Ken Morse, Camera Trainee: Simon Walsh, Camera Assistants: Donal Gilligan, Assistant Editors: Nuala Roche, Dolores Hegarty, On-Line Editor: Mark Nolan, Gaffer:

Maurice Swan, Sound: Kieran Horgan, Sound Mixer: Brian Masterson, Associate Producer: Sarah Power, Production Executives: Kieran Corrigan, Mattie Fox, Editor: Gaye Lynch, Director of Photography: Declan Quinn, Producer: Nuala O'Connor, Director: Philip King. A Hummingbird Production in association with BBC TV, Radio Telefís Éireann, YLE. © Hummingbird Productions Ltd, 1994.

Christy Moore Uncovered (2001) 6 × 25 min.
Producer: Julian Vignoles
Singer and songwriter Christy Moore performing many of his most famous songs and discussing them with those involved in their creation.

Clothing and Donegal (1999) 25 min.
Director: Peter Kelly
An episode of the series *The Last Resource* dealing with the impact of factory closures in the late 1990s on Donegal, the traditional home of clothing and textiles industries in Ireland. Presenter Kathy Donaghy is a native of the area and gives a personal perspective.
Credits Presented by Kathy Donaghy, Research and Script: Mary Brophy, Camera: Neal Boyle, Sound: Billy Roarty, Post-Production: Esras Facilities, On-Line Editor: Garry Creevey, Production Accountant: Gaby Smyth, Editor: Gerry Nelson, Series Producer: Fintan Drury, Director: Peter Kelly. Produced by Esras Films for Radio Teilifís Éireann. © 1999.

Col. James Fitzmaurice: Transatlantic Pioneer (1998) 25 min.
Director: Tim Costello
Profile of the Irish aviator who flew the first east to west flight across the Atlantic Ocean. The film features dramatic reconstruction.

Connemara and its Ponies (1971) 30 min.
Director: David Shaw Smith
How ponies are bred and trained in Connemara to fit into farm life and prepared for export. The film suggests that there are links between the toughness of the animals and that of the people who breed them.
Credits Production Company: David Shaw Smith Productions, Producer: David Shaw Smith, Director: David Shaw Smith, Photography: David Shaw Smith, Script: Michael Killanin, Assistant Producer: Henry Kennedy, Editor: Rory O'Farrell, Narrator: Padraic Ó Raghallaigh, Dubbing: Pat Hayes, Music: Noel Kelehan, Singer: Drowsy Maggie.

Conquest of Light (1975) 10 min.
Director: Louis Marcus
Film detailing how Waterford Glass is made with an emphasis on visual/aesthetic qualities of the process rather than industrial/economic questions.
Credits Production Company: Louis Marcus Films Ltd, Producer: Louis Marcus, Director: Louis Marcus, Editor: Louis Marcus, Script: Louis Marcus, Photography: Robert Monks, Sponsors: Waterford Glass Ltd, Music: Vic Flick, Narrator: Dennis Brennan, Sound: Peter Hunt, Assistant Cameraman: David Murphy, Dubbing: Trevor Pyke, Creative Consultant: Harry Pesin, Lab: Technicolour.

Convoy Mills (1955; stock date) 14 min.
Director: Fr. Tommy Doherty

An account of the manufacture of Donegal Tweed with a strong emphasis on the machines and mechanical processes involved.

Credits Production Company: Irish Shell, Director: Fr. Tommy Doherty.

Cork Draws the Sportsmen (1965) 20 min.

Producer: George Grafton Green

Promotional film detailing the sporting sights of Co. Cork. Almost half of the film is concerned with coverage of the Carrolls International golf tournament.

Credits Production Company: Rank Special Features, Producer: George Grafton Green, Script: Frank Driscoll, Narrator: Tim Turner, Assistant Producers: George Fleischmann, Anthony Barrier, Production Manager: Edward Candy, Editor: Roy Drew, Photography: Peter Cannon, Ray Gallard, William Hooker, Albert Werry.

Country Magazine: January 1955 (1955) 9 min.

Producers: Jet Film Services

Silent promotional newsreel featuring scenes from the Irish countryside.

Cradle of Genius (1958) 50 min.

Director: Paul Rotha

Discussion of the history of the Abbey Theatre filmed shortly after the old building was gutted by fire in 1958. The film features interviews with famous Abbey performers and a historic reunion between Barry Fitzgerald and Sean O'Casey, who had not spoken to one another in years. The film was nominated for an American Academy of Motion Picture Arts and Sciences Award in 1962.

Credits Producer: Tom Hayes, Director: Paul Rotha, Script and Narration: Frank O'Connor, with: Barry Fitzgerald, Siobhan McKenna, Harry Brogan, May Craig, Ria Mooney, Shelah Richards, Sean O'Casey.

Crystal Clear (196?) 11 min.

Director: Brendan Stafford

The history of Waterford Glass, with some footage of the glass-blowing process and particular reference to the skills of the workers.

Credits Producer: Fred O'Donovan, Director: Brendan Stafford, Narrator: Eamonn Andrews, Script: John D. Sheridan, Photography: Robert Monks, Sound: Tommy Meyers, Editor: Dorothy Stimson, Special Processes: Broadcasting and Theatrical Productions Ltd.

Darkroom (2002) 50 min.

Director: Ian Thullier

Reflections on the life, death and art of photographer Harry Thullier Jr., who died under mysterious circumstances in Italy. His younger brother directed the film, which touched on aspects of their lives which were shared and tried to come to terms with those that were not.

Dear Boy: The Story of Micheál MacLiammóir (1999) 52 min.

Director: Donald Taylor Black

Biography of actor Micheál MacLiammóir exploring how the persona he created for himself encapsulated his dilemma as a homosexual in mid-twentieth-century Ireland.

Credits In Memoriam: Mary Manning (1906-1999). Special thanks: Edwards-MacLiammóir Estate (Michael Williams), Gate Theatre (Michael Colgan/Curator, Special Collections), BBC Sound Library and Archive, Mary Cannon, David

Gallery, Film Institute of Ireland, Fingal County Council, Gráinne Humphreys, the Estate of Denis Johnston, Gerard Larchet, Ann Quain, RTÉ Sound Archives (Ian Lee/Rob Canning), Sáirséal agus Dill, Michael B. Yeats. Film Archive Sources: BBC Television Archive, Gael-Linn, the Irish Film Archive of the Film Institute of Ireland (Sunniva O'Flynn), RTÉ Programme Archive (Barbara Durack), Footage from *Othello* provided by Castle Hill Productions, Inc., Additional Archive Sources: Bord Fáilte Éireann, Fergus Bourke, G.A. Duncan, the *Examiner*, Roderick Fenning, Albert Fenton, Gate Theatre, *Irish Independent*, *Irish Press*, *Irish Times*, Carmel and Sheila Leahy, Mary-Rose McMaster, Mander and Michenson Theatre Collection, North-Western University Library, Illinois, Noel Pearson, Richard Pine, RTÉ Reference and Illustrations Library, Alexander Ross, Michael Travers. Extract from 'Micheál Mac Liammóir' read by Paul Durcan. Executive Producers: Anna Carragher (BBC NI), Kevin Dawson (RTÉ), Rod Stoneman (BSÉ), Additional Camera Assistants: Sarah Francis (Dublin), Marc E. Hillygus (New York), Neil Purcell (London), Jill Tufts (Boston), Additional Sound Recordists: Pat Hayes (Dublin), Tim Hunt (London), Additional Rostrum Camera: Nico Vermeulen, Graphic Design: Dave Moran, Key Grip: Philip Murphy, Assistant Grip: Dave Keith, Electricians: Maurice Swan, Stephen Doyle, Colourist: Gary Curran, Production Coordinators: Katie Lincoln, Ruth Riddick (USA), Camera Assistant: Declan King, Dubbing Mixer: Tony Russell, On-Line Editor: Mark Nolan, Sound Recordist: Kieran Horgan, Researcher: Veronica Jane O'Mara, Consultant: Christopher Fitz-Simon, Music: Michael Howard, Narrator: T. P. McKenna, Associate Producer: Richard Pine, Photography: Sean Corcoran, Editor: Maurice Healy, Produced and Directed by: Donald Taylor Black. A Poolbeg production for Radio Telefís Éireann, BBC Northern Ireland, with the assistance of Bord Scannán na hÉireann/the Irish Film Board. © 1999.

Dear Daughter (1996) 42 min.
Director: Louis Lentin
The traumatic experiences of Christine Buckley at the Goldenbridge Orphanage and on her subsequent search for her birth parents who left her in the care of the institution. The film features dramatic reconstructions. Notable for having initated a wave of allegations and investigations in other religious and secular caring institutions. The Sisters of Mercy added a rider to the programme which offered psychological counselling to victims of abuse.
Credits Goldenbridge Girls: Ann Armstrong, Julie Cooney, Shelia Doyle, Bernadette Fahy, Caroline Hunt, Kathleen O'Neill. Thanks to: Sister Catherine Dooley and the Goldenbridge Community of the Sisters of Mercy. Cast: Mary Moynihan, Peggy Hannon (Anna West), Emmanuel Eke (Ariwodo Kalunta), Zoe Dunbar, Jasmine Quinlan, Noreen Brady (Christine), Jean Rooney (Miss Berry), Ruth O'Connell (First Teenager), Mide Ní Bhriain (Second Teenager), Tani Benlis (Nun), Ber O'Hara (Redhaired Lady), Caroline Walsh (Nurse), Claire O'Reilly, Juliette Rahill, Aoife Doyle, Emer O'Keefe, Eoin Bell, Elizabeth Bell, Yvonne Flynn, Declan Flynn, Sara Cambell, Ruth Cambell, Kathy Stokes (Children), Marie Ni Chinsealach (Secretary), Pat Reilly (Granny Martin), Frank Melia (Danny Martin), Margaret Twomey (Sister Gabriel). Narrator: Bosco Hogan, Music: Paul Murphy/Barry Grace at Ear Two Ear. Produced with the assistance of Bord Scannán na hÉireann/the Irish Film Board. Executive Producer for Bord Scannán na hÉireann/the Irish Film Board: Rod Stoneman, Legal Advisor: Eugene Fanning at Arthur Cox, Accountant: Declan Lernihan at GLD, Wardrobe: Vera Patterson, Production Design: Gerry O'Donovan, Production Manager: Patricia Canning, Electricians: Maurice Swan, Terry

Mulligan, John McCullagh, Martin Holland, Casting: Dorothy Mac Gabhann, Rosary Beads: Ann Armstrong, Therapist: Bernadette Fahy, Sound Mix: Paddy Gibbons at Avondale, Assistant Camera: Oisín Kelly, Jo Gibney, Sound Recordists: Darby Carroll, Pat Hayes, Lighting Camera: Peter Dorney, Nick O'Neill, Editor: Jörgen Andréason, Post-Production Facility: Post 22, Produced and Directed by Louis Lentin. A Crescendo Concept in conjunction with Sablegrange Ltd for Radio Telefís Éireann 1996.

'Dragon's Teeth' (1990) 37 min.
Director: Tom Collins
What the barriers on the roads of Northern Ireland mean both in terms of the physical logistics of getting from one place to another and for the concept of Ireland they imply.
Credits Special Thanks to: Raymond McMahon. Music: 'First We Take Manhattan' Leonard Cohen © CBS, 'Leaders of Men' Joy Division © Zombie Music, 'Careering' PIL © Virgin. Photography: Donal Gilligan, Sound Recordist: Simon Ward, Boom Operator: Jack Armstrong, Additional Photography: Connor Hammond, Conor Kelly, Cian De Buitléar, Johnny Gogan, Assistant Editor: Bernie Maloney, Additional Sound: Joe Chalbers, Radio Research: Sara Mackie, Drivers: Nancy Bohanan-Doherty, Sean Semple, Equipment and Hire Facilities: Filmbase, Editing: Windmill Lane, Dubbing and Titles: RTÉ, Film Processing: Technicolor, Editor: Martin Duffy, Producer: Therese Friel, Director: Tom Collins. A DeFacto Film and Video Production © 1990.

Dr. Browne Also Spoke (1992) 52 min.
Director: Frank Stapleton
A fifty-minute one-on-one interview with former minister for health Dr Noel Browne by Michael D. Higgins, TD, which takes place during a train journey. The film features a short excerpt from *Our Country* and other archival material interspersed with the conversation.
Credits Telegael. Interview and Script: Michael D. Higgins, Camera: Billy Keady, Sound: Liam Saurin, Paul Delaney, Gerry McBride, Editors: Cóilín Ó Scolaí, Alan Esslemont, Dubbing Mixer: Enda Boner, Technicians: Ciarán Ó Tuairisc, Aengus Cullinan, Production Assistants: Glyn Carragher, Deirdre Cosgrove, Orla Maloney, Music: Hercules Dux Ferrarial Nomos No. 1, Sean O'Riada, 'The Fool' by P. H. Pearse, Archive – Radio Telefís Éireann, Liam O'Leary Film Archives, Lecture 'Church and State in Modern Ireland' at Queen's University Belfast. In Acknowledgement: Phyllis Browne, Iarnród Éireann/Irish Rail. Producer: Catherine Tiernan, Director: Frank Stapleton. An Ocean Film Production in Association with Radio Telefís Éireann © Ocean Film Productions 1992.

Dublin – Capital of Ireland (1946) 10 min.
Producer: David Barry
Silent, colour tourist film highlighting historical, literary, aesthetic, sporting and architectural interests of Dublin city.

Dubliners – Sean agus Nua / Dubliners – Old and New (1971) 20 min.
Director: Louis Marcus
Juxtaposition of 'old' Dublin with contemporary footage which uses both English- and Irish-language commentary. The English-language voice over is used ironically, reflecting nostalgia, while the Irish voice over addresses contemporary issues.

Credits Production Company: Gael-Linn, Producer: Louis Marcus, Director: Louis Marcus, Editor: Louis Marcus, Photography: Robert Monks, Narration: Brendán Ó hEithir, Sponsors: Roinn na Gaeltachta.

Dust on the Bible (1989) 52 min.
Director: John T. Davis
Scenes of the activities of street preachers in Belfast juxtaposed with footage from the turbulent streets of Belfast.
Credits Director: John T. Davis, Associate Producer: Brendan Hughes, Photography: John T. Davis, Sound: Deke Thompson, Editor: Sé Merry Doyle, Commissioned by: Channel Four.

D-Watch (1999) 6 × 25 min.
Director: Niamh Walsh
'Reality' series following the Phibsborough branch of the Dublin Fire Brigade and Ambulance Service. Features a mixture of pieces to camera and video shot on location during callouts.
Credits Special thanks to: Captain Eamon O'Boyle, Grainne McAleer, James Hickey, Bill Powderly, Phillip O'Dwyer, Assistant Editor: Therese McNamee, Transcripts: Colum Dolan, Assistants to the Director: Ray Cremin, Barry Egan, Sound Consultant: Stephen McDowell, Production Assistant: Zoe Liston, Grading: Dave Gibson, Mixer: Bobby O'Reilly, Music: Niall Byrne, Second DVC Director: Ruan Magan, Editor: Guy Montgomery, Filmed and Directed by Niamh Walsh, Produced by Adrian Lynch, Darragh Byrne. A Graph Films Production for RTÉ © 1999.

'East Wall Amateur Footage' a.k.a. 'A School Day: Snapshots from Church Road' (untitled) (1939–40) 20 min.
Footage of Dublin schoolchildren attending their communion and confirmation ceremonies in 1939 shot by a Catholic priest eager to document the events.
Credits Director/Cameraman: Fr Courtney.

Éire / Ireland (1955) 11 min.
Director: Arthur Guest
British-produced overview of Irish economic relationship with the UK.
Credits Production Company: Educational Foundation for Visual Aids, Producer: Arthur Guest, Director: Arthur Guest, Photography: Arthur Guest, Narrator: Liam O'Leary.

Erin – Through the Mists of Time (1990) 50 min.
Directors: Éamon and Cian de Buitléar
Images of the Irish landscape discussed with an eye for mythological and anthropological curiosities which are relevant to them. Part of BBC's *The Natural World* series.
Credits Narrated by: Peadar Lamb, Filmed and Directed by Éamon and Cian de Buitléar, Film Editor: Susanne Outlaw, Paul Clark, Dubbing Mixer: Steve Stockford, Music Composed and Arranged by: Paddy Moloney, Performed by: the Chieftains with Éamon de Buitléar. The BBC wishes to thank: John Feehan, John McNamara, Daithí Ó Hógáin, Nuala Roche, Office of Public Works, the North Western Regional Fisheries Board. Production Assistant: Sheila Fullom, Unit Manager: Marney Shears, Producer: Pelham Aldrich-Blake. A BBC TV production in association with WNET 13 New York. Series Editor: Mike Salisbury. The Natural World. © BBC Bristol 1990.

Errigal (1970) 14 min.
Director: Patrick Carey
Donegal's Mt Errigal becomes part of a mythical story of a battle between two mountains
fought with storms as weapons.
Credits Production Company: Aengus Films, Producers: Joe Mendoza, Patrick Carey,
Director/Photography: Patrick Carey, Editor: Ann Chegwidden, Composer: Brian
Boydell, Music Supervisor: Peter Hunt, Music Director: Tony Anscombe, Produc-
tion Assistant: Penny Cabot, Judith Toner, Narrator (English): Brian Carey, Narra-
tor (Irish): Niall Toibín.

Eucharistic Congress 1932 (1932) 38 min.
Director: Fr Frank Browne SJ
Footage of the celebrations and events making up the Eucharistic Congress of 1932 fea-
turing many civil and religious figures of the day.
Credits Director/Photography/Editing: Fr Frank Browne SJ

Everybody's Business / Gnó Gach Einne (1951) 20 min.
Director: Tony Inglis
Docudrama on the risks of improper hygiene in shops and restaurants.
Credits Production Company: National Film Institute of Ireland, Director: Tony Inglis,
Animations: Tony Inglis, Script: Quentin Dobson, Narrator: Tom Studley, Sound:
Josephine Hyland, Stephen MacAonghusa, Translator: Seamus Ó Seoghda, Sponsor:
Department of Health. Cast: Gerard Healy, Nora O'Mahony, Maureen O'Sullivan,
Bean Ní Cathain, Annette O'Gorman Quinn, Rory Kilkenny.

*Faithful Departed: The Dublin of James Joyce's Ulysses in the Photographs of
William Lawrence* (1967) 10 min.
Director: Kieran Hickey
Vistas of Dublin city in the early twentieth century as featured in photographs from the
William Lawrence Collection. A voice over reads extracts from *Ulysses* and provides
some general information on the social conditions of the time.
Credits Director: Kieran Hickey, Editor: Patrick Duffner, Script and Production: Des
Hickey, Music Supervision: Bill Somerville-Large, Camera: Sean Corcoran with
Roland Hill, Photographs from the William Lawrence Collection courtesy of the
National Library of Ireland, Commentary spoken by: Jack MacGowran, Sound
Mixer (Recordist): Doug Turner, Recording Studios: De Lane Lea Studios, Eamonn
Andrews Studios, BAC Films.

The Family (1978) 27 min.
Director: Bob Quinn
Profile of the 'Atlantis' commune in Donegal. The film begins with a dramatised sequence
featuring a traditional 'nuclear' family to provide contrast with what is to follow.
First Broadcast in 1991.
Credits Jenny James introduced her family at Atlantis. Suburban Family: Derek Young
(husband), Anne Brogan (wife). Narrator: Kevin McHugh, Electrical Supervisor:
Eddie Bolger, Production Assistant: Dympna Cullen, Film Cameraman: Seamus
Deasy, Film Editor: Brendan Deasy, Film Editor: Victor Curtis, Dubbing Mixer:
Brian Lynch, Series Producer: Bob Collins, Production: Bob Quinn (Cinegael).

Féach in Derry (1987) 25 min.

Editor: Proinsias Mac Aonghusa

Compilation of interview segments from the Irish-language news magazine programme *Féach / Look* shot in Derry in 1970 and 1972.

Credits Déanta ag foireann 'Féach' 1970 agus 1972. Léiritheoirí: Eoghan Harris, Pat O'Connor, Eagarthóir: Proinsias Mac Aonghusa © RTÉ 1987.

Fishing Village

Director: Liam O'Leary

Film depicting the lives of fishermen.

Flaxen Heritage (1953) 14 min.

Director: Burrell Smith

American-produced portait of the production of Irish linen in Northern Ireland.

Credits Production Company: Major Films, Schenectady, New York, Director: Burrell Smith, Sponsors: the Irish Linen Guild.

Fleá (a.k.a. *Fleadh Ceoil*) (1967) 23 min.

Director: Louis Marcus

Cinéma vérité portrait of a traditional music festival being held in Kilrush, Co. Clare in 1967. The film won the Silver Bear at the Berlin Film Festival in 1967, a diploma of honour at the Moscow Film Festival, the Critics Award at La Felguera Catholic Film Festival in Spain and was nominated for an American Academy of Motion Picture Arts and Sciences Award in 1968.

Credits Director: Louis Marcus, Script: Brendán Ó hEithir, Photography: Robert Monks, Nick O'Neill, Réne de Clercq, Narrator: Chris Curran, Studio Sound: Peter Hunt.

Fleadh '73 (1973) 25 min.

Director: Gerry Murray

An account of the traditional music festival held in Listowel, Co. Kerry in 1973.

Credits Interviewer: Tony McMahon, Photography: Ken Murphy, Simon Weafer, Sound: Alan Seavers, Re-Recording Mixer, Bob Bell, Editor: Patrick Duffner, Producer, Director: Gerry Murray.

The Flying Boats at Foynes (1989) 50 min.

Producer: Jim Sherwin

Nostalgic account of the aviation age in Ireland in the 1940s, with particular focus on the flying boats. The film features footage of Maureen O'Hara at the 1989 dedication of a museum to the flying boats at Foynes and extensive archival material including scenes of Éamon de Valera.

Credits Narrated and Produced by: Jim Sherwin, Graphic Design: Dorcas O'Toole, Music: Donal Hurley, Rostrum Camera: Nico Vermeulen, Special Adviser: Margaret O'Shaughnessy, Aviation Historian: Tony Kearns, Electrical Supervisors: Tony Lawles, John Griffin, Tony McCabe, Sound: Pat Johns, Darby Carroll, Naom Schneider, Dave Owens, Jim Rillie, Joe O'Dubhghaill, Cameras: Ken Murphy, Bob Monks, Michele Taverna, Mike Hutton, Ed Bowdring, Research/Production Assistant: Phil Healy, VT Editor: Gerry Nelson, Silhouette Pictures Ltd, Film Editor: Arthur McGuinness.

For Better or Worse? (2003) 4 × 40 min.

Producers/Directors: Betty Purcell, Paul Larkin, Kevin Cummins

Series charting the experience of divorce for several Irish couples. Each episode dealt with a different issue, using the same set of couples to discuss the topic.

Credits Reporters: Fiona Mac Carthy, Mick Peeld, Researchers: Janet Couchman, Pat Neville, Programme Assistant: Barbara Kavanagh, Sonia Patterson, Graphic Design: Elena Doyle; Colourist: Linzi Khan, Opening Music: Tom Unwin, Electrical Supervisor: Kevin O'Toole, Assistant Camera: Simon Culliton, Eoin Keating, Sound Recordists: Alan Seavers, Pat Murray, Stephen Spoor, Post-Production Sound: Jim McDonnell, Lighting Cameramen: Cedric Culliton, Kieran Slyne, Video Editor: Mercedes Garvey, Producers/Directors: Betty Purcell, Paul Larkin, Kevin Cummins. © RTÉ 2003.

'Fr Browne Forestry Film' (untitled) (1933) 3 min.
Director: Fr Frank Browne, SJ
Film fragment commissioned by the Faculty of Agriculture of University College Dublin to illustrate lectures on forestry. It is not known whether the film housed by the Film Archive is the complete work.

Credits Director/Photographer/Editor: Fr Frank Browne, SJ, Sponsors: Albert College, Faculty of Agriculture of University College Dublin.

Freedom Highway (2000) 90 min.
Director: Philip King
Music and the sense of rebellion, as exemplified in the writings of both Irish and international songwriters and performers.

Credits Director: Philip King, Writer: Nuala O'Connor, Producer: Sarah Power, Photography: Cian de Buitléar, Associate Producer: Tina Moran, Music Supervisor: Kevin Laffey, Executive Producer: Kieran Corrigan. A Hummingbird Production for RTÉ, The Irish Film Board, ZDF and BBC Scotland. © RTÉ 2000.

Gaelic Girls (1997) 27 min.
Director: Enda Murray
The experiences of Clan na Gael, an Australian-based ladies Gaelic Athletic Association football team during the 1996 football season. Screened as part of RTÉ's *True Lives* series.

Credits Camera: Peter Robinson, John Curtis, Enda Murray, Additional Camera: Monique Potts, Thomas Harding. Respect for the Music: Tribe of Ssenkrad, Norwich, Ceol Batucada, Drogheda, Cran, Droheda, Shaylee Wilde, Sydney, 'Still Haven't Found What I'm Looking For' by kind permission of U2. Thanks to: In Sydney: Ger, Sue, Fiona, Petrina, Mal and Clan na Gael, Monique, CaTV, C@talyst, Triple J Radio, Warehouse Crew, Grainne and Joey, Maffew, John Boyle O'Reilly's Tree, in Coventry: Mike at the Depot, Fran and Helen, Simon, Andy, Mary and Phil, Ralph Brown, in Drogheda: Paul Lennon, Tony Clayton-Lea, Ben Corcoran, Colin Blakey, Mrs Murray, The Murrays from the banks. Thanks to everyone who lent a hand, Editing: Enda Murray, Dominic Day, On-Line Editor: Dominic Day, Assistant Producer: John Curtis, Produced and Directed by: Enda Murray. Special thanks to the Gaelic Athletic Association and the *Star* newspaper. For Big Sean 1917-1996 Onwards and Upwards. Firbolg Films © 1997.

Gael-Linn (1966) 30 min.
Producer: Wynford Jones
BBC Wales documentary about the activities of Gael-Linn in the preservation of the Irish language and its basis in the cultural and economic community structures of the west of Ireland.

Credits Reporter: Jeffrey Iverson, Camera: Eric Warrilow, Sound: Barry Lanchester, Film
Editor: Peter James, Producer: Wynford Jones.

A Game of Chance (1973) 20 min.
Director: Jim Mulkerns
Briskly edited public-information docudrama recounting the story of a man who sleeps
too late then drives quickly and recklessly to work, severely injuring a motorcyclist
and bringing shame on his family.
Credits Director: Jim Mulkerns, Script: Richard Power, Narrator: Niall Tobín.

Gem of the Sea (1933) 10 min.
Director: uncredited
A 'Magic Carpet of Movietone' presentation of one of the Father Hubbard Educational
Films series. The film profiles 1930s Ireland with a religious emphasis, but also fea-
tures strikingly modern images of Dublin city.
Credits Producers: Father Hubbard Educational Films. Distributors: Magic Carpet of
Movietone.

The Ghost of Roger Casement (2002) 2 × 50 min.
Director: Alan Gilsenan
Historical profile of political agitator and activist Roger Casement, whose trial for trea-
son and homosexual diaries have hindered appreciation of his achievements in the
arena of fundamental rights. Winner of the Irish Film and Television Academy Best
Documentary Series Award.
Credits Thanks to: The Casement Family, Royal Irish Academy, National Library of Ire-
land, National Maritime Museum, UK Public Records Office, the Roger Casement
foundation, Pauric Dempsey, Dr Helen Forde, Banna CIRS Unit, Conor Brennan,
Eoin Ó Maille, Phil Gonzales, Dr Augusto Gomez, Fernando Fidalgo, Ireland
House – NYU, Edmund Lynch, Frank McCarry, Catherine Magee, John O'Ma-
hony, Martin Mahon, Mountjoy Prison, Gerry and Joan Murray, Dr Philip Smyly, Dr
John de Courcey Ireland. Archive: Anti-Slavery International, Argos Films, British
Film Institute, Cinemateca Brasileira, Dr Roger Saywer, Felix Rosensteil's Widow
and Son, Film Institute of Ireland, Gael-Linn, ITN Archive/Reuters, Kerry County
Library, National Library of Ireland, National Maritime Museum, National Photo-
graphic Archive, RTÉ Library Sales, Société du Cinéma du Pantheon, National
Archives and Records Administration. Narrator: Alan Gilsenan, Voice of Roger
Casement: Declan Conlon, Consultants: Angus Mitchell, Dr Roger Sawyer, Ros-
trum: Nico Vermeulen, Dubbing Mixer: Simon Flanagan, Assistant Editor: Brian
O'Brien, Graphics: John Kennedy, On-Line Editor: Eoin McDonagh, Colour Grad-
ing: Gary Curran, Original Music: Ray Harman, Singer: Gemma Hayes, Sound:
Ross Bartley, Joe Dolan, Camera: Richard Kendrick, Additional Camera: Ross Bartley, Mike Charlton, Neal Boyle, Peter Dorney, Production Manager: Katherine
O'Connor, Editors: Oliver Fallen, Martin Duffy, Research: Kim Bartley, Distributed
by: RTÉ International, Executive Producer for the Irish Film Board: Rod Stoneman,
Executive Producer for RTÉ: Kevin Dawson, Writer/Director: Alan Gilsenan, Producers: John Murray, Kim Bartley. A Crossing the Line Films Production for RTÉ.
© 2002. In association Bord Scannán na hÉireann/the Irish Film Board.

Glimpses of Erin (1934) 8 min.
Producer: James A. Fitzpatrick
Travelogue featuring standard touristic images of Ireland in the 1930s. The film makes a

reference to 'the establishment of the new Republic', which testifies to the maker's lack of knowledge of and concern with political and social realities.

Credits Produced and narrated by: James A. Fitzpatrick.

God Bless America (1996) 6 × 50 min.

Director: Alan Gilsenan

A series of profiles of American personalities, one per episode. Each episode focuses on impressions of America filtered through the experiences and views of its subject.

Credits Series Producer: Colin Bell, Director: Alan Gilsenan. A Granada Production for ITN.

Gold in the Grass (1964)

Director: Kevin O'Kelly MscAg

Promotional film encouraging modernisation of Irish agriculture. The voice over tends to be scientific rather than conversational.

Credits Production Company: Rex Roberts Studios Ltd, Director, Script, Narration, Photography: Kevin O'Kelly MscAg., Sponsors: Goulding Ltd Presentations.

Good Night, Safe Home, and God Bless (1998) 50 min.

Director: Brian Reddin

Memories of Ireland's showbands and the heydays of the dance halls consisting mostly of interviews with the musicians.

Credits Thanks to: Eddie Kelly, Michael Coppinger, Paddy Cole, T. J. Byrne, Sean Lucey, Tommy Murphy, Shay Healy, John Keogh, Paddy Brennan – Limerick Rock 'n' Roll Club, Kelley, Everyman Theatre – Cork, Brendan Lockary, Ierne Ballroom – Dublin, Tom Doherty, Michael O'Hanlon Jnr., Dave Glover, Oliver O'Brien, Irish Film Archive – Film Institute of Ireland, the *Irish Independent*, the *Irish Times*, Dublin Corporation Public Libraries, Dublin and Irish Collections, Researcher: Kim Baatley, Sound: Enda Cahill, Eddie Quinn, Camera: Ken O'Mahony, Sound Dubbing: Joe Ó Dubhghaill, Editor: Guy Montgomery, Producer, Director: Brian Reddin. Adare Productions for RTÉ and BBC (NI) © 1998.

Graceville (1997) 52 min.

Director: Bob Quinn

The story of a group of Conamara famers who travelled to the United States in the 1880s to work on a Native American reservation.

The Great Houses of Ireland (1975) 11 min.

Director: James Morris

Brief overview of some historial houses in Ireland with reference to their literary heritage and by inference their place in Irish culture.

Credits Production Company: Rory O'Farrell Film Productions, Producer: Rory O'Farrell, Director: James Morris, Script and Narration: Desmond Guinness, Photography: Brian Lynch, Music: Shawn Davey, Gaffer: Joe Madden, Sponsors: Bord Fáilte Éireann.

The Green Fields of France (1998) 50 min.

Director: Alan Gilsenan

Details of the Irish role in the First World War, featuring poetry excerpts from writers and poets.

Credits Dedicated to the memory of the Irish who died in World War One. Voices: Frank McGuinness (Patrick MacGill), Peter Fallon (Francis Ledwidge), John Banville

(Thomas Kettle), Paul Buckley, Tom Burke, David Collins, Daniel Costello, Peter Holmes, Paul Keeley, Conor Lambert, Jim Luke, James McClatchie, Michael MacElhatton, Séamus Maloney, Padraig Murray, David Pearse, Myles Purcell, Joan Sheehy, Hugh Sloan, Jayne Snow, and Brendan Behan. Archive Material Courtesy of: the Imperial War Museum, and Blackstaff Press, Fr Browne SJ Collection, Caliban Books, Dublin Fusiliers Society, Irish Academic Press, Col. Francis Law, Joe Little, the Longman Group, Myles Dungan, National Army Museum, RTÉ Archive. Yellow Asylum Films would like to thank: Tom Burke, Seán Connolly, Dublin Fusiliers Society, Myles Dungan, Margaret Ward, Pauline O'Rourke, Deirdre Scully, Valerie McCarthy and Marsha Hunt. Legal Advisor: James Hickey, Rostrum: Nico Vermeulen, Telecine/Colourist: Dave Gibson, Tape Operator: Fionnuala Gilmartin, Assistant Editor: Tony Brady, On-Line Editor: Colm O'Brien, Title Sequences: Dave Quinn, Dubbing Mixer: Paddy Gibbons, Archive Research: Liam Wylie, Super 8 mm Photography: Alan Gilsenan, Editor: Lee Hickey, Producer: Martin Mahon, Director: Alan Gilsenan. A Yellow Asylum Films Production for Radio Telefís Éireann.

Guinnessty (1997) 50 min.

Director: Philippa Walker

Mildly scandalous BBC profile of the Guinness family. Part of the *Modern Times* series.

Credits With thanks to: Guinness Brewing Worldwide Ltd, British Pathé, British Movietone News, BBC Television Library. Narrator: Peter Egan, Photography: David Barker, Orlando Stuart, Sound Recordists: Darby Carroll, Steve Whitford, Dubbing Mixer: Colin Martin, BBC Unit Manager: Jane Hewertson, Production Managers: Nicki Riley, Denise Lesley, Film Editor: John Dinwoodie, Assistant Producer: Annabel Hobley, Produced and Directed by Philippa Walker. A Philippa Walker Production.

Hallelujah Love and Stuff (1996) 4 × 35 min.

Director: Darragh Byrne

Four different Irish weddings viewed from preparation to conclusion (in one case, to cancellation). Each episode took a very different couple, drawing comparisons between life styles, social classes and attitudes to morality, religion and sexuality.

Credits Production Accountant: Alison O'Leary, Assistant Camera: Michael O'Dubhann, Sarah Francis, Robert Marshall, Sound Recordist: Stephen McDowell, Lighting Camera: Ronan Fox, Ciaran Tanham, Richard Kendrich, Assistant Producer: Jeanne O'Hagan, Audofile: Enda Bonner, Telegael, Titles by: Virtual Light, Editor: Guy Montgomery (Anner Facilities), Music: Niall Byrne, Associate Producer: Adrian Lynch, Producer and Director: Darragh Byrne. A Graph Films Production for Radio Telefís Éireann © 1996.

Hands (1978–88) 28 min. each episode

Director: David Shaw-Smith

Traditional Irish arts and handicrafts filmed as they are created by artists and artisans, many of whom have been practising their art for generations. Episodes included demonstrations of the art of making currachs, patchwork, basket weaving and cabinet making.

Credits Script and commentary: Benedict Kiely, Music: Jolyon Jackson with Paddy Glacken and Matt Molloy, Sound Recordist: Cormac Duffy, Dubbing Mixer: Pat Hayes, Director/Photography: David Shaw-Smith, Producer: David Shaw-Smith for Radio Telefís Éireann.

The Hard Man (1995) 50 min.

Director: Joe Lee

Profile of Michael Kelly, a former criminal now reformed and dedicated to training local Limerick youth to play soccer as a means of keeping them out of delinquency and crime. The film details the social environment from which Kelly emerged and emphasises the role of alcohol in his descent and of religion in his redemption.

Credits Research: Jas Brady and Brian Kelly, Associate Producer: Brian Kelly Co-produced by Nessbury Entertainments Ltd in association with Merlin Films Production Ltd, Kieran Corrigan and Günther Falkenthal. Production Manager: Seamus McInerney, Production Assistant: Margaret Jennings, Trainee PA: Mary O'Toole, Lighting Cameraman: Sean Corcoran, Assistant Camera: Shane Deasy, Sound Recordist: Ray Cross, Electrician: Graeme Haughton, Film Editor: Dermot Diskin, Assistant Editor: Linda Nartey, Original Music: John Flatley, Music Production: Ken Ralph, Recorded at Sun Street Studio, Sound Dubbing: Richard King, Rostrum Camerawork: Chris Shelly at Frameline, On-Line Editor: Clive Pearson, Graphics: Terry Monaghan, Editing Facilities: Film Base, Transfers: Purple Room, Labs/On-Line Facilities: CFS. the producers wish to acknowledge the support of: Pat Burke, Iarnród Éireann, Cussens & Co. Crane Hire, RT Communications, Army Press Office. Special thanks to: the Kelly Family, Breda Lenihan, Tony Frattaroli, the Nash Family, Kieran Hanlon, Kieran Judge, the Mullan Family, Siobhan O'Donoghue – Media Desk Ireland, Anne Even, Miguel Photo Studio, Mike Smith, Limerick Leader, Hanratty's Hotel, Limerick City Football Club, Derek Cronin, Clarkes Courtyard Studio, Stephen O'Halloran, Colm Waters, Dick Conroy, John Lonergan, the Type Bureau, Mark Long, Brian Norman, Charlie Prichard, Joe Chalmers, Ted Shorthouse, Joe Duffy, Derek Cunningham, Network Insurances. Producer: Jas Brady, Director: Joe Lee. A Pyramid Production for ZDF/ARTÉ and Radio Telefís Éireann. © Pyramid Productions 1995. Zasto Zena Zasto.

The Hard Road to Klondike / Rotha Mór an tSaoil (1999) 52 min.

Director: Desmond Bell

The story of Yukon prospector Mici MacGabhain, who emigrated from Ireland but longed for the pleasures of home. The film won an Irish Film and Television Academy Award for Best Documentary in Irish.

Credits Narrator: Stephen Rea, from the original book by Seán Ó hEochaidh edited by Proinsias Ó Conulain, translated into English by Valerie Iremonger. Thanks to: the Macgowan Family, Stephanie McBride, Cathal Ó Searchaigh, Martin Desht, David Meyer, Vivienne Pollock, Johanna Samuel, Archive: Alaska Motion Picture Archives, Association Frères Lumière, Bord Fáilte, National Film Archive, London, Canon Doherty, Department of Irish Folklore, University College Dublin, Dr Irving Snider, Filmfinders, Huntley Film Archives, Irish Film Archive of the Film Institute of Ireland, J. Fred MacDonald, Jean Duncan and Doug Field, Mansfield Library University of Montana, National Film Board of Canada, National Library of Ireland, Producers Library Service, North Hollywood, California, Radio Telefís Éireann, Silver Bow Archive Butte, TnaG, Ulster Folk and Transport Museum, Ulster Museum, University of Alaska, Fairbanks, US Library of Congress, US National Archives, World Museum of Mining Butte, Yukon Film Archive. Extracts from: Levi and Cohen: *The Irish Comedians* (1898), *What Happened on 14th Street* (1898), *The Kiss in the Tunnel* (1899), *The Great Train Robbery* (1903), *The Lad from Old Ireland* (1910), *An American in the Making* (1912), *The Battle of Elderbrush Gulch* (1913), *The Heart of the Indian* (1913), *The Girl Alaska* (1920), *The Red Kimono* (1925), *The Darkening Trail* (1926), *Aran of the Saints* (1932), *Rotha Mór an Tsaoil* (1967).

Additional Music by Ian Hill. Camera: Giulio Biccari, Ross Keith, Steve Schecter, Tim Olson, Desmond Bell, Jonathan Woods, Assistant Camera: Cian Bell, Sound: Karen Boswall, Elisa Zazzera, Mervyn McKay, Irish Language Consultant: Lillis Ó Laóire, Production Assistants: Carmel O'Brien, Justine Faram, Paula Holt, Mark Williams, Production Manager: Madeleine Sheahan, Archive Research: Declan Smith, Margaret Johnson, Polly Pettitt, Script Consultant: Susan Schulman, Irish Language Editor: Carmel O'Brien, Dubbing Mixer: Dave Bogie, On-Line Editor: Andy McGregor, Imaging Editor: Martin Thornton, Executive Producer for the Irish Film Board/Bord Scannán na hÉireann: Rod Stoneman, for RTÉ: Clare Duignan, for TnaG: Anne McCabe, Editor: Roger Buck, Producer: Sylvia Stevens, Director: Desmond Bell. A Faction Films Production in association with Glass Machine Productions for RTÉ and BBC Northern Ireland in association with TnaG. Produced with the assistance of the Irish Film Board, Napier University and Udarás na Gaeltachta. © 1999.

Harvest (1934) 13 min.
Director: Desmond Egan
Silent colour amateur film drawing attention to the antiquated methods used by Irish farmers in gathering wheat. The film bears interesting similiarities to Eisenstein's *Old and New* and Dovzhenko's *Earth*.
Credits Director/Cameraman: Desmond Egan, Film Stock: Kodak.

Harvest Emergency (1997) 51 min.
Director: Liam Wylie
History of the harvest emergency of 1946 where volunteers from the city saved rural crops threatened by adverse weather conditions. The film also recounts the failed efforts of film pioneers Colm O'Laoighre and Kevin O'Kelly to make a documentary on the subject as it was happening.
Credits Interviewees: James Bannigan, John Bannigan, Maura Behan, Edward Brady, Liv Butler, Dennis Cotter, John Fagan, Teresa Fallon, Mary and Anthony Gaughan, Stephen Hunt, Brian Kelly, Mary and Jack Leake, Professor John Luce, P. J. MacCabe, Phyllis Meegan McMillan, Alfie Mitchell, Colm O'Laoghaire, Dr Michael O'Sullivan, Anthony Winston Forbes, the producers wish to thank everyone who contacted us with stories and information about the voluntary harvest scheme of 1946. Thanks to: Maynagh Lee, Garald A. Smyth, Thomas Duff, Breda Tobin, Martin Mahon, Aine O'Halloran, Alina Carr, Ashlyn Ward, Bernice Turner, Damien Downes, Joe Duffy, Mark Curran, Debbie Ging, Eoin Ryan, Gerry Farrell, Ned Keating, Martin Farrell, Arthur Cox Solicitors, Kevin Williams, Irish Film Archive, the Gilbert Library, the National Library, the National Archives, Ian Lee, RTÉ Radio Archive, Rob Canning, Majella Breen, RTÉ Sound Library, Film Base, Fingal County Council, Kevin Monahan, James Joyce Centre, Tony Varley, Professor Cormac O'Grada, East Anglian Film Archive, All at Treasure Films, Mike Kelly IPU, RTÉ. Archive Footage filmed by: Colm O'Laoghaire and Kevin O'Kelly, 'The Harvest Volunteer' written by Willie Reilly, Words supplied by: James Murphy, Performed by: Tim Dennehy, Engineered by: Catherine Considine, Camera: Nicholas O'Neill, Sound Recordist: Darby Carroll, Production Manager: Seamus Duggan, Production Assistant: Margaret Maggan, Rostrum Camera: Nico Vermuelen, Music Consultant: Nuala O'Connor, Assistant Editor: Irina Maldea, On-Line Editor: Derek Shoebridge, Grader: Gary Curran, Dubbing Mixer: Cecily Loughman, Editor: Emer Reynolds, Executive Producer: Rod Stoneman, Producer and Director: Liam Wylie. In memory of the late Kevin O'Kelly. Grant Aided by the Arts

Council An Chomhairle Ealaíon. Produced with the Assistance of Bord Scannán na hÉireann/the Irish Film Board. A Red Lemonade Production © 1997.

A Harvest of Healing (1989) 27 min.
Director: Dermod McCarthy
The care of mentally ill and intellectually disabled persons in St John of God's Centre, Dublin. Features scenes of dramatic reconstruction.
Credits Mr and Mrs Armstrong: Brian McGrath, Fidelma Murphy, Camera: Nick O'Neill, Sound: Darby Carroll, Dubbing: Pat Hayes, Script: Desmond Forristal, Narration: Bill Golding, Editor: Daibhi Doran, Director: Dermod McCarthy. A Radharc/RTÉ film. RTÉ © 1979.

The Harvest is Rich (1966) 28 min.
Director: Michael McGarry
Film on commercial sea fishing industry in Ireland.
Credits Producer: Peter Owens, Director: Michael McGarry, Camera: Colm O'Laoghaire, Sponsors: An Bord Iascaigh.

Heart on the Line (1990) 61 min.
Director: John T. Davis
A study of the mindset of country music writers and performers in Nashville, including veterans of the trade and rising young stars. The focus is on how the individual artists respond to the challenge of self-expression in their medium set by either personal difficulties or industrial prejudices.
Credits Thanks to: Tree International, Nashville Songwriters Association International, Country Music Association, Broadcast Music Incorporated, Jeff Young, Cowboy Pat, Maralyn 'Mama' Price. Special thanks: Ross Graham. Film Editor: Sé Merry Doyle, Photography: David Bakker, Additional Photography: John T. Davis, Bestor Cram, Camera Assistant: Liz Dinolfo, Assistant Film Editor: Bernadette Moloney, Sound Recordists: Deke Thompson, Glenn Trew, Music Mix: Philip Donnelly, Brian Masterson, Dubbing Mixer: Colin Martin, Graphics: Alan Driver, Production Facilities, Nashville: Film House, Production Secretary: Carol Moorhead, Production Accountant: Brendan Byrne, Researcher: Angie Sifford, Production Manager: Fiona Moore, Associate Producer: Ross Graham, Producer: Brendan Hughes, Director: John T. Davis. A DBA TV Production for Channel Four. 1990.

Hearts and Souls (1995) 50 min.
Director: Donald Taylor Black
Behind the scenes of the No Divorce Campaign before the referendum of 1995. *Cinéma vérité* style documentary featuring several press conferences as well as observational scenes of the campaign managers at work.
Credits Electrician: John McCullagh, Video Technician: Michael Reilly, Camera Trainee: Alison Moxey, Video Grading: Glenn Kyte, Additional Sound: David Jones, Karl Merren, Darby Carroll, Gerry McBride, Additional Camera: Declan Emerson, Peter Dorney, Nick O'Neill, Researchers: Karen O'Connor, Veronica Jane O'Mara, On-Line Editor: Mark Nolan, Sound Recordist: Brendan Campbell, Dubbing Mixer: Tony Russell, Camera: Sean Corcoran, Picture Editor: Maurice Healy, Executive Producer for Radio Telefis Eireann: Mary Raftery, Produced and Directed by Donald Taylor Black. A Poolbeg Production for Radio Telefís Éireann. © 1995.

The Heritage of Ireland (1978) 6 × 25 min.

Director: Louis Marcus

Historical series consciously designed for export attempting to examine the roots of Irish culture through a view of its past.

Credits Presenter: Douglas Gageby, Photography: Robert Monks, Producer: Louis Marcus, Director: Louis Marcus.

Hindesight (1993) 40 min.

Director: Joe Lee

Study of the photographs and postcards of John Hinde, for many the man most responsible for the touristic image of Ireland marketed around the world.

Credits Director: Joe Lee, Camera: John T. Davis, Editor: Sé Merry Doyle, Producers: Seamus McInerney, Margaret Jennings.

Hobo (1991) 90 min.

Director: John T. Davis

Following the stories of several homeless Americans wandering the country in search of something ineffable found only by relentless travelling and transience. The film interviews several subjects but follows one in particular as he moves from place to place across the United States.

Credits Film Editor: Sé Merry Doyle, Assistant Editor: Emer Reynolds, Photography: John T. Davis, David Barker, Sound Recordist: Stephen McCarthy, Deke Thompson, Music: Philip Donnelly Special thanks to Beargrease, Seattle Slim, Steam Train, Scott Caribou Minot Louis, Big Red, Duffy, Mr Green, Sweet Genevieve, Katie Jennings, Bruce Duffy, Northern Light Productions Boston. Dubbing Mixer: Richard King, Graphic Design: Mbbi Phoenix, Production Secretary: Carol Moorhead, Researcher: Fiona Keane, Production Executive: Peter Flood, Production Manager: Brendan Byrne, Associate Producer: Stephen 'Doc' McCarthy, Producer: Brendan Hughes, Director: John T. Davis. DBA Television Belfast for BBC TV.

Home (1998) 4 × 25 min.

Director: Liam McGrath

Series examining the habitations and attitudes towards habitat of people from varying social classes.

Credits Photography: Harry Purdue, Ciaran Tanham, Sound Recordists: Philippe Fayias, Sephan McDowell, Paul Emerson, Sound Editor: Paul Fitzgerald, Dubbing Mixer: Cecily Loughman, Telecine Colourist: Dave Gibson. [Thanks to omitted.] Research: Dearbhla Regan, John Erraught, Film Editor: Jim Dalton, Producers: Lesley McKimm, Robert Walpole, Director: Liam McGrath. A Treasure Films Production for Radio Telefís Éireann 1998.

Home (2002) 26 min.

Director: Patrick Hodgins

A study of homelessness in Dublin, profiling three individuals living on the streets. Part of the *Townlands* series.

Credits Lighting Cameraman: Des Doyle, Assistant Camera: Eoin Keating, John Waters, Trainee Camera: Pat Nangle, Location Sound: Philippe Fraujas, Research: Catherine Carolan, Production Assistant: Iseult O'Siochain, Editors: Patrick Hodgins, Niamh Fagan, On-Line Editor: Gordon Prenter, Assistant Editors: Claudine Fauvret, Janis Twomey, Kit Yuen Lee Groves, Sound Design: Philippe Fraujas, Sound Editor: Peter Carey, Mixer: Peter Blayney, Director: Patrick Hodgins, Producers:

Petra Conrow, Patrick Hodgins, Camera Equipment: DIT Aungier St., VFG, Stock: Kodak Ireland, Laboratory: Colour Film Services, Print: Film Lab North, Negative Cutting: TKT, Opticals/Titles: Studio 51, Gordon Prenter, Editing Facilities: DIT Aungier St., Filmbase, Lightworks: Lightworks/Eurotek, Sound Post-Production: Lime Street Sound, Ardmore Sound. Thanks to: Lara Bradley, Pat O'Donoughue, Paco Hayes, Jacqui Corcoran, Philip Gray, Breege Rowley, Vernon Dolan, Grainne Gavigan, Eoin Holmes, Peter Robertson, Ian Palmer, Shane O'Neill, Michael Holland, Terry Cromer, Marc Long, Eoin Kilfeather, Poco Loco, Windmill Lane, Picture Company. Special thanks: John McNamee, the Salvation Army: George Gillane, Pat Archer, Danny Alcock, Jimmy Thompson, St Vincent de Paul: Seamus McGovern, Simon Community: Greg Maxwell, Focus Ireland: Margaret Gorman, and to the staff and residents of the Model Lodging House, Simon Night Shelter/Usher's Island, the Back Lane Hostel, Grangegorman Night Shelter, York House. This film was made with the support and assistance of Bord Scannán na hÉireann, the Arts Council, Media Production Unit, DIT, RTÉ. © Vertigo Films/Patrick Hodgins 2000.

Home Movie Nights (1996–8) 25 min. each episode
Director: Alan Gilsenan
Home movies shot by various individuals over time are run together with the comments by people in some way involved or connected to them.
Credits Camera: Richard Kendrick, Sound: Ross O'Callaghan, Graphics: Hubert Montag, John Kennedy, Title Music: Roger Bolton, VT Operator: Fionnuala Gilmartin, Editor: Colm O'Brien, Archive Consultant: Liam Wylie. With thanks to the Irish Film Archive of the Film Institute of Ireland. Production Secretary: Jessica Moss, Co-Producer: Martin Mahon, Producer: Isabel Morton, Director: Alan Gilsenan. A Yellow Asylum Films Production for RTÉ.

Hoodwinked: Irish Women Since the 1920s (1997) 3 × 35 min.
Director: Trish McAdam
Series documenting the history of women in Irish politics. Composed substantially of newsreel footage and of interviews with various persons either directly involved or with a background in history.
Credits Archive Libraries: David Dillon Collection, Derek Spiers Collection, Irish Labour History Museum and Archive, National Library of Ireland Collection, Radio Telefís Éireann Radio and Film Archive, University College Dublin, the Fr Browne SJ Collection, the Irish Film Archive of the Film Institute of Ireland. Archive Sources: BBC Worldwide, Bord na Mona, British Council, British Movietone News, British Pathé News, the *Donegal Vindicator*, G. A. Duncan, Gael-Linn, Government Departments Archives, Irish Countrywomen's Association, Irish Distillers Group, the *Irish Independent*, Irish Shell Ltd, the *Irish Times*, Jennifer Leslie, Lila Hyland, Lisburn Camera Club, McConnells Advertising, Michelle Copper, Mrs Flynn for Jack of All Maids, Peter Lennon, Pictorial, Radharc, Rex Roberts, Sighie Humphreys Collection, Sony Music Ireland. Many thanks: Barbar Durack, Cathal Black, Donal Lunny, Donald Taylor Black, Dynphna Halpin, James Hickey, John Burgan, Josephine Doran, Mark Kilroy, Mary McGuigan, Grainne McAleer, Renne Perraudin, Terry Trench. Executive Producer for Bord Scannán na hÉireann/the Irish Film Board: Rod Stoneman, Executive Producer for Radio Telefís Éireann, Claire Duignan, Title Design: Public Communication Centre, Title Animation: Studio Zenith, Trainee Producer/Director: Barry Dignam, Research Team: Mary Jones, Neil Regan, Fionnuala O'Connor, Daire O'Connel, John Killen, Harriet

Devlin, Sue Gogan, Liam Wylie, Music: Bow Lane Studios, Production Manager: Anneliese O'Callaghan, Production Accountant: Jim Doyle, Sound: Phillippe Faujas, David Harris, Sound Mixer: Ciarán O'Tuairise, Director of Photography: Ciaran Tanham, Additional Camera: Declan Emerson, Mick O'Rourke, Ivor Fitzpatrick, On-Line Editor: Neil McLauchlan, Editor: Catherine Creed, Series Consultant: Mary Jones, Produced and Directed by Trish McAdam. Produced with the assistance of Bord Scannán na hÉireann/the Irish Film Board, Commission of the European Communities – DGS, with the support of DOCUMENTARY, an initiative of the MEDIA Programme of the European Communities. An East Lane Films Production in association with Radio Telefís Éireann. 1997.

Housing Discrimination (a.k.a. *Fintona, Fintona: Housing Discrimination*) (1953) 7 min.
Date: 1953.
Producers: Dept of External Affairs, Information Division
Discriminatory housing policies in Fintona, Co. Tyrone are exposed in this polemical public information film which claims that large Catholic/nationalist families are being denied public housing in Northern Ireland because their presence in key electoral districts would upset the unionist hold over the vote.
Credits Sponsors: Dept of External Affairs, Information Division, Filmed by: George Fleischmann.

How Far Home (1997) 38 min.
Director: Brendan J. Byrne
Profile of Gerry Conlon following his release from prison after his wrongful conviction for the Guildford pub bombing. The film details his subsequent (and consequent) inability to integrate with contemporary society and his ongoing psychological and emotional difficulties.
Credits With special thanks to: Gerry Conlon and Family. Thanks also: Martin Donnelly, Joey Cashman, Michael Golembo. Original Music: Robyn Robins, Philip Donnelly, Research: Gerard McCartney, Archive: Universal Pictures, ITN, Los Angeles Fixer: Lionel Mill, Assistant Editor: Jane Tubb, Assistant Camera: Liam McGrath, Lincoln Ascott, Sound Recordists: David Kilpatrick, Marc Hitchens, Dubbing: Ian Burns, Davy Lamb, Production Manager: Fiona Moore, Photograpy: John T. Davis, Film Editor: Greg Darby, Executive Producer: Ros Franey, Producer and Director: Brendan J. Byrne.

The Hungry Land (1950) 17 min.
Producer: James Ginnell
Agricultural film promoting the use of lime. The film instructs farmers on how to apply lime to fields in need of fertilisation.
Credits Producer: James Ginnell, Photography: James Ginnell, Sponsors: the Irish Sugar Company.

ICA: 60 Years A Growing (1970) 30 min.
Producer: Christine MacDiarmada
History of the Irish Countrywomen's Association celebrating their diamond jubilee which argues for a prominent yet traditional role for women in contemporary Irish society.
Credits Production Company: ICA Film, Producer: Christine MacDiarmada, Production Consultants: Ireland Film, Script and Narration: John O'Donoghue, Editor: Rory O'Farrell, Dubbing: Pat Hayes.

If I Should Fall From Grace (2001) 90 min.

Director: Sarah Share

Portrait of singer and songwriter Shane MacGowan, whose self-destructive personality (and alcoholism) is seen to be linked with his creativity.

Credits Director: Sarah Share, Producer: Cilian Fennell, Executive Producers: Larry Masterson, Sarah Share, Rod Stoneman, Micheál Ó Meallaigh, Non-Original Music: Shane MacGowan, the Pogues, Editor: Orla Daly, Sound: Finny Byrne, Enda Cahill, Joe Ó Dubghaill, Research: Kirsty Fitzsimons, Assistant Camera : Anthony Kavanagh, Hazel Masterson, Harry Purdue, On-Line Editor: Richard Kendrick, Rostrum: Nico Vermuelen. Companies: Bord Scannán na hÉireann/the Irish Film Board, Emdee 2000 Productions, TG4.

I gCillín na mBháis 1980-81 / In the Cell of Death 1980–81 (1998) 50 min.

Director: Sonia Nic Giolla Easbuig

An account of the 1980–1 hunger strikes told through first-hand accounts by survivors interviewed by an off-camera researcher.

Credits In ómós do Sissie 'william'. Trachtaire: Donal MacGiolla Easbuig. Mí\le Buíochas do: Laurence, Bik, Tackie, Leo, Mary Doyle, Gerry A., Deirdre, Caoilfhionn, Lena, Falls Community Council, Newhill Community Centre, Michelle Devlin, Glenn, SpringVale Training Centre, Bill Roulston, Colourmaster, Eamonn, Seán Cathal, Cúan, Mick Melvin, Sedbastian, Seán, Keran, Roisín, Fiona, Denise, Conan, John Barr, Paddy S., Anne, Frank, Niall, Teach Leanna mhic Giolla Easbuig, RTÉ, BBC, Martin McCauley, Dan Devenney, Derek Speirs, Brian Campbell, APRN, Fionnuala, Siúbhan, Liam, Chatch, Bríd Ní Shírín, J.C.G., Leon, Christy Moore, Máire Ní Bhraonain, Liam, Norah, agus gach duine eile a chudaight leis an gclár seo a chríochnú. Scriopt: Seán Mac Fhionngháile, Stuideo: SpringVale Media Suite, Áiseanna: Kairos Communications, Telegael, Graificí: Dearadh Dubh, Eagarthóir Coimisiúnaithe: Micheál Ó Meallaigh, Ceol Nuachmtha: Denis Woods, Amhrán 'Music From the Blocks', 'A Rebel's Heart', 'Something Inside So Strong', Terence O'Neill, Brendan 'Bik' McFarlane, Ceamaraí: Tim Lawless, Seamus Caulfield, Fuaim: Pól Mac Phaidín, Fuaimrian: Ciarán Ó Tuairisc, Teidil: Siobhán Bric, Eagarthóirí: Cóilín Ó Scolaí, Bernadette Nic Giolla Bhríghde, Comh-Léirtheoir: Laurence McKeown, Léirtheoir/Stiúrthóir: Sonia Nic Giolla Easbuig, Deánta le cab-hair ó: Údarás na Gaeltachta. Leiriú de chuid Ligid Teoranta do TnaG © TnaG 1998.

Incognitus (2002) 26 min. each episode

Director: Rónan Ó Donnchadha

Mockumentary series charting the 'forgotten' histories of 'unknown' Irishmen whose adventures encompass the gamut of native and diasporic experiences.

Credits Cartlann: RTÉ, Ulster Folk and Transport Museum, Rex Features, Ceamara: Martin Birney, Fuaim: Damien Clifford, Eagarthóir: Darren Chan, Áiseanna: 2BCut, Léiritheoirí: Evan Chamberlain, Cristín Reddin, Stiúrthóir/Léiritheoir: Rónan Ó Donnchadha, Léiritheoir Feidhmiúcháin: Brian Reddin, Subtitles: Margaret Ní Cheannabháin, TMI. Léiriú le Adare Productions do TG4. 'Incognitus' © TG4 2002.

In Flags or Flitters: Pictures of Dublin (1991) 53 min.

Director: Donald Taylor Black

City profile which attempts to redress the mythology of Dublin by using critical artists and documentaries on social problems of the past to problematise more romantic impressions. Contains many interviews and much archival footage.

Credits The producers would like to thank: Irish Film Institute (Archive Section), RTÉ Programme Library, RTÉ Sound Archive, RTÉ Sound Library, Anner, Bord Fáilte, Majella Breen, British Motor Industry Heritage Trust, British Pathé News Ltd, P. J. Carroll and Company, Dardis Clarke, Dept. of Foreign Affairs, Dublin Youth Theatre, Jim Duggan, Emdee Productions, Peter Fallon and the Trustees of the Literary Estate of Patrick Kavanagh, Eugene Finn, Gael-Linn, Irish Life, Paddy Kelly, Michael Kierans, Thomas Kinsella, Glen Kyte, Rossa Lyons, Liam Mooney, Passion Machine, Radharc Films, Rank Film Distributors, Joe Scully, David Shaw-Smith, Viewtech Rank Aldis, Yellow Asylum. Archive Consultants: Barbara Durack (RTÉ), Sunniva O'Flynn (IFI), On-Line Editor: Mark Esdale, Sound Dubbing: Bob Bell, Telecine Transfers: Screen Scene, Video Editor: Jim Colgan, Executive Producer: James Hickey, Producer and Director: Donald Taylor Black. A Poolbeg Production for Radio Telefís Éireann. © Poolbeg Productions 1991.

Insurrection (1966) 6 × 25 min.*
Director: Louis Lentin
Docudrama charting the events of the 1916 rising with an unusual level of objectivity. Stylistically informed by the work of Peter Watkins.
Credits A Boy: Tony Hayes, Cathal Brugha: Joe Lynch, Capt. Bowen-Colthurst: Henry Comerford, Miss Carney: Eithne Lydon, Sir Roger Casement: Conor Farrington, Volunteer Casey: Donal McCann, 2nd Lieutenant Chalmers: Peter Mayock, Tom Clarke: Jim Norton, Coade: Padraig Faye, Michael Collins: Michael McAuliffe, James Connolly: Ronnie Walsh, Jimmy Doyle: Brendan Sullivan, Patrick Doyle: Tony Doyle, Colonel Fane: John Franklyn, Desmond Fitzgerald: Barry Cassin, James Fox: Patrick Laffan, Miss Julia Grenan: Sabina Coyne, Sergeant Hearne: Taolach O hAonghusa, Colonel Hodgkin: David Kelly, A Housewife: Anna Manahan, Lieutenant King: Tom Ascough-Patterson, 1st Looter: Loretta Clarke, 2nd Looter: Patricia Turner, General Lowe: Denis McCarthy, An Old Man: Cecil Nash, Sean MacDermott: Padraig Ó Gaora, Stephen McKenna: Robert Charles, Lieutenant Mahony: Michael Murray, Section Commander Malone: Michael Ryan, Commander Mallin: Gerry Sullivan, Countes Markievicz: Joan O'Hara, General Sir John Maxwell: Howard Marion Crawford, Adjutant Morgan: Robert McLernon, Richard Murphy: Brian Waldron, Constable O'Brien: Patrick Layde, Elizabeth O'Farrell: Sheelagh Cullen, British Officer: Chris Raphael, Volunteer Officer: Michael Murphy, The O'Rahilly: Kevin Flood, P. H. Pearse: Eoin Ó Suilleabhain, William Pearse: Patrick Waldron, Joseph Plunkett: Declan Harvey, Colonel Portal: Peter Kennerley, Captain Pragnell: Bill Skinner, Air-Mechanic Pratt: Robert Carlile Jnr., George Reynolds: Jimmy Caffrey, William Ronan: Kevin McHugh, Jim Ryan: Sean McCarthy, George Bernard Shaw: Michael Monaghan, 1st Shawlie: May Cluskey, 2nd Shawlie: Maureen Toal, Mr Francis Sheehy-Skeffington: Brendan Mathews, British Soldier: Martin Crosbie, Michael Stalnes: Ray Macken, A Volunteer: Tom O'Rafferty, James Walsh: Niall O'Brien, Tom Walsh: Anthony Hennigan, A Woman: Lillian Rapple, and Members of the Defence Forces by Courtesy of the Minister of Defence and through the Cooperation of the Officers, NCO's and Men of the Eastern Command. Narrator: Ray McAnally, Script: Hugh Leonard, Lighting Cameraman: Bestick Williams, Film Sound: Pat Kavanagh, Film Dubbing: Fintan Ryan, Outside Broadcast Cameras: Aidan Maguire, Outside Broadcast Sound: Pierce Ivory, Sound Effects: Jim O'Loughlin, Lighting: Randall Miles, Sound: Bill Fogarty, Senior Cameraman: Tony Barry, Film Editors: Bob Hill, Michael Stoffer, Video Tape Editor: Ted Crowley, Stills Photography: Eddie McEvoy, Unit Organiser: John Baragwanath, Production Assistants: Noeline Coffey, Janet Wynne, Floor Manager:

Mike Purcell, Technical Operators Manager: Tony Williams, Production Manager: Charles Roberts, Historical Advisor: Dr Kevin Nowlan, Research: Maureen O'Farrell, Brendan Cahir, Costume Design: Lona Moran, Music: A. J. Potter, Film Sequences Directed by: Michael Garvey, Design: Alpho O'Reilly, Producer, Director: Louis Lentin. A Telefís Éireann Production. Radion Telefís Éireann Acknowledges the Assistance Derived from Max Caulfield's Book 'The Easter Rebellion'.

* The print viewed was an edited compilation running approximately 1 hr 20 min. Credits as per this print.

INTO Battle (1946) 3 min.
Producers: Irish National Teachers Organisation
An account of the 1946 teachers' strike, featuring scenes from mass meetings and signings.
Credits Producers: Irish National Teachers Organisation, Photography: Breandán Ó Se, Padraig Ó Nuallain.

Ireland (1967) 30 min.
Director: George Sluizer
Strikingly photographed film which discusses Irish history and economy as well as featuring its landscape. The film frequently juxtaposes illustrations from the past with scenes from the present.
Credits Production Company: Vincent Corcoran Productions, Co-Producer: Patrizia Giri de Teramata, Director: George Sluizer, Script: George Sluizer, R. B. D. French, Narrator: Philip O'Flynn, Music: Brian Boydell, Conductor: Philip Martell, Orchestra: RTÉ Symphony Orchestra.

Ireland (1968) 16 min.
Director: Colm O'Laoghaire
Educational overview of Irish history, economy, landscape, sport, etc. produced for the McGraw Hill Company in conjunction with the Dept of External Affairs.
Credits Producer: Colm O'Laoghaire, Director: Colm O'Laoghaire, Adviser: Clyde F. Kohn PhD., Chairman, Dept. of Geography, University of Iowa, Production Company: McGraw Hill Films, Sponsors: Dept of External Affairs. © 1968 Government of Ireland.

Ireland – A Television History (1981) 13 × 50 min.
Producer: Jeremy Isaacs
A comprehensive history of Ireland up to and including 'the troubles' presented by historian Robert Kee.
Credits Producer: Jeremy Isaacs, Writer/Presenter: Robert Kee, Photography: Philip Bonham-Carter, Ken Lowe. A BBC/RTÉ production.

Ireland Invites You (1965) 20 min.
Director: Jim Mulkerns
Promotional film directed at travel agents in which the voice over achieves overwhelming speed and detail.
Credits Commissioned by: Bord Fáilte Éireann, Editor: Ted Hickey, Commentary: Bart Bastable, Camera: Jim Mulkerns, Val Ennis, Director: Jim Mulkerns.

Ireland – Isle of Sport (1959/60) 27 min.
Director: Kenneth Fairbarn

Profile of Ireland as a sporting nation. The film concludes with footage of children participating in an art exhibition sponsored by Caltex Oil, one of the film's co-sponsors.

Credits Producer: Anthony Gilikson, Director: Kenneth Fairbarn, Narrator: Eamonn Andrews, Photography: Douglas Ransom, Editor: Nicholas Gurney, Music Composer and Conductor: Edwin Astley, Sponsors: Texaco Ireland Ltd, Caltex Oil.

Ireland: The Heritage of the Past (1974) 8 min.
Director: Kieran Hickey

Montage of archeological and architectural sites in Ireland which progresses from Stone Age Cairns to Georgian Houses in Dublin.

Credits Production Company: BAC Films, Director: Kieran Hickey, Photography: Sean Corcoran, Editor: Patrick Duffner, Script: Des Hickey, Sponsors: Bord Fáilte Éireann.

Ireland: The New Convention Country (1966) 13 min.
Director: Robert Monks

Promotional film advertising Ireland as a modern country suitable for international conventions.

Credits Producer: Robert Monks, Director: Robert Monks, Sponsors: Bord Fáilte Éireann.

Ireland: The Tear and the Smile (1959) 50 min.
Director: Willard Van Dyke

American-produced (CBS TV) two-part programme examining the state of Ireland in the twentieth century. Features interviews with many prominent literary and political figures.

Credits Production Company: CBS News/Twentieth Century, Producer: Burton Benjamin, Director: Willard Van Dyke, Narrator: Walter Kronkite, Sponsor: Prudential Insurance Company of America.

An Irish-American Story (1996) 30 min.
Director: Cob Carlson

American-produced biographical portrait of Irish emigrant Mary Crehan Dillon, who landed in the United States in 1911 and proceeded to forge a new destiny for herself and others of her family who chose to follow her. The film was directed by her grandson.

Credits Camera, Editor, Producer, Director: Cob Carlson, Additional Camera: Peter Kreiger, Additional Sound: James Kiely, Additional Music Recording: Bob Nolte, Recording Mix Engineer: Ken Volpe, Patron Saints: Kevin Mason, Mae Dillon Carlson, John O'Connor, Sound Mix: Tom Aguello, Color Timer: Rod Bingaman, Titles: Charlotte Davis, Animation Stand: Matt Williams, Negative Matching: American Film Studios, Film Prints: Cinelab, © 1996. A Cob Carlson Production.

Irish and Elegant (1957) 10 min.
Director: Derrick Knight

Profile of the work of Cybil Connolly, Irish clothing designer. Models wearing her designs stand posed against the landscape, suggesting a relationship between the elegance of the clothing and that of the natural environment.

Credits Production Company: Technical and Scientific Films/Film Producers Guild, Producer: Cyril Randell, Director: Derrick Knight, Sponsors: Irish Linen Guild, Photography: Charles K. French, Editor: Terence Twigg, Sound: Ronald Abbott, Sidney Rider, Models: Mola Ross, Pat O'Reilly, Molly Frith.

Irish Boy: The Story of Sean (1970) 15 min.
Director: Kieran Hickey
Encyclopedia Britannica short giving basic details about Irish life through the 'story' of a young boy who tells us of his life.
Credits Production Company: BAC Films, Director: Kieran Hickey, Photography: Sean Corcoran, Script: Des Hickey, Editor: Patrick Duffner, Sponsors: Department of Foreign Affairs, Encyclopedia Britannica. © 1972.

Irish Children (Rural Life in Western Ireland) (1948) 11 min.
Producers: Encyclopedia Britannica Films Inc.
Profile of 'Seán and Mary O'Reilly', children living in 1940s Clare and growing up in a comfortable, traditional, rural environment.
Credits Producers: Encyclopedia Britannica Films Inc., in collaboration with Conrad M. Arensberg PhD., Columbia University. © 1948.

Irish Cinema: Ourselves Alone? (1995) 52 min.
Director: Donald Taylor Black
A history of Irish cinema featuring clips from older and more recent films. The film formed part of the Centenary of Cinema series.
Credits Film Extracts Courtesy of: Academy of Motion Picture Arts and Sciences © 1990 & 1993 AMPAS, Aeon Films, Association Freres Lumiere, BAC Films, Cathal Black Films/Black Star Films, British Film Institute, CNC/Les Archives du Film, Channel Four Television, Cinegael, Clarence Pictures, the Cooper Family, Derry Film and Video Workshop/Jane Balfour Films, Hilton Edwards Estate, Granada Television, Mrs Richard Hayward, Irish Film Archive, Desmond Leslie, Little Bird, Lumiere Pictures, Metro-Goldwyn-Meyer, Miramax Films, National Film and Television Archive, Ploygram Film International, RTÉ Programme Archive, Rank Film Distributors, Republic Entertainment INC., Reuters Television Library, Samson Films, Soverign Pictures Inc., Temple Film and Television Productions, Turner Entertainment Co., Twentieth Century Fox Film Corporation, Vision International, Warner Bros., Yellow Asylum. Thanks to: Mary Albert, Ambassador Cinema, Dublin, BBC TV, Paddy Barrett, Peter Canning, Una Carmody, Tom Casey, Darryl Collins, Colm Connolly, Jane Doolan, Sé Merry Doyle, Andrew Eaton, Jan Faull, Ferndale Films, Film Base, Film Institute of Ireland, Gaiety Theatre, Dublin, Paula Gelfon, John Hill, Irish Film Archive, Irish Film Centre, Junior Dublin Film Festival, the Leslie Family, Declan McLoughlin, John O'Leary, the Purple Room, Roinn na Gaeltachta, Screen Scene, Tracey Seaward, Sheamus Smith, Temple Bar Properties, Windmill Lane Pictures. Electrician: Tony Swan, Camera Assistants: Shane Deasy, Conor Kelly, Assistant Editor: Lisa Murphy, Telecine: Gerry Hoban, Glenn Kyte, Graphics: Ian Jacobs, Stills Photographer: John Morris, Archive Liaison: Barbara Durack (RTÉ), Sunniva O'Flynn (IFA), Sound Recordists: Brendan Deasy, Raymond Cross, Paul Delany, Dubbing Mixer: Cecily Loughman, On-Line Editor: Derek Shoebridge, Post-Production Supervisor: Jim Duggan, BFI Executive Production Manager: Esther Johnson, Series Consultant, Film Copyright Coordinator: Grainne Humphreys, Music: Bill Whelan, Photography: Seamus Deasy, Editor: Maurice Healy, Narrator: Gabriel Byrne, Writer: Kevin Rockett, Executive Producers: Clare Duignan (RTÉ), Rod Stoneman (BSE), Colin MacCabe, Bob Last, Produced and Directed by: Donald Taylor Black. Produced with the support of investment incentives for the Irish film industry provided by the government of Ireland. Made by Centenary Productions in association with Poolbeg Productions for Radio Telefís Éireann with the assistance of Bord Scannán na hÉireann/The Irish Film Board; © 1995.

The Irish Condition (1993–4) 6 × 45 min.

Director: Louis Marcus

Series documenting both Irish history and contemporary attitudes to the questions as raised then and as confronted now by the Irish people. Features interviews with several prominent historians.

Credits Camera: Seamus Deasy, Sound: Brendan Deasy, Editor: Joe Marcus, RTÉ Library Research: Denis McArdle, Joe Scully, Barbara Durack, Principal Archive Film Photography: Robert Monks, Narration: Doireann Ní Bhriain, Recorded by: Patrick Gibbons, On-Line Editor: Mark Nolan, Tape Operator: Michelle Grarke, Telecine: Glenn Kyte, Gerry Hoban, Assistant: Sarah Tanham, Title Graphics: Ian Jacobs, Facilities: Screen Scene, Dubbing: Moynihan Russell, Acknowledgements: Cumann Lúthchleas Gael, Department of the Táoiseach, Gael-Linn, IBEC, Irish Film Archive, Director: Louis Marcus, A Louis Marcus Production for Radio Telefís Éireann. © Radio Telefís Éireann 1994.

The Irish Empire (1999) 5 × 50 min.

Directors: Alan Gilsenan, Dearbhla Walsh, David Roberts

Five-part historical series exploring how the Irish 'colonised' the world through emigration.

Credits Narrator: Fiona Shaw, Music: Deborah Mollison, Script Consultant: Fintan O'Toole, Series Consultants: Paddy Fitzgerald, Centre for Migration Studies, Omagh, Piras Mac Éinrí, Irish Centre for Migration Studies, Cork, Patrick O'Sullivan, Irish Diaspora Research Unit, Bradford. Thanks to: Peggy O'Brien, Kathleen Bernard, Aidan O'Hara, Chris Ryan, Nora Lambert, John Maguire, Pete Hamill, Siobhan Benet, Anita Best. [Archive sources omitted.] Editor: Emer Reynolds, Research: Niamh Barrett, Olive Howe, Siobhan McHugh, Jane Manning, Sheila Brosnan, Mary Doran, Archive Research: Steve Bergson, Titles and Graphic Design: Laura Brooks, Production Manager: Thérèse Randall, Jo-Anne McGowan, Production Assistants: Jessica Moss, Máire Doherty, Post-Production Supervision: Jim Duggan, Lisa Murphy, Screen Scene Dublin, Photography: Peter Dorney, Ross Keith, Richard Craske, Pablo Anello, Donal Gilligan, Olivier Raffet, Breffni Byrne, Ciaran Tanham, Wade Fairley, Ronan Fox, Bob Perrin, Tony Gailey, Sound: Joe Dolan, Bruno Strapko, Craig Lapp, Richard Day, Kenny Oelbert, Joël Flescher, John Duvall, Chris Bollard, Rob Stalder, John P. Scott, Paul Finlay, Tom Ronan, Sound Editor: Niall Brady, Dubbing Mixer: Cecily Loughman, On-Line Editor: Shayne Murphy, Telecine: Glenn Kyte, Business Affairs: Annette Waldron, Simon Birtles, John Russell, Jonathan Kelly, Ivan Garel-Jones. Based on an original idea by: Patrick Bishop, Executive Producers: James Mitchell, André Singer, Chris Hilton, Commissioning Editors: Clare Duignan, Paul Evans, Bridget Ikin and John Hughes, Series Producer: Ritchie Cogan, Director: Alan Gilsenan.* Produced in association with the Australian Film Finance Corporation, Programme Rights Company, with assistance from NSW Film and TV Office, and with the support of investment incentives for the Irish film industry provided by the government of Ireland; A Little Bird, Café, Hilton Cordell Productions, production for RTÉ, BBC Northern Ireland, SBS Independent. © 1999 Little Bird, Café, Hilton Cordell, PRC, AFFC and NSWFTO.

* Subsequent episodes have different directorial credits.

Irish Gossamer (1957) 25 min.

Producer: Colm O'Laoghaire

Tourist film purporting to show the textures and patterns of Ireland which have inspired Irish textiles. The film is not actually concerned with textiles. It uses images of a loom at work as a starting point only.

Credits Producer: Colm Ó Laoghaíre, Commentary: Denis Brennan, Music: Gerard Victory, played by the Rádio Éireann Light Orchestra, Extra Music: Courtesy of Gael-Linn, Fashion Sequence: Miss Irene Gilbert, Fibres: Crock of Gold and Gaeltarra Éireann, Sponsors: the Dept of Foreign Affairs.

The Irish in Me (1959) 8 min.
Director: Herman Boxer
American-produced tourist film following an American girl visiting her Irish grandfather and feeling at one with the culture and landscape.

Credits Sponsors: Universal International Colour Parade, Director: Herman Boxer, Photography: Ed Drews, Editor: Ernest Folk, Narrator: Marvin Miller, Music: Howard Jackson.

Irish Pastoral (1936) 10 min.
Producer: Truman Talley
A 'Magic Carpet of Movietone' travelogue featuring views of a rugged, rural Ireland including 'a fair colleen' singing a love song.

Credits Presented by: Magic Carpet of Movietone, Producer: Truman Talley, Editor: Lew Lear, Narrator: Ed Thorgersen, Distributor: Fox. © 1936.

Irish Rising 1916 (1966) 15 min.
Director: Geroge Morrison
An account of the Irish rising of 1916 with some contemporary footage to create a sense of the results of the rebellion. The film is largely composed of the archival footage used in director George Morrison's 1959 feature *Mise Éire*. It was distributed internationally with a script to be read by local television presenters in their own language.

Credits Producer: George Morrison, Director: George Morrison, Distributor: the Dept of External Affairs, Music: Seán Ó Riada, Orchestra: RTÉ Symphony Orchestra. Produced with the cooperation of the 1916 Commemoration Committee.

Irish Village (1959) 23 min.
Director: Jim Clark
Profile of Crookhaven, Co. Cork: 'an ordinary place with nothing special about it except that it is dying'. In spite of the dramatic voice over lamenting poverty, emigration and lack of progress, the images of rural life are mostly cheerfully touristic.

Credits Research Film Productions Ltd. present a film by James Clark. Music composed and conducted by Ian MacIntyre, Sound: Bob Allen, Production Assistant: Rex Hipple. RCA.

'It must be done right!' (2000) 52 min.
Director: Bob Quinn
Profile of actor Donal McCann. Subtitled 'A collage by Bob Quinn', the film mixes interview commentary, footage from a public interview with McCann, and clips from his work on film and television as well as stills illustrating his stage performances.

Credits Interview: Gerry Stembridge, Participants: Robert Ballagh, Sebastian Barry, Bernardo Bertolucci, Gabriel Byrne, Sinéad Cusack, Lelia Doolan, Rachael Dowling, Michael D. Higgins, Neil Jordan, Pat Laffan, Hugh Leonard, Tom Murphy, Wieland Schutz-Kiel, Jim Sheridan, John Turturro, Research: Sara Mackie, Jennifer Reynolds, Stills: Abbey Theatre Archive, Tom Lawlor, Terenure College, Paddy Cleary, Caroline Fitzgerald, Oliver Maguire, Out of Joint Productions, Executive

Producers: Rod Stoneman (Bord Scannán na hÉireann), Clare Duignan (RTÉ), Cameras: Billy Keady, Christine NÍ Conchubhair, Vinnie Cunningham, Peter Millar, Sound Recording: Iarla Ó Maoláin, Conor McBrierty, Derek Hehir, Mark Alexander, Sound Mixer: Ciarán Ó Tuairise, On-Line Editor: Julian Charlton, Editor: Gordon Bruie. The Producers wish to thank: Galway Film Fleadh and Miriam Allen for their cooperation. Thanks to: Pat Collins, Fr Pat Grace, Vinnie Morris, Irish Film Institute, Abbey Theatre, Phyllis Ryan, Morgan O'Sullivan, Hugh Linehan, Joan O'Hara, Mairéad Donnelly, Clare Austin, Catherine Buchanan, Sarah Jordan, Kerry Henchy, Audrey O'Reilly, Barbara Durack, Telegael. Archive Print Sources: *Strumpet City*, *Faith Healer*, *Juno and the Paycock*, *The Silver Tassie*, *Two Gallants*, *Access to the Children* (RTÉ), *The Pallisers* (BBC), *The Fighting Prince of Donegal* (Walt Disney), *Poitín*, *The Bishop's Story* (Cinegael), *Angel* (Channel Four), The Miracle (Polygram), *The Dead* (Carlton International), Illuminata (John Turturro), *The Nephew* (World 2000 Ent. Ltd.). Producer: Tom Collins, Researcher/Director: Bob Quinn. A De Facto Films Production for Radio Teilifís Éireann and Bord Scannán na hÉireann © De Facto Films 1999.

Jack B. Yeats: Assembled Memories 1871–1957 (1981) 37 min.
Director: Thaddeus O'Sullivan
Profile of painter Jack B. Yeats which presents him within the context of his life and times, locating him within the canon of great Irish artists.
Credits Production Company: Arbor International in association with the British Arts Council, Producer: Margaret Williams, Director, Script, Photography: Thaddeus O'Sullivan, Narrator: Bosco Hogan, Additional Photography: Cathal Black, Joe Comerford, Peter Harvey, Patrick Walsh, Editor: Charles Rees, Music: John Tams, Graeme Taylor, Location Sound: Pat Hayes, Dubbing Mixer: Peter Maxwell, Singer: Mick Lally, Sponsors: RTÉ.

James Gandon – A Life (1996) 58 min.
Director: Sé Merry Doyle
Biography of English architect James Gandon, whose eighteenth-century neo-classical buildings still dominate Dublin's urban landscape. Features some dramatic reconstruction.
Credits Director of Photography: John T. Davis, Script: Jimmy Duggan, Music: Niall Byrne, Narrator: Michelle O'Connor, Location Sound: Brendan Campbell. Cast: Christopher Casson (James Gandon), Cathy Brennan (The Maid); Art Director: Marie Tierney, Make-Up: Tara McHugh, Research: Ríonach Ní Neíll, Niamh Barrett, Production Assistant: Niamh Barrett, Administrative Assistant: Anne King, Titles: Anastasia Clafferty, Camera Assistant: Liam McGrath, Lighting Assistant: Pearse McKenna, Grips: Garry Keane, Film Editing: Dermot Diskin, Sé Merry Doyle, assisted by: Linda Nartey, On-Line Editor: Mark Nolan, Dubbing: Pat Hayes, Sound Studios: Ardmore Studios, Beacon Studios, Rostrum Camera: Ken Morse, Robbie Ryan, John T. Davis, Illustrations: Alan Lambert, Production Back-Up: Anakana Schofield, Ronán O'Muirgheasa, Robbie Ryan, Keith Little, Marcus MacConghaill. Loopline films say thank you to: the Office of Public Works and Elevation Ireland, Cosgrave Homes, John Sisk & Son, Cholmeley Cholmeley-Harrison. Copyright material courtesy of The biography of James Gandon by Hugo Duffy, the Irish Architectural Archive, the National Library of Ireland, the National Gallery of Ireland, the Dublin City Archives, the Bank of Ireland Archive, the Royal Irish Academy, the National Portrait Gallery – London, the Royal Collection © Her Majesty Queen Elizabeth II, Yale Centre for British Art, Paul Mellan Collection, the Irish

Linen Centre, Leeds City Art Gallery, Sir John Soanes' Museum, Metropolitan Museum of Art, Lisburn Museum, the Dublin Historical Society, the Irish Air Corps, the Courtauld Institute of Art, the Honourable Society of the King's Inn Library, the British Museum, the British Library, Sothebys, Dublin Public Libraries, Gael-Linn, C. P. Curran, Dublin Port and Docks Board, David Davison & Associates, Major Cholmeley Harrison, the Dublin Civic Museum. We also thank: Elizabeth Kirwan and the National Library of Ireland, Maria McFeeley and the National Gallery of Ireland, Mary Clark of Dublin City Archives, Ray Murphy, Eve Stewart, Emo Court, Brendan O'Donoghue, Terry Allen, the Custom House, Seán McQuaid, Jimmy Doyle, Barry O'Kelly, Bank of Ireland, Brian Freeman – Drumcondra Cemetery, Col. Furlong, Michael Leenane – the King's Inns, Brendan Ryan, Albert Byrne – the Four Courts, the Captain and Crew of Asgard II, John Scannel, the Gilbert Library, Trinity College Dublin, the Dublin Civic Museum, Tessa and Jeffrey Le Froy, Michael Bohan, the Flowing Tide, F. & S. Shipping, Gandon Editions, Marie Sheahan, Melanie Scott, Martin Mahon, Dave Nolan, Colm Nolan, Giselda Volodi, Brendan Coyle, Fiona Keane, Seamus Lynam, Bridget McNulty and Michael O'Doherty – Office of Public Works. Produced by: Bernadine Carraher, Director: Sé Merry Doyle. Loopline Films in association with Radio Telefís Éireann, the Office of Public Works. © 1996.

James Joyce's Dublin (1968) 25 min.
Director: Michael O'Connor
Profile of James Joyce's impressions of Dublin city.
Credits Director: Michael O'Connor, Script: Ulick O'Connor, Photography: Michael O'Connor, Narrators: Donal Donnelly, Ulick O'Connor.

John Charles McQuaid: What the Papers Say (1998) 2 × 50 min.
Director: Peter Kelly
Following the release of the private papers of former archbishop John Charles McQuaid, John Bowman presents extracts and puts them in their context in presenting the story of the man's career.
Credits Written and presented by: John Bowman, Acknowledgements: Blackrock College Archive, Bord Fáilte, Dublin Diocesan Archive, IRFU Archive, Irish Film Archive, Irish National Archive, National Library of Ireland, Rahdarc Archive, RDS Archive, Reuters Television Library, RTÉ Film Archive (Barbara Durack and Stephen D'arcy), RTÉ Stills Library, RTÉ Sound Library (Robert Canning), St Vincents Hospital. Additional Research: Christine Thornton, Production Assistant: Mary Brophy, Production Accountant: Gaby Smyth, Film Camera: Neal Boyle, Assistant Camera: Ruairí O'Brien, Sound: Billy Roarty, Post Production: Esras Facilities, On-Line Editor: Garry Creevey, Video Grading: Glenn Kyte at Screenscene, Film Editor: Dáibhí Doran, Producer: Fintan Drury, Directed by: Peter Kelly.

John F. Kennedy in The Island of Dreams (1993) 40 min.
Director: Darragh Byrne
An account of the visit by former US president John F. Kennedy to Ireland in 1963 with some commentary on his symbolic status as a member of the Irish diaspora.
Credits Special thanks to: Charles and Anne Byrne, Niall Byrne, Ali O'Leary, Eilish Pearce, Dr's Peggy and York Moore-Lewy and Family, Dr Margaret MacCurtain, Francis Moore-Lewy, John and Betty Maher, Candida McMahon, Joan and Brendan O'Cleirigh, Peter Moorehead, Jeanette Doyle, Dave Powers, Dave Farrell, Brian Lynch, Niamh Daly, The JFK Library, Boston MA, Killian Schurman, Michael

O'Cleirigh, Dr. David Nolan, Brian Scanlan, Mary Cough, Sean Reidy, the Embassy of the United States of America, Staff at Cherry Orchard Hospital, Dublin, the JFK Trust, New Ross, Siobhan O'Donaghue, Moritz Schurmann, Billy O'Hanrahan, Gerry McCarthy, Clare Duignan, Gilroy McMahon Architects, the Office of Public Works, Michael Fitzsimons, Nicholas O'Neill, Brian Ormond, John Lawlor, Brian Moran, Andrea Pitt, Mike Kelly, the Irish Film Institute, Derry O'Brier, CTT, Jacqueline Beusse, Dr Joe Mulholland, Patricia Masterson, Tom Kenny, the National Library, Dr Aiden Meade, Richard Kearney, Annette Byrne, Ken Manning, Tom Aherne, Louis Eaves, Garv. Acknowledgements: Standard 8 mm footage from: Andy Nathan, Frank Nolan, S. O. P. O'Ceallachain, Judy Heffernan, Finbar McCarthy, Excerpts from 'The River' and 'Aran' courtesy of Jan De Fouw, 8 mm Telecine – BBC London, Map courtesy of the Neptune Gallery, Photography – the *Irish Times*, 'Kennedy in Ireland' courtesy of the JFK Library, Boston, MA, Cloud sequence courtesy of BBDO South, Atlanta, GA, Ulster Bank, Visnews, Aer Lingus. With the support of DOCUMENTARY, an initiative of the MEDIA programme for the European Communities and with the support of Farrell and Associates Group. Voice-over artist: Olwen Fouere, Graphics: Pixamation, Audio File: Peter Fletcher, Sound Recordist: Steve Shanahan, Lighting Cameraman: Ronan Fox, Seamus Deasy, Additional Film Footage: Finn Van Gelderen, Editor: Guy Montgomery, Anner Facilities, Music: Niall Byrne, Script and Research: Brian Lynch, Directed by: Darragh Byrne, Co-produced by: William Maher and Darragh Byrne. A Graph Production for Radio Telefís Éireann.

John Huston: An tÉireanach / John Huston: Irishman (1996) 50 min.
Director: Brian Reddin
Profile of legendary director John Huston, who became an Irish citizen in 1963 and was later instrumental in lobbying for government support for an indigenous film industry.
Credits Subtitles: Eamonn Mac Niallais of TMI for TnaG. Copyright TnaG, 1996. Griangrafanna le caoinchead ó: Jim Horgan, Joe Dillon, Stan Sheilds – Connacht Tribune, Michael Hackett, Ingrid Craigie, Frank Patterson, Karen O'Connor, Examiner Publications Ltd., Dan Martin Ryan, Paddy Linehan, Paddy Burke's, Eddie Raftery, Scannstoc le caoinchead ó: Bord Fáilte, Gael-Linn, Irish Film Archive, Kevin McClory, Michael Ferron, Radio Telefís Éireann, First Independent Films, Angelica Huston taifeadta le caoinchead ag 'Smasbox Studios', California, Tráchtaire: Brendán Ó Dúil, Taighdeoir/Agallóir: Traolach Ó Buachalla, Taighdeoir: Ciarán Gallagher, Ceamara: Ken O'Mahony, Fuaim: Karl Merren, Réamonn de Brún, Ceol: Rónan Johnston, Fuaimrian: Joe Ó Dubhghaill, Eagarthóir: Guy Montgomery, Áiseanna: Anner Facilities, Pine Valley Studios, Scríbhneoirí Scripte: Brian Reddin, Traolach Ó Buachalla, Léiritheori/Stiúthóir: Brian Reddin. Léiriú de chuid Adare Productions do TnaG. © 1996.

Jonathan Swift (1967) 30 min.
Director: Kieran Hickey
A portrait of the life and career of Jonathan Swift which attempts to debunk some of the common romantic myths about him and portray him as a bitter and unhappy man.
Credits Director: Kieran Hickey, Script: David Thomson, Narrators: Cyril Cusack, Patrick Magee, Alan Badel, Siobhán McKenna.

The Joy (1997) 4 × 45 min.
Director: Donald Taylor Black

Series chronicling the lives of prisoners and warders at Dublin's Mountjoy Prison (men's and women's facilities) through a series of interviews.

Credits The prisoners featured in this documentary have been convicted in the Irish Courts of a range of crimes. We acknowledge the cooperation of the Prison Service in facilitating this film. Thanks to Governor John Lonergan, Staff and Prisoners for their help and assistance. Graphics: Laura Brooks, Video Grading: Glenn Kyte, Additional Sound: Trevor O'Connor, Brendan Deasy, Paul Emerson, On-Line Editor: Mark Nolan, Sound Recordist: Karl Merren, Associate Producer: Veronica Jane O'Mara, Camera: Sean Corcoran, Editor: Maurice Healy, Executive Producer: James Hickey, Produced and Directed by: Donald Taylor Black. A Poolbeg Production for Radio Telefís Éireann; © Poolbeg Productions 1997.

Julie's Story (2000) 50 min.
Director: Alan Gilsenan
Profile of writer Julie Parsons, formerly of New Zealand, now resident in Ireland.

Credits Thanks to: 1999 New Zealand Listener Book Festival, Kimberley Villari and Jayne Waysmuth, Macmillan Publishers, Mrs Kosenof, Muriel and Keith Kear, Mr and Mrs Dunn, Des and Anne O'Sullivan, Wren and Norla Green, Elizabeth Dobbs, Gay Johnson, Rory Parsons and Simon Parsons, Camera: Nick Finlayson, Ivars Berzins, Richard Kendrick, Sound: Terry King, Scott George, Joe Dolan, Assistant Editor: James Halford, Tape Operator: Janice Toomey, Rostrum Camera: Nico Vermuellen, Colourist: Paul Byrne, On-Line Editor: Colm O'Brien, Dubbing Mixer: Paddy Gibbons, 'Joyita' Photographs: Robin Wright, Family Footage and Photographs used by kind permission of Simon Parsons, Editor: Lee Hickey, Associate Producer (New Zealand): Brad Mercer, Producer: Martin Mahon, Director: Alan Gilsenan. A Yellow Asylum Films Production for Radio Telefís Éireann RTÉ.

The Kickhams (1992) 51 min.
Director: Brendan J. Byrne
Profile of the Belfast Gaelic football team based in the Ardoyne area and the cultural and political complications which result from their activities.

Credits With special thanks: Ardoyne Kickhams GAC, Joe Byrne and Family. Film Editor: Carl Haber, Photography: Peter Dorney, Sound Recordist: Mervyn Moore, Original Music: Mairtin O'Connor, Jimmy Faulkner, Produced by Brendan J. Byrne, Gil Rossellini, Francesco Catalano, Developed in association with BFI, DBA TV Belfast, PELCICULA FILMS, Glasgow, Additional Photography: John T. Davis, Conor Hammond, Alan Young, Rostum Camera: Ken Morse, Additional Sound: Alan Dickinson, Production Team: Carol Moorehead, Tore Sansonetti, Sabrina Battaglia, Additional Editors: Giorgio Conti, Roberto Olivieri, Tonino Dominici, Fausto Biaggiotti, Archive Research: Tom Cowles, Archive: Ulster Television, Legal Advice: Chilton Jones, Post Production Facilities: Fono Roma, Sound Mixer: Renato Giannelli, Sound Editor: Giorgio Conti, Digital Telecine and Titles Design: Technosound Video, Rome, Opticals: Studio 51, London, Musicians: Mairtin O'Connor (accordion), Jimmy Faulkner (guitars), Neil Martin (uileann pipes), Original Music recorded by Paul Ashe-Browne, the Barn Studio, Wicklow, Ireland, 'No Frontiers' written by Jimmy McCarthy, performed by Mary Black, 'On Eagle's Wings' performed by Deirdre Harrison and Ardoyne Youth Choir. Thanks also: Frank McCorry, Pat Murphy, Paddy McArdle, Briege Mooney, Frank McCallan, Pauline Larkin, Joe Lavery, Gerard Byrne, John Murphy, Jimmy Fennel, Greg Darby, Catherine Creed, Peter Flood, Dominic Fitzpatrick, Olivia Garret, Peter Millar, Holy Cross Church – Ardoyne, Ardoyne Fleadh Cheoil Committee '92, Marcas O'Murchu Ceilí Band,

Flying Fox Films, Writer and Director: Brendan J. Byrne. Hot Shot Films and Rossellini & Associati. © Channel Four Television London, 1993.

The Late Dr. Plunkett (1975) 27 min.
Director: Desmond Forristal

Docudrama on the life and death of Oliver Plunkett, archbishop of Armagh, who was executed in 1681. 'Interviewees' played by actors discuss the Archbishop with an off-screen reporter.

Credits Production Company: Radharc/RTÉ, Producer: Dermod McCarthy, Director, Script: Desmond Forristal, Interviewer: Dermod McCarthy, Photography, Editor: Brian O'Reilly, Sound: Patrick Carey, Art Direction: Lona Moran, Wardrobe Supervisor: Joan O'Rourke, Wigs: Maureen Carter. Cast: Edward Golden, Barry Cassin, Arthur O'Sullivan, Maire Ni Dhomhaill, Niall O'Brien, Geoffrey Golden, Edward Byrne, Hilton Edwards.

Leading the Way: A Story of Farming in Ireland 38 min.
Producer: Vincent Corcoran

Promotional film in favour of modernisation and cooperative farming. The film features sequences of dramatic reconstruction.

Credits Producer: Vincent Corcoran, Photography: Vincent Corcoran, Camera: Robert Monks, Assistant Cameramen: Seamus Corcoran, Paddy Lockhart, First Assistant Director: Matt Hennigan, Voice Over: Philip O'Flynn, Music: Ian O'Henry and Quintet, Technical Advisor: Theo O'Keane, Liaison: Dermot Jordan, Eoin O'Kelly, Sponsors: Esso Petroleum Co. Ireland Ltd.

The Leaving (1999) 4 × 25 min.
Director: Darragh Byrne

Series following the lives of students from two radically different secondary schools in their leaving-certificate year. It compares the expectations and social classes of the different students.

Credits The producers would like to thank: Thomas Hogan, Lia Dennehy, Debbie Wright, Sarah Barrett, their Families and Friends, and all who took part in the making of this series. Special thanks: the Students and Staff at Scoil Mhuire, Cork and Jobstown Community College, Frank McCarthy, Ronan Connolly. Assistant Editor: Therese McNamee, Production Assistant: Zoe Lison, Researcher/Assistant Producer: Emily Vargas, Sound Recordist: Stephen McDowell, Martin Birney, Lighting Cameraman: Ciaran Tanham, Additional Footage: Richard Kendrick, Michael O'Rourke, Ken O'Mahony, Mixer: Bobby O'Reilly, Music: Niall Byrne, Editor: Guy Montgomery, Director: Darragh Byrne, Producers: Adrian Lynch, Darragh Byrne. A Graph Films Production for RTÉ © 1999.

A Letter from Ulster (1943) 44 min.
Director: Brian Desmond Hurst

The experiences of American servicemen in Northern Ireland during the Second World War.

Credits Producer: William MacQuitty, Driector: Brian Desmond Hurst.

Life for the Soil (1966)
Director: John Armstrong

Agricultural film promoting the development of bogland for peat harvesting through modern methods.

Credits Director: John Armstrong, Sponsors: Celtic Film Productions, Bord na Móna.

Lifeline (1949) 20 min.
Director: William J. Moylan
Promotional film highlighting the importance of shipping to the Irish economy. The film
features scenes of dramatic reconstruction.
Credits Producer: William J. Moylan, Director: William J. Moylan, Script: P. P. Maguire,
Narrator: Bart Bastable, First Assistant Director: Stanley Moore, Photography:
George Fleischmann, Denis Courtney.

The Light of Other Days (1971) 50 min.
Director: Kieran Hickey
Irish life at the turn of the century in the photographs of Robert French. Extension of the
short *Faithful Departed* with a slightly broader focus.
Credits Production Company: BAC Films, Director: Kieran Hickey, Narrator: Colin
Blakely, Maeve Kean, Editor: Patrick Duffner, Script: Des Hickey, Photography:
Sean Corcoran, Roland Hill, Editor: Patrick Jones, Robert Ballagh, Sound Record-
ing: Douglas Turner, Dialogue Editing: Dea Lane Studios, Singer: Frank Patterson,
Instrumentalist: Edward Beckett, Sponsors: Esso Teoranta, Photographs: Robert
French from the William Lawrence Collection, National Gallery, Photographic
Printing: Richard Dann Studios.

The Little People (1970) 7 min.
Director: Richard Taylor
Speculation on the role of small industry and traditional crafts in the face of the change
from local to global culture in the twentieth century.
Credits Production Company: Vincent Corcoran Productions Ltd, Producer: Vincent
Corcoran, Director: Richard Taylor, Photography: Vincent Corcoran, Assistant
Cameraman: Robin Boyd, Script: Tony Gray, Narrator: Michael Hority, First Assis-
tant Director: Dodd Humphries, Editor: Perry Holder, Assistant Editor: Jerry Reid,
Electricians: Tommy Curran, Sound, Liam Saurin, Pat Hayes, Terry Eiffe, Sponsors:
Shell BP (Ireland) Ltd.

A Long Way to Go (1978) 30 min.
Director: Joe McCarthy
The struggle of disabled persons to find a place in the broader community as seen
through the eyes of a halfway house community in Goatstown, Dublin.
Credits Presented by: St Michael's House, Consultant Editors: Dr Barbara Stokes, St
Michael's House, Dr Michael Mulcahy, Stewart's Hospital, Mr Pat Maloney, St.
Michael's House, Narration: Pat Nolan, Sound: Paul O'Flynn, Lighting: Cine Elec-
tric Ltd, Sound Mixer: Pat Hayes, Production Assistant: Marie Penston-Graham,
Animation: Aidan Hickey, Film Editor: James Morris, Director/Camera: Joe
McCarthy, Producer: Jim Sherwin. A Strathin Enterprises Film, 1978.

Look Up and Live: Ireland in Transition (1965) 2 × 27 min.
Director: Portman Pagett
American-Produced (CBS TV) two-part programme in the tradition of CBS's *Ireland:
The Tear and the Smile* which surveys contemporary Irish social and political live,
interviewing prominent thinkers and speakers.
Credits Production Company: CBS News, Producer: Pamela Islett, Director: Portman
Pagett, Script, Interviewer: Ben Flynn, Narrator: Martyn Green, Photography:
Robert Monks, Sound: Liam Saurin, Editors: George Loughran, Richard Sarna, Liai-
son: Richard J. Walsh, Robert J. Allen, Sponsors: National Council for Catholic Men.

The Love that Dare Not Speak Its Name (2000) 50 min.

Director: Bill Hughes

A history of homosexuality in Ireland and the issues faced by campaigners for gay rights.

Credits 'Come Out Everybody' written and performed by Maria Walsh and Carole Nelson of Zrazy. All colour photographs by: Christopher Robson. Special thanks to: Gráinne McAleer, Kevin Dawson, John Cooney, Caroline Matthews, Lydia Prior, Norma O'Connor, Stephen D'Arcy, Lillian Mohin, Sunniva O'Flynn, Gary Hodkinson, Monica O'Connor, Máire Harris, Gerry Ryan, Paul Russell. Archive: Irish Film Archive, RTÉ Film Library, the Abbey Theatre, RTÉ Stills Library, Glasgow Women's Library, Magill Magazine, the *Irish Times*, the National Library of Ireland, the Dept of Foreign Affairs, the Dublin Writer's Museum, Gael-Linn, the Onlywomen Press, the Gate Theare Dublin. Programme Consultants: Ailbhe Smyth, Christopher Robson, Kieran Rose, Make-Up: Patsy Giles, Rostrum Camera: Nico Vermeulen, Researchers: Carol Ann O'Brien, Ruth O'Looney, Camera: Ronan Fox, Ciaran Tanham, Christian O'Brien, Sound: Stephen McDowell, Karl Merren, Production Team: Vernon Crowley, Peter Greene, Louise Howe, Kelley McMenamin, Production Coordinator: Ruth O'Looney, Graphics: Kirsten Clarke, Melanie Langlotz, David Sarbell, Offline Editors: Pat Hodgins, Gordon Prenter, Pat McKinley, Zaini Daragh, On-Line Editor: Dave Burke, Executive Producer: Declan Farrell, Producer/Director: Bill Hughes. A Radius Television Production for RTÉ © 2000.

Luke (1999) 71 min.

Director: Sinéad O'Brien

Profile of folk singer Luke Kelly, whose life experience mirrors aspects of the development of political consciousness in 1960s and 1970s Ireland. The film features interviews with many prominent Irish people including Bono, Noel Pearson, Christy Moore, John Hume and Gerry Adams.

Credits Production Coordinator: Joan Lambe, First Assistant Director: Daisy Cummins, Archive Research: Christine Thornton, Foreign Archive Research: Sinéad Murphy, Additional Research: Ann Marie Eviston, Trumpet Solo: Earl Gill, Sound: Brendan Deasy, Assistant Camera: Donal Gillan, Conor Kenny, Camera Trainee: Sinéad Murphy, Additional Sound: Karl Merren, Pat Hayes, Kieran Horgan, Electrician: Maurice Swan, Make-Up: Barbara Conway, Post-Production Facilities: Windmill Lane Pictures, Metrocolor London Ltd, Originated on 16 mm Kodak Eastman stock, On-Line Editor: Colm O'Brien, Ian O'Brien, Colourist: Gerard Ward, Dubbing Mixer: Paddy Gibbons at Number 4 Studios, Legal Services: James Hickey, Insurance: Network Ireland, Film Archive Courtsey of: Radio Telefís Éireann, Irish Film Archive of the Film Institute of Ireland, the Ed Sullivan Show courtesy of Sofa Entertainment, London Weekend Television, Cultural Fantasists Ltd, BBC, Aspekt Telefilm Production GMBH, Telepool, YLE Finish Broadcasting Company, ITN, Radharc, O'Connor O'Sullivan Advertising, the National Library of Ireland, Beamish & Crawford, Ian Campbell, Philip Donnellan Estate, Barbara Durack – RTÉ Programme Archive, Photo Credits: RTÉ Photo Library, the Kelly Family, Roy Esmonde, Paddy Monaghan, Ronnie Drew, John Sheahan, Terry Fagan, Terry Connaughton, Colm Henry, Eileen Whiting, Emmett O'Connell, Kate Thompson, Monitor Syndication, Main Photo Stills: Richard Dann, Bronze Bust of Luke Kelly by: Rosie Rathdonnell. Luke Kelly Collection available on the Outlet label nationwide. All efforts have been made to source ownership of the archive material used in this film. If any ommissions have occurred, they are entirely unintentional. Researched by: Sinéad O'Brien, Original Music: Richie Buckley, Story Consultant: Mary Maher, Narration written by: Judy Friel, Narrated by: Stephen Rea, Director of Photography: Cian de Buitléar, Editor: Stephen O'Connell. Special thanks: Ian Campbell, Peggy Seeger, Sunniva O'Flynn, Jill Donnellan, Mick McCarthy, Deirdre Drew, Terry Fagan, Harriet Roche, Johnny Giles, John Sheahan, Paddy Reilly, Barney McKenna, Sean Cannon, Des Hanafin, Eamon Campbell, Mick O'Riordan, Ray Treacy, Michael Doolan, Oliver Hougham, St Lawrence O'Toole CBS, Jimmy Whelan, Kate Thompson, Dave Quinn, Martin Crowe at Windmill Lane Pictures, Fiona Tate at the Charles Parker Archive, Birmingham, Clare Gillam at the National Sound Archive, London, Mary Hardy, Eamon Dignam, Terry Connaughton, Michael Holland at Kodak Ireland Ltd, Directed by: Sinéad O'Brien, Produced by: Noel Pearson. Produced by Ferndale Films for Radio Telefís Éireann, Bord Scannán na hÉireann/the Irish Film Board and Irish Nationwide Building Society. © RTÉ 1999. Worldwide Distribution Ferndale Films Ltd.

The Madness from Within (1998) 50 min.
Director: Colm Magee

The first notable film attempt to document the years and events of the Irish Civil War and to examine the consequences of the civil war mentality for contemporary Irish culture.

Credits Presenter: Bryan Dobson, Music: David Downes, Opening Animation: Rory Kelleher, Camera: Donal Wylde, Sound Recordist: Jim Wylde, Film Editing: Robert Duffy, Research: Sheila Ahern, Sinead Canning, Produced and Directed by: Colm Magee. © Radio Telefís Éireann 1998.

Male Rape: Men Overcoming Rape and Sexual Abuse (1996) 44 min.
Director: Liam McGrath

The experiences of several males who have been either raped or sexually abused. The film features dramatic reconstructions.

Credits Director: Liam McGrath, Producer: Garry Keane, Film and Dialogue Editing: Emer Reynolds, Assistant Editor and Sound Editor: Mick Mahon, Lighting: Conor O'Mahony, Camera Operators: Garry Keane, Liam McGrath, Production Assistant: Alison Toomey, Assistant Sound Editor: Dave Burrows, Music: Gavin Harte, Sound F/X Recording: Benny Lynch, Kelly-Ann O'Neill, Graphics: Anastasia Clafferty, Rostrum Camera: Ken Morse, Post-Production Facility: the Loopline, Couriers: City Air Express, Sound Studio: Interference, Laboratory: Rank, Lawyers: Arthur Cox & Co., Accountants: Brendan Murphy & Co., Insurance: Network Insurances, Sound Transfers: Ardmore Studios, Windmill Lane, Film Stock: Kodak, Telecine: Screen Scene, Dubbing: Richard King, World Wide, Negative Cutters: Tri-Ad. Special thanks: Leslie Bailey, Niamh Barrett, Olive Braiden, Begina Byrne, Denis Conroy, Shelia Cooke, Mark Corcoran, Joe Chalmers, Tadhg Conway, Joe Coughlin, John Cronin, John T. Davis, Daniel Jewesbury, Martin Egan, Christy Fleming, Mick Foley, Film Base, Rita and Pat Haugh, Ben Haugh, Steward Hedrington, Pat Hodgins, Roisin Hogan, Andria Johnston, Jim, Peg and Trish Keane, Damien Kearns, Justin Kilvan, Max Krzyzanowski, John Leinster, Shane Lynch, Mark Marshall, Martin Mahon, Jim and Rita Mahon, Sé Merry Doyle, Neil Mockter, Paddy Moran, Dorothy Morrissey, Anne Mithcell, Dominica McGowan, Denis and Hannah McGrath, Kieran McGrath, Helen McCreery, Linda Nartey, Grace O'Malley, Edel O'Brien, Damien O'Donnell, Fergus O'Farrell, Val O'Kelly, Anne O'Leary, Vera O'Leary, Ger O'Loughlin, Deirdre O'Neill, Dylan O'Neill, Paul O'Neill, Michael O'Reilly, Aiden Quigley, Declan Reddy, Maeve Reynolds, Fintan Ryan, Robbie Ryan, Anakana Schofield, Joe and Marie Sheerin, Jon Sibbons, Ailbhe Smith, Jim Thomson, Shelia Vereher, Cathi Weldon. Executive Producer for Bord

Scannán na hÉireann/the Irish Film Board: Rod Stoneman, Executive Producer for Radio Telefís Éireann: Martin Mahon. A Scratch Films Production for Bord Scannán na hÉireann/the Irish Film Board and Radio Telefís Éireann 1996.

March of a Nation (1949) 16 min.

Director: E. J. H. Wright

A newsreel account of the festivities surrouding the declaration of the Republic, including speeches by Irish politicians and foreign diplomats.

Credits Production Company: Paramount Pictures Corporation, Director: E. J. H. Wright, Script: John Stagg, Narrator: P. P. O'Reilly, Production Assistant: Arthur Smith, Photography: Georg Feischmann, Ronald Ream, Sound: Leonard Dudley, Editor: Albert Stockwell, Victor Stocker, Music: J. W. Hall.

The Marshall Plan at Work in Ireland (1950)

Director: Jim Mellor

Account of how $200 million will help to update and preserve Irish agriculture, including details of modernisation, rural electrification and peat harvesting.

Credits Production Company: Editorial Film Productions, Producer, Director: Jim Mellor, Script: Arthur C. Marshall, Narrator: Jack Ralph, Photography: Brendan Stafford, Assistant Cameraman: Liam O'Leary, Editor: Dudley Birch.

Men for the Harvest (1963) 25 min.

Director: Chloe Gibson

A portrait of the seminary at St Patrick's College, Maynooth. The film's original soundtrack was lost after its first screening in 1963. It was recovered and subsequently restored for a special screening at the Irish Film Centre on 25 May 1998.

Credits Voice Over: Padraig Ó Raghailaigh, Editor: Roger M. Johnston, Sound: Bill O'Neill, Jim Quinn, Lights: Charles Scott, Writer/Director: Chloe Gibson. A Telefís Éireann Production © 1963. Camera: Seamus Smith, Michael Monaghan.

Miles and Miles of Music (1975) 20 min.

Director: Éamon de Buitléar

Profile of musician and music archivist Séamus Ennis, featuring encounters with many other traditional singers.

Credits Featuring: Séamus Ennis, Design: Nora Butler, Sound: Pat Hayes, Photography/Production: Éamon de Buitléar.

Mise Éire / I am Ireland (1959) 90 min.

Director: George Morrison

Archival compilation charting the history of Ireland to 1919, with particular empahsis on the years 1916–19. The film focuses on the struggle for Irish independence, drawing on certain elements of penal history to establish the framework for the years which are of primary concern. The first part of an incomplete trilogy. Followed by *Saoirse?*

Credits Director/Producer: George Morrison, Writer: Seán Mac Réamoinn, Narrators: Liam Budhlaeir, Pádraigh G. O'Raghallaigh, Aindreas O'Gallchoir, Director of Photography: Vincent H. Corcoran, Music Composed and Conducted by: Seán O'Riada, Orchestra: the Radio Éireann Symphony Orchestra, Instrumentalist: Tomas Reck, Sound: Peter Hunt, Gene Martin, Assistant Editors: Louis Marcus, Caitríona O'Briain, Theodora Fitzgibbon, Seán O'Briain, Historical Consultant: Tomás P. O'Neill. Gael-Linn.

Mists of Time (1968)

Director: Patrick Carey

The mysteries of Ireland's megalithic monuments are examined in the context of pagan mythology.

Credits Director/Photography: Patrick Carey, Editor: Jeannine Bradlaugh, Production Assistant: Penny Cabot, Commentary: Tom St John Barry. An Aenghus Films production for RTÉ.

The Moon on My Back (1996) 40 min.

Director: Jonathan White

The story of poet and AIDS campaigner Pat Tierney. The film features dramatic reconstructions.

Credits Based on the autobiography *The Moon on My Back* by Pat Tierney. Cast: John Conway (Pat on Hill), Bernard Nally (Pat in Corridor), Himself (Pat in Caravan), Jenny Blogan (Pat's Mother), Anthony Brophy (Drug Addict), Neil Heneghan (Christian Brother), Matt Ryan, Pat Shaughnessy (Boys on Motorbike). Photography: Donald Gilligan, Sound: Simon Willis, Ray Cross, Editor: Sé Merry Doyle, Production Assistant: Muirinn Lane-Kelly, Production Coordinator: Julia Roddy, Camera Assistant: Harry Purdue, Clapper/Loader: Frank Monaghan, Mark Byrne, Assistant Editors: Linda Nartey, Marino Marolini, Original Score Performed and Produced by Philip Donnelly, Stills Photography: Daniel De Chena, Michael Durand, Art Director: Padraig O'Neill, Set Dresser/Buyer: Orflaaith Stafford, Wardrobe: Monica Ennis, Jill Graves Power, Make-Up: Matthew Guinnane, Gaffer: Con Dempsey, Riggers: Kevin McCarthy, Mike Casey, Carpenter: Ben Rilot, Sound Mixer: Pat Hayes, Titles: Screen Scene, Laboratories: Metrocolour, Executive Producer for Bord Scánnan na hÉireann/the Irish Film Board: James Flynn, Executive Producer for Radio Telefís Éireann: Mary Callery. Special thanks to: Rod Stoneman, Claire Duignan, Cian De Buitléar, Paul Power, Treasure Films, John Higgins and Kevin Greene, Panavision Ireland, Conor O'Toole, Simon Walshe, Brian Shanley, University College Galway, Eamonn De Buitléar, Pat Gilligan, Renmore Barracks, Tricia Murphy, Therese Moylan, Oonagh McArdle, Ann White, Claire Power, the Swan Family, Michael O'Toole, George Birmingham, Network Insurances. Interviewer/Assistant Director: Mick Ruane, Producer: David Power, Director: Jonathan White. A JDM Production for Radio Telefís Éireann and Bord Scannán na hÉireann/the Irish Film Board. © JDM Productions, 1996.

The Morrison Tapes (1995) 4 × 38 min.

Director: Darragh Byrne

Series following the experiences of several Irish people upon emigrating to the United States. The subject of each episode was a different person from a different social background and of a different age.

Credits Special Thanks to: Sharon Beatty, Paul Hardiman, Catriona O'Connolly, TWA Ireland, Emigrant Advice, the American Embassy, James P. Callaghan, Gregory Glynn, Network Insurances, IPU (RTÉ), Dublin Flight Cases Ltd., John Carroll, Peter Moorehead, Film Lighting Facilities, James Hickey, Windmill Lane, Gary Curran, Ann Mitchell, RTÉ Film Processing, Nolan's Pub, Silken Thomas, Long Island 88.7 FM WRHU, Nassau Uniforms Ltd. Production Accountant: Alison O'Leary, Production Coordinator (US): Amy Faust, Research: Marie Keegan, Sound Recordist: Stephen McDowell, Lighting Cameraman: Ronan Fox, Audiofile: Enda Boner – Telefael, Editor: Guy Montgomery, Anner Facilities, Production Assistant: Joanne O'Hagan, Music: Niall Byrne, Associate Producer: Brian Lynch,

Producer and Director: Darragh Byrne. A Graph Films Production for Radio Telefís Éireann © 1995.

Mother Ireland (1988; first broadcast 1993) 55 min.

Director: Anne Crilly

An exploration of the use and abuse of the image of femininity in Ireland, including its religious and political contexts.

Credits 'Mother Ireland' is dedicated to the memory of Miriam James. We gratefully acknowledge the assistance of: Film Base, Pilot's Row Community Centre, Nazareth House Convent School, McIntyre's Butcher Shop, Linenhall Library, Ulster Folk and Transport Museum, Cultra, Dublin Castle (State Papers Office), National Monuments Branch, Trinity College Library, Kilmainham Gaol Museum, National Wax Museum, Central Bank of Ireland, Travellers Centre (Dublin), City of Sheffield Art Gallery, Graves Art Gallery Manchester, AP/RN Photographs, Pace-Maker Photo Agency, Westport Parish, Knock Parish. Special Thanks to: Anne Forbes, Sister Louis, Marie McIntyre, Michael Quirke, Ruby Todd, Chrissie Ward and Family, Denny Elliot, Chris Bratton, Fergus Tighe, Christy Moore, Michael Gallagher, Nuala Crilly, Joe Mulheron, Jackie Crawford, Brian Moore, Marie Bean Ui Ghralaigh, Peter Moloney, Sean Grant, Dan Gilbert, Camerawork Derry, Archive Footage: Movietone, Pathé, R.T.E., John Reilly and Stefan Moore, John McGuirk, RAI, Music: 'Ireland Mother Ireland', 'Larkin', 'Four Green Fields' (Maura Starkie), 'Coast River' (Donal Lunny), Gael-Linn © 1987, 'Roisin Dubh', 'Give an Irish Girl to Me', (Eamon Toland and Malcolm Wray), 'What a Wonderful World' (Helen Brady), Production Equipment: Broadcast Facilities North, Post-Production Facility: Air TV, Rostrum Camera: Rocksteady Rostrum, Editorial Consultant: Annie Goldson, Editor: Mike Shirra, Researched and Directed by: Anne Crilly, Produced by: Derry Film and Video, Anne Crilly, Jim Curran, Stephanie English, Margo Harkin, Tomas Mac Coileain, Geraldine McGuinness, Brendan McMenamin. DFV © 1988.

Mr. Careless Goes to Town (1949) 10 min.

Director: Liam O'Leary

Safety film using dramatic reconstruction to highlight the dangers of failing to follow traffic regulations.

Credits Director: Liam O'Leary, Photography: George Fleischmann, Narrator: Terry O'Sullivan, Editor: Len Green, Sound Supervisor: Arthur Smith, Sponsors: Dept. of Local Government. Cast: Desmond Keane, Liam O'Leary.

My Great Grandmother was a Boxer (1997) 52 min.

Director: Niall Byrne

Was Catherine Moylan's great grandmother a turn-of-the-century female pugilist? A personal investigation featuring scenes of dramatic reconstruction.

Credits For Agnes. Assistant Camera: Declan King, Focus Pullers: Darryl Byrne, Kurt Savage, Clapper Loader: Roger Kenny, Gaffers: Con Dempsey, Graeme Haughton, Electricians: Nick Fitzgerald, Ian Madden, Stephen Doyle, Grips: Oisin Kelly, John Connon, Trainees: Barry Cullen, Conall McCarrigle, Make-Up: Mary Lamb, Carol Walsh, Hair: Edel Cheasty, Casting: Denise Deasy, Rostrum: Ken Morse, Telecine: Glen Kyte, Art Director: Julian King, Assistant Art Director: Laurent Mellet, Costume Designer: Sharon Beatty, PA/Researcher: Maeve Treby, Dubbing Mixer: Bobby O'Reilly, Production Accountant: Alison O'Leary, Executive Producer for Bord Scannán na hÉireann: Rod Stoneman. Cast: Polly Fairclough: Susannah de Wrixon, Young Polly: Kate O'Reilly, Old Polly: June Thorpe, Agnes: Chrissie de

Vesey, Tommy Lynch: Jonathan Shankey, Jack Johnson: Fraser Mushibwe, Tommy Burns: Richard Boyle, Frankie Walsh: Michael Dunleavy, Maid: Ciara O'Callaghan, Bully: Martin Branagan, Young Catherine: Deirdre Walsh, Young Boy AT Wedding: Leon Leonard, Extras: Tara McFadden, Bernard Doyle, Natasha Brerton, Benny Carabini, Brendan Galvin, Clive Jacobs, Thomas Bolger, Jackie Dwyer, Colin Kenney, Fred Tiedt, Brenard Gorman, Noel Young, Carmel Cillen, Frank McQuade, Michael Lynchebaum, Paul Ryan, John Dwyer, Marie King, Peter Houlihan, Gary Coyle, Noel Byrne, Jack Kelly, Siobhan Chambers, Eunan McDonald, Louise Duggan, Emma Walsh, Barabara Kelly, Sarah Cullen, Lorna Doak, Trevor McDonnell, Gavin McDonnell. Thanks to: National Library of Ireland, the Royal Society of Antiquaries of Ireland, the Irish Architectural Archive, St Bartholomew's Church, St Nicholas of Myra Parish Centre, Peter Pearson, An Taisce, Iveagh Trust, Liberties College, Grace Duncan, Glasnevin Cemetery, Gail Heffernan at Jenny Vander, Rufus the Cat, Wigwam, Freda Hoban at Samuel Beckett Centre, Chas Taylor, David Roake, Larry Braysher, Bill Schutte, Alan Martin, Robin Zonenbilck, James Electrical, Cafe Royal, John Morris of British Boxing Board of Control, British Pahte, the *Daily Mail*, the Clarendon in Blackheath, Association Freres Lumiere, Camera Rentals, Film Lighting Facilities, Wave Widger, Murphy's Newsagents, Coffey's School of Drama. Special thanks to: Catherine Morley & Family, Kathleen Morley, Freda, Charlotte Bourke, Ide O'Carroll, Barbara Buttrick, Irish Ex-Boxers' Choir, John McCormac, Paul Ryan, Duffy's Circuc, James Hickey, High Wire Creative Editing, Rod Stoneman, the Arts Council, Mary Callery, RTÉ, Script: Catherine Morley, Niall Byrne, Sound: Paco Hayes, Photographed by: Harry Purdue, Editor: Guy Montgomery, Assistant Producer: Emily Vargas, Producers: Adrian Lynch, Darragh Byrne, Director/Composer: Niall Byrne. A Graph Films Production for RTÉ and Bord Scannán na hÉireann in association with the Arts Council © 1997.

A Nation Once Again (1946) 18 min.
Director: Brendan Stafford
A celebration of the political ideas of nineteenth-century revolutionary Thomas Davis related to the state of 1940s Ireland. The film features scenes of dramatic reconstruction.
Credits Production Company: National Film Institute of Ireland, Director, Photography: Brendan Stafford, Script: John D. Sheridan, Music: Capt. Bowles, Orchestra: Radio Éireann, Assistant Director: Colm Ó Laoghaire.

Navigatio: Atlantean II (1998) 61 min.
Director: Bob Quinn
Sequel to *Atlantean* continuing the thesis that Irish culture owes its roots to peoples of far-flung countries.
Credits Producer: Miriam Allen, Directors of Photography: Edel O'Brien, Norbert Payne, Sound: Enda Bonner, Editor: Mary Crumlish, Music: Roger Doyle, Sponsors: Telefís na Gaelige, Bord Scannán na hÉireann.

Neodrach Éireann / 'The Emergency' in Ireland (1996) 6 × 30 min.
Director: Justin McCarthy
A detailed history of Irish neutrality during the Second World War taking into account events outside and inside the state during that period known as 'the emergency'.
Credits A White Hunter Production for TnaG. Narrator: Mick Lally. Cartlann ó: Lamancha Visnews/Reuters DFAVS, Scéalaí: Mick Lally, Taighdeoirí agus Script: Charlie

McBride, Deirdre Learmont, Justin McCarthy, Adelaide Nic Chárthaigh, Eagarthóir Script: Deirdre Learmont, Ceamara: Billy Keady, Christine Ní Choncubhair, Joe McCarthy, Fuaim: Máire Ní Earcáin, Cathal Ó Méalóid, Réamonn de Brún, Fuaim-riain: RTÉ Commercíal Ents Ltd., Cathal Ó Méalóid, Graificí: Virtual Light, Eagarthóirí: Gordon Bruic, Neil McLauchlan, Léiritheorí, Adelaide Níc Chárthaigh, Justin McCarthy, Stiúrthóir: Justin McCarthy, Léiriú de chuid White Hunter do TnaG © TnaG 1996.

Next Please (1948) 10 min.
Director: William Moylan
Road safety film sponsored by the Dept of Local Government.
Credits Script: P. P. Maguire, Narrator: Bart Bastable, Executive Producer: Desmond Egan, Production Company: Hibernia Films, George Fleischmann, Michael Scott, Director: William Moylan, Sponsor: Dept of Local Government.

Oiche Sheanachais / Storyteller's Night (1934) 10 min.
Producer: Robert Flaherty
Short film featuring storyteller Tomás Ó Díorain relating a tale in Irish to members of the cast of *Man of Aran*.
Credits Production Company: the Dept of Education, Production Facility: Gaumont Studios, London, Producer: Robert Flaherty, With: Tomás Ó Díorain.

Oisín (1970) 17 min.
Director: Patrick Carey
Impressionistic study of the Irish landscape accompanied by natural sounds and birdcalls but no voice over and no musical score. The film was produced to celebrate the European Year of Conservation.
Credits Production Company: Aengus, Producers: Vivien Carey, Patrick Carey, Director: Patrick Carey, Photography: Patrick Carey, Assistant Producer: Joe Mendoza, Editor: Eric Mival, Assistant Editor: Penny Cabot, Sound: Damien Power, Assistant Director: Dodo Humphries, Assistant Cameraman: Liam Miller, Sponsors: the Dept of External Affairs.

On a Paving Stone Mounted (1978) 96 min.
Director: Thaddeus O'Sullivan
Experimental docudrama blending documentary footage with actors recounting the experiences of Irish emigrants living in London. A feature-length extension of *A Pint of Plain*.
Credits Production Company: BFI Production Department, Producer, Editor: Mary Pat Leece, Director, Script, Photography: Thaddeus O'Sullivan, Assistant Cameraman: Dick Perrin, Editor: Roger Ollerhead, Sound: Christopher Swayne, Music: Christy Moore; Cast: Jim O'Neill, Paul Bennett, Frederick Ireves, May Cluskey, Mark Long, Christy Moore. Maureen Toal, Edward de Souza, Gerard Flynn, Paul Copley, Beth Porter, Eamon Kelly, Arthur O'Sullivan, Annabel Leventon, Peter Caffrey, Miriam Margoyles, Olivia Walker, Derrick O'Connor, John Murphy, Anne Balfour, Gabriel Byrne, Billy Murray, Stephen Rea.

The One-Nighters (1963) 40 min.
Director: Peter Collinson
Film following the adventures of the Royal Showband on tour throughout Ireland. The film received a certificate of merit at the Cork Film Festival of 1963.

Credits A TRPS Presentation. Written, Produced and Directed by Peter Collinson, Photographed and Edited by Bob Monks, Sound Recordist: Bill O'Neill, Assistant Camera: Séamus Corcoran, Unit Manager: Jackie Dunne, Production Assistant: Kathy Muldoon, Titles by William McCune. A Collinson & Monks Production.

Operation Shamrock (1997) 50 min.

Director: Simon Wood

The story of German children brought to foster homes in Ireland following the Second World War, some of whom remained and became Irish citizens.

Credits Dedicated to Werner Friedrichs who was the inspiration for this film and who died in June 1997. Thanks to: the German Embassy, Dublin, the Irish Red Cross, Arts Council of Ireland, Irish Times, Glencree Centre for Reconciliation, Eithne Ní Dhalaigh, Dieter Gerlitz, Antje Dingles, Participants: Elizabeth O'Gorman (née Kohlberg), Ernie Berkenheier, Hildegard Jones (née Grabsch), Marlene Byrne (née Grabsch), Gisela Broderick (née Berns), Miriam Carroll, Margarete Birchholz, Eva Remmel, Herbert Remmel, Anna Zakiz, Heidi Schwandt-Boden, Music: Debra Salem, Archive: British Movietone News, Irish Film Archive, Public Records Office, London, Little Girl: Orlaith Graham Wood, Research: Síobhan Morris, Translators: Cathy Molohan, John Quinn, Sound: Mark Alexander, Camera: Michael Quinn, Simon Wood. Peter Millar, Assistant Editor: Michael Crilly, Editor: Dagmar O'Neill, Production Manager: Peter Millar, Associate Producers: Beate Veldtrup, Steve Smith, Produced and Directed by: Simon Wood; A Banter Production for RTÉ in association with the Northern Ireland Arts Council and Northern Visions.

Our Boys (1981; first broadcast 1991) 40 min.

Director: Cathal Black

Drama charting the final days of a Christian Brothers' school intercut with archival footage of public ceremonies and interviews with former students who experienced harsh discipline at the hands of the Brothers and even one Brother who discusses the 'mistakes' that may have been made. The film was not screened on Irish television until ten years after its original completion.

Credits Screenplay: Dermot Healy in collaboration with Cathal Black. The Brothers were played by: Archie O'Sullivan, Michael Lally, Noel O'Donovan, Terry Orr, Kieran Hinds, Vinnie McCabe, Séamus Ellis, George Keegan, With: Paul Bennett (Lay-Teacher), Brendan Ellis, Jimmy Brennan, Dermot Healy (Politicians), Dermot Lynskey (Priest), Johnny Murphy (Van Driver), Charlie Roberts, Liam Stack (Surveyors), Tom Jordan (Father), Anne O'Connor (Mother), Boys in Classroom One: Paul Connolly, John Costelloe, Desmond Whelan, Jonathan White, Joseph Brophy, Anthony Pender, Declan Stapelton, Jesse McGee, Liam Elston, Dennis Bowes, Declan Kenny, Georgie Bowes, Tony Murray, Terry Quirk, Georgie Walter, Liam Calfcart, Paul Kinsella, Laurence Kinsella, Michael Doyle, Pat Bowes, Gerard Kinsella, Christy Kelly, Morgan Blackmore, Christopher Tierney, Robert Meade, James McSherry, Peter Kavanagh, Francis Donoghue, Derek Whelan, John Lynch, Vincent Merriman, Patrick Coleman. Interviews with: Damian Moore 'They used to say, no bodily contact and we used to get beaten up when we wrestled.' The Brother – John C. Moore 'This whole question of the emotional area is very much, to me, a very recent development.' Tony McMahon 'Never in my life have I had such an intense feeling of coldness inside me.' Camera and Lighting: Thaddeus O'Sullivan, Camera Assistant: Art O'Laoghaire, Sound Recordist: Michael Ostroff, Sound Mixing: Pat Hayes, Production Crew: Jacinta Deignan, Barbara Bradshaw, Geraldine O'Reilly, Brendan Ellis, Anne O'Brien, Philip Boxburger, Niall Meehan, Ruth Bradshaw,

Christy McGinn, Asistant Director: Liam Mulcahy, Pick-Up Photography, Camera and Lighting: Shane O'Neill, Props: Nuala McKernan, Assistant Director: John Lawlor, Camera Assistant: Aidan McGuinness. Post-Production Crew: Track Laying: Rob Selleck, Sound Transfers: Tim Morris, Sound Recordist: Kieran Horgan, Couriers: Maggie Mooney, Transport: MZU 330; Film Editor: Sé Merry Doyle, Director: Cathal Black. 'Our Boys' could not have been made without the following people: Jacinta Deignan, Barbara Bradshaw, Joe Bowes, Dermot Healy, Morris Russell Avis, Editing. This film was made with the financial assistance of the Arts Council of Northern Ireland, An Comhairle Ealaion (the Arts Council), the National Film Studios of Ireland. Produced by Cathal Black © in association with Radio Telefís Éireann.

Our Country (1948) 7 min.
Director: Liam O'Leary

Campaign film for Clann na Poblachta, a new political party contesting the general election of 1948. It features pieces to camera delivered by its leaders interspersed with footage of contemporary Ireland which includes images of poverty and emigration previously unseen on Irish screens.

Credits Director: Liam O'Leary, Script: Maura Laverty, Narrator: Noel Hartnett, Camera: Brendan Stafford, Studios: Elstree Studios. Liam O'Leary (shopkeeper). Irish Civic Films.

Our Neighbours' Children (1960) 10 min.
Director: Colm Ó Laoghaire

Profile of St Mary's Hospital, Baldoyle, an institution devoted to the care of disabled children.

Credits Presented by: Lever Bros (Ireland) Ltd, Commentary: Ray McAnally, Camera: Jim Mulkerns, Assistant: Val Ennis, Recording: Peter Hunt Studios, Location Sound: Donal Shanahan, Writer/Producer/Director: Colm Ó Laoghaire on behalf of Baldoyle orthopaedic hospital building fund committee (Little Willie), Dublin, Ireland.

Paddy Carey: Film Maker (1999) 55 min.
Director: Peter Canning

Profile of documentarist and cinematographer Patrick Carey, director of *Yeats Country* and *Oisín*, featuring excerpts from many of his films.

Credits Special thanks to: Vivien Carey, Clodine Carey, Piers Carey, Don Haig (National Film Board of Canada Montreal), Sandra Swann (National Film Board of Canada London Branch), Simon Brown (the British Film Institute UK National Film and TV Archive (London)), Reuters Viznews (London), Columbia Tristar International Television (London), the Museum of the Moving Image (London), Canal Plus Images (Pinewood Studios Buckinghamshire), Ted Shorthouse (Colour Film Services London), Eric Liknaitzky (Contemporary Films London), Linda Middleton (TVP Transfer Facility House London), Abigail Hughes (BBC Enterprises London), Linda Ayton (Secretary to Fred Zinnemann), Nordisk Film Broadcast AS (Copenhagen), John Turpin (National College of Art and Design, Dublin), the Danish Embassy (Dublin), The Irish Department of Foreign Affairs, Sunniva O'Flynn, Liam Wylie (The Film Institute of Ireland, the Irish Film Archive), Rod Stoneman (Chief Executive Bord Scannán na hÉireann/the Irish Film Board), Sandford Park College, Castleknock College, Muiris MacConghail, Tin Whistle: Paddy Moloney (the Chieftains), Script and Interviewing: Peter Canning, Narration: Gabriel Byrne,

Research: Clodine Carey, Peter Canning, RTÉ Programme Archive: Barbara Durack, Pauline Godwin, Graphic Design: Elena Doyle, Graphics Operator: Martha Powell, Rostrum Camera: Nico Vermuelen, Lorraine Sherry. Filming in Ireland: Lighting: Jim Butler, Eddie Bolger, Sound: Pat Doyle, Darby Carroll, Michael Murray, Martin Cronin, Camera: Robert Monks, Production Assistant: Carmel Duignan. Filming in Canada: Production Manager: Chris Medawar, Lighting: Guy Remillard, Sound: Hans Oomes, Margot McMaster, Camera: Tony Lanzelo, Douglas Munro, Camera Assistant: Dean Mitchell, Production Assistant: Marie Penston. Filming in England: Sound: Pat Johns, Lighting Cameraman: Godfrey Graham, Assistant: Darryl L. Byrne, Production Assistant: Nuala Malone, Video Grading: Glen Kyte (Screen Scene), Sound Dubbing: Bob Bell, Audio Post-Production: Peter Fletcher, Video Post-Production: Alan Magrath, Video Editors: Mercedes Garvey, Tommy Mongey, Production Assistant: Marie Penston, Producer/ Director: Peter Canning. © RTÉ 1999.

Páisti ag Obair / Children at Work (1973) 10 min.
Director: Louis Marcus
From the premise 'play is the work of the child', this film explores the activity and movements of children at play in Dublin Montessori schools. The film won an International Critics Award at the Cork Film Festival in 1973, was selected as Oustanding Film of the Year at the London Film Festival and nominated for an American Academy of Motion Picture Arts and Sciences Award.
Credits Production Company: Gael-Linn, Producer, Director, Script: Louis Marcus, Photography: Robert Monks, Sponsors: Roinn na Gaeltachta.

'Patrick Fergus: Sheep Farmer' (untitled) 20 min.
No director credited.
First-person account of the life of Patrick Fergus, a Co. Mayo sheep farmer. The film was part of an episode of the RTÉ television series on agricultural affairs entitled *Landmark*.
Credits Production Company: RTÉ.

Partition Protest Parade (1946) 6 min.
No director credited.
Silent agit-prop featuring footage of anti-partition protest march in Dublin. This film and its companion piece *Treasna an Teorann* may have been directed by Liam O'Leary.
Credits Aiséirge present.

'Patriots to a Man': The Blueshirts and Their Times (2000) 50 min.
Producer: Nick Coffey
The history of the Irish proto-fascist political organisation which rose and fell in the 1930s.
Credits Cameras: Tony Cournane, John Curtis, Neilus Dennehy, Brendan Frawley, Paddy Higgins, Michael Lee, Seamus Rushe, Donal Wilde, Picture Editor: Zaini Darragh, Additional Video Editing: Neil Agney, Donal O'Neill, Post-Production Sound: Peter Fletcher, Additional Research: Ben Kelly, Executive Producer: Edward Mulhall, Writer/Producer: Nick Coffey. © RTÉ News 2000.

Peil (1962) 60 min.
Director: Louis Marcus
Profile of Gaelic football, one of the main sports of the Gaelic Athletic Association.
Credits Director: Louis Marcus, Sponsors: Gael-Linn.

A Pint of Plain (1975) 40 min.

Directors: Thaddeus O'Sullivan, Derrick O'Connor

Experimental docudrama blending documentary footage with actors recounting the experiences of Irish emigrants living in London. A trial run for the feature *On a Paving Stone Mounted*.

Credits Directors: Thaddeus O'Sullivan, Derrick O'Connor, Script: Thaddeus O'Sullivan, Derrick O'Sullivan, Sound: Giles Foster, Photography: Dick Perrin.

Pobal (1970) 25 min.

Director: Louis Marcus

Overview of aspects of Irish life featuring footage shot in various parts of the country. During production this film was entitled *Meascra Muintire* / The People of Ireland.

Credits Photography: Robert Monks, Sound: Peter Hunt, Commentary: Brendán Ó hEithir, Narrator: Niall Tobín, Music: Seán Ó Riada, Orchestra: Ceoltoriri Cualann, Sponsors: Gael-Linn, the Department of the Gaeltacht, Eastmancolour.

Poochers (1989) 17 min.

Director: Denis McArdle

The experiences and lives of traditional Dublin scrap merchants. The film features interviews with several different members of this dying profession.

Credits Poochers: Kevin Murphy, Thomas Salinger, Tom Maher, Ollie Bolger, Gene Hughes, Camera Operator: Stephen Kane, Michael Masterson, Dubbing: Bobby Bell, Brian Lynch, Production Manager: Susan Brennan, Supervising Editor: Anne O'Leary, Editor: Richard West, Music: 'the Hell-Fire Club', Writer/Producer/Director: Denis McArdle. Thanks: BAC Films Ltd, Kodak Ireland Ltd, Hammond Lane Metal Co., Tony O'Leary, Amanda Sutton, Philip Davison, Gunther Wulff, Sally Ann O'Reilly, Laoise Mac Reamoinn, Simon O'Leary, Keith Durham, Bobby Bell. A Dun Laoghaire School of Art Production. 1989.

Portrait of Dublin (1951) 19 min.

Director: Liam O'Leary

Touristic overview of Dublin. Financed by the Cultural Relations Committee, but never released because of personal difficulties between director Liam O'Leary and the Committee.

Credits A Film for the Cultural Relations Committee of Ireland Commentary: John Jordan, Harp Music: Margaret O'Leary, Additional Music: Annie Keelan, Gerald Victory, Our Lady's Choral Society, and Radio Éireann Orchestra, Sound Recording: Peter Hunt, Production, Camera: Brendan J. Stafford, Script, Direction, Editing: Liam O'Laoghaire. Acknowledgements: Maura Lafayette, Messrs Faber & Faber, Louis McNeice, Mrs H. Cummins, Patrick Henchy and the Staff of the National Library, the National Film Institute of Ireland.

Portrait of the Irish Artist (2001) 60 min.

Director: Seán Ó Mórdha

Overview of the emergence of a distinctive voice in Irish twentieth-century art, including theatre, literature, poetry and painting, profiling the most famous artists involved. Similar in subject to the director's earlier *Art of the State*.

Credits Film Archivists: Barbara Durack, Arthur Keating, Lighting Cameraman: Cian de Buitléar, Camera Assistant: Conor Kelly, Sound Recordist: Karl Merren, On-Line Editor: Nicky Dunne, Post-Production Supervisor: Jim Colgan, Colourist: Tim Waller, Dubbing Editor: Michael Reilly, Sound Dubbing: John Fitzgerald, Executive

Producer: Kevin Dawson, RTÉ Concert Orchestra Conducted by Proinnsias Ó Duinn, Music: Bill Whelan, Film Editor: Ben Yeates, Associate Producer: Kitty Mullany, Producer/Director: Seán Ó Mórdha. An Araby Production for RTÉ. © 2001.

Power for Progress (1956) 18 min.
Director: Gerard Healy
Promotional film detailing the importance of the efficent operation of the electricity grid using water and turf sources.
Credits Producer, Photography: George Fleischmann, Director, Script: Gerard Healy, Narrator: Eamon Andrews, Sound: Leevers Rich, Editor: Etta Simpson, Sponsors: the Electricity Supply Board.

Power in the Blood (1989) 76 min.
Director: John T. Davis
Religiously inspired Nashville singer Vernon Oxford tours Northern Ireland to acclaim and popular success.
Credits Director, Producer: John T. Davis, Photography: David Barker, Sound: Deke Thompson, Editor: Sé Merry Doyle, Commissioned by: BBC.

Private Dancer (2001) 50 min.
Director: Alan Gilsenan
The lives of lapdancers in Dublin.
Credits Special thanks to: Angela, Annie, Beatrice, Celena, Chayanne, Claire, Cynthia, Joanne, Katerina, Mia, Morna, Pices, Portia, Sally-Anne, Samantha, Sara, Victoria, Sita and S. H. Researcher: Simone Ache, Stills Photography: Pat Redmond, Publicist: Carmel White, Electrician: Gerry Donnelly, Assistant Camera: Mark Flynn, Post-Production coordinator: Pauline O'Rourke, Assistant Editor: Cathal Geaney, Tape Operator: Ciaran Hynes, Colourist: Paul Byrne, On-Line Editor: Colm O'Brien, Dubbing Mixer: Paddy Gibbons, Sound: Joe Dolan, Camera: Richard Kendrick, Editor: Dee Hickey, Producer: Martin Mahon, Director: Alan Gilsenan. A Yellow Asylum Production for RTÉ © 2001.

The Promise of Barty O'Brien (1951) 50 min.
Director: George Freedland
Docudrama concerning the hopes and dreams of an Irish farmer aspiring to become an engineer.
Credits Director: George Freedland, Script: Sean Ó Faoláin, Photography: Brendan Stafford, Sound: Peter Hunt, Production Manager: Ulli Picard, Sets: Tony Inglis, Assistant Director: Liam O'Leary. Cast: Eric Doyle, Harry Brogan, Eileen Crowe, Doreen Madden.

Prophet Songs (1991) 68 min.
Director: Alan Gilsenan
Profiles of Irish priests who have left the church.
Credits Director: Alan Gilsenan.

Radharc (1960s–1980s) episodes of varying length
Directors: Desmond Forristal, Joseph Dunn, etc.
Ireland's first and most important independent production unit made this self-titled television series over the course of more than two decades. The producers were Catholic priests and as such the show usually featured a religious aspect, encompassing subjects both banal and cutting edge. The word 'radharc' means 'view' or 'perspective'.

Credits Radharc Team: Joseph Dunn, Patrick Cunningham, Sean Dunne, William Fitzgerald, Donal Flavin, Desmond Forristal, Peter Lemass, Con O'Keefe.

Radharc in Retrospect (1997–) 25 min. each episode
Producers: Esras Productions (for RTÉ)
Compilation of short documentaries from the *Radharc* series.
Credits Esras Productions for RTÉ.

Real Men Don't Wear Togs (1999) 25 min.
Director: Jennifer Keegan
Reflections by the regular swimmers at Dublin's famous 'Forty Foot' bathing site, a former male preserve which is also now frequented by females. The programme was dedicated to Billy Wyse, who drowned after it was made. Broadcast as part of a series entitled *Obsessions*.
Credits Sound Recordist: Stephen McDowell, Lighting Cameraman: Ciaran Tanham, Underwater Camera: Richard Kendrick, On-Line Editor: Tony Kavanagh, Dubbing Mixer: Bobby O'Reilly, Editor: Liz Walshe, Production Manager: Hilary Mc Loughlin, Creative Consultant: Dearbhla Walsh, Producers: Anna Devlin, Marina Hughes, Director: Jennifer Keegan. Special thanks to Tommy Ryan, Billy Wyse and all those who facilitated the making of this film. Dedicated to the memory of Joe and all who have swum here. In special memory of Billy Wyse, who drowned tragically shortly after the making of this film. Produced by Venus Film & TV Productions for RTÉ. © 1998.

Rebellion (1998) 3 × 50 min.
Director: Brian Hayes
An extensive account of the 1798 rebellion broadcast as part of the bicentennial commemorations. The series featured dramatic reconstruction, computer animation and a variety of illustrative techniques.
Credits Presenter: Cathal O'Shannon, Consultant Historians: Dr Dáire Keogh, Prof. Thomas Bartlett, Original Music Composed and Performed by: John Walsh, Stills Photography: Dennis O'Farrell, Illustrations and Archive Research: Gabrielle Brocklesby, Archive Sources: The President's Collection Áras an Uachtaráin, the National Gallery of Ireland, the National Library of Ireland, Folklore Department UCD, the Board of Trinity College, Dublin, Irish Film Archive, Monaghan County Museum, the Ulster Museum, the Linenhall Library, Belfast, Belfast Public Libraries, Campbell College, Belfast, Public Record Office of Northern Ireland, Public Record Office, Kew, the Royal Collection © Her Majesty Queen Elizabeth II, the Bridgeman Art Library, the National Portrait Gallery, London, the Scottish National Portrait Gallery, e.t. Archive, London, the National Maritime Museum, London, Getty Images, London, the National Army Museum, Chelsea, Pathé News Library, the Rt Hon. Sir Richard Needham, Photothéque des Musées de la Ville de paris, Réunion des Musées Nationaux, Paris, Musée de la Marine, Paris. Opening Animation: John Hayes, Animated Graphics: Susan Bresnihan, Tim Redfern, Graphic Design: Paul Scott, Rostrum Camera: Nico Vermeulen, Lorraine Sherry, Electrical Supervisor: Eddie Bolger, Location Camera (Paris): Nick Dolan, Grips: Simon Culliton, Richard Egan, Malcolm Huse, Oisín Kelly, Steadicam Operator: Tim Lawless, Sound Recordist: Eddie Duffy, Post-Production Sound: Peter Fletcher, Gerri McCaffery, On-Line Editors: Justin Byrne, Fred Dowdall, Declan Lucas, Alan Magrath, Assistant Editor: Nathan Nugent, Research: Eileen Heron, Mick Peelo, Production Assistants: Rosemary Clarke, Denise Dunne, Production Co-ordinator: Monica Cowley,

Lighting Cameraman: Breffni Byrne, Video Editor: Seán Farrell, Director: Brian Hayes, Writer and Executive Producer: Kevin Dawson. RTÉ © 1998. RTÉ gratefully acknowledges the assistance of the Government's 1798 Commemorative Committee. RTÉ wishes to thank: The National Gallery of Ireland, the National Museum of Ireland, the National Library of Ireland, the Brigade of the American Revolution Fort Lee, New Jersey, Bernard Browne, Comóradh '98, Bill Murray, the Carrickbyrne '98 Committee, Chris Forrestal, the Office of Public Works, An Garda Siochána, the Army Press Office, the Army Equitation School, An Taisce, Trinity College, Dublin, Bank of Ireland, the Guinness Hopstore, Kilmainham Gaol Museum, Na Piobairí Uileann Teo, St Werburgh's Church, Dublin, the Brazen Head, Dublin, Rathaspick House, Co. Wexrod, W. B. Nunn Ltd, Wexford, the Honourable Society of Kings Inns, Dublin, Newman House, Dublin, Loreto Abbey, Rathfarnham, Dublin, Ambassade de France en Irlande, the Royal Ulster Constabulary, Belfast City Council, Antrim Borough Council, Ards District Council, the Ordnance Survey, Gerry Hamilton, John Danaher.

Rebellion: Ireland 1913–1923 (1963) 50 min.
Director: George Morrison
An account of the Irish struggle for independence featuring substantially the same material as the films *Mise Éire* and *Saoirse?*
Credits Production Company: Television Reporters International, Director: George Morrison, Script: Robert Kee, Music: Sean Ó Riada, Supervising Editor: Leonard Trumm.

Reeling in the Years (1999) 10 × 25 min.
Producer: John O'Regan
Archival compilation series featuring television footage from the 1980s overlaid with popular music from the period.
Credits Acknowledgements: Associated Press TV News, Irish International Group, ITN Archive/Reuters, Mercury Records, THE *Sunday Tribune*, RTÉ Archive: Barbara Durack, Pauline Goodwin, Arthur Keating, Paddy Lockhart, Production Secretary: Colette Wallace, Vista Operator: Denise Naughton, Graphic Design: Shirley Dalton, Audio Dubbing: Peter Fletcher, Video Editor: Nathan Nugent, Research: Janet Couchman, Producer: John O'Regan. RTÉ © 1999.

Requiem for a Civilisation (1992) 52 min.
Director: Frank Stapleton
Meditations by Dr Noel Browne on the culture of western Ireland, seemingly embodied in its rugged landscape and stone walls and yet which has faded away with time.
Credits Director: Frank Stapleton, Writer/Presenter: Dr Noel Browne, Producer: Catherine Tiernan, Music: Peadar Ó Riada, Editor: J. Krystoph Romanowski, Photography: Cian de Buitléar, Bill Keady, Featuring: Colette Shaughnessy, Colm MacCába. Ocean Film Productions.

Return to the Island (1965) 28 min.
Director: George Fleischmann
Tourist film using the premise of John Huston's adoption of Irish citizenship to revisit the usual locations, primarily focusing on Connaught and Munster. The film features footage of a young Angelica Huston riding a horse with her father.
Credits Producer: George Grafton Green, Director, Executive Producer: George Fleischmann, Production Manager: Edward Caundy, Script: Liam Nolan, Narrator: Tom

St John Barry, Editor: Ray Drew, Photography: Reg Coast, Peter Cannon, Sound: Alfred Witcomb, Arthur Craven, John Morris, Anthony Barrier, Sponsors: Rank Organisation Special Features, Bord Fáilte, Aer Lingus.

Revival: Pearse's Concept of Ireland (1980) 70 min.
Director: Louis Marcus
Study of the writings and teachings of Padraig Pearse which attempts to explain why he gave his life in the 1916 rebellion. Features scenes of reconstruction.
Credits Producer, Director: Louis Marcus, Photography: Robert Monks, Sound: Peter Hunt, Editor: James Morris, Production Manager: Seamus Byrne, Wardrobe Supervisor: Jack Gallagher, Assistant Cameraman: Art O'Laoghaire, Assistant Editor: Sé Merry Doyle, Production Consultant: Brendán Ó hEithir, Technical Advisor: Seamus Ó Buachalla, Narrators: Andy O'Mahony, Denis Brennan, Readers: John Kavanagh, Niall Toibín, Sponsors: Dept of the Taoiseach. Cast: John Kavanagh (Pearse). © 1980.

Rhapsody of a River (1965) 12 min.
Director: Louis Marcus
Life along the River Lee in Co. Cork.
Credits Director: Louis Marcus, Music: Seán Ó Riada, Editor: Louis Marcus, Sponsors: Gael-Linn, Dept. of External Affairs.

The Road to America (1993) 85 min.
Director: Paddy Breathnach
The battle for qualification for the 1994 World Cup by the Irish team recounted with behind-the-scenes footage intercut with match highlights.
Credits Sponsor: ESB, Director: Paddy Breathnach, Producer: Robert Walpole, Editor: James E. Dalton, Photography: Cian de Buitléar, Seamus Deasy, Sound: Brendan Deasy, Simon J. Willis, A Treasure Films Production for RTÉ.

The Road to God Knows Where (1988) 51 min.
Director: Alan Gilsenan
The experience, effects and meaning of emigration in 1980s Ireland are examined using a combination of interviews with emigrants, commentators and politicians. The film also features inserts of a stand-up comic performing in various locations, adding a surreal element. Made as part of Channel Four's *The Irish Reel* series. Followed by *Road II*.
Credits Comedian: Karl McDermott, Poem: Patrick Finlay, Music: Pogues, Aslan, Light A Big Fire, U2, Various Others, Archive Footage: RTÉ. US Crew: Bob Gorelich (Assistant Cameraman), Mathew Price (Sound), Mark Pancza (Sparks), UK Crew: Jasper Fforde (Assistant Cameraman), Allun Curnock (Sound), Andy Martin (Sparks). Production Assistant: Anneliese O'Callaghan, Electrician: Albert Cassels, Still Photography: Muiris Moynihan, Production Accountant: Frank Moiselle, Legal Advisor: James Hickey, Graphics: Gunher Wulff, Boom Operator: Paul Delaney, Assistant Editor: Jeanine Hurley, Sound Editor: Emer Reynolds, Dubbing Mixer: Tony Amscombe, Assistant Cameraman: Keith Durham, Sound Recordist: Kieran Horgan, Production Manager: Mary Alleguen, Researcher: Fiachra Ó Marcaigh, Film Editor: Martin Duffy, Lighting Cameraman: Thaddeus O'Sullivan, Producer: Martin Mahon, Director: Alan Gilsenan, Series Producer: David Hammond. Yellow Asylum Productions for Channel Four. © Channel Four 1988.

Road II (2001) 54 min.

Director: Alan Gilsenan

Sequel/follow-up to *The Road to God Knows Where*, revisiting the original film, some of the original interviewees, and the country itself thirteen years later. In spite of indigenous funding, the film failed to match its predecessor in either quality or impact.

Credits Participants: Aslan, Conor Brennan, Philip Campbell, Mary Couglan TD, Christy Dignam, Henry McDonald, Katy McGuinness, Tom McLaughlin, Clio McNicholl, Michael Mulcahy, Peter O'Brien, Paul O'Donovan, Catherine Owens. Thanks to: Aer Rianta, the Belfast Telegraph, Jordan Rourke, Stephen Darcy, Martin Duffy, Lorcan Ennis, Sarah Joyce, Liffey Valley Shopping Centre, the Linenhall Library, Karl MacDermott, Clodagh Miskelly, Meals on Wheels, Niall O'Baill, Councillor John Ryan, Trinity Inn (NY), Archive Courtesy of: RTÉ, Channel 4, 'The Road to God Knows Where' Photography by Thaddeus O'Sullivan and Edited by Martin Duffy, Production Secretary: Lynn Caldwell, Post-Production Coordinator: Pauline O'Rourke, Colourist: Gerard Ward, On-Line Editor: Alan Sullivan, Assisstant Editor: Janice Toomey, Dubbing Mixer: Paddy Gibbons, Sound: Joe Dolan, Mary Harkin, Karl Merren, John Duval (US), Dan Harrison (UK), Camera: Richard Kendrick, Ross Keith (US), Mike Charlton (UK), DV Footage: Alan Gilsenan, Additional DV Material: Mark Waldron, Executive Producer for Bord Scannán na hÉireann/the Irish Film Board: Rod Stoneman, Executive Producer for RTÉ: Kevin Dawson, Researcher: Olive Howe, Editor: Emer Reynolds, Producer: Martin Mahon, Director: Alan Gilsenan. A Yellow Asylum Production for Bord Scannán na hÉireann/the Irish Film Board and RTÉ. © Yellow Asylum Films 2001.

Rocky Road to Dublin (1968) 70 min.

Director: Peter Lennon

Personal statement by director Peter Lennon regarding the state of the country in the late 1960s, with emphasis on the influence of the church in education and social life and on the pervasive social and political stagnation.

Credits Producer: Victor Herbert, Director, Writer, Narrator: Peter Lennon, Photography: Raoul Coutard, Georges Liron, Editors: Lila Biro, Philippe DeLasalle, Guy DeLooz, Sound: Tom Curran, Sound Engineer: Antoine Bonfanti, Trainee Photographer: Mole Richardson, Music: the Dubliners and Luke Kelly, Production Manager: Anthony Lennon.

Route 66 (1985) 104 min.

Director: John T. Davis

Life along America's most famous highway.

Credits Director: John T. Davis, Producer: Malcolm Frazer, Photography: Peter Greenhaigh, Sound: Steve Phillips, Editor: David Leighton, Commissioned by: Central TV. A Coproduction by Central and Iona Productions.

Rural Vocational Education (1950) 29 min.

Film promoting the introduction of the vocational education system in rural communities. The emphasis on practical training is balanced by fleeting references to sporting activities.

Safe Cycling (1949) 6 min.

Director: Liam O'Leary

Safety film using dramatic reconstruction about the dangers of improper cycling in Dublin city.

Credits Script: Liam O'Leary, Photography: George Fleischmann, Len Green, Editor, Sound Supervisor: Arthur Smith, Narrator: Terry O'Sullivan.

Saints Went Marching Out (1967) 18 min.
Producer: George Grafton Green

Pro-European film arguing that Ireland's missionary past has meant that Ireland and the Irish have always been part of Europe and the European mainland in one capacity or another.

Credits Producer: George Grafton Green, Sponsors: Department of Foreign Affairs, Assistant Producer: George Fleischmann, Script: Vincent Mulchrone, Narrator: Tom St John Barry.

Samuel Beckett: Silence to Silence (1984) 78 min.
Director: Seán Ó Mórdha

Introduction to the writer and his work featuring scenes of dramatic reconstruction.

Credits Voice: David Warrilow, Old Man: Seamus Forde, Beginning to End: Jack Mac-Gowran, Krapp's Last Tape: Patrick Magee, Happy Days: Billie Whitelaw, Waiting for Godot: Barry McGovern, Des Cave, Ill Seen Ill Said: Susan Fitzgerald, Narration: Tony Doyle, Commentary: Declan Kiberd, Adviser: Richard Ellmann, Flautist: Bill Dowdall, Singer: Austin Gaffney, Pianist: Jeannie Reddin, RTÉ Academica String Quartet, Lighting Cameraman: Peter Dorney, Sound: Tony McHugh, Brian Lynch, Dubbing Mixer: Tony McHugh, Electrical Supervisor: Michael Murray, Design: Lona Moran, Wardrobe: Vera Paterson, Graphic Design: Al O'Donnell, Rostrum Cameraman: Nico Vermeulen, Stills Photographer: Peter Harding, Production Assistant and Research: Kitty Mullany, Film Editor: Martin Duffy, Marc Gleeson, Producer/Director: Seán Ó Mórdha.

Saoirse? / Freedom? (1961) 90 min.
Director: George Morrison

Archival compilation charting the years from 1919 to 1922 up to the outbreak of the Civil War. The second part of an incomplete trilogy. Preceded by *Mise Éire*.

Credits Director/Producer: George Morrison, Writer: Seán Mac Réamoinn, Narrators: Liam Budhlaeir, Pádraigh G. O'Raghallaigh, Aindreas O'Gallchoir, Director of Photography: Vincent H. Corcoran, Music Composed and Conducted by: Seán O'Riada, Orchestra: the Radio Éireann Symphony Orchestra, Instrumentalist: Tomas Reck, Sound: Peter Hunt, Gene Martin, Assistant Editors: Louis Marcus, Caitríona O'Briain, Theodora Fitzgibbon, Seán O'Briain, Historical Consultant: Tomás P. O'Neill, Laboratory: Cinetone, Amsterdam. Gael-Linn.

An Saol 'Gay' / The Gay Life (1992) 27 min.
Director: Louis Marcus

Profile of Ger Philpott, writer, activist and campaigner for equal status for homosexuals in Ireland.

Credits Ceamara: Robert Monks, Fuaim: Liam Saurin, Eagarthóir: Joe Marcus, Cúntóiri Láthair: John Moore, Brendan Geraghty, Eagarthóir Fístéipe: Mark Nolan, Fístéip: David Little, Aston: Sarah Tanham, Áiseanna: Screen Scene, Fuaim-mheascadh: Moynihan Russell, Stiúrthóir: Louis Marcus Léiriú de chuid: Louis Marcus do RTÉ. © RTÉ 1992.

Scannán – Sceala Éireann / Film – Stories of Ireland (1943) 5 min.
Director: Liam O'Leary

Collected amateur footage shot silently and in colour by Liam O'Leary. Features images of Gaelic League Rally, harpist Margaret O'Leary and the Youghal Gaeltacht.
Credits Director, Photography: Liam O'Leary, Film Stock: Kodak.

An Scéalaí Deireanach? / The Last Storyteller? (2002) 50 min.
Director: Desmond Bell
Biographical and socio-cultural profile of storyteller and folklorist Séan Ó hEochaidh featuring dramatic reconstructions of some of the tales he gathered in the course of his life and work. Ó hEochaidh died at the age of eighty-eight shortly before production was completed.
Credits Eagarthóir: Roger Buck, Léiritheoir: Margo Harkin, Scriobhneoir/Stiúrthoir: Desmond Bell. Asylum Pictures do chuid TG4 i gcomhar le RTÉ agus Bord Scannán na hÉireann/the Irish Film Board.

Science and the Farmer (1952)
Director: George Fleischmann
Instructional film urging modernisation of Irish farming methods.
Credits Director: George Fleischmann, Script: John D. Sheridan, Narrator: Denis Brennan, Sponsors: Department of Agriculture.

Screening in the Rain (1930)
Director: Norris Davidson
Silent footage of Abbey Theatre actors and other Dublin personalities attending a party in the gardens of the Spanish Embassy in 1930. Among those pictured are Mary O'Moore, Grace McLoughlin, Judge Johnston, Lord Longford, Hilton Edwards and Micheál MacLiamóir. The film was first screened in the Peacock Theatre in 1930.
Credits Director/Cameraman: Norris Davidson.

See You at the Pillar (1967) 20 min.
Director: Peter Bayliss
Tourist film featuring urban scenes overlaid with a comical voice over, laced with quotations from famous Irish authors, actors, poets, politicians, playwrights and wits.
Credits Writer/Director: Peter Bayliss, 'Conversationalists': Anthony Quale, Norman Rodway; Quotations from: Thomas Davis, H. V. Morton, William Dawson, Flann O'Brien, Oliver Goldsmith, Sean O'Casey, James Joyce, G. B. Shaw, Seamus Kelly, Dean Swift, Michael MacLiammoir, Oscar Wilde, Compiled by: Seamus Kelly (Quidnuc), Music and Songs provided by 'the Croppies'; An Associated British Pathé Production.

A Sense of Loss (1972) 135 min.
Director: Marcel Ophuls
An account of 'the troubles' in Northern Ireland which attempts to give a sense of how the victims of violence were reacting to events.
Credits Produced and Directed by Marcel Ophuls, Edited by Marion Kraft, Director of Photography: Simon Edelstein, Second Unit Direction by Edouard Fenwick, Assistant Director: Ana Carrigan, Additional Photography by Elliott Erwitt, Production Manager: William Stitt, Assistant Editor: Anne Lewis, Assistant Cameraman: Claude Paccaud, Sound Engineer: Claude Pellot, Chief Electrician: Alain Borga, Chaffeur and Social Guide: Robert Moon, Research Assistant: Kathy Keville, Re-Recording: Richard Vorisek, Contributing Journalist: John Whale of the *Sunday Times*, Executive Producer: Max Palevsky, Cinema X/Société Suisse de Télévision, 1972.

Seven Ages: The Story of the Irish State (2000) 7 × 55 min.

Director: Seán Ó Mórdha

Seven-part series charting the seven decades of Irish history using old and new interviews and a mixture of newsreel and contemporary scenes. An 'official' history for the new millennium, the series was even released on DVD.

Credits Film Archivist: Barbara Durack, Sound Archivist: Noel Sheils, Electrical Services: Maurice Swan, Dave Durney, Sound Recordists: Karl Merren, Brendan Deasy, Camera Assistants: Donal Gilligan, Conor Kelly, Graphic Design: John Talbot, Assistant Editor: Sarah McCarthy, On-Line Editor: Emmanuel Stratford, Lighting Cameraman: Cian de Buitléar, Executive Producers: Clare Duignan, Liam Miller, RTÉ Concert Orchestra Conducted by: Prionnsias Ó Duinn, Music: Bill Whelan, Film Editor: J. Patrick Duffner, Associate Producer: Kitty Mullany, Producer/Director: Seán Ó Mórdha. An Araby Production for RTÉ in association with BBC Northern Ireland © RTÉ 2000.

1798 Agus Ó Shin / 1798 and Since (1998) 50 min.

Director: Louis Marcus

An exploration of the 1798 rebellion which relates the events of two hundred years before to the present day. The film strongly emphasises the links between political groups of the time and attempts to debunk popular historical myths.

Credits Ceamara: Ken O'Mahony, Fuaim: Finny Byrne, Eagarthóir: Joe Marcus, Tráchtaire: Doireann Ní Bhriain, Rostram: Ken Morse, Taighde Fístéipe: Denis McArdle, Telecine: Glenn Kyte, Amhránaí: Lillis Ó Laoire, Fuaim Stiúdeo: Derek Doyle, Áiseanna: High Wire, Dubáil: Éanna Ó Cnáimhsí, Comhairleoir Staire: Thomas Bartlett; Buíochas: Abbey Films, Caisleán Bhaile Átha Cliath, Alan L. Carey, Comóradh '98, Event Communications, Irish Film Archive, An tAth Lory Kehoe, Leabharlann Náisiúnta na hÉireann, Leabharlann RTÉ, Linen Hall Library, Tommy McArdle, Músaem Chontae Loch Gaimain, Músaem Náisiúnta na hÉireann, Prísún Chill Mhaighneann, Alastair Smyth, Ulster Museum; Stiúrthóir: Louis Marcus. Léiriú de chuid Louis Marcus do Telefís na Gaelige i gcomhar le RTÉ. © TnaG 1998.

Shellshock Rock (1978) 52 min.

Director: John T. Davis

Profile of the underground punk music scene in late 1970s Belfast.

Credits Director/Producer: John T. Davis, Photography: John T. Davis, Alwyn James, Tommy McConville, Sound: Derek Booker, Mary James, Editor: John T. Davis, Ross Graham.

Short Story – Irish Cinema 1945–1958 (1986) 62 min.

Director: Kieran Hickey

A history of the brief boom period in Irish filmmaking between 1945 and 1958 which argues in favour of the continued development of the indigenous industry.

Credits Director: Kieran Hickey, Production: BAC Films.

A Silence Broken (1996) 50 min.

Director: Claire O'Loughlin

Promotional film for Strokestown Famine Museum.

Credits Camera: Seamus Seasy, Producer, Director: Claire O'Loughlin. A Krino Production for RTÉ.

The Silent Order (1948) 15 min.
Director: George Fleischmann
The life of Irish monks at a monastery in Co. Tipperary.
Credits Production Company: Hibernia Films, Producer: Michael Scott, Director, Photography: George Fleischmann, Sound: Peter Hunt, Narrator: Richard Massingham, Choir: St Peter's, Phibsboro.

Slaying the Dragon (1995) 50 min.
Director: Gerry Gregg
A profile of Irish trade unionism produced on the occasion of the May Day celebrations of 1994. Features extensive interview/speech material from Professor J. K. Galbraith.
Credits Director of Photography: Seamus Deasy, Editor: Nuala Roche, Sound Recordist: Brendan Deasy, Dubbing Mixer: Pat Hayes, Camera Assistants: Shane Deasy, Simon Walsh, Production Assistant: Bernie O'Connor, Electrician: Maurice Swan, Film Processing: Frank Moran, Radio Telefís Éireann, Telecine: Glenn Kyte, Post-Production Facilities: The Loopline, Graphics: Anastasia Claggerty, Music: Danny Sheridan, Supervising Editor: Sé Merry Doyle, Executive Producer: Oliver Donohoe, Director: Gerry Gregg. Made with the help of Commission of the European Union, Irish National Teachers Organisation, Quinnsworth, Crazy Prices, Lifestyle Sports and Leisure. A Vermilion film for Congress in association with Radio Telefís Éireann. 1995.

So This is Dyoublong? (1999) 35 min.
Director: Nuala Cunningham, Ciaran O'Connor
Profile of James Joyce and his world presented by Senator David Norris. The film features scenes from the shooting of the biographical drama *Nora* and from Norris's stage show.
Credits Script: David Norris, Nuala Cunningham, Photography: Ciaran O'Connor, Editor: Dympna Grieve, Sound Recordists: John Harte, Philip Graham, Additional Camera: Dympna Grieve, Camera Assistant: Niall Connolly, Rostrum Camera: Nico Vermeuler, Sound Effects: Karen Williams, Researcher/Production Assistant: Trish Drinan, Production Secretary: Kaye O'Toole, Post-Production Facilities: New Decade TV. [Song and photograph credits omitted.] Associate Producer: Linda Cardiff, Executive Producer for RTÉ: Peter Feeney, Producer, Director: Nuala Cunningham, Ciaran O'Connor. A New Decade Production in Association with RTÉ.

Southpaw (a.k.a. *Francis Barrett – Southpaw, Southpaw – The Francis Barrett Story*) (1998) 76 min.
Director: Liam McGrath
Profile of Irish Olympic boxer Franics Barrett, the first member of Ireland's travelling community to compete for Ireland in an international sporting event. The film was selected for screening at the Sundance Film Festival in 1999.
Credits Special thanks to: the Barrett Family and everyone at Hillside Galway. Thanks to all who helped in the production of this film, especially Sé Merry Doyle, the McDonagh family and all at Yeats Close, Neasden, London. The Olympic footage was reproduced with the consent of the International Olympic Committee. [Song list omitted.] Line Producer: Lesley McKimm, Production Coordinator: Emma Richardson, Additional Photography: Seamus Deasy, Garry Keane, David Scott, Additional Sound Recordists: Brendan Deasy, Greg Bailey, Focus Pullers: Donal Gilligan, Simon Walsh, On-Line Editor: Alan Sullivan, Assistant Editor: Kimmo Hirvonen, Sound Editors: Annette Stone, Anthony Litton, Gráinne D'Alton,

Production Accountant: Jim Gillespie, Production Assistants: Niamh Barrett, Rachel O'Flanagan, Telecine: Dave Gibson, Dubbing: Cecily Loughman, Title Design: John Power, Newspaper Archive: Dublin Corporation Public Libraries: Dublin and Irish Collections, Additional TV Archive: RTÉ Archive, Executive Producer for Radio Telefís Éireann: Clare Duignan, Executive Producer for Bord Scannán na hÉireann/the Irish Film Board: Rod Stoneman, Series Editor for Channel Four: Peter Moore, Narration: Eamonn Hunt, Sound: Simon J. Willis, Music: Dario Marianelli, Editor: James E. Dalton, Director of Photography: Cian de Buitléar, Producers: Robert Walpole, Paddy Breathnach, Director: Liam McGrath. Produced with the support of investment incentives for the Irish film industry provided by the government of Ireland. Filmed on location in Ireland. A Treasure Films Production for Radio Telefís Éireann and Bord Scannán na hÉireann/the Irish Film Board and Channel 4. A Hillside Productions Production for Treasure Films Ireland. © Treasure Films 1998. Distributors: Downtown Pictures.

Spencer Freeman Collection: Sweepstake Scenes Ireland (1940) 9 min.
Advertising film which subverts the prohibition on advertising the sweepstakes in the cinema by filming the sweepstakes parade in Dublin.
Credits Acknowledgements: Irish Hospitals Sweepstake.

Spotlight on the Army (1952)
Director: George Fleischmann
Credits Director: George Fleischmann, Script: Gerard Healy, Narrator: Denis Brennan, Sponsors: Department of Defence.

Spré Rosy Ryan / Rosy Ryan's Dowry (1997) 53 min.
Director: Traolach Ó Buachalla
A study of the social impact of the filming of *Ryan's Daughter*. The film explores both the positive and negative results of the arrival of a full-scale well-financed film crew to a relatively isolated rural area where several locals spoke only Irish.
Credits Buíochas ó chroí ag dul do: Munitir Chorca Dhuibhne, Mícheál De Mórdha, Frances Uí Chinnéide, Munitir Fheiritéar, Neil Ní Chinnéide, Aingeal and Breandán Ó Buachalla, Kyle Clifford, Adrian Cronin, Anne McCabe, Proinsias Ní Ghráinne, Scannstoc le caoinchead: Radío Telefís Éireann, Joe Creedon, An Bhlarna, 'Ryan's Daughter' le caoinchead Turner Entertainment Co., Grianghrafanna le caoinchead: Ken Bray, Mícheál De Mórdha, Kevin Coleman, Bab Feiritéar, Pat Hennessy, Maria Simonds-Gooding, Pádraig Tyers, Seamus Ware, Tadhg Ó Coiléain, Tráchtaire: Doireann Ní Bhriain, Ceamara: Ken O'Mahony, Paul Warde, Fuaim: Eddie Quinn, Measchtóir Fuaime: Joe Ó Dubhghaill, Pine Valley Studios, Eagarthóir: Guy Montgomery, High Wire, Léiritheoir Feidhmiúcháin: Brian Reddin, Stiúrthóir/Léiritheoir: Traolach Ó Buachalla, Léiriú de chuid Adare Productions do TnaG © 1997.

A State of Crisis (1995) 50 min.
Director: Michael Hewitt
A history of the arms crisis of 1969–70 in which several prominent Irish politicians, including future Taoiseach Charles J. Haughey, were accused of conspiring to supply weapons to Northern Irish paramilitaries.
Credits Reporter: Mike Milotte. Thanks to: Radio Telefís Éireann Archives, ITN, BBC, the *Irish Times*, Researchers: Diarmaid de Paor, Jim Jennings, Production Assistant and Additional Research: Kevin Cummins, Programme Coordinator: Mike Travers,

Graphic Design: Maura Osborne, Rostrum Camera: Nico Vermeulen, Electricians: Tony Lynch, Dermot O'Grady, Kevin O'Toole, Stedicam: Brian Drysdale, Tim Lawless, Second Unit Director: Diarmuid Lavery, Location Sound: Ray Haughey, Post-Production Sound: Peter Fletcher, Music: Aisling Drury-Bryne, Brian Longridge, Lighting Cameraman: Roy Bedell, Editor: Mark Quinn, Producer/Director: Michael Hewitt, Produced by: Deirdre Younge. © Radio Telefís Éireann, 1995.

States of Fear (1999) 3 × 56 min.

Director: Mary Raftery

Series focusing on the exploitation and abuse of children in state institutions. Each episode was followed by an advertisement for helplines. The film won the Irish Film and Television Academy award for Best Documentary in English of 1999.

Credits RTÉ would like to thank: Sunniva O'Flynn, the Irish Film Archives, IFC, John McDonnell, Barnardos Film Archives, UK, National Museum of Ireland, Dr Pat Wallace, Limerick Institute of Technology, University College Cork, Office of Public Works, Dermot O'Sullivan, Turner Entertainment Co., Narrator: Áine Lawlor, Researcher and PA: Sheila Ahern, Lighting Cameramen: Tom Curran, Óisin Kelly, Location Sound: Stephen Spoor, Electrical Services: Jimmy Butler, Gordon O'Toole, On-Line Editor: Fred Dowdall, Stills Research: Veronica O'Mara, Rostrum Camera: Lorraine Sherry, Nico Vermuelen, Graphic Design: Derek Ryan, Original Paintings: Katy Simpson, Dubbing: Vincent Kilcullen, Editor: Séan Farrell, Written, Produced and Directed by Mary Raftery. © RTÉ 1999.

Stories from the Silence (1990) 57 min.

Director: Alan Gilsenan

The story of AIDS and HIV in Ireland highlighting the social difficulties faced by sufferers.

Credits Photography: Pat Shine, Director: Alan Gilsenan.

Sunday After Sunday (1985) 70 min.

Director: Louis Marcus

The history of the Gaelic Athletic Association from 1885 to 1985 with a strong emphasis on the community/club basis of the membership. The film incorporates some discussion of the social and political context in which the association was both originally founded and still exists.

Credits Photography: Robert Monks, Sound: Liam Saurin, Script Adviser: Brendan O'hEithir, Narrator: Mick Lally, Music: Artane Boys Band, Musical Director: Joe Lynch, Camera Assistant: Art O'Laoghaire, Second Unit: Nick O'Neill, Darby Caroll, Paul O'Flynn, Frank Scott, Studio Sound: Pat Gibbons, Picture Sources: Clare County Library, David Guiney, Gill & Macmillan, Kenny's Bookshop Galway, National Library of Ireland, Film Sources: Irish Film Institute, Mr James C. Gaynor, Wexford, Gaumont News, Movietone News, Pathé News. Extracts from the films *Peil* and *Christy Ring* and from the newsreel *Amharc Éireann* by courtesy Gael-Linn, Video Extracts Adviser: Maurice Reidy, Librarian: Barbara Durack, Produced and Directed by Louis Marcus. A Louis Marcus Production in association with Radio Telefís Éireann and with the assistance of An Rannóg Spóirt, An Roinn Oideachais, Comóradh an Chéid, Cumann Lúthchleas Gael. © Cumman Lúthchleas Gael 1985.

Super Trouper (1994) 52 min.

Director: John McColgan

Profile of veteran stage and screen entertainer Maureen Potter featuring a range of clips from her performances.

Credits Special Thanks to: Jack O'Leary, Archive Excerpts from: RTÉ's *Christmas With Maureen* 1970–1972, RTÉ's *Maureen Potter Show* 1973, *Gaels of Laughter*, *O'Dea's Company*, Archive Excerpts Featured: Jimmy O'Dea, Danny Cummins, Barbara Brennan, Patricia Cahill, Joe Linnane, Thelma Ramsey, Vernon Hayden, Ursula Doyle, Riordan's Sketch Featured: John Cowley, Tom Hickey, Maura Deady, Frank O'Donovan, Annie D'Alton, *Juno and the Paycock* Featured: John Kavanagh, Donal McCann, Seamus Forde, Joe Sevino, Geraldine Plunkett, *Portrait of the Artist* (RTÉ, 1977) Featured: T. P. McKenna, Rosaleen Linehan, Des Perry, Maureen Potter at Clontarf Castle With: Val Fitzpatrick, Musical Director: Chris Kenevey, Additional Archive Stills Courtesy of: John Finegan, Sound Dubbing: Tony Russell, Additional Music: Chris Kenevey, Production Manager: Claire Wilde, 2nd Camera: Declan Emerson, Electricians: Brendan Walls, Graeme Haughton, Graphic Design, Niall O'hOisín, Sound Recordists: Paul Emerson, Brendan Campbell, Lighting Cameraman: Ciaran Tanham, Off-Line Editor: Gareth Young, On-Line Editor: Derek Shoebridge, Produced and Directed by: John McColgan. A Tyrone Production for RTÉ. © 1994.

They Called Him God (1998) 60 min.
Director: Colm O'Callaghan
Profile of Irish soccer star Paul McGrath, whose class and racial background have been important challenges in his life.

Credits Reporter, Researcher: Dave Hannigan. Special thanks to: Paul McGrath and Family, Frank Mullen and Family, the Court Hotel, Killiney, Bob Hennessy, Lynne Laffan, Barry Mackleston, Original Music: Infinite AM, Stills: Billy Strickland/INPHO Phot., Graphic Design: Shirley Dalton, Rostrum Photography: Lorraine Sherry, Lighting Cameraman: Aidan McGuinness, Sound Recordist: Paul Tynan, Electrical Services: Brian Looby, Production Assistant: Niamh Guckian, Post-Production Sound: Terry Gough, VT Editor: Tom Bannon, Director, Producer: Colm O'Callaghan. © RTÉ 1998.

This is Dublin (1990) 53 min.
Director: Bernadine Carraher
Montage of cityscapes, buildings and building sites with a voice over tracing the foundations of Dublin city which have subsequently been covered by modern edifices. The film makes extensive use of a musical score by young Irish bands.

Credits Bands & Music: 'Red Cow' BIRD, 'Celtic' Lance Hogan, 'Ocean Floor' Sony Condell, 'Ingrid Bergman' the Dixons, 'The Tinker's Daughter' Simon O'Dwyer, 'Forfeit Trials' the Harvest Ministers, 'Sylvie' Miss Brown to You, 'The Heartland' A Rhythm, '18 Miles from Memphis' the Tennessee Hennesseys, 'Higher' Shake, 'At Last Our Time is Here' BIRD, 'Brown Rabbit' the Swinging Swine, 'Midnight Blues' Interference, 'Judgement Day' the Fireflys, Music Score: Fergus McGovern, Stills and Script: B. Carraher, Cameras: Eric Johnson, Editor: John Fisher, Produced and Directed by Bernadine Carraher. 1990 BC Productions.

This is Ireland (1966) 13 min.
Producer: Morton Schindel
American-produced overview of Irish scenes reproduced from the 1964 book of drawings by Miroslav Sasek.

Credits Producer: Morton Schindel. Adapted from the book by: Miroslav Sasek. Script: Marianna Morris, Sponsors: SIM, Narrators: Philip O'Flynn, Jean Francois Lalet, Production Consultants: Philip Newport, Tom Sheehy, Produced at Western Woods Studios, Weston, Connecticut, USA.

Three Moons (1995) 37 min.

Director: Jim Sheridan

Profile of Hong Kong/Irish designer John Rocha focusing on his influences, his interest in and involvement with Irish culture and the preparations for a show.

Credits Acknowledgements: John Gleeson, Frank Gleeson, Mary Moylan, Cuan Hanley, Monica Gambrielle, Reiko Tanaha, Cléa van der Grijn, Sinéad O'Connor, Lighting Cameraman: Cian de Buítléar, Gerry MacArthur, Sound Recordist: Simon Willis, Stephen McDowell, Martin Birney, Camera Assistant: Carl Hayden, Production Assistant: Ann Brehany, Assistant to the Director: David A. Donohue, Production Manager: Noëlette Buckley, Post-Production Sound: Peter Fletcher, Editor: Ray Roantree, Producer: Arthur Lappin, Director: Jim Sheridan. A Hell's Kitchen Production for Radio Telefís Éireann. 1995.

Tide on the Turn (1963) 14 min.

Producers: Rank Organisation

Part of the Rank Organisation *Look at Life* newsreel detailing the industrialisation and modernisation of Ireland, featuring footage of shipbuilding, oil refining and other endeavours. The film argues that emigration is no longer an economic necessity.

An Tine Bheo / The Living Flame (1966) 35 min.

Director: Louis Marcus

Account of the struggle for Irish independence featuring interviews with veterans of the conflict. The film argues that 'the living flame' of recent history still influences both the people and the landscape of contemporary Ireland.

Credits Production Company: Gael-Linn, Director: Louis Marcus, Script: Brendán Ó hEithir, Photography: Robert Monks, Sound: Peter Hunt Studios, Music: Seán Ó Riada, Narrators/Interviewees: Eoin Ó Suilleabhain, Christ Curran, Seamus Forde, Vincent Dowling, Howard Marian Crawford.

An tOileanach a d'Fhill / Return of the Islander (1970) 35 min.

Director: Jim Mulkerns

An Aran islander working in London returns home to experience the joys of community life and fishing on the open sea. Features scenes of dramatic reconstruction and visual references to *Man of Aran*.

Credits Sponsors: Department of the Gaeltacht, Producer: George Fleischmann, Director: Jim Mulkerns, Camera: Val Ennis.

Tomorrow Begins Today / Inniú's Amárach

Promotional film showing how Bord na Móna, the Irish Peat Authority, has benefited the country and the lives of its workers.

Top of the Morning (1935) 18 min.

Director: SOS

Promotional film for the Irish sweepstakes disguised as a travelogue because regulations prevented film advertising of the lottery at that time.

Credits Presented by: the Irish Travel Club, Directed by: SOS, Photography: Joseph Evans.

To Save a Life (1965)

Director: George Morrison

Docudrama about water safety. The film won a diploma of Merit at the 6th International Documentary Film Festival, Milan, 1965.

Credits Director: George Morrison, Sponsor: Dept of Local Government.

To the Waters and the Wild (1970) 30 min. each episode
Director: Éamon de Buitléar
Follow-up series to the 1960s *Amuig Faoin Spéir*, shot in colour and still peppered with the illustrations of Gerrit Van Gelderen.
Credits Production Team: Éamon De Buitléir, Gerrit Van Gelderen.

Tourism is Everybody's Business (1978) 14 min.
Producer: Joe Byrne
Details of Bord Fáilte's contribution to Ireland's economy which also encourages ordinary people to help out.
Credits Production Company: Marshall Smith Films, London, Producer: Joe Byrne, Script: Joe Byrne, Aidan O'Hanlon, Brian Keogh, Art Direction, Production Design: Murakami Film Ltd, Photography: Michael Delaney, Sponsors: Bord Fáilte Éireann.

Travellers (1999) 84 min.
Directors: Alen MacWeeney and John T. Davis
Revisiting the subjects of photographer Alen MacWeeney's 1960s series of images of traveller families in Dublin and Galway.
Credits Directors: Alen MacWeeney, John T. Davis, Editor: Sé Merry Doyle

Treasna an Teorann / Crossing the Border (1946) 6 min.
No director credited.
Silent agit-prop featuring footage of anti-partition march across the Northern Ireland border. This film and its companion piece *Partition Protest Parade* may have been directed by Liam O'Leary.
Credits (non-print source) Aiséirge present.

The Troubles (1981) 4 × 50 min.
Director: Richard Broad
An account of the events in Northern Ireland from the late 1960s which incorporated some historical background. Broadcast around the same time as *Ireland – A Television History*.
Credits Producers: Richard Broad, Ian Stuttard, Thames Television, Writer: Taylor Downing, Narration: Rosalie Crutchley.

Twelve Days in July (1997) 50 min.
Directors: Margo Harkin, Michael Hewitt, Dearbhla Walsh
An account of the build-up to the Orange Order parade in Portadown, which was the occasion for sectarian antagonism and rioting.
Credits Thanks to: Claire Dignam, The Garvaghy Road Residents Coalition and the Garvaghy Road Community, Clifford Forbes, Cecil Johnston, David Jones, Hilda Winter, Sanda, the Orange Order, Star of David Accordion Band and the Rathdown Defenders Flute Band. Narrator: Veronika Hyks, Production Unit: Johnny Golden, Eileen Curran, Lea Aglett, Resident Consultants: Dominic Bryan, Neil Jarman, Camera: Deirdre Noonan, Sound: Marty Kennedy, Assistant Edtior: Paul Harris, Photography: David Barker, Michael Quinn, Directors: Margo Harkin, Michael Hewitt, Dearbhla Walsh, Editor: Alex Board, Co-Producer: Fionnuala Sweeney, Producer: Margo Harkin. A Besom Production for Channel Four. © Channel Four Television Corporation, 1997.

Ulster (1940) 11 min.

Director: Ralph Keene

A profile of the industrial landscape of Northern Ireland with particular emphasis on its
contribution to the Allied war effort.

Credits A Standard Film Production. Presented by: Donald Taylor, Producer: Alexander
Shaw, Director: Ralph Keene, Camera: Jo Jagle, George Noble, Commentary: St
John Ervine, Narrator: Robert MacDermot, Music: Richard Addinsell, Musical
Director: Muir Mathieson, Recordist: A. Rhind.

Ulster Heritage (1949) 16 min.

Director: Stanley Willis

Northern Irish film focusing on the life of a 'typical Ulster farming family' which deals
exclusively with agricultural life, making no references to the political context.

Credits Producer: Ronald H. Riley, Director, Script: Stanley Willis, Production Com-
pany: RHR in association with the Film Producers Guild, Photography: Josef
Ambor, Editor: Sheila Willson, Music: Nigel Warrack, Narrator: Allan McLelland,
Music Engineer: Ron Abbott, Westrex Recording System.

The Uncle Jack (1996) 80 min.

Director: John T. Davis

Semi-autobiographical study of director John T. Davis's eccentric uncle, a Northern Irish
architect who designed cinemas. The film explores Davis's own reasons for becoming an artist through his relationship with his uncle.

Credits Producer: Brendan J. Byrne, Script, Director, Photography: John T. Davis, Production Company: Holywood Films.

Urban Cowboys (1996) 20 min.

Director: Erin Cotter

Short documentary focusing on the problem of horses in Dublin's suburban housing
estates. Part of Channel Four (UK)'s *Short Stories* series.

Credits Narrator: Jason O'Mara, Photography: Roger Chapman, Luke Hallam, Sound:
Craig Lines, Production: Mary McCarthy, Jo Newberry, Diane Palliser, Dubbing
Editor: David Hindmarsh, Radio Report courtesy of Anna Livia FM, Research:
Niamh O'Connor, Editor: Nicky Ager, Assistant Producer: Briget Deane, Producer:
Christine Alderson, Director: Erin Cotter. An Ipso Facto Films Production for
Channel Four. © Channel Four 1996.

A Vertical Man (1998) 60 min.

Director: Paul Swann

Profile of composer Seán Ó Riada featuring reconstructed sequences in which Ó Riada
is played by an actor wearing his actual clothes.

Credits Producer: Nigel Warren Green, Director: Christopher Swann, Music: Seán Ó
Riada, Narrator: Patrick Bergin, Music Performed by: the Irish Film Orchestra,
Leader: Christopher Warren Guest, Conductor: John McGinn, Choir and Orchestral
Management: Catriona Walsh, Soloist: Aliona MacDonagh, Music Consultant:
Peadar Ó Riada. Thanks to: DDFH and B Advertising, The Fitzwilliam Hotel Group,
Aim Media Specialists, Gael-Linn. Produced with the support of investment incen-
tives for the Irish Film industry provided by the government of Ireland. Poetry: W. H.
Auden, John Montague, Seamus Heaney, Gaffer: Stephen Beuin, Electrician: Gareth
Baldwin, Grip: Wally Sullivan, Standby Props: Martin Carey, Dresser: Tina Brophy,
Make-Up Artist: Rosie Blackmore, Costume Designer: Sue Wain, Production Office:

Helen Hadden, Gearoid Ó Duinnin, Tom Stevens, Legal: Eugene Fanning, Greg Casey, First Assistant Director: Mick Walsh, Rostrum: Ken Morse, Telecine Rushes and Neg Conforming: Mike Fraser Ltd., Assistant Cameraman: Russel Deason, 2nd Unit Camera: Ciaran Tanham, Sound: Brendan Campbell, Lighting Cameraman: Peter Robertson, Colourist: Vincent Narduzzo, Dubbing Mixer: David Woolley, On-Line Editor: Henry Stein, Editor: Gerry Nelson, Co-Producer (Ireland): Oliver Fallon, Co-Producer (UK): Frances Peters, Executive Producers: Brian Conroy, Rod Stoneman, Kevin Menton, Nigel Warren Green. Young O'Riada: Tom O'Leary, The Aisling: Zeena Eate. Irish Screen © 1998.

The Village (1967) 70 min.
Director: Mark McCarty
Ethnographic/anthropological profile of Dunquin, Co. Kerry. There is no voice over, but opening title cards direct viewers to consider it a document of a dying way of life.
Credits University of California Extension Media Center. Producer: Colin Young, Anthropologist: Paul Hockings, Filmmaker: Mark McCarty, Sound Recording/Additional Photography: Mike Hall, Paul Hockings, Alex Prisadsky, Re-Recording: Don Worthen, Traditional Music: Arranged by Seán Ó Riada, Played by Ceoltóirí Cualann. Produced by the UCLA Ethnographic Film Program, Co-Directors Walter Goldschmidt, Colin Young, UCLA, Funded by the Ford Foundation Grant to UCLA. for International and Comparative Studies.

The Visitation (1948)
Directors: Henry Cooper, John Page
Details of the missionary work of the Medical Missionaries of Mary in Nigeria.
Credits Producer: Andrew Buchanan, Narrator: Robert Speaight, Music: M. De Wolfe, Choral Prologue and Epilogue: Westminster Chathedral Choir, Director, Camera-work (Nigeria): John Page, Unit Manager (Nigeria): Joan Duff, Direction (Ireland): Henry Cooper, Camerawork (Ireland): George Fleischmann, Charles V. Francis, Editor: James Anderson.

Voice of Generations: The Story of Peig Sayers (1998) 50 min.
Director: Brendán Feiritéar
Sentimental account of the life of Peig Sayers with extracts from her writings and several scenes of reconstruction. The film adds some interview material with contemporary historians and commentators, but is primarily focused on visualising the familiar details of her life.
Credits Actors: Neasa Mistéal, Boscó Ó Conchúir, Christy Mac Gearailt, Frances Uí Chinnéide, Fionnán Ó hÓgáin, Helen Ni Shé, Aisling Feiritéar, Sinéad Ní Chonchúir, Michelle Ní Dhálaigh, Gráinne de Mórdha, Rúth Ní Longáin, Colm Ó Bric, Mícheál de Mórdha, Páidín Ó Catháin, Dáithí Mac Gearailt, Donie Ó Dubhshláine, Pádraig Ó Murchú, Ciarán Ó Slatara, Mícheál Ó Slatara. Acknowl-edgements: Dept. of Irish Folklore, University College Dublin, Catherine Duggan, the Blasket Centre, Máire Mac Conghail, An tAth. Tomás Ó hÍceadha, Jackie, Kerry and Dan Sheehan, Barbara Durack, RTÉ Archive, Tomás Mistéal, Cartlann RnaG, Canon Jackie Mac Ginneá. Narration: Bríd Ní Neachtain, Neasa Ní Annracháin, Seán Ó Murchú, Seán Rowantree, Cóilín Ó Scolaí, Music Arrangement: Stiofán Ó Cuanaigh, Violinist: Máire Bhreathnach, Production Assistant: Eleanor Finucane, Facilities: Telegael, Sound: Máire Ní Earcáin, Réamon de Brún, Sound Mix: Enda Boner, Camera: Billy Keady, Christine Ní Chonchúbhair, Editor: Cóilín Ó Scolaí, Written and Directed by Brendán Feiritéar. © Radio Telefís Éireann 1998.

Voyage to Recovery (1952) 17 min.

Director: Gerard Healy

Docudrama on the treatment of TB drawing attention to the unnecessary social stigma attatched to the disease as well as the treatment process itself.

Credits Presented by: the Minister for Health, Produced by: the National Film Institute with the cooperation of: the Dept of Health and Staffs of Ballyowen Sanatorium, Dublin, St Mary's Chest Hospital, Dublin, Western Regional Sanatorium, Galway, Script, Direction: Gerard Healy, Photography: George Fleischmann, Sound: Movietone News. Cast: Edward Golden, Gerard Victory, Joe Lynch, Seathrún Ó Goilí, Joan O'Hara, Micheál Ó hAonghusa, Máire Ní Chatháin, Barry Cassin, Breffni O'Rourke, Pauline Delaney.

The Waters of Providence (1949) 55 min.

Director: Fr Frank Browne, SJ

A history of the Providence Woollen Mills in Foxford, Co. Mayo which charts the intercession of Sister Mary Arsenius of the Irish Sisters of Charity, who founded it. The film details the operation of the mill, but also highlights its centrality to the community.

Credits Director: Fr Frank Browne, SJ

Waves (1973) 25 min.

Director: Patrick Carey, John Taylor

The Atlantic Ocean batters the coast of the Aran Islands. The film focuses on the movement of the waters and their collision with the land, making no reference to human habitation or geographical specificity.

Credits Director/Photography: Patrick Carey, John Taylor, Assistant Camera Operator: Dodo Anderson, Assistant: Dave Humphries, Editor: Eric Mival, Dubbing Mixer: Ken Scrieveman. Aengus Films.

W. B. Yeats: A Tribute (1950) 21 min.

Directors: George Fleischmann, John D. Sheridan

Pictorial study of Co. Sligo, where W. B. Yeats was raised, and Dublin, where he worked. The images are accompanied by excerpts from Yeats's poetry. The film received a certificate of merit at the Venice Film Festival in 1950 and was selected for screening at the Edinburgh Film Festival.

Credits Production Company: the National Film Institute, Directors: George Fleischmann, John D.Sheridan, Photography, Editor, George Fleischmann, Script: John D. Sheridan, Sound: Peter Hunt, Narration: Cyril Cusack, Music: Eamonn Ó Gallchobhair, Readers: Michael MacLiammoir, Siobhan McKenna, Sponsors: the Department of External Affairs (Cultural Relations Committee).

W. B. Yeats: Cast a Cold Eye (1989) 90 min.

Director: Seán Ó Mórdha

Detailed study of the life and work of the poet, reflecting on the art and politics which affected him.

Credits Based on Richard Ellman's *Yeats: The Man and the Masks*. Narrator: T. P. McKenna, Voice of W. B. Yeats: Bosco Hogan, Music: Seoirse Bodley, Lighting Cameraman: Peter Dorney, Assisstant Cameraman: Declan Emerson, Sound Recordist: Pat Hayes, Dubbing Mixer: Peter Smith, Studio Sound: Dermot Moynihan, Electricians: James McGuire, Dave Durney, Accountant: Cooney Corrigan, Rostrum Cameraman: Nico Vermuelen, Graphic Design: Ali O'Donnell, Production Assistant: Kitty Mullany, Film Editing: Jim Duggan, Teresa Smith, Executive

Producers: Nigel Williams, Derek Bailey, Producer/Director: Seán Ó Mórdha. We thank: Michael York, Anne Yeats, Mary Ellman, Society of Authors, National Library of Ireland, Abbey Theatre, Thor Ballylee, Coole Park, Royal Borough of Kensington, Aer Lingus, Dr Pott. Araby Productions for BBC Northern Ireland and RTÉ.

We'll Fight and No Surrender: Ulster Loyalism and the Protestant Sense of History (1990) 55 min.
Director: Desmond Bell
A video document exploring the culture of loyalism in Northern Ireland which concludes, 'for a people with no dream of the future, the past constantly beckons'.
Credits Narrator: Patricia Murphy, Editor: Jim Duggan, Production Crew: John Armstrong, Liam Doyle, Marcus Free, Gerald Hoban, Ronan Kelly, Victor Lacher, Fergal Spelman, Technical Assistance: Frank Clarke, Writer/Director: Desmond Bell. Made with the assistance of the School of Communications, NIHE Dublin. A Glass Machine production grant aided by the Arts Council/An Comhairle Ealaion.

Whitefriar Street Serenade (1990) 52 min.
Director: Seamus Carraher
Profile of working-class Whitefriar Street (Dublin) and its inhabitants.
Credits Producer: Bernice Donoghue, Director, Script: Seamus Carraher, Photography: Art O'Laoghaire.

Who Fears to Speak of '98? (1948) 16 min.
Director: Kevin Anderson.
Commemorative documentary detailing the festivities celebrating the 150th anniversary of the 1798 rebellion. Features footage of 1916 veterans and members of the government attending.
Credits Director: Kevin Anderson, Production Company: Abbey Films, Photography: George Fleischmann, Script: Liam O'Leary, Narrator: Cyril Cusack, Singer: Sean Mooney.

Would You Believe? (1990s–2000s) 30 min each episode
Directors: Various
Religious-themed weekly television series produced by RTÉ. A pale succcessor to *Radharc*.
Credits Rostrum Camera: Eric Ryan, Electrical Services: Jim Butler, Lighting Cameraman: Breffni Byrne, Location Sound: Eddie Duffy, Post-Production Sound: Peter Fletcher, Video Editor: David Whelan, Producer/Director: Julian Vignoles.

The Years of Change (1997) 6 × 30 min.
Director: Louis Marcus
A compilation of *Amharc Éireann* newsreel footage with a voice over documenting the years during which the Gael-Linn service operated and positing that they constitute the most important years in recent Irish history.
Credits Amharc Éireann was produced for Gael-Linn by Colm Ó Laoghaire Principal Cameraman/Director: Jim Mulkerns, Acknowledgement: Irish Film Archive. *The Years of Change*: Editor: Joe Marcus, Narrator: Eamonn Lawlar, Facilities: Picture Company, Telecine: Glenn Kyte, Screen Scene, Dubbing: Éanna Ó Cnáimhsí, Telegael, Series Advisers: Tomás Mac Gabhann, Seán Mac Reeamoinn, Written and Directed by: Louis Marcus.

A Year 'Til Sunday (1999) 51 min.

Director: Pat Comer

An account of the Galway senior football team's successful bid for the 1998 All Ireland Football Championship.

Credits Many thanks to the Galway Senior Football Team and Management and a special thanks to all their families, friends and supporters. Camera: Pat Comer, Additional Photography: Ken O'Mahony, Michael O'Dubhain, Reamonn Mac Donnacha, Trevor Laffey, Patrick Barron, Paul Fennell, Pascal Brooks, Sound: Enda Cahill, Colm O'Mealoid, Finbarr Byrne, Iarla O'Maolain, Colm Kirwan, Pat Lavelle, On-Line Editor: Alan Sullivan, VT Operator: Paul Byrne, Assistant Editor: Nicky Fennell, Production Assistant: Imelda Kelly, Production Coordinator: Dearbhla McNulty, Legal Services: John Given, A&L Goodbody, Rostrum Camera: Ger Conway, Track Laying: Mick Mahon, Kirstin Sheridan, Post-Production Sound Number 4: Paddy Gibbons, Simon Flanagan, Facilities: Windmill Lane Pictures Ltd., Colourist: Dave Gibson, Post-Production Coordinator: Pauline O'Rourke, Technical Support: Declan Hogan. Special Thanks: Leonard Ryan and Setanta, Croke Park, Victor Finn and MCPS, Mary Callery, Michael Hyland, Clare Duignan, Mike Kelly, Paul Power, Robert Walpole, Tommie Gorman, Aidan Goulding, Steve McQueen, Thomas Hardiman, Pat Collins, John Sheehan and Eleanor McCarthy, Fergus Tighe, Rupert H. Murray, Tony Ryan, Mick Tarpey, Brian Carty, Tommy Varden and Michael O'Muircheartaigh, Chris Crehan, Mellers Power, Adrian Devane, Stephen D'Arcy, Eoin Joyce, Brendan Coffey, the Breffni Bar, the Vatican Pub, the Red Gap, An Chistin, MacNamara's Pub, James Finlan, JDM, Galway Film Centre, all at Windmill Lane Pictures, Ollie Jennings, the Dalton Family, the Healy Family, Sal Comer, Therese and Harry, Jeff Canavan. Film Editor: James E. Dalton, Producer: David Power, Director: Pat Comer. A Comer & Co. / Power Pictures Production for RTÉ. Power Pictures © Comer & Co. / Power Pictures 1998.

Yeats Country (1965) 18 min.

Director: Patrick Carey

Pictorial study of the landscape of Co. Sligo, where W. B. Yeats was raised. The images are accompanied by excerpts from Yeats's poetry. Very similar in style and approach to *W. B. Yeats: A Tribute*. The film won a Golden Bear at the Berlin Film Festival, a diploma of merit at the Edinburgh Film Festival, first prize at the Chicago Film Festival, and First Prize for best colour short at the Barcelona International Film Festival. It was nominated for an American Academy of Motion Picture Arts and Sciences Award in 1966.

Credits Production Company: Aengus Films, Producers: Joe Mendoza, Patrick Carey, Director, Photography: Patrick Carey, Narrators: Tom St John Barry, Niall Toibín, Editor: Anne Chegwidden, Music: Brian Boydell, Sound: Peter Hunt, Literary Advisers: T. R. Henn, Liam Miller, Sponsors: the Dept of External Affairs.

'Youghal Gazette' (untitled) (1910–22) various durations

Directors: James and Thomas Horgan

Generic title given to a selection of documentary footage taken between 1910 and 1922 (roughly) in Youghal, Co. Cork by the Horgan Brothers.

Secondary filmography

Non-Fiction

7 Up (UK, 1963) Dir: Michael Apted.

An American Family (US, 1973) Dir: Craig Gilbert.

A propos de Nice (Fra., 1930) Dir: Jean Vigo.

Arctic Outpost (Can., 1960) Dir: John Feeney.

The Arrival of a Train (Fra., 1895) Dirs: Pierre and August Lumière.

The Atomic Café (US, 1982) Dirs: Kevin and Pierce Rafferty, Jayne Loader.

At the Derby (UK, 1896) Dir: Robert Paul.

Berlin (Ger., 1927) Dir: Walter Ruttman.

The Black Cruise (Fra., 1926) Dir: Léon Poirier.

Bloody Sunday (UK, 1994) Dir: Tony Stark.

The Bridge (Neth., 1928) Dir: Joris Ivens.

Burden of Dreams (Ger., 1982) Dir: Les Blank.

A Cattle Drive in Galway (UK, 1908) Dir: Robert Paul.

Chang (US, 1927) Dirs: Merian C. Cooper, Ernest B. Schoedsack.

Chronique d'un été / Chronicle of a Summer (Fra., 1961) Dirs: Jean Rouch, Edgar Morin.

City of Gold (Can., 1957) Dirs: Tom Daily, Colin Low, Wolf Koenig.

The Civil War (US, 1990) Dir: Ken Burns.

Congorilla (US, 1929) Dirs: Mr and Mrs Martin Johnson.

Culloden (UK, 1964) Dir: Peter Watkins.

Daughters of the Troubles (US, 1996) Dir: Marcia Rock.

The Dead: 25 Bloody Years (UK, 1994) Pro: Peter Dale.

Drifters (UK, 1929) Dir: John Grierson.

Endgame in Ireland (UK, 2001) Dir: Mick Gold.

Fall of the Romanov Dynasty (USSR, 1927) Dir: Esfir Shub.

Grass (US, 1925) Dirs: Merian C. Cooper, Ernest B. Schoedsack.

Harlan County, USA (US, 1976) Dir: Barbara Kopple.

How the Myth Was Made (US, 1978) Dir: George Stoney.

The Importance of Being Dublin (UK, 1973) Dir: Norman Cohen.

Ireland: Behind the Wire (UK, 1974) Dir unknown.

Journey Into Spring (UK, 1957) Dir: Ralph Keene.

'last night, another soldier' (UK, 1973) Pro: Eric Davidson.

The Life of an American Fireman (US, 1905) Dir: Edwin S. Porter.

Life on the Great Southern and Western Railway (UK, 1904) Dir: Louis de Clerq.

The Living Stone (Can., 1958) Dir: John Feeney.

London to Killarney (UK, 1907) Dir: Arthur Melbourne-Cooper.

Lonely Boy (Can., 1961) Dirs: Wolf Koenig, Roman Kroitor.

The Long Journey Home (US, 1997) Dir: Thomas Lennon.
Looking for the Man of Aran (UK, 1995) Dir: Sebastian Eschenback.
Loyalists (UK, 1998) Dir: Peter Taylor.
Man of Aran (UK, 1934) Dir: Robert Flaherty.
Man with a Movie Camera (USSR, 1929) Dir: Dziga Vertov.
The Memory of Justice (Ger. / US, 1976) Dir: Marcel Ophuls.
Moana: A Romance of the South Seas (US, 1926) Dir: Robert Flaherty.
Moscow (USSR, 1927) Dir: Denis Kaufman.
Nanook of the North (US, 1922) Dir: Robert Flaherty.
Night and Fog / Nuit et brouillard (Fra., 1955) Dir: Alain Resnais.
Olympia (Ger., 1938) Dir: Leni Riefenstahl.
The Plow that Broke the Plains (US, 1936) Dir: Pare Lorentz.
Pompiers à Lyons (Fra., 1896) Dir: Lumière Assoc.
Provos (UK, 1997) Dir: Peter Taylor.
Rain (Neth., 1929) Dir: Joris Ivens.
Rien que les heures (Fra., 1926) Dir: Alberto Cavalcanti.
The River (US, 1936) Dir: Pare Lortenz.
Roger & Me (US, 1989) Dir: Michael Moore.
A Sense of Loss (US, Swiss., 1972) Dir: Marcel Ophüls.
Sherman's March (US, 1986) Dir: Ross McElwee.
Shoah (US, 1985) Dir: Claude Lanzmann.
The Sorrow and the Pity (Fra., 1971) Dir: Marcel Ophüls.
The Thin Blue Line (US, 1988) Dir: Erroll Morris.
Titicut Follies (US, 1967) Dir: Frederick Wiseman.
Touring Great Cities: Dublin (UK, 1974) Dir: Harry Cowdy.
Triumph of the Will (Ger., 1934) Dir: Leni Riefenstahl.
The Unfinished War (UK, 1976) Dir: David Elstein.
Whaling Ashore and Afloat (UK, 1908) Dir: Robert Paul.
The Yellow Cruise (Fra., 1929) Dir: Léon Poirier.

Fiction

Anne Devlin (Irl., 1984) Dir: Pat Murphy.
Battleship Potemkin (USSR, 1925) Dir: Sergei Eisenstein.
The Bishop's Story (Irl., 1994) Dir: Bob Quinn.
Budawanny (Irl., 1987) Dir: Bob Quinn.
Caoineadh Airt Uí Laoire (Irl., 1975) Dir: Bob Quinn.
Criminal Conversation (Irl., 1980) Dir: Kieran Hickey.
Down the Corner (Irl., 1977) Dir: Joe Comerford.
Earth (USSR, 1930) Dir: Alexander Dovzhenko.
End of St. Petersberg (USSR., 1927) Dir: Vsevelod Pudovkin.
Exposure (Irl., 1978) Dir: Kieran Hickey.
Freaks (US, 1932) Dir: Tod Browning.
A Hard Day's Night (UK, 1964) Dir: Richard Lester.
In the Name of the Father (Irl., 1993) Dir: Jim Sheridan.
Irish Wives and English Husbands (UK, 1907) Dir: Arthur Melbourne-Cooper.
The Italian Job (UK, 1969) Dir: Peter Collinson.
I Went Down (Irl., 1997) Dir: Paddy Breathnach.
The Lad From Old Ireland (US, 1910) Dir: Sidney Olcott.
The Last Picture Show (US, 1971) Dir: Peter Bogdanovich.
The Magdalene Sisters (UK, 2002) Dir: Peter Mullan.
A Man for All Seasons (UK, 1966) Dir: Fred Zinnemann.

Michael Collins (Irl. / US, 1996) Dir: Neil Jordan.
Monty Python's Life of Brian (UK, 1979) Dir: Terry Jones.
Partie d'écarte (Fra., 1895) Dirs: Pierre and Auguste Lumière.
Les Quatres Cent Coups / The 400 Blows (Fra., 1959) Dir: François Truffaut.
The Quiet Man (US, 1952) Dir: John Ford.
Ryan's Daughter (UK, 1970) Dir: David Lean.
Sinful Davey (UK, 1969) Dir: John Huston.
Sinners (Irl., 2001) Dir: Aisling Walsh.
Traveller (Irl., 1981) Dir: Joe Comerford.
Trojan Eddie (Irl., 1996) Dir: Gillies McKinnon.
Up the Junction (UK, 1967) Dir: Peter Collinson.
Withdrawal (Irl., 1979) Dir: Joe Comerford.

Bibliography

Aitken, Ian (1990) *Film and Reform: John Grierson and the Documentary Film Movement*, London, Routledge.

Aitken, Ian (ed.) (1998) *The Documentary Film Movement: An Anthology*, Edinburgh, Edinburgh University Press.

Alfalfa (1968) 'That Wonder in Your Eye', *Take One*, 2:1, March.

Anderson, Carolyn and Thomas W. Benson (1991) *Documentary Dilemmas: Frederick Wiseman's Titicut Follies*, Carbondale and Edwardsville, Southern Illinois University Press.

Anstey, Edgar (n.d.) 'The March of Time', *The Movie*, 7:124.

Aristotle (1970) *The Poetics of Aristotle*, trans. Preston H. Epps, Chapel Hill, University of North Carolina Press.

Ashcroft, Bill, Gareth Griffiths and Helen Tiffin (eds) (1995) *The Post-Colonial Studies Reader*, London, Routledge.

Barnouw, Erik (1993) *Documentary: A History of the Non-Fiction Film*, 2nd rev. edn, Oxford, Oxford University Press.

Barsam, Richard (1988) *The Vision of Robert Flaherty: The Artist as Myth and Filmmaker*, Bloomington and Indianapolis, Indiana University Press.

Barsam, Richard (1992) *Non-Fiction Film*, rev. edn, Bloomington and Indianapolis, Indiana University Press.

Barthes, Roland (1989) *Mythologies*, trans. Annette Lavers, London, Paladin Grafton.

Barton, Ruth (1999) 'Feisty Colleens and Faithful Sons: Gender in Irish Cinema', *Cineaste*, 24:2–3, 40–5.

Baudrillard, Jean (1999) *Revenge of the Crystal: Selected Writings on the Object and its Destiny 1968–1983*, trans. Paul Foss and Julian Pefanis, London, Pluto.

Begg, David (1997) 'The Danger Posed to Democracy by the New Media Monopolies', in Damien Kiberd (ed.), *The Media in Ireland: The Search for Diversity*, Dublin, Open Air, 59–67.

Berger, John (1972) *Ways of Seeing*, Harmondsworth, Penguin/BBC.

Bhabha, Homi K. (1995) Signs taken for Wonders', in Bill Ashcroft, Gareth Griffiths and Helen Tiffin (eds), *The Post-Colonial Studies Reader*, London, Routledge.

Biskind, Peter (1979) *Hearts and Minds*, in Louis Jacobs (ed.), *The Documentary Tradition*, 2nd edn, New York, W. W. Norton.

Bluem, William (1965) *Documentary in American Television: Form, Function, Method*, New York, Hastings House.

Bordwell, David and Kirstin Thompson (2001) *Film Art: An Introduction*, 6th edn, McGraw Hill.

Brassell, Bruce R. (1996) 'Bullets, Ballots and Bibles: Documenting the History of the Gay and Lesbian Struggle in America', *Cineaste*, 21:4, 17–21.

Breen, John (1994) 'The Empirical Eye: Edmund Spenser's A View of the Present State of Ireland', *Irish Review*, 16, Autumn/Winter.

Breen, Richard, Damian F. Hannan, David B. Rottman and Christopher T. Whelan (1990) *Understanding Contemporary Ireland: State, Class and Development in the Republic of Ireland*, Dublin, Gill & Macmillan.

Brown, Terence (1995) 'Ireland, Modernism, and the 1930s', in P. Coughlan and A. Davis (eds), *Modernism and Ireland: Poetry in the 1930s*, Cork, Cork University Press, 24–42.

Browne, Noel C. (1951) 'Health Education Through The Film', *National Film Quarterly Bulletin of the National Film Institute of Ireland*, 1:4, March, 11–12.

Browne, Vincent (1996) 'The Rocky Road to Dublin', *Film West*, Summer, 34–6.

Browne, Vincent (1999) 'Airbrushing History: The Irish Soldier and the First World War', Film West, 35, February, 40–2.

Brydon, Diana (1995) 'The White Inuit Speaks', in Bill Ashcroft, Gareth Griffiths and Helen Tiffin (eds), *The Post-Colonial Studies Reader*, London, Routledge, 136–42.

Budhlaeir, Liam G. (1965) 'Tráchtaireacht Scannán', *Vision*, 1:4, Autumn, 25–6.

Burch, Nöel (1978) 'Two Recent British Films and the Documentary Ideology', *Screen*, 19:2, Summer, 119–29.

Burch, Nöel (1990) *Life to Those Shadows*, Berkeley, Los Angeles and London, BFI/University of California Press.

Butler, Pat (1998) 'An Open Letter to Harvey O'Brien, Critic, re Ballyseedy', *Film Ireland*, February/March, 46.

Calder-Marshall, Arthur (1963) *The Innocent Eye: The Life of Robert J. Flaherty*, London, W. H. Allen.

Carty, Ciaran (1995) *Confessions of a Sewer Rat: A Personal History of Censorship and the Irish Cinema*, Dublin, New Island Books.

Casey, Mike (1998) 'Toke'nism', *Film West*, 32, 48–50.

Charney, Leo and Vanessa R. Schwartz (eds) (1995) *Cinema and the Invention of Modern Life*, Berkeley and Los Angeles, University of California Press.

Christie, Ian (1994) *The Last Machine*, London, BFI/BBC.

Clarke, Donald (1998/1999) 'The Real Boxer', *Film Ireland*, December/January, 14–16.

Collins, Mike (1996) 'Bíonn an Fhirinne Searbh', *Film Ireland*, June/July, 17–18.

Collins, Mike (1997) 'Peeping Toms and Dirty Rats', *Film Ireland*, April/May, 24–5.

Collins, Noreen (1998) 'Twelve Days in July', *Film West*, 34, October, 20–2.

Collins, Pat (1996) 'Home Movie Nights', *Film West*, Summer, 20–2.

Comiskey, Ray (1983) 'There's Many a Slip . . . ', *Irish Times*, 20 October.

Corless, Damian (1998) *Pulp Friction: Irish Feuds and Public Ructions*, Dublin, Kaysons Publications.

Corner, John (1996) *The Art of Record*, Manchester, Manchester University Press.

Corr, Alan (2001) 'After the Deluge', *The RTÉ Guide*, 13–19 October, 4–6.

Coughlan, Patricia, and Alex Davis (eds) (1995) *Modernism and Ireland: The Poetry of the 1930s*, Cork, Cork University Press.

Dahlgren, Peter (1996) *Television and the Public Sphere: Citizenship, Democracy and the Media*, London, Sage.

Dalsimer, Adele M. (ed.) (1993) *Visualising Ireland: National Identity and the Pictorial Tradition*, London, Faber & Faber.

Daly, John (2001) 'De Buitlear Did It', *Irish Independent Weekend*, 13 January, 22–4.

Devane, Fr. Richard S. J. (ed.) (1943), *The Irish Cinema Handbok*, Dublin, Parkside Press.

Dornfield, Barry (1998) *Producing Public Television: Producing Public Culture*, Princeton, NJ, Princeton University Press.

Dowling, Jack, Lelia Doolan and Bob Quinn (1969) *Sit Down and Be Counted: The Cultural Evolution of a Television Station*, Dublin, Wellington.

Doyle, Diarmuid (1999) 'A Match of Games and Sets', *Sunday Tribune*, 17 January, 3.

Dunkley, Chris (1976) 'Carey on Filming', *Radio Times*, 19 May–4 June, 13.

Dunn, Joseph (1986) *No Tigers in Africa!: Recollections and Reflections on 25 Years of Radharc*, Dublin, Columba.

Dunn, Joseph (1994) *No Lions in the Hierarchy: An Anthology of Sorts*, Dublin, Columba.

Eagleton, Terry (1991) *Ideology: An Introduction*, London, Verso.

Eagleton, Terry (1998) *Crazy John and the Bishop and Other Essays on Irish Culture*, Cork, Cork University Press/Field Day.

Edgell, Stephen, Sandra Walklate and Gareth Wiliams (eds) (1995) *Debating the Future of the Public Sphere: Transforming the Public and Private Domains in Free Market Societies*, Aldershot, Avebury.

Eitzen, Dirk (1995) 'When is a Documentary? Documentary as a Mode of Reception', *Cinema Journal*, 35:1, Fall, 81–102.

Eldridge, John (ed.) (1993) *Getting the Message: News, Truth and Power*, London, Routledge, 1993.

Erens, Patricia (1988) 'Women's Documentary Filmmaking: The Personal is Political', in Alan Rosenthal (ed.), *New Challenges for Documentary*, Berkeley and Los Angeles, University of California Press, 554–65.

Evans, E. Estyn (1992) *The Personality of Ireland: Habitat, Heritage and History*, Dublin, Lilliput.

Fagan, James C. (1950) 'The Institute's Aims', *National Film Quarterly Bulletin of the National Film Institute of Ireland*, 1:2, September, 15–18.

Fanon, Frantz (1963) *The Wretched of the Earth*, trans. Constance Farrington, New York, Grove.

Farrell, Brian (2001) 'Introduction', in Nuala Ní Dhomhnaill (ed.), *100 Years: Ireland in the 20th Century*, Dublin: TownHouse and CountryHouse, v–vi.

Fay, Liam (2000) 'Tried and Trusted', *Sunday Times*, 7 April, 26.

Fay, Liam (2001) 'Dishonest to God', *Sunday Times*, 7 April, 6–7.

Fischel, Anne (1989) 'Engagement and the Documentary', *Jump Cut*, 34, March, 35–40.

Flynn, Arthur (1996) *Irish Film 100 Years*, Bray, Kestrel Books.

Fortune, Antoinette T. (1965) 'Holding Up a Mirror to the Irish', *Vision*, 1:1, January, 25–7.

Gardener, Robert (1996) 'The Impulse to Preserve', in C. Warren (ed.), *Beyond Document: Essays on Nonfiction Film*, Hanover, Wesleyan University Press, University Press of New England, 169–80.

Georgakas, Dan (1996) 'Cinema of the New Deal', *Cineaste*, 21:4, 47–9.

Gerrard, John (1948/1949) 'Ireland and the Documentary', *Sight & Sound*, 17:68, Winter, 164–5.

Gerrard, John (1949) 'Irish Documentaries', *Sight & Sound*, 17:69, Spring, 133–4.

Gibbons, Luke (1984) 'From Kitchen Sink to Soap: Drama and the Serial Form on Irish Television' in Martin McLoone and John MacMahon (eds), *Television and Irish Society*, Dublin, RTÉ/IFI, 21–51.

Gibbons, Luke (1996) *Transformations in Irish Culture*, Cork, Cork University Press/Field Day.

Gilbert, Craig (1988) 'Reflections on *An American Family*, II', in Alan Rosenthal (ed.), *New Challenges for Documentary*, Berkeley and Los Angeles, University of California Press, 288–307.

Gillespie, Elgy (1980) 'Love in a Cool Climate', *Irish Times*, 16 December.

Gillespie, Raymond (1993) 'Describing Dublin: Francis Place's Visit, 1698–1699' in Adele Dalsimer (ed.), *Visualising Ireland: National Identity and the Pictorial Tradition*, London, Faber & Faber, 99–117.

Gorham, Maurice (1967) *Forty Years of Irish Broadcasting*, Dublin, RTÉ Talbot.

Graham, Brian (ed.) (1997) *In Search of Ireland: A Cultural Geography*,London, Routledge.

Graham, Colin (2001), *Deconstructing Ireland: Identity, Theory, Culture*, Edinburgh, Edinburgh University Press.

Grant, Barry Keith (1992) *Voyages of Discovery: The Cinema of Frederick Wiseman*, Urbana and Chicago, University of Illinois Press.

Grant, Barry Keith, and Jeannette Sloniowski (eds) (1998) *Documenting the Documentary: Close Readings of Documentary Film and Video*, Detroit, Wayne State University Press.

Grierson, John (1947) 'A Time for Enquiry', *Documentary 47*, Programme for the First International Festival of Documentary Films, Edinburgh, 31 August–7 September, 3–7.

Grierson, John (1948) 'A Film Policy for Ireland', *Studies*, 37: 147, September, 283–91.

Griffiths, Gareth (1995) 'The Myth of Authenticity', in Bill Ashcroft, Gareth Griffiths and Helen Tiffin (eds), *The Post-Colonial Studies Reader*, London, Routledge, 237–41.

Guynn, William (1998) 'The Art of National Projection: Basil Wright's *Song of Ceylon*', in B. Grant and J. Sloniowski (eds), *Documenting the Documentary*, Detroit, Wayne State University Press, 1998, 83–98.

Harris, Bernard and Grattan Freyer (eds) (1981) *The Achievement of Seán Ó Riada: Integrating Tradition*, Ballina, Irish Humanities Centre and Keohanes.

Heaney, Mick (1998) 'Who Fears not to Speak of '98?' *Sunday Times*, 31 May, 11.

Heidegger, Martin (1971) *Poetry, Language, Thought*, trans. Albert Hofstader, New York, Harper & Row.

Heider, Karl G. (1976) *Ethnographic Film*, Austin, University of Texas Press.

Herman, Edward S. and Noam Chomsky (1988) *Manufacturing Consent: The Political Economy of the Mass Media*, New York, Pantheon Books.

Hill, John (1980) 'Real to Reel, Reel to Real', *Film Directions*, 3:11, 17–19.

Hill, John (1999) 'Filming in the North', *Cineaste*, 24:2–3, Spring/Summer, 26–7.

Hill, John, Martin McLoone and Paul Hainsworth (eds) (1994) *Border Crossing: Film in Ireland, Britain, and Europe*, Belfast, Insitute of Irish Studies/BFI.

Hill, John, and Pamela Church Gibson (eds) (1998) *The Oxford Guide to Film Studies*, Oxford, Oxford University Press.

Holt, Eddie (1996) 'Talk Television', *Irish Times*, 10 April, 11.

Horgan, Donal (1988) *Echo after Echo: Killarney and its History*, Cork, Blackface.

Horrigan, Bill (1993) 'Notes on AIDS and its Combatants', in Michael Renov (ed.), *Theorizing Documentary* London, Routledge, 164–73.

Howe, Stephen (2000) *Ireland and Empire: Colonial Legacies in Irish History and Culture*, Oxford, Oxford University Press.

Hyndman, Marilyn (1992) 'Resisting Cultural Arrest', *Film Ireland*, November/December, 16–17.

Inglis, Tom (1998) *Moral Monopoly: The Rise and Fall of the Catholic Church in Modern Ireland*, 2nd edn, Dublin, UCD Press.

Izod, Richard, and Richard Kilborn, with Matthew Hibberd (eds) (2000) *From Grierson to the Docu-soap: Breaking the Boundaries*, Luton, University of Luton Press.

Jacobs, Louis (ed.) (1979) *The Documentary Tradition*, 2nd edn,New York, W. W. Norton.

Jameson, Frederic (1992) *The Geopolitical Aesthetic*, Bloomington and Illinois, Indiana University Press.

Jameson, Frederic (1998) *The Cultural Turn: Selected Writings on the Postmodern, 1983–1998*, London, Verso.

Kearney, Richard (1997) *Postnationalist Ireland: Politics, Culture, Philosophy*, London, Routledge.

Kehoe, Paddy (1997) 'Tragedies of Kerry', *RTÉ Guide*, 7 November, 18.

Kehoe, Paddy (1998) 'Irish Heartbeat', *RTÉ Guide*, 10 July, 14–16.

Kelly, Peter (1996) 'Through a Lens Darkly', *Film Ireland*, August/September, 25.

Kennedy, Brian P. (1993) 'The Traditional Irish Thatched House: Image and Reality 1793–1993', in Adele M. Dalsimer (ed.) *Visualising Ireland: National Identity and the Pictorial Tradition*, Boston and London, Faber & Faber

Kenny, Conor (1993) 'Shooting Back', *Film Ireland*, 37, February/March, 16–17.

Kenny, Kevin (ed.) (2003) *New Directions in Irish-American History*, Madison, University of Wisconsin Press.

Kelly, Mary (1984) 'Twenty Years of Current Affairs on RTÉ' in Martin McLoone and John MacMahon (eds), *Television and Irish Society: 21 Years of Irish Television*, Dublin, RTÉ/IFI.

Kepley, Vance Jr. (1986) *In the Service of the State: The Cinema of Alexander Dovzhenko*, Madison, University of Wisconsin Press.

Keyssar, Hélène (1996) 'The Toil of Thought: On Several Nonfiction Films by Women', in Charles Warren (ed.), *Beyond Document: Essays on Nonfiction Film*, Hanover, Wesleyan University Press, 101–36.

Kiberd, Damien (ed.) (1997) *Media in Ireland: The Search for Diversity*, Dublin, Open Air.

Kiberd, Declan (1995) *Inventing Ireland: The Literature of the Modern Nation*, London, Jonathan Cape.

Kilborn, Richard and John Izod (1997) *An Introduction to Television Documentary: Confronting Reality*, Manchester, Manchester University Press.

Kuehl, Jerry (1988) 'History on the Public Screen II', in Alan Rosenthal (ed.), *New Challenges for Documentary*, Berkeley and Los Angeles, University of California Press, 444–53.

Kuhn, Annette (1978) 'The Camera I: Observations on Documentary', *Screen*, 19:2, Summer, 71–83.

Lane, Jim (1993) 'Notes on Theory and the Autobiographical Documentary Film in America', *Wide Angle*, 15:3, July, 21–35.

Lavery, Dermot (1992) 'Power in the Lens', *Film Ireland*, 32, November/December, 18–21.

Lavie, Smadar (1990) *The Poetics of Military Occupation: Mzeina Allegories of Bedouin Identity under Israeli and Egyptian Rule*, Berkeley and Los Angeles, University of California Press.

Lee, J. J. (1989) *Ireland 1912–1985: Politics and Society*, Cambridge, Cambridge University Press.

Lee, Joseph and Gearóid Ó Tuathaigh (1982) *The Age of deValera*, Dublin, Ward River.

Lennon, Peter (1964a), 'Climate of Repression', *Guardian*, 8 January, 10.

Lennon, Peter (1964b), 'Students in Blinkers', *Guardian*, 9 January, 8.

Lennon, Peter (1964c), 'Turbulent Priests', *Guardian*, 10 January, 10.

Lennon, Peter (1964d), 'Grey Eminence', *Guardian*, 11 January, 10.

Lesage, Julia (1978) 'The Political Aesthetics of the Feminist Documentary Film', *Quarterly Review of Film Studies,* 3:4, Fall, 507-23.

Lesage, Julia (1989) 'The Fictions of Documentary', *Jump Cut*, 3;4, March, 507–23.

Linehan, Hugh (2000) 'Davis's Inferno', *Irish Times*, 28 January, 13.

Lovell, Terry (1983) *Pictures of Reality*, London, BFI.

Lukács, Georg (1971) *History and Class Consciousness: Studies in Marxist Dialectics*, trans. Rodney Livingstone, London, Merlin.

Lynch, Declan (2000) 'It's Yesterday Once More', *Sunday Independent*, 24 September, 10L.

Lyons, F. S. L. (1973) *Ireland since the Famine*, 2nd edn, London, Fontana.

Lysaght, Charles (2003) 'When is an Archive not the Whole Story?' *Irish Times*, 10 January, 13.

MacBride, Sean (1951) 'A Native Film Industry', *National Film Quarterly Bulletin of the National Film Institute of Ireland*, 1:3, Spring, 26.

MacDermott, Eithne (1998) *Clann na Poblachta*, Cork, Cork University Press.

Macdonald, Kevin and Mark Cousins (1996) *Imagining Reality: The Faber Book of Documentary*, London, Faber & Faber.

MacKillop, James (ed.) (1999) *Contemporary Irish Cinema from The Quiet Man to Dancing at Lughnasa*, Syracuse, Syracuse University Press.

MacLochlainn, Alf (1966) 'Documentary is Dead', *Vision*, Spring, 12–13.

MacLochlainn, Alf (1967) 'A New Description of the Cinema', *Scannán*, February, 7.

Macorelles, Louis (1971) *Living Cinema: New Directions in Contemporary Film-Making*, trans. Isabel Quigly, London, George Allen & Unwin.

Mac Réamoinn, Seán (1996) *The Church in a New Ireland*, Dublin, Columba.

Mamber, Stephen (ed.) (1974) *Cinema Verite in America: Studies in Uncontrolled Documentary*, Cambridge, MA, MIT.

Manning, Maurice (2001) 'Blueshirts: Fascists or Defenders of the Free Speech?', *Irish Independent*, 12 January, 12.

Marcus, Louis (1965) 'Film Scripting and Direction', *Vision*, 1:3, Summer, 14–15.

Marcus, Louis (1967) 'A Dearth of Documentary', *The Irish Film Industry*, Dublin, Irish Film Society, 18–24.

Marcus, Louis (1992) 'Creating Reality', *Film Ireland*, 32, November/December, 12–13.

McAvera, Brian (1990) *Art, Politics and Ireland*, Dublin, Open Air.

McCarthy, Thomas (1978) *The Critical Theory of Jürgen Habermas*, London, Hutchinson.

McCracken, Kathleen (1999) 'Poetic Documentary: The Films of John T. Davis' in James MacKillop (ed.), *Contemporary Irish Cinema from The Quiet Man to Dancing at Lughnasa*, Syracuse, Syracuse University Press, 11–21.

McCurtain, Margaret (1993) 'The Real Molly Macree', in A. Dalsimer (ed.), *Visualising Ireland: National Identity and the Pictorial Tradition*, London, Faber & Faber, 9–21.

McDowell, Shelia (1989) 'Louis Marcus: One Man Show', *Film Base News*, 11, March/April, 6.

McIlroy, Brian (1988) *Irish Cinema*, Dublin, Anna Livia Press.

McIlroy, Brian (1998) *Shooting to Kill: Filmmaking and the 'Troubles' in Northern Ireland*, Wiltshire, Flicks Books.

McKeone, Marion (1998) 'In the Frame: An Interview with Alan Gilsenan', *Sunday Business Post*, 11 November, 41–2.

McLoone, Martin (ed.) (1996) *Broadcasting in a Divided Community: Seventy Years of the BBC in Northern Ireland*, Belfast, Institute of Irish Studies.

McLoone, Martin (2000) *Irish Film: The Emergence of a Contemporary Cinema*, London, British Film Institute.

McLoone, Martin and John MacMahon (eds) (1984) *Television and Irish Society: 21 Years of Irish Television*, Dublin, RTÉ/IFI.

McNally, Brenda (1998) 'An All-Digital Millennium', *Tracking*, Summer, 3–5.

McNally, Frank (1996) 'Talk Radio', *Irish Times*, 17 January, 16.

Metz, Christian (1974) *Language and Cinema*, trans. Donna Jean Umiker-Sebeok, The Hague, Mouton.

Michelson, Annette (ed.) and Kevin O'Brien (trans.) (1984) *Kino–Eye: The Writings of Dziga Vertov*, Berkleey and Los Angeles, University of California Press.

Moody, T. W. and F. X. Martin (eds) (1967) *The Course of Irish History*, Cork, Mercier.

Morash, Christopher (2002) *A History of Irish Theatre 1601–2000*, Cambridge, Cambridge University Press.

Morrison, George (1979) 'The Making of *Mise Éire*', *Irish Times*, 28 December.

Nietschmann, Bernard (1993) 'Authentic, State, and Virtual Geography in Film', *Wide Angle*, 15:4, October, 4–12.

Mullen, Pat (1935) *Man of Aran*, New York, E. P. Dutton.

Ní Chanainn, Áine (1992) *The Pioneers of Audio Visual Education in Ireland*, Dublin, n.p.

Ní Dhomhnaill, Nuala (ed.) (2001) *100 Years: Ireland in the 20th Century*, Dublin, TownHouse and CountryHouse.

Nichols, Bill (ed.) (1976) *Movies and Methods: Vol. 1*, Berkeley and Los Angeles, London, University of California Press.

Nichols, Bill (ed.) (1985) *Movies and Methods: Vol. 2*, Berkeley and Los Angeles, London, University of California Press.

Nichols, Bill (1991) *Representing Reality: Issues and Concepts in Documentary*, Bloomington and Indianapolis, Indiana University Press.

Nichols, Bill (2001) *Introduction to Documentary*, Bloomington and Indianapolis, Indiana University Press.

O'Brien, Harvey (1999) 'Documenting Ireland', *Cineaste*, 24:2–3, 64–9.

O'Brien, Harvey (2000) 'Projecting the Past: Historical Documentary in Ireland', *Historical Journal of Film, Radio and Television*, 20:3, 335–50.

O'Brien, Harvey (2001) 'Somewhere to Come Back to: The Filmic Journeys of John T. Davis', *Irish Studies Review*, 9:1, Autumn, 167–77.

O'Brien, Harvey (2003) 'Culture, Commodity, and Céad Míle Fáilte: US and Irish Tourist Films as a Vision of Ireland', in Kevin Kenny (ed.), *New Directions in Irish-American History*, Madison, University of Wisconsin Press, 248–62.

O'Connor, John, (1993) 'Ground Breaker', *Film Ireland*, October/November, 20–3.

O'Donnell, Fr. E. E., SJ (ed.) (1997) *Father Browne's Titanic Album*, Dublin, Wolfhound.

O'Donoghue, Donal (1998a) 'Who Fears to Speak?', *RTÉ Guide*, 10 April, 14.

O'Donoghue, Donal (1998b) 'Soul Survivors', *RTÉ Guide*, 1 May, 12–14.

O'Donoghue, Donal (1998c) 'Rebellion', *RTÉ Guide*, 8 May, 6–8.

O'Donoghue, Siobhán (1993/1994), 'Documenting the Present and Past', *Film Ireland*, 38, December, 8.

O'Kelly, K. (1951) 'O! To be an ESB Man,' *Sunday Press*, 19 August.

O'Kennedy, Leon (1959) 'Films and the Magic of Irish History,' *Scannán*, 4:1, November, 12–13.

O'Laoghaire, Colm (1957) 'Gael-Linn "Vest-Pocket" Documentaries', *Irish Film Quarterly Bulletin of the National Film Institute of Ireland*, March, 9–11.

O'Leary, Liam (1945) *Invitation to the Film*, Tralee, The Kerryman.

O'Leary, Liam (1990) *Cinema Ireland 1896–1950*, Dublin, The National Library of Ireland.

O'Mahony, Catherine (2003) 'Chavez Film Labelled "Best in the World"', *Sunday Business Post*, 15 June, 17.

O'Neill, Kevin (1993) 'Looking at the Pictures: Art and Aftfulness in Colonial Ireland', in Adele M. Dalsimer (ed.), *Visualising ireland: National Identity and the Pictorial Tradition*, London, Faber & Faber.

O'Neill, Martha (1990) 'Real Lives and Television: The Terror of Judgement', *Film Base News*, 17, April/June, 15–16.

O'Regan, John (ed.) (1993) *John T. Davis: Works*, Dublin, Gandon.

O'Shea, Brendan (1948) 'Documentaries Need Sponsors', *Irish Cinema Quarterly*, Winter, 21–3.

Paget, Derek (1998) *No Other Way to Tell It: Dramadoc/docudrama on Television*, Manchester, Manchester University Press.

Paget, Derek (1999), 'Tales of Cultural Tourism', in Alan Rosenthal (ed.), *Why Docudrama? Fact–Fiction on Film and TV*, Carbondale and Edwardsville, Southern Illinois University Press.

Parry, Benita (1995) 'Problems in Current Theories of Colonial Discourse', in Bill Ashcroft, Gareth Griffiths and Helen Tiffin (eds), *The Post-Colonial Studies Reader*, London, Routledge, 36–44.

Perris, Arnold (1985) *Music as Propaganda: Art to Persuade, Art to Control*, Greenwood.

Pettitt, Lance (1999) 'A Construction Site Queered: "Gay" Images in New Irish Cinema', *Cineaste*, 24:2–3, Spring/Summer, 61–3.

Pettitt, Lance (2000) *Screening Ireland: Film and Television Representation*, Manchester, Manchester University Press.

Pine, Richard (2002) *2RN and the Origins of Irish Radio*, Dublin, Four Courts.

Pius XI (1936) *Vigilanti Cura/On Motion Pictures*

Ponech, Trevor (1997) 'Visual Perception and Motion Picture Spectatorship', *Cinema Journal*, 37:1, Fall, 85–100.

Pym, John (1988) 'Ireland – Two Nations', in Alan Rosenthal (ed.), *New Challenges for Documentary*, Berkeley and Los Angeles, University of California Press, 480–7.

Quinn, Bob (1996) 'ArtFilmArtFilmArt', *Film Ireland*, October/November, 33.

Quinn, Bob (2001) *Maverick: A Dissident View of Broadcasting Today*, Kerry, Brandon.

Rabiger, Michael (1992) *Directing the Documentary*, 2nd edn, Boston, Focal.

Reeves, Nicholas (1999) *The Power of Film Propaganda: Myth or Reality?*, London, Cassell.

Renov, Michael (ed.) (1993) *Theorizing Documentary*, London, Routledge.

Riis, Jacob A. (1997) *How the Other Half Lives: Studies Among the Tenements of New York*, Harmondsworth, Penguin.

Roberts, Graham (1991) 'Esfir Shub: A Suitable Case for Treatment', *Historical Journal of Film, Radio and Television*, 11:3, 149–59.

Robinson, Tim (1993) 'Listening to the Landscape', *Irish Review*, 14, Autumn, 21–32.

Rockett, Kevin (1980a) *Film and Ireland: A Chronicle*, London, A Sense of Ireland .

Rockett, Kevin (1980b) 'Interview with Louis Marcus', *IFT News*, 3:12, December, 9–13.

Rockett, Kevin (1996) *The Irish Filmography*, Dublin, Red Mountain.

Rockett, Kevin (2001) '(Mis-) Representing the Irish Urban Landscape', in Mark Shiel and Tony Fitzmaurice (eds), *Cinema and the City: Film and Urban Societies in a Global Context*, Oxford, Blackwell, 217–28.

Rockett, Kevin, Luke Gibbons and John Hill (1988) *Cinema and Ireland*, London, Routledge.

Rosen, Philip (ed.) (1986) *Narrative, Apparatus, Ideology: A Film Theory Reader*, New York, Columbia University Press.

Rosenheim, Shawn (1996) 'Interrogating History' in Vivian Sobschack (ed.), *The Persistence of History*, London, Routledge/AFI, 1996, 219–34.

Rosenstone, Robert A. (1996) *Visions of the Past: The Challenge of Film to Our Idea of History*, Cambridge, MA, Harvard University Press.

Rosenthal, Alan (1971) *The New Documentary in Action: A Casebook in Film Making*, Berkeley and Los Angeles, University of California Press.

Rosenthal, Alan (ed.) (1988) *New Challenges for Documentary*, Berkeley and Los Angeles, University of California Press.

Rosenthal, Alan (ed.)(1999) *Why Docudrama? Fact-Fiction on Film and TV*, Carbondale and Edwardsville, Southern Illinois University Press.

Rothman, William (1997) *Documentary Film Classics*, Cambridge, Cambridge University Press.

Ryall, Tom (1978) *Teaching Through Genre*, Screen Education, 17.

Sacerdos (1950) 'National Film Institute: Its Functions', *National Film Quarterly Bulletin of the National Film Institute of Ireland*, 1:2, September.

Savage, Robert J. (1996) *Irish Television: The Political and Social Origins*, Cork, Cork University Press.

Schofield, Carey (1994) *Ireland in Old Photographs*, Boston, Little, Brown.

Sheehy, Ted (1996) 'The Windhover', *Film Ireland*, October/November, 16–17.

Sheehy, T. J. M. (1950a) 'An Irish and Catholic Documentary', *The Irish Catholic*, 9 March.

Sheehy, T. J. M. (1950b) 'Apply to Navan', *The Irish Catholic*, 30 March, 5.

Sheehy, T. J. M. (1967) 'The Tourist Film', *Vision*, 3:3, Summer, 4–5.

Sheeran, Patrick (1988) 'Genius Fabulae: The Irish Sense of Place', *Irish University Review*, 18:1, Autumn, 191–206.

Sheridan, John D. (1950) 'The Yeats Film', *National Film Quarterly Bulletin of the National Film Institute of Ireland*, June, 11.

Sherman, Sharon R. (1998) *Documenting Ourselves: Film, Video and Culture*, Lexington, KT, The University Press of Kentucky.

Shiel, Mark and Tony Fitzmaurice (eds) (2001), *Cinema and the City: Film and Urban Societies in a Global Context*, Oxford, Blackwell.

Slide, Anthony (1967) 'A British Film Pioneer in Ireland', *Vision*, 3:1, Winter, 5–6.

Smyth, Gerry (1997) *The Novel and the Nation: Studies in the New Irish Fiction*, London, Pluto.

Snyder, Robert L. (1994) *Pare Lorentz and the Documentary Film*, Reno and Las Vegas, University of Nevada Press.

Sobshack, Vivan (ed.) (1996) *The Persistence of History*, London, Routledge.

Sontag, Susan (1977) *On Photography*, New York, Dell.

Sorlin, Pierre (1980) *The Film in History*, Rowman & Littlefield.

Stites, Richard (1991) 'Soviet Movies for the Masses and for Historians', *Historical Journal of Film, Radio and Television*, 11:3, 243–53.

Swann, Paul (1989) *The British Documentary Film Movement 1926–1946*, Cambridge, Cambridge University Press.

Tallents, Stephen (1932) *The Projection of England*, London, Faber & Faber.

Taylor, Richard (1998) *Film Propaganda: Soviet Russia and Nazi Germany*, 2nd rev. edn, London, I. B. Tauris.

Tester, Keith (1994) *Media, Culture and Morality*, London, Routledge.

Tobias, Michael (ed.) (1998) *The Search for Reality: The Art of Documentary Filmmaking*, California, Michael Wiese.

Walker, Rev. Reginald, CSSp. (1950) 'National Film Institute: Ways and Means', *National Film Quarterly Bulletin of the National Film Institute of Ireland*, June, 6.

Warren, Charles (ed.) (1996) *Beyond Document: Essays on Nonfiction Film*, Hanover, Wesleyan University Press, University Press of New England.

Warren, Mark E. (1995) 'The Self in Discursive Democracy', in Stephen K. White (ed.), *The Cambridge Companion to Habermas*, Cambridge, Cambridge University Press, 167–200.

Watson, Iarfhlaith (2003) *Broadcasting in Irish: Minority Language, Radio, Television and Identity*, Dublin and Portland, Four Courts.

Weinberger, Elliot (1996) 'The Camera People', in C. Warren (ed.), *Beyond Document: Essays in Nonfiction Film*, Hanover, Wesleyan University Press, University Press of New England.

Welch, David (1983) *Propaganda and the German Cinema 1933–1945*, Oxford, Oxford University Press.

Whelan, Bernadette (1999) '$elling the Mar$hal Plan in Ireland: The Promi$e of Barty O'Brien', *Film West*, 35, February, 32–3.

White, Gerry (2003) 'Arguing with Ethnography: The Films of Bob Quinn and Pierre Perrault', *Cinema Journal*, 42:2, Winter, 101–24.

White, Harry (1998) *The Keeper's Recital: Music and Cultural History in Ireland, 1770–1970*, Cork, Cork University Press/Field Day.

White, Stephen K. (1995) *The Cambridge Companion to Habermas*, Cambridge, Cambridge University Press.

Whyte, J. H. (1980) *Church and State in Modern Ireland 1923–1979*, 2nd edn, Dublin, Gill & Macmillan.

Williams, Raymond (1983) *Keywords*, rev. and expanded edn, London, Fontana.

Winston, Brian (1993) 'The Documentary Film as Scientific Inscription', in Michael Renov (ed.), *Theorizing Documentary*, London, Routledge.

Winston, Brian (1995) *Claiming the Real: The Documentary Film Revisited, Griersonian Documentary and its Legitimations*, London, BFI.

Winston, Brian (1999) 'Documentary: How the Myth was Deconstructed', *Wide Angle*, 21:2, March, 70-86.

Wright, Basil (n.d.) 'Real Life on the Screen', *The Movie*, 7, 121–3.

Youdelman, Jeffrey (1988) 'Narration, Invention, and History' in Alan Rosenthal (ed.), *New Challenges for Documentary*, Berkeley and Los Angeles, University of California Press, 454–64.

Other sources

Active or Passive? green paper on broadcasting, government of Ireland, 1995.

Barton, Ruth and Harvey O'Brien (eds) *Keeping it Real: Issues and Directions in Irish Film and Television* (forthcoming, Wallflower Press, 2004).

Bunreacht na hÉireann / The Constitution of Ireland.

Cork Film Festival programmes (various).

Dublin Film Festival programmes (various).

Galway Film Fleadh programmes (various)

Irish Film Centre programmes (various).

O'Donoghue, Francis 'Louis Marcus: Documentary Filmmaker', MA dissertation, University College Dublin, 1994.

Index

1798 rebellion 63, 103–4, 132–3
1916 Rising
    events of 67, 74, 93, 139 nn5–6
    films about 51, 111–14, 116,
        120–1, 132, 157–8
    legacy of 68, 78, 88, 106, 108, 169,
        171–2, 210

abortion 204, 207–8, 209, 211, 230
actuality 9–10, 24, 34
agriculture 35, 40, 41–2, 64, 78, 79,
    91, 98, 151, 255
Amharc Éireann 104–6, 118, 123,
    124, 139 n7, 141, 148, 161, 238
Aran of the Saints 36–41, 49, 50, 54
Atlantean 193, 194–202, 207, 208,
    223–4
autobiography 197, 221–2

Barnouw, Eric 11, 12, 66, 260
Barsam, Richard 45, 144
Barthes, Roland 119–20
Barton, Ruth 204, 207
Bell, Desmond 246–7
Black, Donald Taylor 230, 241–3,
    247, 250, 253–4
Bord Fáilte 66, 88, 90, 150–1, 167,
    176
Britain
    film productions 45, 89, 109, 155,
        166, 188, 212
    before Irish independence 22, 24,
        110–11, 114–15, 134

as location 29, 70, 73, 82, 152
and Northern Ireland 104, 141,
    206
see also colonialism
British Broadcasting Corporation
    (BBC) 110, 131, 141, 148, 156,
    159, 181, 208, 245
British documentary movement 12,
    40, 73, 79, 80, 109, 146
Brown, Terence 52–3
Browne, Dr Noel 74, 81–2, 100 n12
Browne, Fr Frank 31–6, 38–9, 44,
    79–80, 135, 158, 161

Canada 108, 146
Carey, Patrick 145–50
Carlson, Cob 247
cartography 18–20
Catholic church
    in films 26, 38, 57, 80, 92, 125,
        171–6
    scandals 100 n12, 174, 193, 214,
        228–35
    social/political influence 32–3, 239,
        59–63, 73, 153, 159, 207, 213
children 26–7, 39, 70, 72, 194,
    209–10, 212, 226, 230
cinéma vérité 12, 144, 155, 163–6,
    172, 178, 203, 230, 241, 255
civil war (Irish) 30, 71, 101, 104, 108,
    111, 113, 133–6, 137
Clann na Poblachta 67, 69–71, 100
    n12

clothing/textile industries 80–1, 90, 183

Collins, Michael 7, 111–15

colonialism 7–8, 18–19, 22–4, 38, 43, 64, 85–6, 91, 111, 119, 130, 192, 254

communism 73, 176–7

community video 205, 246, 253

Constitution (Irish) 5, 59–60, 62, 129, 132, 143, 185, 204

Cork Film Festival 106, 107, 108, 177, 218, 244

Corner, John 9, 10, 75–6, 213–14, 255, 256, 258

Davidson, Norris 40, 46, 50, 100 n15

Davis, John T. 217–18, 248, 254

Dear Boy: The Story of Micheál Mac Liammóir 243, 247

Dear Daughter 230–5, 241, 244

De Buitléar, Éamon 149, 182

De Valera, Éamon 115
  in films 65, 115, 121, 175, 185
  in politics 29, 49, 59, 71, 100 n12, 111, 161
  as president 106, 121, 124, 143
  in public life 60, 63

digital television 239–40

distribution 40, 56, 73, 88, 105–6, 145, 166, 176–7, 195, 218, 250, 253

divorce 193, 204, 209, 230, 241, 257–8

docudrama 32, 49, 66, 74–8, 82, 135, 157–8, 181–2, 229, 231

Doyle, Sé Merry 227, 236 n3, 254

Eagleton, Terry 102–3, 130, 138

education 39, 59, 61, 104, 156, 171, 181, 228–9

emergency services 24, 256, 258–9

emigration 70, 77, 80, 192, 208–9, 212, 215, 247, 256

ethnography 30, 36–8, 195–6, 249

Eucharistic Congress 1932 32–4, 38–9, 49, 54, 131

Evans, E. Estyn 17–18

Family, The 184–5

Fanon, Frantz 7, 85, 193

Faithful Departed 152

fascism 33, 35, 46

feminism 127–8, 185, 203–8

First World War 32, 134–5, 215

fisheries 151

Fitzpatrick, James A. 51

Flaherty, Robert 29, 30, 31, 37, 40, 50, 149, 166
  see also Man of Aran

Fleá 163–5, 170, 172, 183

Fleischmann, George 79, 84, 86–7, 95, 151, 160

folklore 19, 31, 34–5, 40, 116, 155

Free Cinema 155

Gaelic Athletic Association (GAA) 27, 162, 169, 172, 249

Gael-Linn 103–6, 109, 116–18, 123, 142, 155, 156, 161–8, 181, 248

geographic montage 18, 20–1, 28, 53

Gibbons, Luke 2, 4, 7–8, 16, 20, 50, 52, 88–9, 150, 180, 237

Gilsenan, Alan 134, 208–17, 244, 253

government sponsorship 49, 57, 62–3, 66, 74–6, 81–2, 86, 118

Graham, Brian 2, 18

Graham, Colin 7, 8, 194

Great Famine 59, 64, 169

Grierson, John 10, 28, 30, 45, 48, 54, 56–8, 68, 80, 88, 149, 166

Griersonian documentary 2, 6, 56–7, 146, 166, 259

Habermas, Jürgen 237–8

Harvest 31, 35, 41–3, 50, 79

Haughey, Charles J. 126–7, 160, 179–80, 208

Hearts and Souls 241, 245

Heidegger, Martin 2, 17, 21, 53, 102
Heider, Karl 36–8, 42
Hickey, Kieran 109, 152, 159, 180–1
hidden camera 95, 160
historiography 101–2
homelessness 160, 234, 259–60
Home Movie Nights 213–14, 216
homosexuality 211, 242–3
Horgan Brothers 25–8, 51, 67
Housing Discrimination 66, 79, 95–9, 118, 187, 248
Howe, Stephen 8, 129–30, 193
How the Myth Was Made 40–1, 49

ideology (definition) 101–3
Industrial Development Authority (IDA) 81, 88, 210, 212
Inglis, Tom 59, 100 n12, 228–9, 230, 232, 239
Insurrection 145, 157–8, 182, 231
interactive mode 12, 174–5, 241–2, 247–8
Irish Amateur Film Society 31
Irish Empire, The 215
Irish Film Archive 21, 25, 32, 36, 55 nn3–5, 67, 69
Irish Film Board 178, 195, 213
Irish Film Society 61, 62–3, 67, 73, 107, 162, 165, 177
Irish language
  and broadcasting 126, 238–9
  documentaries in Irish 104–5, 132, 161–2, 167, 182
  as subject 64, 112, 117, 195
  see also Gael-Linn; Telefís na Gaelige (TnaG); TG4
Irish Republican Army (IRA) 22, 27, 73, 104, 127, 135, 206
Irish Rising 1916, The 120–2, 157

Joy, The 241–2, 245
Joyce, James 94, 152, 253
  Ulysses 22, 52, 152

Kearney, Richard 4–7, 71, 192, 240
Kiberd, Declan 4, 7–8, 44, 48, 52, 64, 85, 225
Kickhams, The 247
Kopple, Barbara 246

Lane, Jim 221–2
Late Late Show, The 156–7, 176, 232
Lemass, Seán
  in politics 95, 103, 106–7, 118, 124, 150, 162, 175, 208
  and television 141, 143–4, 180
Lennon, Peter 157, 170–8, 233
literature 8, 44, 52, 92–3, 136, 213, 216
Lumière Brothers 21–4, 51

MacBride, Seán 67, 69–74, 81–2, 100 n12
McGrath, Liam 243–4, 249, 259
McIlroy, Brian 4, 188
McLoone, Martin 4, 16, 46, 181, 193, 195, 204
McQuaid, Archbishop John Charles 62, 159, 174
MacWeeney, Alen 218, 226–8
Man of Aran 44–51
  see also Flaherty, Robert
Marcus, Louis
  advocacy 165–6, 173
  early works 162–3
  and Gael-Linn 118, 155, 163–7, 248
  historical subjects 109, 116, 121–3, 131, 133, 169
  other subjects 168–9, 181, 243, 254
military 24, 63, 65
Mise Éire 29, 52, 93, 99, 101–25, 142, 178, 250
modernism 30, 52–4, 107, 155, 191, 201
modernity 22, 28, 51–4, 64, 92, 125, 191, 204

Monks, Robert 150, 153, 155, 163
Morrison, George 99, 104–10
'Mother and Child' scheme 73, 100 n12
Mother Ireland 205–6, 208, 224, 231, 245
Mulkerns, Jim 104, 118, 148–9, 151, 167–8, 182, 252–3
Mullen, Pat 46, 49
music
    film scoring 136–7, 148, 151, 157, 162, 209, 215
    popular 126, 211–12, 253
    role in culture 115–17, 153–5, 218–20, 250–2
    traditional 163–5, 183–4, 198

Nanook of the North 21, 30, 37, 45
nation 4–8, 125, 199, 252
National Film Institute of Ireland (NFI) 57, 61–3, 69, 73, 86, 107, 159
nationalism 6, 16, 27, 35, 52, 91, 127, 133, 186, 192, 198, 239
    in historical documentary 63–5, 101–29
    in Northern Ireland 95–8, 205–6, 247–8
nationality 6–9
Nation Once Again, A 63–5, 88, 99, 103, 121, 138
nature (as subject) 20, 35, 41–3, 45, 146, 182
Neitschmann, Bernard 2, 18
Nelson pillar 22–3, 68, 91
newsreels 25, 29, 51, 79, 104–5, 118
Nichols, Bill 3, 9, 11–13, 58, 103, 147, 175, 191, 196, 203, 237–8
Northern Ireland
    broadcasting 141, 205, 245
    in documentaries 95–9, 139–40 n7, 160, 187–8, 218, 220–1, 245–8
    and 'Irish' history 113, 118, 121, 124, 132, 211

objectivity 12, 33, 58, 71, 135, 163
observation 12, 144, 146–7, 155, 172, 241, 256, 259
Oisín 147–9
Ó Laoghaire, Colm 65, 90, 104, 110, 118, 137–8
O'Leary, Liam 61, 65, 66–74, 76, 78, 82, 92–3
Ó Mórdha, Seán 131, 135, 136–7
One-Nighters, The 153–5, 163, 165
ontology 10, 76, 102, 135
oral tradition 43, 116, 128–9, 131, 135, 156, 197, 208, 230, 248, 250
Ó Riada, Seán 106, 114–17, 137, 153, 157, 162, 165, 198
Our Country 57, 65–74, 82, 84, 95, 131, 139, 170–2, 176, 195, 209, 224

painting and illustration 19–20, 27, 28, 40, 52, 218, 228
Paget, Derek 75–6, 85
parody 27, 86, 175, 196, 210–11
partition 66, 69, 95–7
Pearse, Padraig 7, 63, 93, 112, 121, 169, 186, 209
perception 11, 17, 28, 238
Pettitt, Lance 4, 49, 160
photography 20, 23, 25, 31, 110, 152, 182, 207, 218, 221, 226–8
picturesque, the 19, 23, 40, 42, 45
place (concept of) 17–21
poetry 35, 41, 43–4, 46–7, 48, 53, 88, 146–7, 163, 169, 219, 253
political violence 112–13, 187–8, 245–8
postcolonialism 7–8, 85, 134, 192–4, 198–201, 219, 240
postmodernism 6, 12, 37, 130, 181, 191–4, 196, 201, 211–12, 216, 252
postnationalism 6–7, 193–4, 201, 216–17
prisons 160, 221, 241–3, 248

Promise of Barty O'Brien, The 77–8
propaganda 33, 66–7, 70–1, 76, 97,
    102, 116, 172, 178
public health 66, 67, 82–4, 213,
    244–5
public service broadcasting 118,
    141–5, 156, 239–40
    see also Radio Telefís Éireann
    (RTÉ)

Quinn, Bob 144, 178, 180–1, 184–5,
    186–7, 194–203, 223, 230

Rabiger, Michael 13, 75, 80, 241
Radharc 126, 149, 156, 158–61, 168,
    179, 181, 187, 229, 234, 248
Radio Telefís Éireann (RTÉ)
    commercial enterprises 133
    establishment of 141–5, 155, 159
    policies and operations 126, 156,
        161, 179, 182, 185, 187, 201,
        208, 212, 229–30, 232–4,
        238–9, 258–9, 261
    productions/coproductions 126–8,
        131–8, 147, 181, 242, 249
    rebellion at 144, 178–81
    series and programmes 156–7,
        163, 194, 214–15, 229, 230,
        232, 241–2, 249, 252, 255–6,
        257
    see also public service broadcasting
realist fiction films 181
reflexivity 7, 12, 37, 191, 195–6, 201,
    206, 214, 221–3, 226
Renov, Michael 43, 183
revisionism 125, 129–30, 132, 136–9,
    169
rhetorical form 3, 39, 56, 58, 95, 118,
    144, 160, 261
road safety 76–7, 182
Road to God Knows Where, The 155,
    209–13, 224, 253, 256
Robinson, Mary 194, 254
Rockett, Kevin 4, 29, 46, 49, 51, 97,
    181, 186

Rocky Road to Dublin 73, 145, 170–8,
    180, 183, 193, 201, 209–10,
    212, 224, 233
Rouch, Jean 12, 37, 41

Said, Edward 7, 8, 85
Savage, Robert 3, 141
Second World War 9, 63, 78, 97
Sense of Loss, A 187–8, 246
Seven Ages 131–2, 135, 136–7
Shaw-Smith, David 182–3
Sheridan, John D. 65, 86–7
Sherman, Sharon 31, 34–5, 44, 47
shipping industry 78–9
social documentary 12, 36, 56–8, 75,
    212, 259
Southpaw 249–50, 259
Soviet cinema 10, 12, 25–7, 30, 35,
    41–2, 70, 107–8, 113, 126,
    164–5
sports (as subject) 27, 91, 92–3,
    162, 173, 206–7, 241, 247,
    248–50
Stafford, Brendan 65, 78, 92
state, the 4–5, 8, 58–65, 84, 92, 97,
    144, 171, 207, 209–10, 232–4,
    258
States of Fear 193, 231, 233–5, 244
subjectivity 12–13, 28, 37, 39, 48,
    221–2, 225, 256
Synge, John Millington 40, 45, 85

Telefís na Gaelige (TnaG) 201, 238
TG4 86, 132, 239
theatre 93, 202
Tine Bheo, An 121–2, 133, 157, 163
tourism 29, 41, 50, 78, 82, 84–90, 95,
    150–2, 166, 182, 248
Travellers 218, 226–8
travelling community 226–8,
    249–50
Trinity College 51, 64, 94, 173
Triumph of the Will 9, 33, 65, 68
TV3 238–9
Twelve Days in July 245–6

Uncle Jack, The 201, 218–25
unionism 96, 124, 132, 140 n7, 220
United States of America (US/USA)
  film productions 49, 51, 80, 89,
    170, 206, 221
  influence 58–9, 71, 98, 144, 153,
    240
  as location/subject 213, 216,
    217–20, 256
  Marshall Aid programme 77–8
  television productions 98–9, 109,
    125, 166, 190 n11, 256
University College Dublin 32, 35

Vigilanti Cura 61–2, 143
voice of documentary 11–12
Voyage to Recovery 66, 79, 82–4, 93

war of independence 29, 51, 71, 103,
  108, 114
Waterford Crystal 151, 168
Waters of Providence, The 79–80
Watkins, Peter 157
W. B. Yeats – A Tribute 86–8, 93,
  112, 145–6, 250
White, Harry 116, 250
Williams, Raymond 4–5, 51, 102,
  144, 179
Winston, Brian 6, 10, 37, 56
Wiseman, Frederic 9, 12

Yeats, Jack B. 27, 40
Yeats, W. B. 44, 48, 67, 86–8, 93,
  112–13, 145, 253
Yeats Country 145, 146–7, 167